BOUNDARIES OF MORPHOLOGY AND SYNTAX

Edited by

LUNELLA MEREU
Università degli Studi di Roma Tre

JOHN BENJAMINS PUBLISHING COMPANY
AMSTERDAM/PHILADELPHIA

The paper used in this publication meets the minimum requirements of American National Standard for Information Sciences — Permanence of Paper for Printed Library Materials, ANSI Z39.48-1984.

Library of Congress Cataloging-in-Publication Data

Boundaries of morphology and syntax / edited by Lunella Mereu.
        p.   cm. -- (Amsterdam studies in the theory and history of linguistic science. Series IV, Current issues in linguistic theory, ISSN 0304-0763 ; v. 180)
    Papers presented at the European Colloquium on "The Boundaries of Morphology and Syntax," which was held Oct. 25-27, 1997, Università degli Studi di Roma Tre.
    Includes bibliographical references and index.
    1. Grammar, Comparative and general--Morphosyntax Congresses. I. Mereu, Lunella. II. European Colloqium on "The Boundaries of Morphology and Syntax" (1997 : Università degli Studi di Roma Tre) III. Series.
P290.368   1999
415--dc21   99-15509
ISBN 90 272 3686 0 (Eur.) / 1 55619 957 0 (US) (Hb; alk. paper)   CIP

John Benjamins Publishing Co. • P.O.Box 75577 • 1070 AN Amsterdam • The Netherlands
John Benjamins North America • P.O.Box 27519 • Philadelphia PA 19118-0519 • USA

FOREWORD

The present collection of articles grew out of papers presented at the European Colloquium on "The Boundaries of Morphology and Syntax" which was held at the Dipartimento di Linguistica of the Università degli Studi di Roma Tre in the period 25-27 October 1997. It was attended by linguists, mostly Europeans but also North Americans, from eleven countries.

I would like to express my gratitude to all the speakers who greatly helped making the Colloquium a successful event. I also thank the numerous participants whose contributions kept the discussion lively and interesting.

ACKNOWLEDGEMENTS

I acknowledge the financial support of the Università degli Studi di Roma Tre and in particular the 1996 Research Committee (Francesco Paolo Ricci, chairman), as well as the Humanities Committee of the Comitato Nazionale delle Ricerche (Paolo Ramat, chairman). I also acknowledge the financial support of the Dipartimento di Linguistica (Raffaele Simone, head of Department). Thanks go to the Saritel Company (a Telecom Italia Group Company) for sponsoring the Colloquium.

A special thanks to Biancamaria Tedeschini Lalli, the Rector of my University in 1997, for introducing the Colloquium.

This volume, and the Colloquium itself, would not have been possible without the help of Giuseppina Vecchioni and the other administrative and technical staff members of my Department. Thanks also to my English speaking colleagues, Patrick Boylan, Elisabeth Glass and David Hart for their constant assistance.

Annarita Puglielli was generous in her support; Mara Frascarelli worked hard as my assistant for the Colloquium and formatted papers for the present volume; I thank them both.

Special thanks go to Raffaele Simone, who has contributed so much to make the Colloquium a success, not only with his professional experience but also with his friendly encouragement; I am in debt to him also for his help and suggestions in the various stages of the preparation of this volume.

I finally wish to thank my family, Franco and Chiara, who patiently endured my frequent absences both during the Colloquium and while preparing this volume.

LUNELLA MEREU

Rome, January 14, 1999

P291 Bou

BOUNDARIES OF MORPHOLOGY AND SYNTAX

AMSTERDAM STUDIES IN THE THEORY AND HISTORY OF LINGUISTIC SCIENCE

General Editor

E. F. KONRAD KOERNER

(University of Ottawa)

Series IV – CURRENT ISSUES IN LINGUISTIC THEORY

Volume 180

Lunella Mereu (ed.)

Boundaries of Morphology and Syntax

CONTENTS

INTRODUCTION

Linguistics has always been concerned with the problem of defining the boundaries among the different levels of analysis it distinguishes. Indeed, establishing where one level ends and the other begins has often been an object of discussion in theoretical approaches to linguistic data. Recently, under the influence of computer science, the boundary question has been seen as a problem of interface among the different components of the grammar and interesting issues about the autonomy of each component and the kinds of interaction among them have emerged.

This volume is specifically focused on the interface between morphology and syntax, although, as we will soon see, the morpho-syntax-pragmatics and the morpho-syntax-semantics interfaces will be considered too.

The morphology-syntax interface is one of the linguistic areas in which recent research has been particularly rich in providing interesting results through broad cross-linguistic investigations and solid theoretical apparatuses. As a matter of fact, most morphological and syntactic studies have been recently concentrated on the morphological richness of many typologically-different languages. Agreement, case-marking, cliticization and incorporation phenomena, old and basic themes in linguistics, have been among the phenonema to which most attention has been recently devoted. Think of Nichols' (1986) characterization of languages as being either 'head-marking' or 'dependent-marking' languages, or of Jelinek's (1989) distinction between 'pronominal argument' and 'lexical argument' languages. Both concepts are related to languages in which the morphological richness is relevant for syntax: the former specifically refers to the possibility that languages have to morphologically mark syntactic relations "either on the head of a constituent, or on the dependent" (Nichols 1986:56-57);[1] the latter distinguishes between languages with "morphologically-bound person-marking elements (clitics and affixes)

---

[1] As Nichols points out, there are also 'double-marking languages', that is languages that morphologically mark both the head and the dependent member of a constituent, and languages that do not present morphological marking on either.

that fill the clausal argument positions" (Jelinek 1989:118), the so-called pronominal argument languages in which full or lexical NPs are adjuncts or pragmatically-marked constituents, and lexical argument languages, that is languages with no bound forms to express argumenthood.[2]

An extreme formal characterization of 'morphologically-oriented' languages is represented by Baker's studies first on incorporation phenomena
(1988) and next on polysynthetic languages (1996). He provides an analysis of
morphologically-oriented languages within both the Principle and Parameter
(Chomsky 1981) and the Minimalist approaches (Chomsky 1995) of generative
grammar, and works out his Polysynthesis Parameter (or Morphological Visibility Condition). According to this parameter, a very complex word in polysynthetic languages may contain a set of morphemes which are either agreement morphemes (or pronominal affixes) or incorporated roots, both related via
coindexing to the NPs which express the arguments of the head containing
them.[3]

In more theoretical and abstract terms the recent Minimalist approach of
generative grammar (Chomsky 1992, 1995) recognizes the central role that
morphology has in syntactic theory. Think of the morphological material corresponding to agreement, tense, mood or other grammatical properties represented in the syntactic tree as heads of different functional projections, and of
the conditions concerning the movement of these heads as "driven by morphological requirements" (Chomsky 1995:262).[4]

Also in typological studies, and in particular in grammaticalization theory
(Traugott & Heine 1991; Hopper & Traugott 1993, among others), word formation processes have shown the strict relationship between morphology and
syntax, both in diachronic and synchronic analyses of grammatical phenomena.
In other words both the synchronic variation among different languages or
dialects and the diachronic change among different stages of the same language
have been seen as changes from syntactic to morphological processes (see

---

[2] Of course most of the properties we are referring to have been already studied before the
eighties. Consider, for example, Jelinek's (1989) characterization of pronominal argument languages; this is remeniscent of Boas' (1911) and Sapir's (1911) studies on Amerindian languages at the beginning of the century.
[3] This means that the relationship between the verb and the NPs which bear thematic roles is
mediated by those morphemes attached to the verb; thematic role assignment is made 'visible'
via morpheme coindexation with a NP argument by agreement or head movement (in case of
incorporation).
[4] In more technical terms the movement condition states: "Move raises α only if morphological
properties of α itself would not otherwise be satisfied in the derivation" (Chomsky 1995:261).

Givón 1976, 1984; Lehmann 1982, 1985, as examples of applications of this line of research to morphologically-oriented languages).

However the morphological richness of some languages is relevant for syntax not only in the sense that certain kinds of morphemes express syntactic relations. In fact other syntactic properties such as constituent order are involved in those languages. The correlation between rich agreement and/or case-marking and the lack of 'rigid word order' is well-established in linguistics (see Givón 1984, among others). In more recent analyses in formal syntax the distinction between 'rigid word order' and 'free word order' languages has been reinterpreted in terms of configurationality by Hale (1981, 1983), who distinguishes two types of languages, 'configurational', the rigid word order type, and 'non-configurational', or the free word order type. Configurational languages are those languages in which the grammatical functions of subject and object are encoded by phrase structure, that is languages that have fixed position in the syntactic tree; non-configurational languages are those languages in which the grammatical functions above-mentioned are not distinctively encoded by phrase structure. In other words, as Bresnan (1995) and Austin & Bresnan (1995) point out, in non-configurational languages conceptual units are not necessarily expressed by means of phrases, that is word *groups,* but by means of word *shapes,* that is by often non-contiguous words provided with the same formal endings (case and/or inflectional morphology). Once more it is true here that morphology competes with syntax, as languages rich in word structure may recur less in fixed phrase structure forms (Bresnan 1995).[5]

As already implied in Jelinek's (1989) definition of pronominal argument languages, the variation in constituent order that non-configurational languages show is due to the pragmatic properties that sentences realize, as typologists have often pointed out (see Givón 1984). Here Mithun's (1987) studies on word order are particularly relevant; as she explains, word order is not syntactically determined in all languages, but there are languages which express pragmatic functions such as topic or focus not simply through prosody or the linear progression from given to new information. She speaks about languages with a 'pragmatically-based system' as languages in which "Constituents appear in descending order of newsworthiness" (Mithun 1987:325) and which are highly polysynthetic.

---

[5] This does not mean that it is not possible to recover the functional organization of sentences in non-configurational languages. It only means that there is no direct correlation between the overt forms of expression and the syntactic phrase structure representations in these languages.

In formal approaches languages of this kind are included among 'discourse-configurational languages' (Kiss 1995), that is "languages in which topic and focus form key constituents of sentence structure, i.e. languages in which primary sentence articulation serves to express discourse-semantic functions" (Kiss 1995:5).

All this shows that there is not only a strict relationship between morphology and syntax, but also between these and pragmatics. As we all know, however, the relationship between morpho-syntax and semantics cannot be ignored either; the latter must be taken into account too, as many questions related to word order and to other morpho-syntactic phenomena are related to the presence of different classes of verbs, of specific thematic roles, or of aspectual markers. Take, for example, the work on 'unaccusative verbs' by Perlmutter (1978), 'ergative verbs' according to Burzio's (1986) terminology; these works aim at explaining variability in subject-verb order or in cliticization phenomena in Italian and other languages in terms of the distinction among different classes of verbs.

All this highlights the need to study linguistic phenomena more on the basis of the relationship among the different levels of analysis than within one single level each phenomenon mainly belongs too. However, due to the level of refinement and completeness that each of the different components of grammar, from phonology to pragmatics, have reached in modern linguistics, most approaches, formal ones in particular, have worked more in the direction of establishing the autonomy and centrality of the components they are involved with most specifically. This has created conflicts, among which the ones we deal with here: the playoff between morphology and syntax in terms of autonomy and the precedence each claims in interacting with the higher components of grammar. As an example, we may take the Lexical Integrity Principle (Bresnan & Mchombo 1995; Di Sciullo & Williams 1987; Selkirk 1982) which has been proposed to avoid syntactic interference in morphological studies; according to this principle syntax cannot *see* the forms within a word, although in some cases the syntactic need to reconstruct the hidden relationship between a predicate and its arguments within a sentence has been recognized.

This volume is primarily centered on this conflict, that is on focusing on boundary phenomena between morphology and syntax. It suggests possible ways in which they may interact with each other while belonging to separate competence fields, but also focuses on the inevitable links and interactions with the higher components of grammar. Thematically the volume is concerned with the topics and the approaches that are mostly involved in this conflict, both from the morphological and syntactic point of view; it is also concerned with a variety of typologically-different languages from different areas, from European to Afro-asiatic languages, or from American to Austronesian ones.

The papers are grouped into three sections: I. Morphological phenomena and their boundaries; II. Morpho-syntax and pragmatics; III. Morpho-syntax and semantics.

The first section is primarily concerned with boundary phenomena between morphology and syntax. Inflectional morphology phenomena in Romance languages are dealt with in Benincà's and Schwarze's papers, the former within the Minimalist generative approach, the latter within the Lexical-functional approach. Derivational morphology phenomena are analysed in the papers presented by Bisetto & Scalise and van der Auwera, both discussing synchronic data: while Bisetto & Scalise analyse special compound forms in Italian in a generative framework, van der Auwera discusses verbal prefix formations in Dutch according to Grammaticalization theory. Incorporation phenomena are dealt with in Mithun & Corbett's and Svolacchia & Puglielli's papers, the former a typological account of noun incorporation in Mohawk, the latter an interpretation of Somali as a particular type of polysynthetic language. Finally Załęska provides a diachronic analysis of 'modus irrealis' in Polish in grammaticalization terms.

The second section is specifically concerned with the different ways in which grammar expresses pragmatic information, dealing mainly, but not only, with focus-structures or wh-questions. The papers presented by Engdahl, Frascarelli and Kiss illustrate different syntactic approaches to pragmatics. Engdahl shows how a multi-dimensional lexically-based approach such as Head-driven Phrase Structure Grammar can account for different ways (prosodic, morphological and syntactic) of grammaticalizing pragmatic information in English, Catalan and Korean. Frascarelli analyses focus structures in pragmatically-oriented languages according to the Minimalist version of generative grammar, specifically dealing with Somali, some Italian dialects and Selayarese. Kiss deals with a specific focus structure i.e., the cleft construction, in English, analysing it according to the Principle and Parameter version of generative grammar. Blanche-Benveniste provides a syntactic and semantic account of some morpho-syntactically complex ways of questioning about definitions in French, often involving the cooccurrence of interrogative subject [-Human] pronouns, the predicate *be* and reinforced forms. Mereu analyses focus- and wh-structures in two pragmatically-oriented linguistic systems (Somali and Trentino), showing the special ways in which morpho-syntactic resources (use of inflectional morphemes, clitics and word-order) interact with pragmatic information in the two linguistic systems.

The third section is devoted to the interface between morpho-syntax and semantics. Lo Cascio & Jezek's paper discusses a class of Italian verbs which optionally or obligatorily take the pronominal marker *si* when used intransitively. Markantonatou's paper is about the optionality of predicative complements in specific uses of motion verbs in English. Both papers, although from different theoretical perspectives and on different data, stress the importance of the aspectual properties of sentences, rather than of the lexical classes of verbs they are dealing with. Finally Sornicola examines word order variability with Italian one-argument verbs and focuses on the instability of the patterns they give place to, again discarding traditional proposals to explain this data, such as the 'unaccusativity hypothesis' or differences in information structure.

The papers collected in this volume do not aim at proposing a unified answer to handle the multi-level complexity of languages. Rather they present various ways of dealing with this complexity from different, sometimes opposite, theoretical perspectives, all proposing interesting alternative approaches to account for the various forms of expression languages have come to use.

REFERENCES

Austin, Peter & Joan Bresnan. 1996. "Non-Configurationality in Australian Aboriginal Languages". *Natural Language and Linguistic Theory* 14.215-268.
Baker, Mark C. 1988. *Incorporation: A theory of grammatical function changing.* Chicago: University of Chicago Press.
——. 1996. *The Polysynthesis Parameter.* New York & Oxford: Oxford University Press.
Boas, Franz. 1911. *Handbook of American Indian Languages.* Bulletin 40. Washington, D.C.: Smithsonian Institution, Bureau of American Ethology.
Bresnan, Joan. 1995. *Lexical-Functional Syntax.* Unpublished Manuscript, Stanford University (to be published by Blackwell, Oxford).
—— & Sam A. Mchombo. 1995. "The Lexical Integrity Principle: Evidence from Bantu". *Natural Languages and Linguistic Theory* 13.181-254.
Burzio, Luigi. 1986. *Italian Syntax: A government-binding approach.* Dordrecht: Reidel.
Chomsky, Noam. 1981. *Lectures on Government and Binding.* Dordrecht: Foris.
——. 1992. "A Minimalist Program for Linguistic Theory". (*MIT Occasional Papers in Linguistics*, 1.) Cambridge, Mass.: MIT.
——. 1995. *The Minimalist Program.* Cambridge, Mass.: MIT Press.
Di Sciullo, Anna Maria & Edwin Williams. 1987. *On the Definition of Word.* Cambridge, Mass.: MIT Press.

Givón, Talmy. 1976. "Topic, Pronoun and Grammatical Agreement". *Subject and Topic* ed. by. Charles N. Li, 149-188. New York: Academic Press.
——. 1984. *Syntax: A functional-typological introduction.* Vol. I. Amsterdam & Philadelphia: John Benjamins.
Hale, Kenneth L. 1981. *On the Position of Warlbiri in a Typology of the Base.* Bloomington: Indiana University Linguistics Club.
——. 1983. Warlpiri and the Grammar of Non-Configurational Languages". *Natural Languages and Linguistic Theory* 1:1.5-47.
Hopper, Paul J. & Elizabeth Closs Traugott. 1993. *Grammaticalization.* Cambridge: Cambridge University Press.
Kiss, Katalin É., ed. 1995. *Discourse Configurational Languages.* New York & Oxford: Oxford University Press.
Jelinek, Eloise. 1989. "The Case Split and Pronominal Arguments in Choctaw". *Configurationality: The typology of asymmetries* ed. by László Marácz & Pieter Muysken, 117-142. Dordrecht: Foris.
Lehmann, Christian. 1982. "Universal and Typological Aspects of Agreement". *Apprehension: Das sprachliche Erfassen von Gegenständen* ed. by Hansjakob Seiler & F. J. Stachowiak, vol. II, 201-267. Tübingen: Gunter Narr.
——. 1985. "Grammaticalization: Synchronic variation and diachronic change". *Lingua e Stile* 20:3.303-318.
Mithun, Marianne 1987. "Is Basic Word Order Universal?". *Coherence and Grounding in Discourse* ed. by Russell S. Tomlin, 281-328. Amsterdam & Philadelphia: John Benjamins.
Nichols, Johanna. 1986. "Head-marking and Dependent-marking Grammar". *Language* 62:1.56-119.
Perlmutter, David. 1978. "Impersonal Passives and the Unaccusative Hypothesis". *Proceedings of the Fourth Annual Meeting of the Berkeley Linguistic Society*, 157-189. Berkeley: University of California.
Sapir, Edward. 1911. "Noun Incorporation in American Languages". *American Anthropologist* 13.250-282.
Selkirk, Elisabeth O. 1982. *The Syntax of Words.* Cambridge, Mass.: MIT Press.
Traugott, Elizabeth Closs & Bernd Heine, eds. 1991. *Approaches to Grammaticalization.* 2 vols. Amsterdam & Philadelphia: John Benjamins.

I
MORPHOLOGICAL PHENOMENA
AND THEIR BOUNDARIES

BETWEEN MORPHOLOGY AND SYNTAX
ON THE VERBAL MORPHOLOGY OF SOME ALPINE DIALECTS[*]

PAOLA BENINCA'
Università di Padova

0. *Introduction*

The present paper is a tentative description of some quite surprising phenomena of verbal inflection, found in dialects of the Alpine area, in Northern Italy and Southern Switzerland. Though close to each other, the areas involved are not contiguous, so the phenomena cannot be considered to be a case of spreading from a single source. Instead, we are dealing with spontaneous innovations, which originated independently in different parts of the Romance area. This preliminary conclusion is important in so far as it suggests that the morphological facts that we will illustrate are produced by general principles of grammar, and are not a result of the influence of one variety on the other. A consideration of these phenomena, which are rare but at the same time well documented, can contribute to the debate on the 'deep' nature of morphology in an inflected language. As we will see, they bring to light a morphological process of particle incorporation that appears to coexist with inflection, as we are used to conceiving of it in a fully inflectional language.

Basing myself on the analysis of these phenomena, I will reflect on two

---
[*] The essence of the phenomenon has been presented – together with other similar processes operating between morphology and syntax – at the Linguistic Symposium on Romance Languages held in Los Angeles in 1994 (appeared as Beninca' 1996). I develop here in some detail further aspects of this phenomenology.

I am grateful first of all to Gianni Bonfadini who called my attention to Oscar Keller's work; to Cecilia Poletto, Christina Tortora, Raffaella Zanuttini and Bob Frank for comments on a previous version of the paper and stimulating discussion; to Andrea Calabrese, for sending me a draft of an article of his where he discusses the analysis of Beninca' (1996); I hope that at least some of the problems that have been pointed out by them can find a partial answer in this more detailed version. Lunella Mereu and Shinji Yamamoto carefully read and commented on the final version of the paper, pointing out obscurities and shortcomings that I have tried to correct, and interesting problems that I hope to deal with in the future.

alternative theories of morphology in generative grammar.

The core of the alternative positions that I will take into consideration can be summed up as follows:

Baker's (1985, 1988) Mirror Principle, one of the most stimulating proposals of the last few decades, has indirectly led to the discovery of regularities and an interlinguistic consistency regarding the ordering of morphemes, and an account which implies admitting a precise relation between morphology and syntax. The order of the subparts of a morphological suffix – where it is possible to isolate them – mirrors the order of the syntactic operations that produce its forms and the values it assumes. This implementation has been developed by Pollock (1989) and Belletti (1990) with their theory on Verb movement, which they have precisely connected with the operations that produce a verbal inflected form. In particular, Belletti has based her hypothesis on the fact that person Agreement morphology always appears externally with respect to the formatives characterising Tense. The structure underlying a verbal form thus consists of a sequence of functional projections, which mirrors the order of morphemes:[1]

(1)

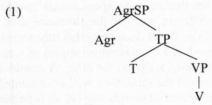

In a structure like this, then, the movement of the verbal head (which is strictly leftward and upward) will produce the correct surface order Verb-

---

[1] For the moment, I adopt a very simple functional structure; in what follows it will become clear that the kind of structure I have in mind reflects the theory illustrated by Cinque (1998), Poletto (1996), Zanuttini (1997), among others, in which the functional structure appears to be as rich as the linguistic facts empirically suggest, and is considered to be part of our knowledge of language.

Abbreviations in the text and in glosses are the following:

ACC	accusative case	PRES	present
AGR	agreement	RECONSTR	reconstructed
AGRS	subject agreement	SING	singular
CONDIT	conditional	SUBJUN	subjunctive
IMPF	imperfect	T	Tense
INDIC	indicative	V	verb (stem)
PLUR	plural	XP	the maximal projection level of a category X

Tense-Person Agreement, as in, for example, *mangiavamo* "we ate-IMPF": V-*mangia*+T-*va*+AGR-*mo*, to be compared with *mangiamo* "we eat-PRES": V-*mangia*+AGR-*mo*.

On the other hand, close consideration of the morphology of natural languages reveals that the Mirror Principle is too strong and unable to deal with a huge amount of irregularities. It is typical of an inflected language to have forms whose components are often impossible to isolate, and which very rarely have a one-to-one correspondence with their functions. Even an agglutinative language such as Hungarian, only ideally has a biunique correspondence 'morpheme-function' (or functional feature), since it often exhibits a fusion of morphemes that become inseparable. For example, in a form such as *gyerek-ek-et* "child+PLUR+ACC", the plural and case morphemes can be isolated: case follows plural. If a possessive is inserted in the singular accusative, it appears as an -*m*- before the case suffix (*gyerek-em-et*), but in the plural it blends with the plural morpheme: *gyerek-eim-et* "child+my.PLUR+ACC"; that is, the plural suffix, which is elsewhere a -*k*- with a predictable vowel, appears as an *ei* inserted before the possessive -*m*-.

Cases of fusion of morphemes are the rule rather than the exception in an inflected language; this means that the functional distribution of morphemes is recognisable only in part. Etymology can often suggest a historical reason for some morphological alternation, but even using devices of this kind, suffixes are almost never completely productive.

Chomsky's (1995) theory offers a radical alternative: inflected forms are drawn from the lexicon endowed with their functional features and are learned and stored as such. The syntax interprets the features and moves the form into the appropriate syntactic position; here the features find their companion and are discharged. When they do not match, the derivation crashes. On this view, it is not the task of the syntax to explain why the inflected forms have the shape they have, nor how they have acquired the features they are endowed with and the function which they have, nor even why the features are 'checked and discharged' in a given order.

This theory could be too weak, if it is not supplemented by an independent principle, which at least specifies, for example, in what order the matching of features has to occur. The regularities that are the empirical basis of the Mirror Principle, a hypothesis concerning the relation between morphology and syntax, become mere coincidence, which does not require any explanation within the syntactic component. The order of the morpheme subparts – where they are recognisable – largely mirrors the order in which the features are checked in Chomsky's (1995) theory; however, this is no longer an empirical generalisation, but rather the chance result of processes which cannot be formalised: the exceptions have more empirical weight than the regularities.

However, typological records are quite impressive: they appear as strong tendencies that – as Joseph Greenberg would say – are unlikely to be the result of chance. If we consider the observed solidarity between phenomena as mere coincidence, we are not pushed by the exceptions to a hypothesised law towards a more accurate recognition of the existing phenomena and a more precise formulation of our theory: instead, we are led to abandon it, perhaps too quickly. For example, the huge number of languages in which person Agreement appears in the verb to the right of Tense, Modality and Aspect morphemes would simply be the consequence of a general tendency to give more visibility to this particular part of inflection (Chomsky 1995:196). In accepting this explanation, one has to take for granted that 'visibility' means 'nearer to the word boundary', and this furthermore has to be understood as 'nearer to the right boundary' in inflectional languages. As these assumptions do not appear obvious, we will take the other option, and try to pursue a perspective where the observed regularities serve as a challenge to discover the principles of the grammar that produce them.

The facts that I will present are, at first sight, clear counterexamples to Baker's theory: they are cases of verbal forms produced by adding to an already complete form with person Agreement a further particle with tense value. The surface order of the suffixes is then exactly the opposite of what is generally found in inflectional languages, in particular of what is found very consistently in Romance languages (including the contiguous dialects). Person Agreement in these languages – where recognisable – is always located at the right end of the verb. In two distinct small dialects areas however we have verb conjugations in which a Tense specification in the form of a particle follows person Agreement morphology.

If inflected forms are learned and stored in the lexicon together with their abstract features, there is no point in wondering why a small set of Romance varieties shows this morphological peculiarity. I would argue here that this question is worth posing, because in doing so we are pushed to attempt generalisation and we happen to find unexpected regularities of minute phenomena at the interface between morphology and syntax. If the regularities appear to be real, this means that a theory of morphology as Chomsky's (1995) is too weak and Baker's is superior from an empirical point of view: the latter produces more detailed and precise descriptions of linguistic phenomena, from which the theory itself can be refined.

1. *Livinallongo verb morphology*

I will first take into account verbal forms of the dialect of Livinallongo (Dolomitic Alps, Northern Italy). The relevant forms of the verb *ester* "be" and *avéj* "have" are presented in (2) and (3) (from Pellegrini 1973, 1974). For readers not familiar with the syntactic typology of Northern Italian Dialects, an elucidation of the forms is in order. The 2nd person singular has an obligatory subject clitic *te*; the 3rd singular has a subject clitic *l* (*el* when initial; *la* if the subject is feminine); the 3rd plural has a subject clitic *i* (*le* if the subject is feminine); *l* is also the dummy subject of impersonal and meteorological verbs. As in many varieties of this area, the 1st person singular and the 1st and 2nd plural do not have a subject clitic. The 3rd person plural is identical with the 3rd singular; as is the case in many northern Italian varieties, plural Agreement is only expressed by the subject clitic. The distribution of obligatory subject clitics in the paradigm – 2nd singular, 3rd singular and plural – remains a mystery, but it is widely attested and does not have any bearing on the phenomenon at issue.

(2) *ester* "be"

a. PRES INDIC	b. IMPF INDIC	c. IMPF SUBJUN	d. PRES SUBJUN
son	*sonve*	*ke sonse*	*ke sombe*
t es	*t eve*	*ke t ese*	*ke te siebe*
l è	*l eva*	*ke l esa*	*ke l siebe*
son	*sonve*	*ke sonse*	*ke sombe*
sei	*seive*	*ke seise*	*ke siebe*
i è	*i eva*	*ke i esa*	*ke i siebe*

(3) *avéj* "have"

a. PRES INDIC	b. IMPF INDIC	c. IMPF SUBJUN	d. PRES SUBJUN
e	*eve*	*ke ese*	*ke ebe*
t as	*t ave*	*ke t ase*	*ke t asbe*
l a	*l ava*	*ke l asa*	*ke l abe*
on	*onve*	*ke onse*	*ke onbe*
ei	*eive*	*ke eise*	*ke eibe*
i a	*i ava*	*ke i asa*	*ke i abe*

Compare each person of the present indicative of both verbs with the corresponding persons of the other tenses; these latter appear to be made of the present indicative plus an invariable formative, specific for each tense: *ve* for the imperfect indicative, *se* for the imperfect subjunctive, *be* for the present subjunctive (1SING: PRES INDIC *son* "I am", IMPF INDIC *son-ve*, IMPF SUBJUN *son-se*, PRES SUBJUN *son-be*; 2SING: PRES *t as*, IMPF *t a-ve*, IMPF SUBJUN *t a-se*; PRES

SUBJUN *t a-be*).[2] This is not the usual way Romance verbs (in fact, verbs in general in natural languages) inflect.[3]

The paradigm of 'have' is identical. The IMPF INDIC, IMPF SUBJUN and PRES SUBJUN are formed by adding respectively a formative *ve*, *se*, or *be* to the inflected forms of present indicative. With lexical verbs we find interesting differences: the verb *sauté* "jump" in (4) illustrates the behaviour of all lexical verbs. In the singular it behaves as Romance verbs, while the phenomenon we are considering appears in the plural (just 1st and 2nd person, the 3rd plural being identical with the 3rd singular, apart from the subject clititc).

(4) *sauté* "spring"

a. PRES INDIC	b. IMPF INDIC	c. IMPF SUBJUN	d. PRES SUBJUN
saute	*sautave*	*ke sautase*	*ke saute*
te saute	*te sautave*	*ke te sautase*	*ke te saute*
el sauta	*el sautava*	*ke l sautasa*	*ke l saute*
sauton	*sautonve*	*ke sautonse*	*ke sautombe*
sautéj	*sautéjve*	*ke sautéjse*	*ke sautéjbe*
i sauta	*i sautava*	*ke i sautasa*	*ke i saute*

Let us consider again just the imperfect indicative and imperfect subjunctive and compare them with the corresponding forms of other Romance varieties: the characteristic formatives that appear at the end of 1st and 2nd plural correspond to the formatives that in other Romance languages appear between the stem and personal suffixes (with a difference in the final vowel that we will come back to later). For example, in Italian we have, for the verb *saltare* "jump":

(5) | | PRES INDIC | IMPF INDIC | IMPF SUBJUN |
|---|---|---|---|
| 1PLUR | *salt-ia-mo* | *salt-a-va-mo* | *salt-a-ssi-mo* |
| 2PLUR | *salt-a-te* | *salt-a-va-te* | *salt-a-s-te* |

In Spanish, for a verb of the same class, *tocar* "touch, play an instrument":

(6) | | PRES INDIC | IMPF INDIC | IMPF SUBJUN |
|---|---|---|---|
| 1PLUR | *toc-à-mos* | *toc-à-ba-mos* | *toc-à-sse-mos* |
| 2PLUR | *toc-à is* | *toc-à-ba-is* | *toc-à-sse-is* |

The Livinallese imperfect indicative and subjunctive show – for all persons

---

[2] In the 3rd SING and PLUR, in fact, the final vowel changes. For the moment, we are idealising the facts; we will turn to this important aspect later.

[3] Auxiliaries are often particularly irregular, learned as they are form by form as single lexical elements due to their highly frequent usage. Because of this, they are for the language learner a continuous source of spontaneous correction during language acquisition. But this is the reason why auxiliaries maintain very old basic forms, preserved from analogy and only affected by regular rules of phonological change.

the case of auxiliaries, only for 1st and 2nd plural in the case of lexical verbs – after the inflected form corresponding to present indicative exactly the formative that in other Romance languages appears before the personal inflection. If we abstract from the final vowel and consider only the consonant, which is characteristic of the Tense (see note 2 above) we see that what precedes this consonant is identifiable as an inflected form of the present indicative.

If we assume with Chomsky (1995) that the fact that in many natural languages person Agreement appears on the right is nothing more than a tendency, we will not be too surprised to find that a particular language does not conform to this tendency. Italian *saltavamo* and Livinallese *sautonve* are lexical forms, stored as such in the lexicon with their Tense and Agreement features, and their phonological form cannot be of any interest from a syntactic point of view. If, on the contrary, we adopt a stronger theory and we consider the morphological sequences above as projected in accordance with the Mirror Principle, the different order of Tense and Agreement projections in the dialect of Livinallongo with respect to the other comparable Romance varieties would be the result of a parameter variation, according to which Functional Heads can appear in different orders in the structure of different languages: in Livinallese we would have Subject Agreement Heads lower than Tense (or Mood) Heads. From this perspective, the difference between Livinallese and other Romance languages is more telling, in fact, even too much so. It forces us to assume a variation in the order of government of functional heads between languages that are in many other respects very close to one another. In particular, many well-known dialects contiguous to Livinallese do not show this pattern but generally conform to that of Italian and Romance one.[4] The following diagram (7a) illustrates the 'Italian pattern', with the Tense projection lower than the AgrS projection; (7b) shows the supposed Livinallese pattern, with the reverse order of TP and AgrSP:

---

[4] There are in fact various isolated cases of particle adjoined to the inflected form in many Northern varieties: they appear not in the entire paradigm of a single tense, but just in one or two persons (1st and/or 2nd plural: see some examples in Beninca' 1996). It is even more difficult to interpret these cases as instances of the different ordering of projections, since they are limited to certain persons of the verbs only.

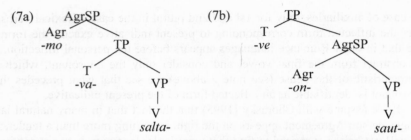

Were this the case, we would expect much more variation in the sequence of functional projections in Romance, in fact many more cases of the type we are considering.[5] As this is not the case, let us try to understand the phenomenon better, and observe the forms of the subjunctive, which differ from the ones we have outlined in an interesting way.

1.1 *The present subjunctive*

While imperfect indicative and subjunctive resemble parallel Romance forms, but with the curious inversion of Tense and Agreement, the present subjunctive cannot be understood in the same way. First of all, the inflected part does not simply correspond to the present indicative, but is already similar to a typical Romance present subjunctive; secondly, the ending is not analysable as a formative of the subjunctive, in the sense that it does not have a correspondent in any Romance variety, as far as I know; it is an invariable *be*, with no vowel alternation depending on the person of the verb, as was the case for the tenses we have seen above.

From a diachronic point of view, a possible origin of the consonant *b* could be the present subjunctive of the verb 'have'; it could derive from a new (or 'wrong') segmentation of the final stage of the regular phonological evolution illustrated by the following table (in many Romance varieties the present subjunctive of 'have' underwent a parallel development: for some data see Rohlfs 1966):

(8) 1SING   ABEAM > *abja*   >   *ajba* >   eba
     2SING   ABEAS > *abjas*   >   *ajbas* > ebe
     3SING   ABEAT > *abja*   >   *ajba* >   eba

---

[5] One case, namely a 1st person plural of the imperfect indicative of a lexical verb, *credonve* "we believed", has been found by Poletto (1993:102) in a dialect not far from this area, and analysed as the result of a different type of verb movement to functional heads. If we see this limited case as the relic of a wider and more complex phenomenon, her hypothesis cannot be maintained.

In the 1st singular this form could be interpreted as an *e* (PRES INDIC) + *ba*, but the remainder of the conjugation is not analysable in this way, on the basis of the actual data, as can be clearly seen the present subjunctive of the verb 'have' is compared with the present indicative:

(9)   a. PRES INDIC   b.*RECONSTR SUBJUN   c. PRES SUBJUN
            e   *ke eba*   *ke ebe*
            t as   *ke t ebe*   *ke t a(s)be*
            l a   *ke l eba*   *ke l abe*

There is still another difference between the regular hypothetical outcome and the actual forms: the final vowels. The regular outcome shows a differentiation of the 2nd singular deriving from the 'palatalising' effect of the dropped final -*s,* as in the other cases of 2nd singular, while the actual forms are not differentiated. This could be, however, a subsequent phenomenon, again very common in Romance, which eliminated – more or less completely – the distinctions of person Agreement in the singular of the present subjunctive. What remains to be explained is why the root of 'have' *e-* < **aj* changed and became identical to the present indicative of 'have'. We can hypothesise that an analogical process took place, starting from the wrong analysis of a diachronically regular present subjunctive, but what has given the analogical process the direction it took remains unexplained. To try to find the cause of this direction is another aspect of the same problem, namely, what is the synchronic analysis of these forms? Even if the starting point of the peculiar morphology of this tense had been the supposed reanalysis, this hypothesis is not able to explain the actual forms, nor the wrong analysis itself. Later we will see more evidence in favour of the idea that the diachronic process did proceed in precisely the way we have just outlined, but this does not help us to understand why it happened. In order to understand the way in which the forms and tenses are connected to one another today, we have to take into account the fact that, even if -*b*- derives from the subjunctive of the verb 'have', it is now an independent particle that adjoins to fully inflected forms.

Regarding this particle we can also consider a different hypothesis, based on the observation of the verb in other varieties, where we find analogous characteristics. Even if it were to prove wrong as a factual reconstruction of the diachronic origin of the phenomenon, it can suggest a possible way to interpret synchronically the Livinallongo conjugation.

In some dialects of the Swiss Lombard area (Northern Italy and Southern Switzerland) we find an agglutinative phenomenon, first described at the end of the past century by Carlo Salvioni (1886) and subsequently refined by Oscar Keller (1938), who also proposed a very insightful analysis. The possibility of interpreting our -be as having the same origin as the particle that agglutinates to the verb in the Swiss dialect gives us a clearer idea of the nature of the process *per se*. We would conclude that the process is the same, while the origin of the particle is a problem to be considered at a different level. The group of facts as a whole can be theoretically interesting only if we keep the two levels distinct, while allowing them to throw light on each other.

2. *Verb morphology of Sonogno*

In the dialect of the Swiss village of Sonogno, studied by Keller in various works and analysed in Keller (1938), a lexical verb presents the forms in (10): a particle -ba adjoins to an inflected form which is already complete as far as Tense and Agreement specifications are concerned.[6]

This dialect presents a different paradigm of subject clitics with respect to the Livinallongo dialect. Again, the pattern is not specific to this dialect, but is widespread in Lombardy and the Italian-speaking part of Switzerland. All persons have subject clitics; the 1st person plural is expressed, as in French and in Lombard, with the 3rd singular verb and a subject *um* "man, one"; the 2nd plural and the 3rd singular in the table below appear to have the same subject clitic, but if we compare forms of verbs beginning with a vowel, we see that the *u* of the 3rd singular masculine is the realisation of *l* before a consonant, while the 2nd plural *u* is maintained in this context too[7] (it is diachronically connected with the pronoun VOS "you").

(10) *kantà* "to sing"

a. PRES INDIC

a	kant-a
ti	kent-a
u	kant-a
um	kant-a
u	kant-é
i	kant-a

b. *ba*-CONJUGATION

a	kànt-e-ba
ti	kent-e-ba
u	kànt-e-ba
um	kànt-e-ba
u	kanté-ba
i	kànt-e-ba

c. IMPF INDIC

a	kantéva, kantéveba
ti	kantìva, kantìveba
u	kantéva, kantéveba
um	kantéva, kantéveba
u	kantìva, kantìvebu
i	kantéva, kantéveba

d. FUTURE

a	kanterò, -òba
ti	kanteré, -éba
u	kanterà, -àba
um	kanterà, -àba
u	kanteré, -éba
i	kanterà, -àba

e. CONDIT

a	kanterýs, -ýzba
ti	kanterýs, -ýzba
u	kanterýs, -ýzba
um	kanterýs, -ýzba
u	kanterýsu, -ýzbu
i	kanterýs, -ýzba

---

[6] The phenomenon is in fact attested in other villages of the same Verzasca Valley; the systematic analysis of Keller is centred on Sonogno, and compared with data from the other villages.

[7] Compare, for ex., in (12) below, 3rd SG *l a* "he has", *l eva* "he had", with 2nd PL *u iva*.

The same pattern appears with the auxiliaries 'be' and 'have'. Notice, for a correct interpretation, that the verb 'have' in (12) has a locative *j* as part of its lexical basis; this is common with other dialects of northern Italy, and is to be compared with colloquial Italian as well, where a locative *ci* is cliticised to 'have', but only when used as a lexical verb.[8]

(11) *ves* "be"

a. PRES INDIC	b. IMPF INDIC
a sunt / somba	*a sera / sereba*
ti se / seba	*ti sira / iveba*
l e / eba	*l era / ereba*
um se / seba	*um sèra / sèreba*
u si / siba	*u sira / sireba*
i e / eba	*era, ereba*

(12) *avek* "have"

a. PRES INDIC	b. IMPF INDIC
a j o /a j oba	*j éva / j éveba*
ti j e /ti j eba	*ti ìva / ìveba*
l a / l aba	*l èva / èveba*
um a / aba	*um èva / èveba*
u j i / j iba	*u ìva, -u / ìve-ba, -u*
j a / aba	*i eva / eveba*[9]

In this dialect, a particle *ba* adjoins to the inflected forms: as in the case of the Livinallongo forms, here too we will conclude that the final vowel is a component of the inflection. We will consider this aspect in a moment. As Oscar Keller shows in his work, the adjunction of *-ba* does not produce a proper tense, as had been asserted in previous reports,[10] but a form that coexists with the form without the particle, and provides a further specification that he terms 'Aktionsart', and we would call Modality. Apparently, the value provided by

---

[8] An interesting fact, which we will not deal with here, is that in this dialect the locative only appears in present indicative and - what is even more intriguing - not with 3rd singular and plural (including the 3rd singular that forms the 1st plural).

[9] For the future and conditional of 'have' and 'be' I only have the following 1st singular forms:

    'have':   *a vrò, a vròba*; CONDIT *a vrýs, a vrýzba*;

    'be':   *a sarò, saròba*; CONDIT *a sarýs, sarýzba*

[10] Carlo Salvioni was the first to report this peculiar conjugation, which he presented as a new creation with the meaning of a simple past; the transcription of the forms was mistaken, and consequently the analysis was wrong. On the basis of more precise data and an accurate etymological reconstruction, Keller is able to exclude the hypothesis put forth by Salvioni, who proposed an agglutination of a past participle of 'have', practically a reduction of a present perfect. Salvioni was uncertain how to analyse the other tenses with *-ba*.

the particle is not unitary, but changes in relation to the basic tense of the verb and the pragmatic context. When added to a tense of the indicative, for example, it has presuppositional value, added to a conditional it can convey a 'not committed' or even an 'irrealis' modality.

Looking at the contiguous dialects, he is able to reconstruct a continuum of different stages of grammaticalization of the particle, which originates from a full manner adverb *ben* "well".[11] We are able to observe the series of steps that the element made from its starting point to the final stage of enclitic (agglutinated) particle: it is important to note that a range of stages coexisting inside one dialect can be found.

2.1 *The vowel endings*

If we seek to reword Keller's theory in a more formal way, we can also face, at this point, the problem of the final vowels: both the inflected form and the form with -*ba* show a vowel -*a* in final position, which has no simple explanation, or clear origin. Put another way, -*ba* appears to adjoin to the inflected form, which, when *ba* is adjoined, looses its own -*a*. Thus, we could also say that it is only a *b* which is inserted inside the inflection, leaving on the right side -*a*, which is still part of the original inflection. From an etymological point of view, the vowel endings of the present indicative -*a* (all persons except the 2nd plural) have no possible source in the diachronic phonology of this dialect and of the dialects of this area. The idea that -*a* represents a further adjunction to person Agreement has also synchronic motivation, because it seems to 'cover' other deeper vowels: the 2nd singular shows metaphony of the root vowel, which is necessarily induced by an underlying -*i* ending. For the verbs of the first conjugation such as the one in (10a), we could hypothesise that the vowel corresponds to the thematic vowel, but this is not tenable for the verbs of the other conjugations, whose thematic vowel is different (as the infinitive shows). Compare the present indicative of the verb *sentì:*

(13) *sentì* "to hear, to feel"

a. PRES INDIC	b. *ba*-CONJUGATION
a sénta	*a sénteba*
ti sìnta	*ti sìnteba*
u sénta	*u sénteba*
um sénta	*um sénteba*
u sintì	*u sintìba*
i sénta	*i sénteba*

When the particle -*ba* adjoins, this -*a* does not appear at the end of the in-

---

[11] The relevant data can be found in Keller (1935, 1938) and in Sganzini (1965-70:303-306).

flected form, but at the end of the compound (inflected form + particle). The final vowel of the inflected form becomes an -e, in this dialect. The -e could either result from a weakening of the original a, or be the vowel underlying the
-a. A third possibility is that this is simply a support vowel, permitting the adjoining of the particle in a way that conforms to the word formation principles
of the dialect. It is difficult to choose among these possibilities: Keller assumes
that the internal -e- results from a weakening of the original -a; the context is an
appropriate one, if we suppose that the adjoining of the particle -ba forms a
new word, where the original -a is found in a 'post-tonic of a proparoxytone'[12]
position, a well known weakening context of internal vowels. These choices
between different interpretations regarding the loss of -a when internal, do not
have any bearing on the explanation of its occurrence when it is in final position, whether it belongs to the inflected form or the agglutinated compound
with -ba; an -a is not expected in either case.

In particular, since -ba is synchronically related to the adverb ben "well",
it is relevant to state that in no other case do we find in this dialect an -a as the
outcome of a final -e(n), be it stressed or unstressed. Keller himself observes
that be(n) becomes -ba only in the varieties where -a is a morphological ending
of the inflected forms and where the adverb is intimately conjoined to the verb.
I would like to go further, taking into account also other facts we know of the
diachronic reconstruction of these varieties. We can observe that in the dialect
of Sonogno -ba has this form even when adjoined to inflected forms that do not
have an -a ending, as is the case with the auxiliaries 'have' and 'be', with modals and with some other 'irregular verbs' (whose behaviour is still to be studied). More importantly, not in all cases is -ba the form of the particle: in the
second person plural of some tenses it appears as -bu, with a vowel -u that
sometimes appears as an ending in other Lombard dialects too: it results from
the agglutination of the subject clitic of this person (< VOS). Therefore, I interpret the form of the particle -ba in the following way: be(n) becomes part of the
inflection of the verb adjoining to a 'subject' clitic -a. To do that, as in other
cases of cliticisation, it has to become 'sticky',[13] that is, it has to lose the vowel

---

[12] For those not familiar with the traditional terminology, the formula refers to the syllable
placed between the stressed and the final syllable, in a word stressed on the antepenultimate.
[13] With this metaphor I am referring to widely discussed processes; on the one hand, we have
words that have to lose their vowel ending when they incorporate enclitics, as the Italian infinitive when it acquires enclitic pronouns; on the other, the processes of grammaticalization generally go hand in hand with phonological impoverishment (see Cardinaletti & Starke 1994 for the
most far-reaching theoretical exposition of this issue). For example, there is reason to believe

that closes it in order to be 'not complete', in order to make itself open to further morphological adjunctions.

If this is correct, we can hypothesise the same of the inflectional -*a* that appears in all persons but the 2nd plural in the simple forms of the verb; thus *kanta, kenta, kanta,* or *senta, sinta, senta* are to be analysed as *kant*v+*a*, *kanti*+*a, kanta*+*a*; and *sent*v+*a, senti*+*a, sent*v+*a*: -*a* again being the 'high subject clitic'. Assuming this to be correct too, we must now consider the change of *a* > -*e* when -*ba* adjoins to the inflected form can be explained in the following ways: either it is a case of weakening of the post-tonic vowel in a proparoxytone, or there is only one -*a* in the structure and it adjoins at the end of the agglutinated form; the internal -*e*- is then either a support vowel or the re-emerging of the deep vowel. I leave this last question open. If we translate the segmentation I have suggested – a further development of Keller's analysis – into a formal structure, we can say that the verb is inserted into the structure with its 'basic' inflection (present indicative), it moves and reaches its final goal when it reaches the 'high subject clitic' -*a*; if a modal head is activated, a -*b*- is inserted in that head; the verb collects it and proceeds to the final step, where -*a* is positioned. When the verb is 2nd plural, we assume that it meets the clitic -*u,* which attaches to it, closing the word and the process of composition ends.

The difference between this language and languages without -*ba* agglutination can be reduced to the fact that in the latter the activation of the modal head remains at an abstract level, without the insertion of an element with phonetic content: the verb moves and adjoins to the activated head, without a visible consequence of a morphological or a phonological nature. The difference is reduced, then, to a different semantic distribution in the lexical inventory: Sonogno has a relatively independent particle bearing an 'irrealis' – or more generically 'modal' value, that in other languages is borne by the inflected form itself.

The idea that a morphological component (which can also be a subcomponent of the lexicon) provides inflected forms with their endowment of features can be accepted, given the kind of phenomena we are considering, if it is inserted in a very detailed functional structure, existing independently in our linguistic competence. Part of the meaning of an inflected form can get lost and be newly expressed by an independent lexical item,[14] in our case a grammati-

that Romance clitic pronouns are phonologically represented by one phoneme, and their final syllabic aspect is the result of phonetic readjustments.

[14] It is perhaps worthwhile to recall that a similar diachronic process is thought to be the origin of the auxiliaries, that develop to compensate for the loss of meaning in inflected forms: for example, Latin had an opposition in the past between simple past and impefect only, while Ro-

calised particle; it is inserted in the appropriate position and the inflected form is attracted by it (in the same technical way as a clitic attracts a verb of which it becomes enclitic).[15]

Finally, it can be briefly pointed out that the grammaticalization process that we have outlined here appears to fit very well into the framework of the theory developed by Cardinaletti & Starke (1994) with respect to the pronouns: their work mentions the possibility of applying to some types of adverb the same ternary classification as they propose for pronouns, namely 'strong-weak-clitic'. The adverb corresponding to 'well' seems a good candidate, as the authors suggest, and as can be deduced from the data we are dealing with. Aspects of word order and meaning relating to French *bien*, English *well*, German *wohl*, Italian *bene* as well as their tendency to phonological reduction seem to suggest a 'weak' form of the adverb; in our Swiss dialects we can observe the cliticisation stage.

2.2 *A note on the tenses*

The tenses involved in the phenomenon of agglutination in Sonogno overlap in part with the tenses of Livinallongo dealt with above. The present indicative appears in both systems as a Tense that can acquire a modal marking: in Livinallongo it gives an imperfect and the subjunctives (present and imperfect),

---

mance languages, in order to distinguish morphologically between the various component values of the simple past, developed a present perfect with an auxiliary. Furthermore, many non-standard varieties also created a very specific past tense with two auxiliarie, and subsequently lost the simple past, in a continuous reorganization of forms in response to different pressures within the overall economy of the system, as it were.

[15] Interesting evidence of the grammaticalization process is given by the following: in very similar dialects of the same valley, a type of future with a modal*olé* "to want" is used (together with the usual Romance formation): when the modal appears with the particle, it can only have the function of the future modal, while without the particle it can be ambiguous:

(i) a   *a voj kantà*
          "I want to sing"
     b   *a voj-ba kantà*
          "I want-well sing" = "I will sing (immediately)"

The same happens with the conditional. Moreover, in a few varieties, for some or all the persons of the verb, it is possible to drop the modal verb completely, leaving to the particle the task of governing the infinitive, on the surface:

(ii) a   *i be da-tal*
          "I well give-you-it?" = "I will give it to you"
     b   *te be vedé*
          "you well see" = "you will see".

In many varieties this type of future coexists with the synthetic type, with a different value (see the detailed report of Keller 1935).

in Sonogno it takes *-ba* with modal values. This behaviour of the present indicative is compatible with the characteristics that have been attributed to the present tense in Italian, and presumably Romance in general, in contrast with English (see Giorgi & Pianesi 1995 for details). In brief, in both varieties, the tenses involved are all compatible with 'irrealis' mood specification.

The most relevant difference between the two dialects is the lack of the present subjunctive in the set of Tenses to which *-ba* adjoins in Sonogno; this is unexpected also because, if the common feature of the tenses involved is the compatibility with an 'irrealis' mood specification, the present subjunctive would have to be in this group. The explanation, though, is, in a way, simple: the present subjunctive is already the result of the agglutination of a particle, which appears again adjoined to an inflected form, a present subjunctive of the Romance type. The adjoined particle is *-g'a* (with a palatalised /g/)[16] which apparently comes from an unetymological segmentation of the present subjunctive of DIRE "to say", in which *-g'a* is the regular outcome of the Latin present subjunctive DICAM, DICAS, DICAT, etc.[17]

(14) *kantà* "sing"
    PRES SUBJUN
    ke kàntig'a
    ti kéntig'a
    u kàntiga
    um kàntiga
    u kantég'a
    i kàntig'a

The analogical processes that bind together the so-called 'athematic verbs' – which can also be considered, from a semantic point of view, 'light verbs'[18] –

---

[16] This dialect shows a palatalisation process affecting velar consonants before *-a* (here it appears to affect only voiced velars; the phenomenon has been widely studied with regard to conservative areas of northern Italy and Switzerland: see references in Haiman & Beninca' 1992).

[17] This is a reformulation of a suggestion made by Keller (1935:187-188), who develops a former analysis by Salvioni.

[18] The whole set is represented by *dire* "say", *dare* "give", *andare* "go", *fare* "do", *stare* "stay". These verbs are called 'athematic' because they lack a thematic vowel, as the vowel that precedes the infinitive ending is part of the stem (the Romance form for *dire* and *fare* is cited and not the Latin one DICERE, FACERE as to limit reference to that stage of development and to the particular varieties in which they have the characteristics of an athematic verb (in Latin they evidently had a partially thematic paradigm); since they have a simple, basic, meaning, they can be considered light verbs from a semantic point of view. The set is not completely stable in the history of the Indo-European languages (some members are lost and later re-acquired); any of them can trigger an analogical process. See, for an example in the verbal morphology of Friulian, Beninca' & Vanelli (1976).

are clear and continually being renewed during the whole history of the Indo-European languages. To limit ourselves to the point at issue, namely the ending -*ga* spreading from the present subjunctive of DIRE to other verbs, we can cite the case of Venetian; an ending -*g*V – where the vowel is an inflectional ending – is extended to DARE STARE FARE from DIRE. The parallel is interesting, but the difference with our phenomenon is even more so: in Venetian it is a matter of analogical infixation (person Agreement is still at the end of the form), while in the case of the Sonogno subjunctive in -*g'a* we have the agglutination of a formative to an inflected form, marked as present subjunctive. The formative is, again, to be interpreted as *g'* plus the 'high subject clitic' *a*.

3. *Back to the Livinallongo morphology*

The phenomenon observed in the Swiss dialect above bears a fundamental similarity to the peculiar morphology of Livinallongo which was our point of departure: a morpheme (a grammaticalised particle) is adjoined to an inflected form, slightly modifying it, without obscuring its morphological completeness. The difference with resepct to Livinallongo is that the particle is not used to produce one of the basic tenses, but types of Modality that in the majority of the Romance dialects do not need a special form of the verb to be expressed. This kind of difference among languages is expected: what in one language finds a specific form that expresses it, in others is apparently silent, synthetically contained together with other values in one form.

Synchronically, both Sonogno and Livinallongo have in their lexicon (a set of) independent particles that express some Tenses or Modalities. The inflected verb, inserted in the structure, moves to check its features: if it meets the particle, this agglutinates to it. But while Sonogno -*ba* has a sure origin from the grammaticalization of an adverb *ben*, "well" – a process whose steps can be seen directly within the dialect and indirectly, when compared with the contiguous dialects – the origin of the Livinallongo particles appears to vary.

We have kept -*be*, whose origin in the Livinallongo dialect is not immediately evident, separated from -*ve* and -*se*, whose identification with the Romance morphemes of tense is clear. While for the latter the proposal of an inversion in the order of functional heads could be well founded, for -*be* it is impossible because no formative of this kind is attested in Romance for the present subjunctive. At the end of Section 2 we saw that -*be* could possibly originate from a incorrect segmentation of the present subjunctive of 'have', a division whose rational, however, is obscure.

The -*ba* of Sonogno can now suggest a possible alternative solution; as the basic value of a subjunctive as opposed to an indicative is a [+irrealis] marking, i.e. a modal value, here again we could be dealing with the grammaticalization of a *ben* "well", specialised for the marking of the present subjunctive. We do not find in the immediately contiguous dialects such strong evidence of the process as that found in Italian Switzerland. However, as we said briefly above, the tendency of this adverb to undergo more or less extreme grammaticalization is a general phenomenon well attested, at least in Indo-European languages. In our dialect, and in general in Northern Italian varieties, *bene* enters in the formation of the subordinating conjunction *se ben che* "although", lit. "if well that", or *can ben che*, lit. "when well that", i.e. "even if", etc.

The facts are not strong enough to support the usage of the parallelism with Sonogno as a means to explain this point of Livinallongo morphology; but if we resume now the alternative hypothesis of an origin from the present subjunctive that we alluded to in Section 2.1 above, we can see the problem in a different light. Whether the *-be* of Livinallongo comes from a grammaticalised weak adverb BENE, or from the present subjunctive of 'have' whose final section has been interpreted as a mobile part of the verb with 'irrealis' modal feature, is a purely etymological problem, perhaps lacking a simple solution. Whatever its origin, we have again an independent particle that is adjoined to an inflected form in the syntax, building a morphological form of the verb. This particle is the formative of the mood 'present subjunctive' and we can assume that it is inserted in the structure in the appropriate position; when the inflected form of the verb is inserted, it moves and the particle adjoins to it. The same happened with *-ve* and *–se*, which were extracted form an originally inflected form, interpreted as mobile, independent parts and inserted separately into the structure. The fact that the tenses involved in the process have all to do with an 'irrealis' interpretation as was the case in Sonogno is important, in the light of the sentence structure proposed by Cinque (1998), where this projection is quite high in the functional verbal 'field'.

I have referred to the particles of Livinallongo as *-be*, *-se* and *-ve*, deliberately disregarding the fact that they vary with the person of the verb. After having analysed the case of the final *-a* of Sonogno and shown that it can derive from a 'high subject clitic', it appears to me possible to maintain that this is the case for the final vowels in Livinallongo as well. Another well represented pattern of high subject clitics of Northern Italian dialects presents the same type of vowels and the same alternations as the endings of the verb in Livinallongo: 1st and 2nd singular and plural are identical and different from the 3rd singular and plural, indicating probably a semantic specification of [+/-deictic] (see Beninca' 1986, Poletto 1993, 1996). The vowels of this type of system are precisely 1st and 2nd *i*, 3rd *a*. Final *-i* normally becomes *-e* in this dialect.

One aspect that deserves investigation is the fact that lexical verbs only show the enclisis of the particle in the plural in Livinallongo (see (4) in the text); in the singular the tenses are formed apparently in the usual way of Romance languages.[19] I hope to come back to this aspect in particular in the future (see other phenomena that involve only plural persons of the verb in Beninca' 1996).

4. *Conclusions*

I am aware that the treatment of the phenomenon I have presented is still in a sketchy form. Much more space would be necessary to discuss the descriptive details and the theoretical consequences, as well as to give the comparative evidence that supports some intuitions. I think the facts presented here demonstrate the importance of looking inside Inflection and trying to describe how it works. If the morphological processes I have chosen have been correctly understood, they support Baker's theory, in so far as they show a morphological ending constructed in the syntax. Even if we follow Chomsky (1995) and accept the idea that some forms are inserted into the syntax as 'ready-made' inflected forms, we are obliged to accept the existence of a process that builds morphology in the syntactic component. In inflectional languages the shape of inflected forms carries over the memory of the syntactic process that produced them in the past.

I have tried to maintain a clear distinction between the knowledge we can obtain through etymology and that which we can hypothesise on the basis of synchronic evidence. It seems to me that each of the two opposed perspectives can be a source of independent evidence for the other.

REFERENCES

AIS *Sprach- und Sachatlas Italiens und der Südschweiz*. Zofingen:Ringer 1928-40.

Baker, Mark. 1985. "The Mirror Principle and Morphosyntactic Explanation". *Linguistic Inquiry* 16.373-415.

——— . 1988. *Incorporation: A Theory of Grammatical Function Changing*. Chicago: University of Chicago Press.

Belletti, Adriana. 1990. *Generalized Verb Movement*. Torino: Rosenberg & Sellier.

Beninca', Paola. 1986. "Punti di Sintassi Comparata dei Dialetti Italiani Settentrionali". *Raetia Antiqua et Moderna: W. Th. Elwert zum 80. Geburtstag* ed. by Gunther Holtus & Kurt Ringger, 457-479 [reprinted in P. Beninca'. 1994. *La Variazione Sintattica*. Bologna: Il Mulino].

——— . 1996. "Agglutination and Inflection in Northern Italian Dialects". *Aspects of Romance Linguistics: Selected papers from the Linguistic Symposium on Romance Languages 24, Los Angeles, 10-13 March 1994* ed. by Claudia Parodi et alii, 59-72.

---

[19] This is a point made by Calabrese (1998) regarding my analysis in Beninca' (1996).

Washington, D.C.: Georgetown University Press.

—— & Laura Vanelli. 1976. "Morfologia del Verbo Friulano: il Presente Indicativo". *Lingua e Contesto* 1.1-62.

Calabrese, Andrea. 1998. "On Fission and Impoverishment in the Verbal Morphology of the Dialect of Livinallongo". Manuscript. University of Connecticut.

Cardinaletti, Anna & Michal Starke. 1994. "The Typology of Structural Deficiency: A case study of the three classes of pronouns". Manuscript, University of Venice [to be published in *Clitics in the Languages of Europe* ed. by Henk van Riemsdijk (*Language Typology*, vol. 8) Berlin: Mouton].

Chomsky, Noam. 1995. *The Minimalist Program*. Cambridge, Mass.: MIT Press.

Cinque, Guglielmo. 1998. *Adverbs and Functional Heads*. New York & Oxford: Oxford University Press.

Giorgi, Alessandra & Fabio Pianesi. 1995. "From Semantics to Morphosyntax: The case of the imperfect". *Temporal Reference, Aspect and Actionality 1: Semantic and Syntactic Perspectives* ed. by Pier Marco Bertinetto, Valentina Bianchi, Jim Higginbotham & Mario Squartini. Torino: Rosenberg & Sellier.

Haiman, John & Paola Beninca'. 1992. *The Rhaeto-Romance Languages*. London & New York: Routledge.

Keller, Oscar. 1935. "Contributo alla Conoscenza del Dialetto di Val Verzasca (Ticino)". *Volkstum und Kultur der Romanen* 8.142-209.

——. 1938. "Aktionsart oder Periphrastisches Perfekt? Die Verbalflexion auf *ba* der Val Verzasca (Tessin)", *Zeitschrif für romanische Philologie* 58.525-41.

Pellegrini, Adalberto. 1973. *Vocabolari Fodòm-Taljan-Tudask*. Bolzano: Ferrari-Auer.

——. 1974. *Grammatica Ladino-Fodoma*. Bolzano: Ferrari-Auer.

Poletto, Cecilia. 1993. *La Sintassi del Soggetto nei Dialetti Italiani Settentrionali*. Padova: Unipress.

——. 1993a. "The Aspect Projection: An analysis of the *passé surcomposé*". *Proceedings of the XVIII Meeting of Generative Grammar, Trieste* ed. by Elisabetta Fava, 289-312. Torino: Rosenberg & Sellier.

——. 1996. "Three Types of Subject Clitics and the Theory of *pro*". *Parameters and Functional Heads* ed. by Adriana Belletti & Luigi Rizzi, 269-300. New York & Oxford: Oxford University Press.

Pollock, Jean-Yves. 1989. "Verb Movement, Universal Grammar and the Structure of IP". *Linguistic Inquiry* 20:3.365-424.

Rohlfs, Gerhard. 1968. *Grammatica Storica della Lingua Italiana e dei suoi Dialetti*. II: Morfologia. Torino: Einaudi.

Salvioni, Carlo. 1886. "Saggi Intorno ai Dialetti di Alcune Vallate dell'Estremità Settentrionale del Lago Maggiore". *Archivio Glottologico Italiano* 9.188-260.

Sganzini, Silvio, ed. 1965-70. *Vocabolario dei Dialetti della Svizzera Italiana*. Vol. II, I. Lugano: Mazzucconi.

Zanuttini, Raffaella. 1997. *Negation and Clausal Structure: A comparative study of romance languages*. New York & Oxford: Oxford University Press.

COMPOUNDING
MORPHOLOGY AND/OR SYNTAX?[*]

ANTONIETTA BISETTO & SERGIO SCALISE
Università di Ferrara - Università di Bologna

0. *Introduction*

The morphological theory known as 'Lexical Morphology' was based on very simple and 'strong' assumptions (cf. Scalise 1984) that can be summarized as follows:

(1)   a.   the computational space in the grammar for morphological operations is a separate component
       b.   the separation between morphology and syntax is absolute
       c.   the formal domain prevails over the semantic one
       d.   "external" data are not relevant

These assumptions were not always explicit but, approximately, this has been the theoretical frame from one of the most productive and inspiring currents of theoretical morphology of the last two decades. Today we know that the assumptions in (1) were simplistic but at the time, they played a crucial role in allowing scholars to isolate homogeneous and clear problems.

All the assumptions in (1) have been challenged over the last twenty years. Let us consider (1b), for example. In order to maintain a clear distinction between morphology and syntax, the so-called 'No Phrase Constraint' (NPC) (cf. Botha 1984) and the 'Lexical Integrity Hypothesis' (LIH) (cf. Di Sciullo & Williams 1987) were proposed.[1] The two principles were intended to block any kind of

---

[*] This paper, which is part of a wider research project, has been written with the financial support of the CNR. We would like to thank the partecipants at the European Colloquium on the Boundaries of Morphology and Syntax for their helpful comments on the oral presentation of this paper.

[1] Abbreviations in the text and in glosses are the following:

CSN =	Construct State Nominal		NPC =	No Phrase Constraint
KP =	the maximal projection level whose head K° can contain the Case marker		MH =	Modern Hebrew
			WF =	Word Formation

relationship between morphology and syntax in both directions: NPC prevents morphology from accessing syntax (cf. 2), while LIH prevents syntax from accessing morphology (cf. 3):

(2) *[[   ]$_{NP}$ + Suf], *[[   ]$_{VP}$ + Suf]

(3) a.   *Maria taglia carte*   →   *Cosa taglia Maria?*
          "Maria cuts paper(e)"   "What does Maria cut?"

     b.   *Maria ha un taglia carte*→ **Cosa ha Maria un taglia?*
          "Maria has a paperknife"   what has Maria a   cut?

     c.   **Maria ha una taglia grandi carte*
                                        Maria has a   cut   big   paper(s)

As stated above, the assumptions in (1) have been called into question and today scholars generally agree on the fact that the subcomponents of the grammar, in order to be descriptively adequate, must interact in some way. Current morphological theories seem more flexible than the lexicalist theories of the 80s because linguistic research has emphasized data that cannot be accounted for by rigidly separationist models.

Consider, for example, a Dutch compound like the following (Booij 1997):

(4) *[kleine-kinderen] gedrag*
     "[little kids] behavior"

This kind of compound includes a phrase; in order to be adequate, a model needs therefore to allow (under certain circumstances) morphological rules of compounding to take a syntactic construction as its base. The Saxon genitive in English (cf. 5b) and particular suffixation processes in Italian (cf. 5c) etc are case in point. An adequate theory of word formation, therefore, must be able to account for composition in all such cases:

(5) a.   composition (Dutch)   *[kleine kinderen] gedrag*
     b.   Saxon genitive (English)   *[a friend of mine]'s*
     c.   suffixation (Italian –ismo/ista) *[me ne frego]ismo*

Theories, however, must be restrictive for the simple reason that languages are characterized by restrictions. Lieber's (1992) 'deconstructing morphology' focused on so-called 'phrasal compounds', that is to say on constructions such as the following in English (cf. 6a) and in Afrikaans (cf. 6b,c):

LIH =   Lexical Integrity Hypothesis

(6) a.   a floor of a birdcage taste
          a pipe and slipper husband

     b.   *lach of ik schiet humor*
          "laugh or I shoot humor"

     c.   *God is dood theologie*
          "God is dead theology"

Such constructions, however, are not true morphological constructions since they do not obey the Lexical Integrity Principle, as can be seen in an analogous type of Italian construction:

(7) *un marito pipa e pantofole*
     "a husband pipe and slippers" (lit.)
     un marito tutto pipa e pantofole
     "a husband entirely pipe and slippers" (lit.)
     un marito tutto casa pipa e pantofole
     "a husband entirely home, pipe and slippers" (lit.)
     un marito tutto casa, chiesa, pipa e pantofole
     "a husband entirely home, church, pipe and slippers" (lit.)
     un marito tutto casa, chiesa anglicana, pipa Peterson e pantofole De F.
     "a husband entirely home, Anglican church, P. pipe and De F. slippers"

Bresnan & Mchombo (1995) maintain that constructions like the above are like 'quotations' and indeed they can even include phrases in 'foreign' languages:

(8) a *mea culpa* look
     the *ich bin ein Berliner* speech
     a certain *je ne sais quoi* quality

The point at issue, then, is not whether morphology and syntax should interact but whether morphological constructions can be entirely accounted for by syntax. Indeed, it is one thing to show that phrases can be input constituents to word formation and quite another to say that the constructions of the morphology (lexical constructions) can be entirely accounted for by syntax. In the latter case morphology would not have a specific domain of its own.

In this paper we want to discuss a particular kind of Italian constructions. On the basis of the data we present, we will claim that it is possible to distinguish between constructions which are exclusively syntactic and constructions which are exclusively morphological. The implicit conclusion is that syntax cannot account for all morphologically complex constructions and therefore that morphology has its own specific domain.

The constructions we will discuss are the following:

(9)   *arruolamento volontari*   "volunteer(s) enlistment"
        produzione scarpe   "shoe(s) production"
        accordatura chitarre   "guitar(s) tuning"
        accreditamento stipendi   "salary (/ies) crediting"
        concessione permessi   "licence(s) allowance"
        trasporto merci   "good(s) transportation"
        asporto rifiuti   "litter(s) removal"
        elaborazione dati   "data processing"
        rinnovo licenze   "license(s) renewal"

Before discussing the properties of these constructions, however, we will briefly illustrate the situation of compounds in Italian.

1. *Italian compounds*

Italian has different types of compound that can be grouped (for the purposes of the present discussion) as follows:

(10) a. lexicalised   *coda di cavallo*   "pony tail"
                       madre perla   "mother of pearl"
                       altoforno   "blast-furnace"
                       bagnomaria   "bain-marie"
                       acquaforte   "etching"
                       acquavite   "brandy"
                       barbagianni   "barn owl"
                       cavolfiore   "cauliflower"
      b. primary   *capostazione*   "station master"
                       nave traghetto   "ferry boat"
                       calza maglia   "panty hose"
                       punto vendita   "point of sale"
                       cassapanca   "chest"
                       caposezione   "department head"
                       vagone ristorante   "dining car"
                       valigia armadio   "suitcase-wardrobe"
                       prete operaio   "worker priest"
      c. N prep N   *ferro da stiro*   "flat iron"
                       permesso di pesca   "fishing licence"
                       rete da pesca   "fishing-net"
                       mulino a vento   "windmill"
                       macchina da cucire "sewing machine"
                       occhiali da sole   "sun glasses"
                       pattini da ghiaccio "ice skates"
                       libro di lettura   "reading book"
                       mezzo da sbarco   "landing-craft"

Lexicalized compounds such as those in (10a) are forms that are no longer compositional from a semantic point of view, in the sense that even though the meanings of the individual words of the complex can be recognized, the meaning of the whole word cannot be obtained through their composition. This is the case of *coda di cavallo*, whose "kind of hairstyle" meaning has little to do with a "tail of a pony", but with the fact that that kind of hairstyle resembles a pony tail.

The compounds in (10b), which we have called 'primary' because of the underived nature of the head constituent (cf. Botha 1984, Lieber 1980, Allen 1978), belong to three different subclasses: i) forms such as *capostazione* and *caposezione* in which the two constituents are joined by a 'specifying' relationship (a *capostazione* is the *capo di una stazione* "head of a station"), ii) forms such as *cassapanca* and *caffè latte* ("coffee and milk") in which a coordination relation holds (a *cassapanca* is a *cassa* "case" and a *panca* "form"), iii) compounds such as *valigia-armadio* and *punto vendita* in which the relationship between the constituents is the so-called 'variable R(relation)' (cf. Allen 1978, Scalise 1983); there is a range of 'possible meanings' relating the two constituents (a *valigia-armadio* is "a suitcase where one can put a lot of clothes as if it were a wardrobe" or "a suitcase whose dimensions are similar to those of a wardrobe", etc.).

In (10c) there are constructions whose structure is 'N preposition N' which have not yet been studied from a theoretical point of view in Italian.[2] We have classified them as compounds because they seem to be 'syntactic atoms' at least to a certain degree. These constructions are mostly opaque to syntax, at least as far as the insertion of lexical material between the constituents is concerned.

It is well known that a compound is a complex word behaving like an atom with respect to syntax, in the sense that syntax has no access to the single word-components (cf. Di Sciullo & Williams 1987). The compoundhood of a word can be tested in different ways, but the main test of compoundhood has always been the impossibility of inserting phonologically realized material between the constituents. So, forms such as those in (11a', b', c', d') are ungrammatical:

(11) a.   *uomo rana*   a'. **uomo piccolo rana*
       "frog man"   "man little frog" (lit.)

---

[2] This kind of constructions have been widely discussed in French. See, among others, Borillo (1997) and the references there cited.

b.	*nave traghetto* "ferry boat"	b'.	**nave appena costruita traghetto* "ship just built ferry" (lit.)
c.	*capostazione* "station master"	c'.	**capo giovane stazione* "master young station" (lit.)
d.	*valigia armadio* "suitcase wardrobe"	d'.	**valigia capiente armadio* "suitcase big wardrobe" (lit.)

In this respect, compounded words behave exactly like derived words. Even in derivatives, modifiers[3] cannot be inserted:

(12) a.	*felicità* "happiness"	**felice molto + ità* "happy very + ity"
b.	*allegria* "cheerfulness"	**molto allegro + ia* "very cheerful + ness"

There are, however, other tests of compoundhood. Ten Hacken (1994) for example, discussed and applied the tests listed below to Dutch:[4]

(13) - semantic specialization
   - head deletion under coordination
   - wh-movement
   - topicalisation
   - insertion (of parentheticals and modifiers)
   - referential opacity
   - anaphoric reference
   - pronominal reference

The tests discussed by Ten Hacken can be applied to Italian compounds as well, though we think that not all of them are significant. Semantic specialization, for example, does not have consequences for (Italian) compounding in that compounds do not generally acquire a specialized meaning. They do so only when lexicalized, not when productively formed such as the meaning of the word *pescecane* "shark" (lit. "fish dog"). Though not yet lexicalized – its meaning can be constructed from its components – the word has a particular

---

[3] Expressions of the kind in (12b) do actually exist: *scienziato atomico* ("atomic scientist") and *flautista barocco* ("baroque flautist") are examples of this phenomenon: *atomico* scopes over *scienza*, the base word in *scienziato*, and *barocco* modifies *flauto* not *flautista*. In this case, however, we are dealing with particular expressions (*flauto barocco* and *scienziato atomico*) concerning objects belonging to a 'natural class'. For discussion of these 'parenthesization paradoxes', see Spencer (1991) for English and Bisetto (1995) for Italian.
[4] Ten Hacken has pointed out that tests such as 'inflection', 'stress' and the Right-hand Rule are not reliable for reasons we cannot go into here.

meaning because of the metaphorical contribution of the word *cane* to the meaning of the whole: *pescecane*, in fact, is a fish which is similar to a dog because of its teeth, voracity, etc. However, this is not true of all primary compounds; in the majority of cases, in fact, the meaning of the compounds does not differ from the meaning of phrases that can be used alternatively (cf. *nave traghetto* "ferry boat" = "boat performing the service of a ferry", *caposezione* "head of a department").

We will thus verify the nature of the compounds in (10b) using the following tests:

(14) i. head deletion under coordination
ii. wh-movement of the head and the non-head constituent
iii. non-head topicalization
iv. pronominal reference

Those in (14) are 'syntactic' tests, that is to say tests which prove the phrasal nature of an expression. Consequently, if the application of the tests gives a negative result, we can say that the expressions in question are not phrases but compounds.

2. *Test results for Italian compounds*

The following are the results obtained when the tests in (14) are applied to primary compounds and to phrases:

(15) Test i.: head deletion under coordination

Compounds a. **la costruzione della nave ospedale e della __ traghetto*
"the construction of the hospital-boat and of the ferry
richiederà tempo
will take time"

a.' **hanno licenziato il capostazione e il __ reparto*
"the station master and the department __ have been fired"

Phrases b. *il trasporto dei passeggeri e __ delle merci sono*
"the transportation of passengers and __ of goods have
migliorati
improved"

b'. *la produzione della carta per banconote e __ delle*
"the production of watermarked paper and ___ of
schede elettorali sono state incrementate
voting papers has increased"

As can be seen, the deletion of the head constituent under coordination is impossible in compounds but possible in phrases.

The test of the wh-movement can be split into two sub-tests, movement of the head constituent and movement of the non-head one. The results of the first sub-test can be seen in the (a-a', b-b') examples in (16): movement is impossible in compounds and not completely acceptable in phrases:

(16) Test ii. wh movement of the head:

Compounds   a.   *che cosa ___ ospedale hanno costruito?
                 "what hospital have they built?"

            a.' *chi hai incontrato ___ stazione?
                 "who did you meet station?"

Phrases   b.   ²che cosa ___ dei passeggeri è efficiente?
                 "what of the passengers is efficient?"

            b'. ²cosa ___ della carta è stata sospesa?
                 "what of the paper has been stopped?"

The wh-movement of the non-head constituent, in turn, gives the following results:

Compounds   c.   *che cosa una nave ___ hanno costruito?
                 "what a boat have they built?"

            c.' *che cosa hai incontrato il capo ___ ?
                 "what did you meet the master?"

Phrases   d.   di chi è efficiente il trasporto ___ ?
                 "of whom the transportation is efficient?"

            d'. di che cosa è stata sospesa la produzione ___ ?
                 "of what has been stopped the production?"

The results we obtain are thus ungrammaticality in compounds and well formedness in phrases.

The results of the topicalization (of the non-head constituent) and pronominal reference tests are shown in (17) and (18) respectively. The two processes are allowed in phrases but not in compounds:

(17) Test iii.: non-head topicalization

Compounds   a.   *ospedale, hanno costruito una nave ___
                 "hospital, (they) have built a boat"

            a'. *stazione, hanno licenziato il capo ___
                 "station, (they) have fired the master"

Phrases   b.   *della carta, è stata sospesa la produzione* ___
"of the paper, has been stopped the production"

b'.   *dei passeggeri, è efficiente il trasporto* ___
"of the passengers, the transportation is efficient"

(18) Test iv.: pronominal reference

Compounds a.   **il punto vendita$_i$ è stato inaugurato da poco, ma*
"the sale point has been opened recently, but
non la$_i$ fanno a rate
they do not buy it on installments"

a'.   **la nave ospedale$_i$ è in esercizio da molto tempo*
"the hospital boat has been in service for a long time
ma non lo$_i$ utilizzano bene
but they do not use it well"

a".   **il capo-stazione$_i$ è simpatico ma la$_i$ dirige male*
"the station master is nice but he manages it badly"

Phrases   b.   *quell'azienda si occupa del trasporto quotidiano del*
"that firm deals with the daily transportation of milk
latte$_i$ ma la sua$_i$ freschezza non è certa
but its freshness is uncertain"

b'.   *la distribuzione della carta$_i$ è in ritardo, ma ne$_i$ abbiamo*
"the distribution of paper is late but we have a sufficient
a sufficienza
quantity of it"

As expected, the (syntactic) tests show that the compounds are syntactically opaque words, viz. are 'syntactic atoms' in the above mentioned sense of Di Sciullo & Williams (1987).

Let us now consider the situation when the tests of compoundhood are applied to the constructions under discussion, i.e., to the above constructions in (9) above and below in (19) which we call 'compound-like phrases'.

3.   *Compound-like phrases*

The compound-like phrase to be analyzed are the following:

(19)   'comp-like phrases'
arruolamento volontari   "volunteer(s) enlistment"
produzione scarpe   "shoe(s) production"
accordatura chitarre   "guitar(s) tuning"
accreditamento stipendi   "salary (/ies) crediting"

concessione permessi	"licence(s) allowance"
trasporto merci	"goods transportation"
asporto rifiuti	"litter removal"
elaborazione dati	"data processing"
rinnovo licenze	"license(s) renewal"
costruzione fabbricati	"building construction"

Such constructions, though at first sight similar to primary compounds like *punto vendita* and *vagone ristorante* (cf. 10 above*)*, are quite different. Their two constituents, in fact, are not bound by a 'possible variable relation' but the non-head constituent (the right-hand element) is the internal complement of the head noun (the left-hand element). The latter, in fact, is a process nominal: process nominals cannot usually occur in sentences not followed by their internal complements (= arguments) (cf. 20a); otherwise a referential reading of the nominal'(if possible) (cf. 20b) is activated:

(20) a. *la costruzione del fabbricato*
        "the construction of the building"

    b. *questa costruzione non mi piace*
        "I do not like this building"

Since the second noun (*fabbricato*) is the internal complement of the process nominal *construction*, the *di* "of" tying together the two constituents is a Case marker.

In Italian it is the nature of the relationship between the two nouns that seems to allow the deletion of the Case marker. Indeed, if we take other constructions whose constituents are not bound by the same relation into account, deletion of *di* is impossible, as the following examples illustrate:

(21)   *negozio di scarpe*   **negozio scarpe*
        shop   of shoes   shop   shoes
        "shoe-shop"

        amico di famiglia   **amico famiglia*
        friend of family"   friend family
        "family friend"

        compagno di scuola   **compagno scuola*
        fellow   of school   fellow   school
        "school fellow"

        tavolo di legno   **tavolo legno*
        table of wood   table wood
        "wooden table"

scarpe di pelle   *scarpe pelle
shoes of leather   shoes leather
"leather shoes"

4. The results for compound-like phrases

Let us now consider the situation when the tests of compoundhood are applied to our compound-like phrases.

(22) Test i.: head deletion under coordination:

a.   [?]il trasporto   passeggeri e il ___ merci sono fallimentari
the transportation passengers and the___ goods are   not convenient
in questa stagione
in this   season
"passenger and freight transportation are not convenient in this season"

a'.   [?]la produzione carta e la ___ schede sono in piena attività
the production   paper and the ___ cards are   in full   service
"paper and card production are in full service"

a".   [?]l' elaborazione dati e la ____ programmi richiedono
the elaboration . data and the ____ programs   demand
tempi lunghi
long   times
"data and program elaboration take a long time"

(23) Test ii.: wh movement of the head (b-b') and the non-head constituent (b"-b"')

b.   *che cosa ___ carta è stata sospesa?
"what paper has been stopped?"

b'.   *che cosa ___ passeggeri è efficiente?
"what passengers is efficient?"

b".   *cosa produzione ___ è stata sospesa?
"what production has been stopped?"

b"'.   *cosa trasporto ___ è efficiente?
"what transportation is efficient?"

(24) Test iii.: non-head topicalization

c.   *carta, è stata sospesa la produzione ___
"paper, has been stopped the production"

c'.   *passeggeri, è efficiente il trasporto ___
"passengers, is efficient the transportation"

(25) Test iv.: pronominal reference

d.   *il trasporto   passeggeri$_i$ è efficiente, ma noi non
the transportation passengers is efficient, but we do not
li$_i$ conosciamo
them know
"passenger(s) transportation is efficient but we do not know them"

d'.   *la produzione carta$_i$ ha avuto un notevole sviluppo, ma noi
the production paper has had   a good   growth, but we
non   la$_i$ compriamo
do not   it   buy
"paper production has had a good growth but we do not buy it"

As illustrated, three of the four tests produce ungrammaticality and we are therefore tempted to conclude that the constructions under examination are compounded words. But if we apply the test of insertion, which is traditionally the main test of cohesiveness, we find the following situation:

(26) a.   produzione accurata scarpe
production accurate shoes
"accurate shoe production"

b.   produzione scarpe estive
production shoes   summer
"summer shoe production"

c.   produzione accurata scarpe estive
production accurate shoes summer
"accurate summer shoe production "

d.   *produzione limitata nel   tempo scarpe
production limited in-the time   shoes
"limited in time shoe production"

Compound-like phrases are thus transparent to insertion (though with some restrictions, since insertion seems to be limited to a one adjective only). An adjective can modify the first noun (26a), the second (26b) or both (26c). What is impossible, however, is the insertion of a parenthetical (26d), an operation which is also not allowed in compounds and which we do not consider a reliable test of compoundhood.

5. *Some tentative conclusions*

Summarizing, the test results for the three different kinds of expressions are illustrated in the following table:

	phrases	comp.-like phrases	compounds
head deletion	+	+(?)	-
wh-movement	+	-	-
topicalisation	+	-	-
insertion	+	+	-
pron. reference	+	-	-

According to three of the five tests compound-like phrases are more similar to compounds than to phrases; nevertheless, we cannot conclude that these constructions are compounds because, besides the fact that the relationship between the two constituents, unlike what happens to compounds, is an argumental relation, they respond positively to the tests of head-deletion under coordination and primarily to insertion.

Constructions of this kind are not easily found in other Romance languages. Germanic languages have expressions which are comparable to the Italian ones, viz. compounds such as the English *car driving* (27a) in which the head noun, *driving*, is a deverbal process noun and *car* corresponds to its internal argument. Constructions like these, however, do not allow either for the internal modification (27a'-a") or head deletion under coordination (27b):

(27) a.   car driving
     a'. *a red car driving
     a"   *a car fast driving
     b.   *a car ___ and truck driving

As such they are to be considered compounds in all respects.

6.   *The real nature of constructions*

The constructions under examination have a parallel in Modern Hebrew (MH), in which there exist particular nominal forms, the so-called Construct State Nominals (CSNs), to which Italian compound-like phrases can be partially compared.

CSNs are words formed by two nouns: the first noun, which is the head of the whole construction, is stress lacking (cf. 28a) when it appears in a construct state, which does not occur when it appears in a NP (cf. 28b); this has a phonological consequence, that of triggering the reduction to 'schwa' of the preceding vowel (28b). The second nominal constituent, which is interpreted as possessor/complement, is not preceded by *shel*, the MH·correspondent of the English preposition/case assigner *of* (and Italian *di*) which must be inserted when a phrase is used (28a):

(28) a. *ha-ca?if (shel ha-yalda)*
the scarf   of   the girl
"the girl's scarf"

b. *cð?if   ha-yaldá*
scarf   the-girl
"the girl's scarf"

Hebrew construct state nominals are complex words but not compounds, as Borer (1988) has shown. For present purposes they differ from compounds as regards the following properties:
i) CSNs (29a), but not compounds (29a'), allow for the direct modification of their possessor/complement:

(29) a. *gan   peyrot   tropyim*
garden   fruit   tropical
"a garden of tropical fruit"

a'. **gan   yeladim   ktanim*
garden   children little
"a kindergarten for young children"

ii) CSNs (30a), but not compounds (30a'), allow for the conjunction of their complement/possessors:

(30) a. *shomer   batim   u-mexoniyot*
guard   houses   and-cars
"guard of houses and cars"

a'. **gan   yeladim   ve-xayot*
garden   children and animals
"a kindergarten and a zoo"

iii) CSNs (31a), but not compounds (31a'), allow for the pronominal reference to their head:

(31) a. *hu bana li   shney batey   ?ec   ve-'exad mi-plastik*
he built for-me   two   houses wood and-one   from plastic
"he built for me two wooden houses and a plastic one"

a'. **hu bana lanu   shney batey xolim   ve-'exad le-zkenim*
he built for us   two   houses sick(s) and-one   for old(s)
"he built for us two hospitals and a retirement house"

From these and other properties of CSNs, Borer concludes that the two kinds of constructions are words formed at different levels of the grammar. More precisely, she claims that Word Formation (WF) is not a component ordered prior to the syntactic component but is parallel to it; WF, she says, "is organized in such a way that its operations may apply, in principle, at any stage of the derivation, given that no well-formedness conditions are violated" (Borer [1988:46]).

We do not want to suggest that formations such as *trasporto latte* are construct state like nominals; as we saw, there are fundamental differences between the two kinds of construction: a) CSNs have a head noun without stress and with phonological 'reduction'; this is not the case for the Italian constructions under discussion;[5] b) the constituents of these Italian constructions are joined by a complement (= argument) relationship because of the process nature of the head-noun; this is not the case with Hebrew CSNs; c) Italian compound-like phrases can accept the direct modification of the head nominal (as we saw in 26), while this is not possible for CSNs, in which modification of the head constituent can only be ambiguous, i.e., an adjective following the possessor/complement can be construed as modifying either the head or the possessor/complement:

(32) *cɔ̃ʔif   ha-yeled   ha-yafe*
     scarf   the-boy   the-pretty
     "the boy's pretty scarf"   and   "the pretty boy's scarf"

Two facts seem relevant to us in CSNs with respect to compound-like phrases: 1) that they are words, like our constructions; 2) that the non-head constituent of the CSNs, (in Italian constructions) is always an obligatory complement (not a possessor), lacks an overt case marker as in the Italian constructions.

7. *The representation*

The constructions we have discussed here are peculiar forms that pertain mainly to labeling and technical languages, that is to say 'genres' in which shortenings are common. We claim then that forms like these are actually phrases with is the following structure:[6]

---

[5] Italian 'construct states' have been studied by Longobardi (1996).

[6] As scholars attending the meeting have kindly suggested to us, the problem could also be solved through incorporation. Since our aim was to show the (syntactic, not morphological) nature of the Italian constructions, we did not examine this proposal.

(33)

```
                DP
          _____
        Spec        D'
                _____
               D          NP
                     _____
                   Spec        N'
                          _____
                         N          KP
                      trasporto  _____
                               Spec        K'
                                      _____
                                     K          DP
                                     e      _____
                                          Spec        D'
                                                 _____
                                                D          NP
                                                e     _____
                                                    Spec        N'
                                                                 |
                                                                 N
                                                             passeggeri
```

where the noun *passeggeri* is the internal argument of the upper process noun *trasporto*. Between the two DPs, following the suggestions of Lamontagne and Travis (1987), Hale & Bittner (1994) and Bittner (1994), we put a functional projection KP whose head K° can contain the Case marker. This Case marker is absent in these constructions, as we saw. The absence of the Case marker, we suggest, is due to the fact that the upper noun is a process nominal keeping some of the properties of the verb from which it is derived (cf. Cinque 1980 and Picallo 1991 among others). As we saw above (cf. (21)), nouns lacking a process interpretation are not allowed to be followed by another noun lacking the Case marker.

Government by a lexical head is what allows for the absence of the determiner in front of the plural or mass noun in argument position (cf. Longobardi 1994).

8. *Conclusions*

For many years, the idea that morphology and syntax are two different components of the grammar has been assumed more on an ideological basis than on an empirical one. Subsequently, several counterexamples have led to the assumption that syntax can also account for morphological constructions.

We currently believe that a) morphology and syntax account for constructions with different properties and that b) it is possible to distinguish between them.

To this end we have examined a type of construction which is 'on the boundary' between morphology and syntax and concluded that we are dealing with syntactic constructions. Even though syntactic tests show that these constructions behave more like morphological constructions than phrasal ones, we have demonstrated that they are not syntactic atoms from the point of view of the insertability of lexical material.

REFERENCES

Allen, Margareth. 1978. *Morphological Investigations*. PhD. Dissertation, University of Connecticut.

Bisetto, Antonietta. 1995. *Tra Derivazione e Composizione: Su alcune formazioni complesse in italiano*. PhD. Dissertation, Università di Padova.

—— & Sergio Scalise. 1997. "L'autonomie de la morphologie". Paper read at the XVI Congrès International des Linguistes, Paris 20-25 July 1997.

Bittner, Maria. 1994. *Kase, Scope and Binding*. Dordrecht: Kluwer Academic Publishers.

Booij, Geert. 1997. "Allomorphy and the Autonomy of Morphology". *Yearbook of Morphology* 10.35-53. Dordrecht: Kluwer Academic Publishers.

Borer, Hagit. 1988. "Morphological Parallelism between Compounds and Constructs". *Yearbook of Morphology* 1.45-66. Holland: Foris.

Borillo, Andrée. 1997. "Identification de Composés Nominaux Basés sur la Relation de Méronimie". *Mots possibles et Mots Existants: Actes du colloque de Villeneuve d'Ascq (28-29 Avril 1997)* ed. by Danielle Corbin, Bernard Fradin, Benoît Habert, Françoise Kerleroux & Marc Plénat, 55-64. Lille: Université de Lille III, U.R.A.

Botha, Rudolph. 1984. *Morphological Mechanisms*. Oxford: Pergamon Press.

Bresnan, Joan W. & Sam M. Mchombo. 1995. "The Lexical Integrity Principle: Evidence from Bantu". *Natural Language and Linguistic Theory* 13.181-254.

Cinque, Guglielmo. 1980. "On Extraction from NP in Italian". *Journal of Italian Linguistics* 5.47-90.

Di Sciullo, Anna Maria. 1993. "The Complement Domain of a Head at Morphological Form". *Probus* 5.95-126

—— & Edwin Williams. 1987. *On the Definition of Word*. Cambridge, Mass.: MIT Press.

Grimshaw, Jane.1990. *Argument Structure*. Cambridge, Mass.: MIT Press.

Hale, Kenneth & Maria Bittner. 1994. "The Structural Determination of Case". Unpublished manuscript. MIT and Rutger University.

Lamontagne, Gregory & Lisa Travis. 1987. "The Syntax of Adjacency". *Proceedings of West Coast Conference on Formal Linguistics*, 173-186.

Lieber, Rochelle. 1980. *On the Organization of the Lexicon*. PhD. Dissertation distributed by Indiana University Linguistics Club, Bloomington.

—— 1992. *Deconstructing Morphology: Word structure in syntactic theory*. Chicago: University of Chicago Press.

Longobardi, Giuseppe. 1994. "Reference and Proper Names: A theory of N-movement in syntax and logical form". *Linguistic Inquiry* 25.609-667.

—— 1996. "Formal Syntax and Etymology: The history of French *chez*". Unpublished Manuscript, University of Venice.

Picallo, Carme M. 1991. "Nominals and Nominalizations in Catalan". *Probus* 3:3.279-316.

Scalise, Sergio. 1983. *Morfologia Lessicale*. Padova: Clesp.

—— 1984. *Generative Morphology*. Dordrecht: Foris.

Spencer, Andrew. 1991. *Morphological Theory*. London: Blackwell.

Ten Hacken, Pius. 1994. *Defining Morphology*. Hildesheim-Zurich-New York: Olms.

THE EFFECT OF NOUN INCORPORATION
ON ARGUMENT STRUCTURE

MARIANNE MITHUN & GREVILLE G. CORBETT

University of California, Santa Barbara - *University of Surrey*

0. *Introduction*

Important discussions of the boundaries between morphology and syntax have focused on cross-linguistic differences in the expression of similar ideas. What is expressed syntactically in one language is sometimes expressed morphologically in another. Morphological and syntactic expressions of possession are compared in Corbett (1987), for example, and passives in Börjars et al. (1997). Particularly frequent in such discussions has been noun incorporation, a kind of noun-verb compounding that yields new verb stems. An example can be seen in the sentence in (1) from Mohawk, an Iroquoian language of northeastern North America. The full Mohawk sentence consists of a verb based on the verb root *-ientho* "plant" compounded with the noun root *-tsi'tsi-* "flower".

(1) Mohawk noun incorporation: (Karihwénhawe Lazore, speaker)

    Waktsi'tsiaiénthon
    wak-tsi'tsi-a-ientho-on
    1SG.PAT-flower-EP-plant-ST
    "I've planted flowers."[*]

---

[*] Mohawk examples are presented here in the community orthography adopted by the six Mohawk communities in Quebec, Ontario, and New York State (Kahnawà:ke, Kanehsatà:ke, Ahkwesáhsne, Thaientané:ken, Ohswé:ken, and Wáhta). We are extremely grateful to the members of these communities who have generously shared their expertise on the language over the years, and especially to Kanerahtenhá:wi Hilda Nicolas of Kanehsatà:ke, Kaia'titáhkhe' Annette Jacobs of Kahnawà:ke, and Rokwáho Dan Thompson of Ahkwesáhsne, for their insightful discussion of issues addressed here. We are also grateful to Brian Butterworth for references to work on speakers' knowledge of lexical frequency, and to Andrew Pawley for discussion about lexicalization. This research has been supported in part by the Ontario Training and Adjustment Board and the Academic Senate, University of California, Santa Barbara (MM), and by the Economic and Social Research Council, UK (grant R000236063) (GGC); this support is gratefully acknowledged.

Translations of single words like these into full English sentences have sometimes fostered an assumption that their differences are negligible, that whether an idea is expressed morphologically in a single word or syntactically in several is an uninteresting accident of form. Several lines of research have aimed at describing morphological structures in syntactic terms (Lees 1960, Postal 1962, Sadock 1980, 1985, Baker 1988, 1995, 1996, among others). This approach has not been uncontroversial. Over the past decade, most discussion of noun incorporation has focused on the issue of whether it should indeed be analyzed as a syntactic process (Di Sciullo & Williams 1987, Rosen 1989, Baker 1995, 1996, and others).

Describing incorporation in syntactic terms could have certain advantages. Already highly articulated models of syntax could be extended to a new domain. If established syntactic principles accounted for patterns of incorporation as well, the principles could be seen to be more general than originally thought and so, in a sense, predictive. The exercise of testing them on incorporation might, furthermore, prompt us to notice facets of the construction that could otherwise go unobserved. On the other hand, if noun incorporation shares important features with other morphological processes, analyzing it in terms of syntactic models alone could prevent us from capturing generalizations in that domain.

Probably the most ambitious treatments of incorporation as a syntactic process have been those of Baker (1988, 1995, 1996, 1997, and elsewhere), who takes Mohawk as his prime example. In his earlier work, Baker defended the view that incorporation in Mohawk was purely syntactic. More recently, he has retreated from this position somewhat to propose that some incorporating constructions should be considered syntactic but others lexical. Unfortunately, as he points out (1995), various criteria for distinguishing syntactic and lexical incorporation do not produce the same classifications of specific items. Furthermore, individual diagnostics do not

---

Abbreviations in the text and in glosses are the following:

AGT	grammatical agent	NOM	nominalizer
CAUS	causative	OPT	optative
CISLOC	cislocative	PAT	grammatical patient
CONTR	contrastive	PL	plural
DIM	diminutive	PRF	perfective
DC	duplicative	PRT	partitive
DU	dual number	PURP	purposive
EP	epenthetic	RFL	reflexive
FACT	factual	REV	reversive
FUT	future	SG	singular
IMPRF	imperfective	ST	stative
INDEF	(fem)/indefinite gender	TRANSLOC	translocative
M	masculine		

always yield clear results for particular forms. The apparently conflicting results are more easily explained once we recognize the significance of the fact that incorporation creates lexical items.

1. *Background*

Several types of evidence indicate that the products of noun incorporation in Mohawk are different in kind from the products of prototypical syntactic processes. The differences are both formal and functional.

1.1 *The lexical integrity of Mohawk words*

It might be wondered whether constructions such as *waktsi'tsiaiénthon* "I've planted flowers" in (1) are truly single words, since they seem to convey the content of a full English sentence. Evidence of different types confirms that they are. Most important are speaker judgments, which are unequivocal on this point. Unlike words, individual morphemes are unintelligible to speakers in isolation. (The unconscious knowledge of morphological structure that speakers exploit to create new words is another matter.)

Other phonological and morphological patterns confirm the solidity of the word as an integral unit. Mohawk words have just one primary stress, usually on the penultimate syllable. Numerous phonological adjustments occur at morpheme boundaries within words but not between words. The order of elements contrasts sharply: morpheme order is rigid and invariant, while word order is almost fully fluid in Mohawk, governed by pragmatic considerations. Both nouns and verbs contain certain obligatory prefixes and suffixes which also serve to signal the beginnings and ends of words. Additional traditional criteria for wordhood are unequivocal as well. Speakers do not pause in the middle of words, searching for the next morpheme, then continue. If for any reason they stop mid-word, they go back and begin afresh, selecting the word as a whole rather than piece by piece.

1.2 *The functions of incorporation*

Languages with incorporating constructions generally contain analytic syntactic counterparts as well. In the Mohawk sentence in (1), the flowers were represented by the incorporated noun root *-tsi'tsi-*, but they could also be identified by an independent word instead, the noun *otsì:tsia'*, as in (2).

(2) Mohawk syntactic counterpart   (Karihwénhawe Lazore, speaker)

Otsì:tsia'   *wakiénthon*
o-tsi'tsi-a'   *wak-ientho-on*
NEUTER-flower-NOUN.SUFFIX   1SG.PAT-plant-ST
"I've planted flowers."

(Most Mohawk noun roots cannot constitute words alone, but must be preceded by a prefix like the neuter *o-* in "flower" and followed by a noun suffix like *-a'*.) This does not mean of course that every noun and verb root in the language occurs in both constructions, only that the parallel structures coexist as structures. Morphological and syntactic counterparts like (1) and (2) would not coexist so systematically if they were identical in function. Their semantic and pragmatic differences are well documented (Mithun 1984, 1986a, Evans [1991:264-292] among others). Essentially, incorporation allows speakers to package components of a concept together in a single word. Such packaging is done for two kinds of purposes, the creation of new labels and the regulation of information in discourse.

Incorporation, like all compounding, serves a basic word-formation function, as a device for creating terms for nameworthy concepts, such as *tewakhwishenhé:ion* (*te-wak-hwish-enhei-on* DC-1.PAT-strength-die-ST) "my strength has died" = "I'm tired". Often the incorporated noun serves to narrow the scope of the verb semantically, creating a verb stem for a more specific kind of activity or state than the verb root alone, as in *ronwatinonhsaníhen* (*ronwati-nonhs-a-nih-en* INDEF.AGT/ M.PL.PAT-house-EP-lend-ST) "one house-lent them" = "they were renting". Renting is a special kind of lending, house-lending for payment. Morphological verbs are used pervasively in Mohawk as syntactic nominals. Objects are often described in terms of their function or appearance, best expressed with verbs, as in *iehwista'ékstha'* (*ie-hwist-a-'ek-st-ha'* INDEF.AGT-metal-EP-strike-INSTRUMENTAL-IMPRF) "one metal-strikes with it" = "bell".

Incorporation has a second kind of function in Mohawk. The alternation between incorporated and independent nouns is used pervasively to regulate the flow of information through discourse. Separate nouns tend to be used to focus individual attention on a newsworthy piece of information, such as a significant new participant or a contrast. Information that is already an established part of the scene, predictable, or incidental, may be carried along by an incorporated noun. During one conversation, a speaker was describing a community program in which seeds were distributed. Her grandson asked permission to plant on her land:

(3) General gardening

Enwá:ton	ken	wahèn:ron
en-w-at-on	ken	wa-ha-ihron-'
FUT-NEUTER-be.possible-ST	Q	FACT-M.AGT-say-PRF

entiéntho'?
en-k-ientho-'
FUT-1SG.AGT-plant-PRF
"May I plant here?, he said."

She continued (in Mohawk): "I said of course you can, I guess. I was very happy that he would learn this right. What was so hard about that? All I did was talk to him, and he did all the work". In the next line, she incorporated the noun *-heht-* "garden".

(4) Incorporated noun: *-heht-* "garden"

Ahsatkáhtho'	*tsi*	*nihohehtí:io*	*nòn:wa.*
a-hs-atkahtho-'	*tsi*	*ni-ho-heht-iio*	*n-onhwa*
OPT-2SG.AGT-see-PRF	that	PRT-M.PAT-<u>garden</u>-nice.ST	the-now

"You should see how nice his garden is now."

Though the noun "garden" had not been used before, the idea of a garden had become an established part of the discussion and did not require special attention. It was accordingly backgrounded by incorporation. The speaker continued again, talking about other people she had seen planting.

(5) Independent noun: *ó:nenhste'* "corn"

Ó:nenhste'	*i:kehre'*	*rotiiénthon.*
o-nenhst-e'	*k-ehr-e'*	*roti-ientho-on*
NEUTER-corn-NOUN.SUFFIX	1SG.AGT-think-IMPRF	M.PL.AGT-plant-ST

"I think they've planted <u>corn</u>."

The corn was significant new information, worthy of a separate word.

Incorporation for discourse purposes can also be seen with presentative verbs, verbs with little semantic content of their own, such as "exist" or "have". The entity and its existence together form a single unit of newsworthy information, so they are often packaged together in a single word, such as *tkahéhtaien* (*t-ka-heht-a-i-en* CISLOC-NEUTER.AGT-garden-EP-lie-ST) "there.a.garden.lies" = "there is a garden there".

The lexical and discourse functions of incorporation are not necessarily distinct. A given combination may both constitute a recognizable lexical item and regulate the flow of information.

1.3 *Productivity*

Incorporation can be highly productive in Mohawk. The pervasiveness of incorporation in the language has sometimes been taken as evidence that it is a syntactic process (Baker [1988:80] and others). The productivity is different in kind, however, from that of many syntactic constructions. It is like that of word-formation processes in general, tied to individual morphemes. The verb root *-ianer-* "be good", for example, never incorporates. The verb *-ken* "see" almost never incorporates, though it frequently appears with an independent noun identifying the object seen. (Only one rare example has ever been encountered, a combination *-ia't-ken* "body-see" = "be conspicuous".) The verb *-ientho* "plant" appears often with an incorporated noun, as in (1). The verb root *-iio* "be good/nice" always incorporates. The productivity of individual verb roots varies along a continuum. Noun stems show a similar range of incorporability: some are never incorporated, some rarely, some often, some usually, some always.

The productivity is ultimately a lexical matter, not fully predictable on grammatical or semantic grounds. The root *-ianer-*, which never incorporates, and *-iio*, which always incorporates, have approximately the same meaning: "be good/nice". The variation is not entirely arbitrary: certain factors contributing to the patterns can be discerned (Mithun 1984). Noun and verb roots denoting recurring elements of nameworthy concepts often appear in names for them, for example. Among the most frequently incorporated nouns are those that are classificatory in useful ways. Mohawk terms for mental activities and states often incorporate the noun *-'nikonhr-* "mind": *tho'nikonhratihénthon* "he is attracted to it" ("it/him-mind-pulls"); those with physical effects on living beings often incorporate the noun *-ia't-* "body": *sakonwaiia'tenhá:wihte'* "they led them away (bodily)" ("again-they/them-body-carry-cause"); those pertaining to more abstract matters often incorporate the noun *-rihw-* "matter, affair, idea, word, fact ...": *iah tehorihwató:ken* "he wasn't consistent" ("not was-he-idea-certain").

It might be expected that incorporating constructions used for discourse purposes should show few constraints on productivity: in principle, all nouns that could represent established information should be incorporable. Even here, however, limitations can be seen. Relatively general terms typically stand in for large sets of more specific ones. There is no grammatical reason why nouns for domestic animals should not be incorporated, but they almost never are. In their place, the general root *-nahskw-* "domestic animal" is used. Similarly, there is no grammatical reason why the word for "bell" should not be incorporated. It is a deverbal nominal ("one metal-strikes with it"), but many deverbal nominals are incorporated (with a nominalizing suffix). In its place, the root *-hwist-* "metal" is incorporated.

(6)   Incorporation of general terms

   Wahatihwistaniion'tá:ko'
   wa-hati-hwist-a-niion't-ako-'
   FACT-M.PL.AGT-metal-EP-hang-CAUS-REV-PRF
   "It (the bell) was taken down (from the church steeple) . . ."

The incorporated noun *-hwist-* is used in this way for a variety of metal objects, including stoves and money. If incorporation were a purely syntactic process, like clefting or topicalization, we would expect the full range of nouns to be incorporated. Incorporating constructions functioning on a discourse level are often highly productive, such as those involving presentative verbs, but it is not unrestricted. The situation is not unlike that of English compounding. The English noun *player* is easily combined with almost any noun for a game, sport, or musical instrument: *Parchesi player, tiddlywinks player.* (Some may of course not be used because of existing formations: *violin player.*) Others are somewhat less productive, such as the English *ache*: speakers know that there is a noun *headache* but no noun *footache*, though it could exist and its meaning would be clear.

1.4 *Transparency*

A feature closely related to productivity is transparency, the degree to which the meaning and structure of a complex form correspond to those of its parts. The transparency of Mohawk incorporating structures has sometimes been taken as evidence of their syntactic status (Baker [1988:80] and elsewhere). A great many complex verbs in Mohawk are indeed fully transparent, like *waktsi'tsiaiénthon* "I flower-planted" in (1). Their meanings are completely predictable from their parts, and the relation between the flowers and the planting is clear. Speakers may not be able to isolate individual morphemes on request, but they know which meanings are represented in the word. Other combinations have idiomatic meanings, but their literal meanings are still readily available to speakers, as in *eniewirahní:non* "she will baby-buy" = "she is expecting". Still others show considerably less transparency, such as *atekhwà:ra* "it has food set on it" = "table". Speakers have expressed surprise at discovering that the word for "table" contains the incorporated noun root *-khw-* "food".

When Mohawk incorporating constructions are examined as a group, it becomes apparent that they show a cline of semantic and structural transparency, ranging from those that are fully transparent, like "flower-plant", through those that are idiomatic but still transparent like "baby-buy", through those whose original meanings can be recovered only with effort, and ultimately to many whose origins are inaccessible. Again, the situation is not unlike that of English compounds. Most speakers are aware of the rationale behind *ice-cream* or *forthcoming*, perhaps somewhat less of *cockpit* and *handkerchief*, and even less of *foolscap* or *rigamarole*.

In part because incorporated nouns can function in Mohawk discourse to keep reference clear, it has been suggested that they differ sharply in referential status from nouns in compounds like English *head-ache*. They are claimed to be syntactically equivalent to free nominals. Sentences like (7) from Baker (1997) have been presented as evidence for this view. (Spelling and morphological analysis have been regularized.)

(7) Referential transparency test: (Baker 1997)

Wa'onkkonhsóhare'
wa'-onk-konhs-ohare-'
FACT-INDEF.AGT/1SG.PAT-face-wash-PRF
"She washed my face."

tanon	*kwa*	*shé:kon*	*ioná:nawen*
tanon	*kwa*	*shé:kon*	*io-na'naw-en*
and	even	still	NEUTER.PAT-be.wet-ST

and it (the face) is even still wet."

When presented with (7) and asked "What is wet?", speakers indeed have little trouble identifying the face. It is significant, however, that such structures are not usual in speech. The contrast points to the need for care in the data-gathering process. Particularly in a language like Mohawk, where so many grammatical choices are triggered by discourse factors, and lexicalization plays a pervasive role, grammatical patterns emerge more systematically in natural speech than in constructed examples. The sentence in (7) was apparently constructed on an English model then presented to bilingual Mohawk speakers for judgments about reference. Even out of context, if speakers construct the Mohawk translation themselves, they come up with a form that differs in a crucial way in the second line.

(8) Speaker-generated Mohawk: (Kanerahtenhá:wi Nicholas, speaker)

... *Shé:*	*ki'*	*wakkonhsaná:wen*
shé:kon	*ki'*	*wak-konhs-a-naw-en*
still	just	1SG.PAT-face-EP-wet-ST
"it's still wet."		(literally "I'm still face-wet")

In the speaker-generated translation, the incorporated noun is repeated in the second clause: "I'm still _face_-wet". When presented with the alternative lacking the incorporated noun, some speakers have hesitated a moment, but all have responded that the incorporated noun should be included.

Even if sentences like (7) were to be taken as evidence that incorporated nouns function syntactically like full lexical noun phrases, it would first have to be demonstrated that the reference of the pronominal prefix *io-* "it" depends on a full antecedent noun phrase. A similar construction can be seen in (9), from a spontaneous conversation.

(9) Referential transparency in natural speech: (Awenhráthen Deer, speaker)

Thí:	tho:	ne:',	ronwatinonhsaníhen
thí:ken	tho	ne:'	ronwati-nonhs-anih-en
that	there	it is	INDEF.AGT/M.PL.PAT-house-lend-ST

"They were renting a house there,

iah	kwí	tekanó:ronhkwe'
iah	kwí	te-ka-nor-on-hkwe'
not	at.all	NEG-NEUTER.AGT-expensive-ST-PAST

and it wasn't expensive at all."

There had been no previous mention of the house in this conversation, so it does appear that the antecedent of ka- "it" in "it wasn't expensive" must have been the incorporated noun -nonhs- "house". The speaker continued (in Mohawk): "That's why, because it wasn't expensive, it used to feel nice. And then they would cook, put a feed on once a month. It was this woman K. We used to go there with my mother to eat. And it was so close, such a short distance ..."

(10) Reference without incorporated noun: (Awenhráthen Deer, speaker)

Tánon'	thó	ki'	ia'teniakwatskà:hon
tanon'	tho	ki'	i-a'-t-en-iakw-atska'nhon-
and	there	just	TRANSLOC-FACT-DC-FUT-1.PL.AGT-dine-PRF

"And we just ate there,

iáh	kwí	tekanó:ron
iah	kwi	te-ka-nor-on
not	at.all	NEG-NEUTER.AGT-be.expensive-ST

and it wasn't expensive at all."

This time the same pronominal prefix ka- appears in "it was not expensive", but there is no noun, incorporated or free, to serve as an antecedent. Was it the food, or perhaps the eating? Reference appears to be constructed by pragmatic inference. Incorporated nouns can certainly aid in inference, but they are not crucial. (Similar points have been made for other languages, as in Cornish 1986 among others.) The fact that incorporated nouns can assist speakers in determining reference is not surprising and does not in itself prove that they are different in kind from the components of compounds. Presented with the sequence *I have a headache; it really hurts,* few English speakers would have problems determining what hurts.

1.5 *The product*

Incorporation is indeed formed according to a regular. pattern in Mohawk: a noun stem representing a semantic patient is compounded with a verb root to yield a complex verb stem. But regularity of formation does not automatically mean that the formation is a syntactic process. Regularities are characteristic of productive grammatical processes in general, both syntactic and morphological. They differ in the nature of their products.

The essential difference between regular syntactic processes and Mohawk noun incorporation is that incorporation produces lexical items. It is not the usual mechanism for on-line production of connected speech. The resulting complex verb stem may then be stored and accessed as a unit on subsequent occasions. Where incorporation is highly productive, as it is in Mohawk, there are large numbers of such derived verb stems, and they appear pervasively in natural speech. There is ample evidence that speakers are generally aware of the fact that they are creating a new word when they use a new combination; such occasions are often accompanied by obvious delight. Fully fluent speakers vary widely in the frequency with which they innovate, and special talents for creating new forms are recognized and appreciated. Listeners generally know whether they have heard a particular combination before. They often describe the circumstances under which they first heard a combination, and they can identify the person who uses it. After visits to other Mohawk-speaking communities, they routinely remark on unfamiliar noun-verb combinations encountered, even when the novel forms are completely regular and transparent. Speakers helping to transcribe and translate tape-recorded speech from other communities constantly point to new combinations in the same way.

These lexical items are not exactly the same units as the phonological words described in section 1.1, but there is a close relationship. For the most part, they are the bases of the phonological words, the units that become phonological words in Mohawk with the addition of inflection. In general, speakers have clearer memories of lexical items than of phonological words. Thus they are likely to know whether or not they have heard the stem *-tsi'tsiaientho-* "flower.plant" of the word *waktsi'tsiaienthon* "I've planted flowers", but not whether they have heard it with all possible pronominal prefixes. Speakers are typically aware of creating something novel when they form a new noun-verb combination via incorporation, but not when they use an existing combination with a different pronoun. Lexical items do not always correspond to stems, but this appears to be the most common state of affairs, particularly in Mohawk.

The fact that incorporation creates lexical items accounts for the continua of both productivity and transparency. The varying degrees of productivity are tied to individual morphemes, as in other word-formation processes. The gradation in transparency arises from two factors, one the initial creation of the forms, the other their subsequent use.

First, words are coined for a purpose, to allow speakers to package single concepts into single words. The purpose may be to add new terms to the stock of vocabulary, or to regulate the flow of information in discourse. Combinations formed for discourse purposes often tend to be transparent, while those formed to enrich the vocabulary may be less so. A new vocabulary item may not be associated with its full range of possible literal meanings. The term *iehwista 'ékstha'* "bell", for example, is literally "one metal-strikes with it", and speakers can generally retrieve its literal meaning on request. It is not used for just any object used to strike metal, however, such as the range of tools ones might find in a garage.

A second factor contributing to the cline of transparency is the fact that the products of the process are lexical items, with their own integrity. They are learned, stored, and accessed as units. As such, they may shift in meaning and function over time, without regard to their original components. These shifts are made possible by a side effect of the creation of lexical items, a reduction in the specification of internal structure.

2.   *Grammatical relations*

The core arguments of Mohawk clauses are generally easy to identify. Every clause contains a finite verb with pronominal prefixes specifying its core arguments, whether independent noun phrases are present as well or not. The prefix on an intransitive verb refers to one participant, like *ra-* "he" in (11).

(11) Intransitive pronominal prefix: (Konwatsi'tsaién:ni Phillips, speaker)

> *Ratákhe'*
> *ra-takh-e'*
> M.AGT-run-IMPRF
> "He is/was running"

The pronominal prefix appears on the verb even if a coreferent nominal also appears in the clause, as in *shaià:ta ratákhe'* "one boy was running". A transitive pronominal prefix refers to two participants.

(12) Transitive pronominal prefixes: (Akwirà:'es Natawe, speaker)

> *Tahshakóhsere'.*
> *ta-hshako-hser-e'*
> CISLOC-M.AGT/3PL.PAT-chase-IMPRF
> "He was chasing them."

Again, either or both participants may be further identified by independent nominals: *Kaspé tahshakóhsere' ne ronón:kwe* "Kaspé was chasing the men."

There are three basic pronominal prefix paradigms, two intransitive sets and one transitive set. The first intransitive set (I), usually termed the Agent set, typically represents participants who instigate and control intransitive events, like the prefix *ra-* "he" referring to the runner in (11). The second intransitive set (II), usually referred to as the Patient set, typically represents participants who are not in control but are affected, such as people who are ill or tired. The transitive set represents an Agent/Patient combination, like *-hshako-* "he/them" in (12). Paradigm choice is categorical and lexicalized with individual verbs, though a semantic motivation can usually be discerned (Mithun 1991). Speakers do not select cases as they speak: some intransitive verbs are simply lexicalized with Set I pronouns, and others with Set II. The appropriate paradigm choice is learned with each verb. There are no independent pronouns equivalent in function to the unstressed pronouns of English. That function is served by the pronominal prefixes, which differ primarily in the fact that they are present in every clause, even when noun phrases are present as well.

Among the third person pronominal prefixes, three genders are distinguished: masculine, feminine/indefinite ("she, one"), and neuter/zoic. (Neuters are used for inanimate objects and zoics for animals, but in most contexts the two categories are expressed with the same forms.) Neuters are represented only when no other participant is present. Thus the prefix on *rá-hsere's* "he's chasing (it)" is simply the masculine singular agent *ra-* "he", the same as the prefix on *ra-tákhe'* "he is/was running". As a result, there is often no formal distinction between transitive and intransitive verbs. The same verb is used for "I'll plant" and "I'll plant it".

(13) Mohawk ambitransitivity

   Enkiéntho'
   en-k-ientho-'
   FUT-1SG.AGT-plant-PRF
   "I'll plant", "I'll plant it"

Spontaneous intransitive use of the verb "plant" was seen in (3) above "May I plant here?". No crop had been mentioned or even selected. In (14), the same verb is clearly used transitively with a nominal identifying the crop.

(14) Mohawk ambitransitivity

   Ó:nenhste'   *enkiéntho'*
   o-nenhst-e'   en-k-ientho-'
   NEUTER-corn-NOUN.SUFFIX   FUT-1SG.AGT-plant-PRF
   "I'll plant corn."

Thus apart from actions directed at persons, which require the specification of two parties in their pronominal prefixes, grammatical transitivity is not systematically distinguished overtly for verb stems, since neuters are not mentioned in the prefixes if any other participant is involved. Some stems never co-occur with a separate nominal identifying a patient, such as *-e-* "go"; such distributional evidence points toward intransitivity. Many others, like "plant", occur sometimes with a separate patient noun and sometimes without. When no such noun is present, the verb may sometimes be interpreted as transitive with specific patient ("I planted it"), and sometimes as intransitive ("I'll do the planting"). The existence of a patient (crop) might of course be implied, just as with the English *eat* (*food*) or *sing* (*a song*).

In any case, it is clear that incorporated nouns are not treated grammatically as core arguments. Because the vast majority of incorporated nouns are neuter, and neuter participants would not be represented by pronominal prefixes in any case, the distinction is not usually evident. In the relatively rare instances where an incorporated noun represents a human being, the pronominal prefix does not refer to it as a core argument. The verb in (15) was used to describe the habits of a monster.

(15) Incorporation of an animate: (Konwatsi'tsaién:ni Phillips, speaker)

> *Ratonkwe'tí:saks*
> *ra-at-onkwe't-isak-s*
> M.AGT-MIDDLE-person-seek-IMPRF
> "He hunts people."

The pronominal prefix *ra-* is intransitive, referring only to "he". If the people eaten were core arguments, the pronominal prefix would be *-hshako-* "he/them", as in (12) above, but such a form is unacceptable. If the role of the incorporated noun is no longer overtly mentioned within the pronominal prefix, can we still say that it is specified? We might be able to maintain that even if it is not specified, it is recoverable, since only semantic patients are incorporated in Mohawk.

In many languages, all verbs containing incorporated nouns are intransitive. In Mohawk, verbs with incorporated nouns may be lexicalized as intransitive, transitive, or both, though, as we have seen, the distinction is not always clear. Often the incorporated noun is a general term that serves to narrow the scope of the verb, so that it denotes a kind of event or state appropriate for a class of entities. An independent nominal (consisting of a noun, descriptive term, demonstrative, or some combination of these) may then further identify the particular entity involved. Incorporation of this type has been termed 'classificatory' (Mithun 1984).

(16) Incorporation with separate nominal: (Konwatsi'tsaién:ni Phillips, speaker)

> *Wahonhiákha'*   *sewahió:wane'.*
> *wa-hon-ahi-ak-h-a'*   *s-w-ahi-owan-e'*
> FACT-M.PL.AGT-fruit-pick-PURP-PRF   one-NEUTER-fruit-be.large-ST
> They went to fruit-pick   apples
> "They went to pick apples."

(The term *sewahió:wane'* is a verb "it is the one that is fruit-large" that has been lexicalized as a nominal "apple".) Structures like that in (16) could be taken as confirmation of the grammatical relation of the incorporated noun, as a patient or object, since it could be analyzed as co-referent with the independent noun phrase which appears to be filling this function.

Yet the incorporated noun and independent noun phrase need not be coreferent. Constructions like that in (17) below are common. The incorporated noun is -*hso 'kw-* "head", but the grammatical arguments of the clause are both masculine, as can be seen by the pronominal prefix *ho-* "he/him". The independent noun refers to the man, not his head.

(17) Coreference not necessary: (Kaia'titáhkhe" Jacobs, speaker)

Ia'thohsò:kweke'	ne raia'táhere'
ia'-t-ho-hso'kw-ek-'	ne · ra-ia't-a-her-e'
TRANSLOC-DC-M.AGT/M.PAT-head-hit-PRF	the he-body-EP-be.set-ST

"He bopped the man who was laid out [in the casket] on the head."

Such constructions, sometimes referred to as 'external possession', are common cross-linguistically. They serve an important function, permitting speakers to cast people rather than their parts as arguments (Mithun 1984).

We might try to salvage the retrievability of grammatical relations by stipulating that when a possessed entity is incorporated, the possessor is automatically registered as a grammatical argument of the clause. The incorporated possession remains the patient (or object). Incorporating a possessed noun does not necessarily entail a change in the argument structure of the clause, however. Possessors appear as core arguments only when the speaker expresses more interest in the effect of the situation on them than on their possessions. The sentence in (18) involves action directed at a possession, the door: "The two reached the door of an old couple". The verb contains the incorporated noun root -*nhoh-* "door", but the pronominal prefix is intransitive: -*hni-* "they two (masculine)". The old folks are the possessors of the door, but they are not sufficiently affected by the event, nor important enough to the narrative, to be portrayed as core arguments of the clause ("they/them-door-reached"?).

(18) Incorporated possession, no argument shift: (Konwatsi'tsaién:ni Phillips)

Iakèn:'ak	iahninhohó:ka'te'
iakèn:'ak	i-a-hni-nhoh-oka't-e'
barely	TRANSLOC-FACT-M.DU.AGT-door-reach-PRF

"They (two boys) just barely reached the door

rotikstén:ha	iatathróna'.
roti-kst-en-ha	i-atat-hrona'
M.PL.PAT-be.old-ST-DIM	M.DU-RFL-married

of an old couple."

It might be hoped that the recoverability of grammatical relations could be rescued by distinguishing alienable from inalienable possession, as proposed in Baker (1997). The man's head in (17) is inalienable (inseparable), but the couple's door in (18) is alienable. We might stipulate that possessors are coreferent with their inalienable possessions: if you hit his head you hit him. Both the head and its owner could then occupy the role of grammatical patient. The distinction between inalienable and alienable possession is in fact expressed formally elsewhere in Mohawk, in the choice of possessive prefixes on nouns (Mithun 1995). Furthermore, inalienable possessions are more often incorporated than alienable ones, and their possessors appear more often as core arguments of the clause.

Neither pattern is a mechanical consequence of alienability marking, however. Situations involving inalienable possessions like body parts simply significantly affect their owners more often than those involving alienable possessions. Alienable possessions may be incorporated as well, and their owners made core arguments, but only if they are substantially affected. Harnesses are classified grammatically in Mohawk as alienable, for example. Yet in (19) "he unharnessed the horses", the horses still appear as core arguments, because the effect of the action on them was more important than its effect on the harness.

(19) Incorporation of alienable possession: (Tekaronhió:ken Jacobs, speaker)

Wahshakohkwenniahrá:ko'		*ne*	*akohsá:tens.*
wa-*hshako*-ahkwenni-hr-ako-'		*ne*	*ako*-hsaten-s
FACT-he/them-harness-be.on-REV-PRF		the	INDEF.PAT-carry-IMPRF
"He unharnessed the horses."			

The grammatical relation of the incorporated noun in Mohawk is thus not specified formally, nor mechanically interpretable from form alone. Grammatically, incorporated nouns are simply modifiers of the verb root. In Mohawk, incorporated nouns typically represent semantic patients, entities centrally involved but not in control of events or states, but this pattern is not a necessary property of incorporated forms. Cross-linguistically, entities invoked by incorporated nouns can be seen to bear a variety of semantic relationships to their associated verbs, most often semantic patients, instruments, and/or locations (Mithun 1984).

The relation of the entity invoked by the incorporated noun to the predication is understood by pragmatic inference, in much the same way as the relation of horses to horseshoes and alligators to alligator shoes in English. Incorporated nouns indicate the involvement of an entity that qualifies the verb in some unspecified way. There is no internal syntactic structure specifying grammatical relations.

The lexical status of incorporating constructions can have important grammatical consequences. Since they are lexical items, their meanings are interpreted as unitary concepts, without formal articulation of the specific roles of the elements to each other. Particularly when they are first formed, the role of the incorporated noun may still be deduced, in part because in Mohawk it is semantic patients that are incorporated. Once a word has been formed, however, it has a semantic life of its own, without regard to its internal structure. As seen in (16) and (17) above, Mohawk transitive verbs containing incorporated nouns may co-occur with independent noun phrases further identifying either the referent evoked by an incorporated noun ("fruit-picking apples") or its possessor ("head-hit the man").

When we examine the range of use of incorporating constructions over longer stretches of speech, however, we see that the relation between an incorporated noun root and external nominal are not limited to these types. The incorporated noun *-renn-* "song" in (20) is neither coreferential with nor the possessor of *o'nó:wa'* "guitar". The incorporated noun *-renn-* is simply an element of the complex verb *-renn-ot-* "sing, play", appropriate for music. Singing/playing can be used intransitively or transitively.

(20) Mohawk incorporation: (Awenhráthen Deer, speaker)

O'nó:wa'	*ne:'*	*thaterennótha'.*
o-'now-a'	ne:'e	t-ha-ate-renn-ot-ha'
NEUTER-guitar-NOUN.SUFFIX	it.is	DC-M.AGT-MIDDLE-song-stand-IMPRF
guitar	it.is	he song-stood
"He played the guitar"		("He song-stood the guitar"???)

It is not difficult to see how the structure in (20) might have come into being. The verb stem *-renn-ot-* "song-stand" = "sing, play" was transparent when first formed, and soon came to co-occur with independent nominals identifying particular songs. With use, speakers became less and less conscious of its original internal structure, and it was simply associated with a concept "sing/play", and easily extended to contexts like that in (20).

A similar situation can be seen with the verb *-nia'kwakwaríhsi* "drink straight down" in (21), literally "neck-straighten". The relation between the incorporated *-nia'kw-* "neck" and the independent nominal "nice liquid" is neither classification nor possession.

(21) Mohawk incorporation: (Margaret Edwards, speaker)

Kwah   thiahania'kwakwaríhsia'te'
kwah   th-i-a-ha-nia'kw-kwari-hsi-'t-'
just   CONTR-TRANSLOC-FACT-M.AGT-neck-be.crooked-REV-CAUS-PRF
just he neck-straightened

> *tsi*   *nikahnekí:io*
> *tsi*   *ni-ka-hnek-iio*
> such   PRT-NEUTER-liquid-be.nice.ST
> such   such a nice liquid
> "He just drank the clear liquid straight down."
>
>   ("He <u>neck</u>-uncrooked <u>the liquid</u>" ???)

The complex verb stem was apparently originally formed by incorporating the semantic patient "neck" into the verb "straighten" ("cause to be uncrooked"). The combination was used in contexts where someone drank something in a single draught, without separate swallows. Once the verb stem was formed, however, its meaning "drink straight down" took over, and its internal· structure faded in the minds of speakers. At that point, it could be extended to contexts like that in (21). It should be noted that such an extension does not entail that speakers cannot retrieve the literal meaning of the expression on request.

3.   *The status of incorporating processes and constructions*

At first glance, it is easy to see the appeal of analyzing incorporation as a syntactic process. First, in many languages, incorporation can seem to produce sentences, like Mohawk *waktsi'tsiaiénthon* "I've planted flowers". In such languages, however, verbs without incorporated nouns can also constitute sentences: *wakiénthon* "I've planted, done my planting".

Second, incorporation operates on morphemes with meanings comparable to those of words in many languages, like *-tsi'tsi-* "flower" and *-ientho* "plant". If such comparisons were sufficient, however, we should consider the formation of the English *un-happy* to be a syntactic process as well, since negation in English is usually accomplished with the word *not*.

Third, incorporation can have syntactic implications, most clearly in its capacity to alter argument structure. It can convert a verb like Mohawk *-ohare* "wash", whose core arguments are the washer and the object washed, to an intransitive verb like *-nonhs-ohare* "houseclean", whose only core argument is the housecleaner (*wa'ḵenonhsóhare'* "I did the cleaning"), or to a different transitive verb like *-konhs-ohare* "face-wash", whose arguments are the washer and person affected by the washing: *wa'ḵhekonhsóhare'* "I face-washed <u>her</u>". Such effects can be produced by derivation as well, with antipassives, causatives and applicatives. In fact even lexical choice can affect argument structure, such as substituting "feed" for "eat", or "enter" for "go". If effect on argument structure is taken as evidence of a syntactic process, then lexical choice should be considered a syntactic process as well.

Specific arguments put forth for viewing incorporation as a syntactic process have depended to some extent on the model of syntax assumed. In a generative framework, noun incorporation has been viewed as the result of syntactic movement (Move-Alpha), which leaves behind a trace coreferent with the incorporated noun (Baker 1988, 1995, 1996). Because of the coreference, the trace is expected to show the anaphoric properties of a lexical noun. The derived complex verb is assumed to be intransitive; any separate nominals that occur with it are adjuncts outside the clause. Arguments for this view contrast it with a different movement process, identified as lexical, that would leave behind an empty pro, an invisible referential pronoun. This process is said to derive a transitive verb. Within this theory, then, arguments for the analysis of incorporation as a syntactic process have focused on anaphora and transitivity.

Unfortunately, the two syntactic tests proposed for anaphora, involving Condition C of the Binding Theory and licensing and agreement, are applicable only to a narrowly restricted set of forms, those whose incorporated nouns are animate. But animate nouns are almost never incorporated in Mohawk, so of the few constructed combinations for which the test might be valid, nearly all are highly unnatural, unacceptable on other grounds, making grammaticality judgments difficult to assess.

A third test proposed for determining the syntactic status of the process focuses on transitivity by examining question formation. It is argued that sentences like (22) cannot be transitive, because there is no object position for the question word (Baker 1995, 1996). The intransitivity is taken as proof of the syntactic status of the incorporation process. (Transcription and morphological analysis have been regularized.)

(22) Picking up: (Baker 1995:18, 1996:323)

    ?*Ónhka'   *tenhsewí:rahkwe'?*
    ónhka'   *t-en-hse-wir-a-hkw-e'*
    who   DC-FUT-2SG.AGT-baby-EP-pick.up-PRF
    *"Who are you going to pick up (a baby)?"

The sentence is actually problematic for other reasons. Picking up a baby is not expressed by incorporating the noun root -*wir*- "baby" into "pick up". It is an action physically affecting an animate being, so the derived stem -*ia't-a-hkw*- "body-pick.up" is used.

(23) Picking up: (Kanerahtenhá:wi Nicholas, speaker)

    Tenhonwaià:tahkwe'.
    t-en-honwa-ia't-a-hkw-e'
    DC-FUT-INDEF.AGT/M.PAT-body-EP-pick.up-PRF
    "She'll pick him up."   ("She will pick him up bodily.")

This verb is transitive, as can be seen from the pronominal prefix -*honwa*- "she/ him"; it may co-occur with a separate nominal identifying the child. It can also be used in "who" questions. Asked whether the noun *-wir-* "child" could be incorporated into the verb *-hkw-* "pick up", speakers consulted are categorical in their judgment: the form would not be Mohawk.

Even if the verb stem *-wir-a-hkw-* "baby-pick.up" did exist, the structure in (22) would be unacceptable for other reasons. If the noun "baby" were incorporated, it would be for discourse purposes, to background established or secondary information. For this reason, it is incompatible with a "who" question, where the focus is on discovering the identity of the one picked up. Nouns incorporated for discourse purposes can of course appear with questions formed with *ka' niká:ien* "which one". "Which" questions presuppose the previous identification of a relevant set of possibilities, just the conditions conducive to incorporation.

The same question test was used to classify the combination *-ks-ohare-* "dish-wash" as syntactic (Baker 1995, 1996). Incompatibility with the question word *nahò:ten* "what" was viewed as a sign of intransitivity, which was taken in turn as proof of the syntactic status of incorporation.

(24) Dishwashing: (Baker 1995:21, 1996:325)
      *Nahò:ten   wahseksóhare'?
      *naho'ten   wa-hse-ks-ohare-'?
      what   FACT-2SG.AGT-dish-wash-PRF
      *"What did you dish-wash?"

The question in (24) is indeed ungrammatical and the verb intransitive. There is no reason, however, that the intransitivity should be taken as proof of the syntactic status of the incorporating process, apart from Baker's own premise that lexical incorporation must create transitive stems. If, however, a lexical process is identified simply as a process that creates lexical items, to be stored and accessed in speakers' minds as units, it is not surprising that it should be able to create intransitive, transitive, and ambitransitive stems, mirroring the range of underived stems. The stem *-ks-ohare-* "dish-wash", for example, was coined as a label for a recurring cultural activity, like ironing or cooking. It does not generally appear with an object nominal because none is necessary. The term *-ksa't-iio-* "child-be.good" = "be a good child" is also intransitive. The stem *-ia't-a-hkw-* "body-pick.up" for picking up a person is typically transitive, occurring with an agent (the one picking up) and a patient (the one picked up). The stem *-hnek-ihr-* "liquid-consume" = "drink" can function either way: *Enhshnekì:ra' ken?* "Will you have a drink?", *Nahò:ten enhshnekì:ra'?* "What will you drink?". The transitivity of lexical items derived by incorporation in Mohawk is not fully predictable by general rule: it depends on the concept to be named.

As Baker realized (1995, 1996), his tests for the syntactic status of incorporation do not yield clear results. Some incorporating constructions would be classified as syntactic in his scheme ("dish-wash", "wood-cut", "baby-pick.up"), some would be classified as lexical ("wood-get", "liquid-drink", "liquid-throw"), and some are un-classifiable because speakers are too uncomfortable with the diagnostic constructions ("meat-buy", "baby-lose", "fruit-pick"). As can be seen, these results do not coincide with any of the usual views of the lexicon. For Baker, the primary issue in the study of incorporation is "the interesting question of how a language learner decides whether a given morphologically complex form is derived lexically or syntactically" (1995:4). If we simply assume that children learn the words they encounter, then deduce patterns for forming more as needed, this problem disappears. The fact that all of the combinations follow a clear pattern simply makes learning them easier.

What it means to say that a process should be viewed as lexical depends of course on the view of the lexicon assumed. One view has been that the lexicon is only the repository of irregularities. A more comprehensive view, and that adopted here, is that the lexicon is the set of lexical items that speakers know. New items may be added to the lexicon at any time. The new items may be borrowed, or they may be constructed according to regular rule, a common phenomenon in a language with morphological processes as rich and productive as those of Mohawk. These processes differ crucially from syntactic processes in that they are not the primary mechanism for producing on-line speech. They create lexical items to be learned, stored, and accessed as units.

Recognition of the fact that incorporation is primarily a word-formation process has several advantages. It permits the uniform treatment of all noun incorporating constructions in Mohawk, constructions which show the same formal characteristics. All are created according to the same word-formation process, by which a noun stem is compounded with a verb root. In all formations, the noun, which invokes a semantic patient, precedes the verb. The noun must be a formal morphological noun stem, with an overt nominalizing suffix if it is deverbal: *wa'ke'serehtahní:non* "I drag-thing-bought" = "I bought a car". If the incorporation would result in a con-sonant cluster, a non-stress-bearing stem joiner -*a*- is added: -'*sereht-a-hninon*- "car-STEM.JOINER-buy".

At the same time, it explains certain rare forms that do not follow the pattern exactly. Incorporation in Mohawk involves the combination of one noun stem with one verb stem. Yet a very few complex verb stems appear to contain two incor-porated nouns, as in (25).

(25) Double incorporation?　　　(Niioronhià:'a Montour, speaker)
  Enkonia'thahónnien
  en-kon-ia't-hah-onni-en-'
  FUT-1SG.AGT/2SG.PAT-body-path-make-BENEFACTIVE-PRF
  "I shall make a path for you" = "I shall guide you"

This construction could be formed only in several diachronic stages. One stage involved the creation of the complex verb stem *-hah-onni* "path-make", a useful vocabulary item. Once it had become an established lexical item, it was reinterpreted as a simplex verb, and again underwent the process, this time incorporating the noun root *-ia't-* "body" to signal an action with a physical effect on another living being.

The lexical status of incorporation also explains its variable productivity. As is typical of word-formation processes, the productivity varies with the individual morphemes combined. It also accords well with what speakers report knowing about their language. The possibility of a mental lexicon containing all the words (stems) of a language has on occasion been rejected, on the grounds that 1) speakers could not possibly keep track of the words they have heard and 2) that such a model would mean that different speakers of the same language must have different lexicons (Baker 1995). The first objection has been laid to rest by numerous studies showing that speakers not only know which words exist, they also have surprisingly accurate knowledge of their relative frequencies (Underwood 1966, Shapiro 1969, Carroll 1971, Gordon 1985, Connine et al. 1990). Work with speakers of Mohawk indicates clearly that they certainly have detailed knowledge about which stems exist in the language and which could but happen not to. Furthermore, we find just the lexical variation among speakers that such a theory would predict. Mohawk is currently spoken in six communities in Quebec, Ontario, and New York State. The majority of the lexicon is shared, but speakers are keenly aware of differences among communities, generations, and even individuals.

Viewing incorporation as a word-formation process also accounts for the variation we find in semantic and grammatical transparency. Many incorporating constructions are fully transparent semantically and grammatically. Speakers are aware of their components, and the combinations yield predictable results. Many others have idiomatic meanings like *eniewirahninon* "she will baby-buy" = "she is expecting", or unpredictable argument structures like *thihania'kw-akwaríhsia'te'* "he neck-straightened" = "he drank it straight down." They may be intransitive or transitive. Moreover, these different features do not covary systematically: a combination with a highly idiomatic meaning may still be fully transparent structurally, and its components easily accessible to speakers. Alternatively, a combination may be regular in every way except for its argument structure, or the accessibility of its components to speakers. The independent variation of these factors poses a problem for models that differentiate two types of incorporation, syntactic and lexical. Different criteria for classification give conflicting results, as discovered by Baker (1995, 1996).

In the end, when all incorporation is understood as a process of word-formation, the various idiosyncrasies are not surprising. Lexical items are created for specific purposes, and are subsequently free to change over time as units, without regard to their original internal structures.

REFERENCES

Baker, Mark. 1988. *Incorporation*. Chicago: Chicago University Press.
———. 1995. "Lexical and Nonlexical Noun Incorporation". *Lexical Knowledge in the Organization of Language* ed. by Urs Egli, P. Pause, Christoph Schwarze, A. von Stechow, & G. Wienold, 3-33. Amsterdam & Philadelphia: John Benjamins.
———. 1996. *The Polysynthesis Parameter*. Oxford: Oxford University Press.
———. 1997. "Conditions on External Possession in Mohawk: Incorporation, argument structure, and aspect". Paper presented at the Symposium on External Possession, University of Oregon, Eugene.
Börjars, Kersti, Nigel Vincent & Carol Chapman. 1996. "Paradigm, Periphrases and Pronominal Inflection: A feature-based account". *Yearbook of Morphology 1996* ed. by Geert Booij & Jaap van Marle, 155-180. Dordrecht: Kluwer.
Carroll, John B. 1971. "Measurement Properties of Subjective Magnitude Estimates of Word Frequency". *Journal of Verbal Learning and Verbal Behavior* 10.722-729.
Connine, Cynthia M., John Mullennix, Eve Shernoff & Jennifer Yelen. 1990. "Word Familiarity and Frequency in Visual and Auditory Word Recognition". *Journal of Experimental Psychology: Learning, memory and cognition* 16.1084-1096.
Corbett, Greville. 1987. "The Morphology/Syntax Interface: Evidence from possessive adjectives in Slavonic". *Language* 63.299-345.
Cornish, Francis. 1986. *Anaphoric Relations in English and French: A discourse perspective*. London: Croom Helm.
Di Sciullo, Anna Maria & Edwin Williams. 1987. *On the Definition of Word*. Cambridge. Mass.: MIT Press.
Evans, Nicolas. 1991. "A Draft Grammar of Mayali". Unpublished Manuscript, Melbourne.
Gordon, Barry. 1985. "Subjective Frequencies and the Lexical Decision Latency Function: Implications for mechanisms of lexical access". *Journal of Memory and Language* 24.631-645.
Lees, Robert. 1960. *The Grammar of English Nominalizations*. Bloomington: Indiana University.
Mithun, Marianne. 1984. "The Evolution of Noun Incorporation". *Language* 60.847-895.
———. 1986a. "On the Nature of Noun Incorporation". *Language* 62.32-38.
———. 1986b. "The Convergence of Noun Classification Systems". *Noun Classes and Categorization* ed. by Colette Craig, 379-98. Amsterdam & Philadelphia: John Benjamins.

——. 1991. "Active/Agentive Case Marking and its Motivations". *Language* 67.510-546.

——. 1995. "Multiple Reflections of Inalienability in Mohawk". *The Grammar of Inalienability* ed. by Hilary Chappel & William McGregor, 633-549. Berlin: Mouton de Gruyter.

Postal, Paul. 1962. *Some Syntactic Rules of Mohawk*. Ph.D. Dissertation, Yale University (published 1979 by Garland Press, New York).

Rosen, Sara T. 1989. "Two Types of Noun Incorporation: A lexical analysis. *Language* 65.294-317.

Sadock, Jerrold. 1980. "Noun Incorporation in Greenlandic". *Language* 56.300-319.

——. 1985. "Autolexical Syntax: A proposal for the treatment of noun incorporation and similar phenomena". *Natural Language and Linguistic Theory* 3.379-440.

Shapiro, Bernard J. 1969. "The Subjective Estimation of Relative Word Frequency". *Journal of Verbal Learning and Verbal Behavior* 8.248-251.

Underwood, Benton J. 1966. *Experimental Psychology*. New York: Appleton-Century-Crofts.

LEXICAL-FUNCTIONAL MORPHOLOGY
AND THE STRUCTURE OF THE LEXICON*

CHRISTOPH SCHWARZE
Universität Konstanz

0. *Introduction*

This paper focuses on representational and interface aspects of morphological structure,[1] morphology being regarded as an autonomous, generative system which operates on the lexicon and helps to provide syntax with words.[2]

Two claims will be made. The first is that Lexical Functional Grammar (LFG) is a suitable framework for the representation of morphological structure

---

* I want to thank Miriam Butt, Bruce Mayo, Lunella Mereu, Veronika Knüppel and Vieri Samek-Lodovici for valuable comments on earlier versions of this paper.

[1] Abbreviations in the text and in glosses are the following:

ADJ	=	syntactic adjective	N	=	syntactic noun
Adj	=	lexical adjective	n	=	lexical noun
ADV	=	adverb	NON_FIN	=	non-finite
A_OBL	=	the oblique case marked by the preposition *a*	NUM	=	number
ARE	=	the inflectional class of those Italian verbs which have -*are* in the infinitive	OBJ	=	direct object
			PERS	=	person
ARG	=	argument	PRED	=	predicate
BARE_PRED	=	bare predicate	PRES	=	present tense
C	=	conjunction	PL	=	plural
CLASS	=	inflectional class	SG	=	singular
c-structure	=	constituent structure	SUBJ	=	subject
D	=	determiner	V	=	syntactic verb
D_PRED	=	derived predicate	v	=	lexical verb
GEN	=	gender	Vinfl	=	suffix of verb inflection
f-structure	=	functional structure			
INFIN	=	infinitive	v/n	=	suffix turning verbs into nouns
It.	=	Italian			
LFG	=	Lexical Functional Grammar	Vprefix	=	verb prefix
MAS	=	masculine			

[2] I will not go into the current theoretical debate about whether there is a domain of grammar called morphology. Among others, Börjars et al. (1996) and Booij (1997) have given careful overviews of the problem and valuable arguments for the reality of such a domain, at least in many languages.

and the syntax-morphology interface. It will be assumed that morphological structure, like syntactic structure, is represented at two levels: at the level of constituent structure (c-structure) and of functional structure (f-structure). Börjars et al. (1996) have already argued that a theory in which functional structure, such as agreement features, grammatical functions, tense, mode and lexical meaning, is represented separately from constituent structure and in which both levels of representation are related to each other by mapping relationships is highly adequate for morphological analysis. They show how such a theory makes it possible to account for morphological phenomena which go beyond mere concatenation of linear surface segments, e.g. suppletion or conversion. In the present paper I will confirm some of their essential points[3] and discuss some more specific issues, widening their analysis to include not only inflectional, but also derivational morphology.[4] I will refer to the theory in its original version (Bresnan 1982)[5], since recent developments have no bearing on most of the points which I will discuss.[6]

A second claim will be made conjointly, namely that a procedural view of the lexicon makes it possible to account for the syntax-morphology interface in a straightforward way. It will be proposed that the lexicon is not only organized according to categories of constituent structure, such as words, stems and suffixes, but also with respect to interface aspects and to storage. Under this perspective, a distinction is made between lexical and syntactic words[7] and between a main and a temporary lexicon.

---

[3] Rather than from comparison of theories, my own position derives from concrete work on the morphology of Romance within the framework of Lexical Functional Grammar, including implementation with a Prolog-based compiler; for detail, see Mayo (1996, 1997). My data will be mostly from Italian, a language with a particularly well developed morphology.

[4] I will not treat here those morphological phenomena which do not involve operations on feature structures, such as the alternation of the thematic vowel -a-, which appears as -e- in the future-and-conditional stems, or the alternation between [k] and [tʃ], as in *specifico* [spe'tʃifiko] "specific (SG)" vs. *specifici* [spe'tʃifitʃi] "specific (PL)". Alternations of this kind may be formulated in the format of phonological rules, but take place within the lexicon and are restricted, if irregular, to given lexical items and, if regular, to given cells of the relevant paradigm.

[5] For a short introduction, cf. Butt et al. (1998), sections 1.3 and 1.4.

[6] An exception must be made, however, for the stripping of grammatical functions connected with nominalization, as discussed in section 2.1 below: linking theory (Bresnan & Kanerva 1989, Bresnan & Moshi 1990) may well yield a better analysis than the one I propose there.

[7] I take the term 'syntactic word' from Di Sciullo & Williams (1987:78ff.). That does not imply that I adopt all aspects of their notion. For example, I do not share their claim that syntactic words have non-compositonal meanings (Di Sciullo & Williams 1987:80). Furthermore, the reader should note that what I call lexical words are not just 'listemes'. In fact, I do not think that the permanent lexicon is just "the prison of the lawless", "incredibly boring by its very

I will first deal with inflectional morphology, to which the distinction between lexical and syntactic words is crucial. Syntactic words are inflected
forms, such as It. *canto* "I sing", *case* "houses", *alti* "high (MAS PL)", and
words which have no inflection, such as conjunctions (e.g. It. *ma* "but"), adverbs (e.g. It. *oggi* "today"), etc. The distinction between lexical and syntactic
words rests upon the following assumptions:

(1) Lexical insertion, i.e. the procedure which puts words into the end
    nodes of c-structures, only accepts syntactic words.

(2) Lexical words are turned into syntactic words by inflectional mor-
    phology.

(3) Syntax checks the lexical category and the functional properties of
    complex words, but does not see their internal c-structure; cf. the
    'lexical integrity principle' (Di Sciullo & Williams [1987:49], Bres-
    nan & Mchombo 1995, Bresnan [1996:13]).

(4) Derivational morphology expands the lexicon, generating additional
    lexical words.

(5) The lexicon contains not only lexical but also syntactic words.

1. *Inflectional morphology*

As has been said above, inflectional morphology turns lexical words into
syntactic words. It does so by combining morphological segments at the c-
structure level and by operations on feature structures at the f-structure level.
Operations on feature structures, however, are not necessarily linked with processes at the c-structure level. Hence, rules of inflectional morphology are of two
types. The rules of the first type are similar to those of syntax, i.e. they generate
branching structures with feature annotations at the c-structure level. Thus, a
form like It. *canto* "I sing" is generated by a branching rule which puts the stem
cant- and the inflectional suffix *-o* together and requires unification of their
features. The rules of the second type add features without creating branching
structures, that is, they turn lexical words into syntactic words without adding a
suffix. Examples are It. nouns like *proprietà* "property". They are both lexical
and syntactic nouns: they are lexical nouns as represented in the lexicon with-

---

nature" (Di Sciullo & Williams 1987:3). To mention just one of the reasons, lexical semantics
shows that there are highly complex systematic relationships between lexical words, such as
antonymy (*short* vs. *long*) and that these may have intricate internal structures, such as implied
negation (*to deny, to refuse*).

out a number feature, and they are syntactic nouns when used in sentences, where they are singulars or plurals; cf. *questa proprietà* "this property" vs. *queste proprietà* "these properties". Another example is given by French adjectives, which will briefly be discussed below.

1.1 *Feature adding operations*

Rules of inflectional morphology add features to lexical words. These features are those which are used a) for agreement and b) to add semantic information at various levels of f-structure, including the sentence. Typical attributes for features of inflectional morphology are person, number, tense, mode, and gender. They are partially encoded in a sublexicon of affixes. Thus, It. *-vo*, an inflectional affix[8] for verbs, as in *anda-vo* "I went" has the following entry:

(6) *vo*, Vinfl, ($\uparrow$ TENSE) = IMPERFECT, ($\uparrow$ PERS) = 1, ($\uparrow$ NUM) = SG

Rules of inflectional morphology, just like the familiar annotated c-structure rules of syntax, pass this information on to the resulting syntactic words. Moreover, still like syntactic c-structure rules, they can introduce features which are not encoded in the lexicon. Thus, the French lexical word *grand* "big" has features which specify a predicate and an argument structure, plus a feature stating that, in noun phrases, its default position is before the noun:

(7) *grand*, adj
     ($\uparrow$ PRED) = 'GRAND (ARG)'
     ($\uparrow$ POSITION) = PRENOMINAL

The syntactic word *grand* inherits these features, and additionally receives the agreement features masculine singular. This is done by a rule which simply adds these agreement features to the features already encoded in the lexical word. In order to write rules of this kind, we need a convention which expresses the difference between lexical and syntactic words. I use lower case letters for lexical words and capital letters for syntactic words. The rule which generates masculine singular adjectives can now be formulated as (8), and the representation of the syntactic word *grand*, which is generated by (8) is (9):

(8) ADJ $\rightarrow$ adj
                        $\uparrow = \downarrow$
                  ($\uparrow$ NUM) = SG
                  ($\uparrow$ GEN) = MAS

---

[8] For reasons that will be explained in section 1.4.2, I do not analyze *-vo* into smaller segments.

(9) *grand*, ADJ
    ($\uparrow$ PRED) = 'GRAND (ARG)'
    ($\uparrow$ POSITION) = PRENOMINAL
    ($\uparrow$ NUM) = SG
    ($\uparrow$ GEN) = MAS

1.2 *Inflectional features and morphological shape*

In the syntactic adjective *grand*, as represented by (9), there is no parallel-ism between morphological f-structure and c-structure: *grand*, as the lexical word represented by (9), is analyzed into four features, belonging to two differ-ent kinds, namely inflectional and non-inflectional ones, whereas at the c-structure level, the word is unanalyzable. This is the consequence of what has been said above: features may be added by non-branching rules. These features typically are NUMBER = SINGULAR, GENDER = MASCULINE and TENSE = PRESENT.

Moreover, there is a class of features which never correspond to segments, namely those which specify inflectional classes. A language has inflectional classes if, within a lexical category, given functional information is expressed by a set of exponents in such a way that each lexical word extracts one, and cannot take other exponents from that set. Thus, the Italian verb has various inflectional classes, among which the *are*-class and the *ere*-class, as illustrated in (10) for the 3rd person present of *cantare* "to sing" and *vendere* "to sell":

(10)	INDICATIVE		SUBJUNCTIVE	
SG	*cant-a*	*vend-e*	*cant-i*	*vend-a*
PL	*cant-ano*	*vend-ono*	*cant-ino*	*vend-ano*

In the LFG framework, the wellformedness conditions given by inflectional classes can be expressed as agreement requirements, more precisely by features which are encoded as properties of lexical words and of inflectional suffixes and which must unify when affixation takes place. Thus, lexical entries for the verb stems and inflectional suffixes involved in (10) can be formulated as fol-lows:

(11) *cant*, v, ($\uparrow$ PRED) = 'CANTARE (SUBJ)', ($\uparrow$ CLASS) = ARE

(12) *vend*, v, ($\uparrow$ PRED) = 'CAPIRE (SUBJ), (OBJ)', ($\uparrow$ CLASS) = ERE

(13) *a*, Vinfl, ($\uparrow$ PERS) = 3, ($\uparrow$ NUM) = SG, ($\uparrow$ TENSE) = PRES, ($\uparrow$ MODE) = INDICATIVE, ($\uparrow$ CLASS) = ARE

(14) *a*, Vinfl, ($\uparrow$ PERS) = 3, ($\uparrow$ NUM) = SG, TENSE) = PRES, ($\uparrow$ MODE) = SUBJUNCTIVE, ($\uparrow$ CLASS) = ERE

(15) *e*, Vinfl, (↑ PERS) = 3, (↑ NUM) = SG, (↑ TENSE) = PRES, (↑ MODE) = INDICATIVE, (↑ CLASS) = ERE

(16) *ano*, Vinfl, (↑ PERS) = 3, (↑ NUM) = PL, (↑ TENSE) = PRES, (↑ MODE) = INDICATIVE, (↑ CLASS) = ARE

(17) *ano*, Vinfl, (↑ PERS) = 3, (↑ NUM) = PL, (↑ TENSE) = PRES, (↑ MODE) = SUBJUNCTIVE, (↑ CLASS) = ERE

(18) *ino*, Vinfl, (↑ PERS) = 3, (↑ NUM) = PL, (↑ TENSE) = PRES, (↑ MODE) = SUBJUNCTIVE, (↑ CLASS) = ARE

(19) *ono*, Vinfl, (↑ PERS) = 3, (↑ NUM) = PL, (↑ TENSE) = PRES, (↑ MODE) = INDICATIVE, (↑ CLASS) = ERE

Once unification has been successful and a syntactic word has been created, the inflectional class feature is not needed any more. Therefore, unlike all other features, it is not passed on to the syntactic word.[9]

Furthermore there is a mismatch between morphological shape and feature structures of a more abstract kind: morphological segments and functional attributes form classes which do not fully correspond to each other. The features which are relevant for inflectional morphology are typically encoded as properties of affixes (or, less typically, as rule annotations). But they may also be encoded as properties of lexical words. Gender, for example, in Italian and other languages, is encoded in inflectional suffixes as well as in stems. And the distribution of irregular or suppletive stems can be accounted for by assuming that inflectional features are encoded in stems. Thus, for noun forms like *uomo* "man", *uomini* "men", number can be said to be encoded not only in the suffixes *-o* (SG) and *-i* (PL), but also in the stems, *uom-* (SG) and *uomin-* (PL). Likewise, tense, person and number can be said to be encoded in the "strong" perfect stems of the Italian verb, e.g. in *diss-i* "I said" vs. *dice-sti* "you said", *fec-i* "I did" vs. *face-sti* "you did", *pres-i* "I took" vs. *prende-sti* "you took". Hence the lexical entries of these strong perfect stems will be said to contain the feature TENSE = PERFECT,[10] plus a feature which constrains the strong stem to the first person in the singular and the third person in both numbers.[11] Thus, the strong stem *diss-* will be represented by the following lexical entries:

---

[9] A feasable alternative to this treatment of inflectional classes is to subclassify stems and inflectional suffixes at the c-structure level, and to formulate morphological rules accordingly. But this would mean complicating the system of morphological rules (unneccessarily).

[10] I use PERFECT to translate the Italian term 'passato remoto'.

[11] In these cases, the distinction between lexical and syntactic words appears to be blurred, since features which typically belong to inflectional suffixes may also be associated with lexical

(20) *diss-*, v

(↑ PRED) = 'DIRE (SUBJ), (OBJ), (A_OBL)'
(↑ TENSE) = PERFECT
(↑ PERS) = 1
(↑ NUM) = SG

(21) *diss-*, v

(↑ PRED) = 'DIRE (SUBJ), (OBJ), (A_OBL)'
(↑ TENSE) = PERFECT
(↑ PERS) = 3

1.3 Syntactic words and the lexicon

Syntactic words may have different status within the lexicon: they may be:

(22) merely virtual, i.e. they are generated by morphological rules, and consequently are regular and transparent; they are not represented as full forms in the lexicon; It. *illustrereste* "you (PL) would illustrate" might be an example;

(23) lexicalized, and also generated by morphological rules, i.e. due to their frequent use, they are stored and processed as a whole, but they are transparent, and can be accessed via the morphological system, e.g. It. *basta* "that's enough";[12]

(24) lexicalized, and not generated by morphological rules, i.e. they may have a feature structure, but an opaque morphological shape at the c-structure level, e.g. It. *è* "is".

At this point, mention should be made of what is generally termed "blocking". Syntactic words of the kind defined in (24) "block" the output of morphological rules. But rather than being a property of the generative morphological system, blocking effects derive from a principle of general lexical

---

stems. But this is only apparently so, since we do not define the difference between lexical and syntactic words in terms of kinds of features, but with respect to lexical insertion.

[12] Highly frequent regular forms like It. *anni* "years", *basta* "is enough", *bisogna* "is necessary", *capito* "understood (participle)", *casa* "house", *cosa* "thing", *credo* "I believe" are likely to be directly represented in the lexicon, but, since they perfectly match the structures of the regular nouns and verbs, they are also generated by morphology. In the corpus of spoken Italian used by De Mauro et al. (1993), these words have the following usage values: *anni* 411 (against only 248 for the singular *anno*), *basta* 161, *bisogna* 207, *capito* 411 (against only 15 for the feminine *capita*), *casa* 347 (against only 12 for the plural *case*), *cosa* 1229 (against only 594 for the plural *cose*), *credo* 317 (against only 7 for the third person *crede*).

management. It seems reasonable, in fact, to think that there is a kind of Lexical Immigration Authority, which controls possible lexical growth. It aims at protecting the items already present in the lexicon from newcomers created by the morphological generative system; it may also prevent borrowings and other lexical innovations. It is related, rather than to grammar and cognition, to the communicative and social aspects of language. Since lexicalization is not independent from frequency of use, the Authority may fail to protect items which are rarely used, making it possible for lexical items to be replaced by others which have the same functional properties.

In the model of morphology we are advocating, there are no transformations or "phonological" adjustment rules. Allomorphy of word stems, as far as it cannot be restated in terms of postlexical rules of phonology, is treated in terms of multiple lexical representations.[13] We will say, for example, that an irregular verb, such as It. *prendere* "to take" has more then one lexically represented stem: *pres-* for the "strong" forms of the perfect (1st and 3rd person of the singular, 3rd person for the plural) and for the past participle, *prend-* elsewhere.[14]

This conception of a variable relationship between the generative system and permanent lexical storage may also account for morphological change. Thus, one of the most visible morphological changes, namely the loss of internal c-structure, as in Lat. *hab-e-o* "I have" > Proto-Romance *ai-o* > It. [ɔ] *ho*, can be described as a passage from situation (23) above to situation (24). It presupposes a further invisible process, namely the passage from situation (22) to situation (23). In fact, loss of internal structure cannot occur as long as a syntactic word is merely virtual (situation [22]) it must be stored and processed as

---

[13] Cf. Booij (1997:32ff.), who discusses this point in more detail and comes to similar conclusions.

[14] If allomorphous forms are not derived (suppletive forms cannot be derived), how can they be said to be forms of the same word? Traditional grammar uses the term 'paradigm' to refer to this kind of relationship, and defines paradigms by writing the inflected forms in the closed lists used in old-fashioned textbooks for language-learners. The question is: how can the notion of paradigm be rendered in a feature-structure morphology? Paradigms obviously cannot be represented as the set of forms derived from a given stem, since in suppletive paradigms, there is more than one stem. One might then think of a paradigm as the set of syntactic words which have the same predicate. Schwarze (1996), however, argues that It. *avere* "to have" and *essere* "to be", used as temporal and passive auxiliaries, do not have a predicate in their feature structure. If that analysis is correct, then the predicate cannot express the unity of the paradigm. The simplest way to express the relationship of inflected forms to a paradigm is to follow the example of traditional grammar, which gives each lexical item a conventional name, its citation form. And, since belonging to a given paradigm is a functional property, it will preferably be expressed as a feature.

a whole in order to undergo changes in its internal c-structure. I will discuss another example in 1.4.3 below.

1.4 Problems

1.4.1 Functional ambiguity. The output of inflectional morphology may seem ambiguous with respect to the functional information needed by syntax. Thus inflectional morphology generates participles like *cantato* "sung", *capito* "understood", regardless of their functional properties. In fact, these participles may be past participles, which receive the lexically-encoded functional structure of the verb they derive from, or passive participles, with the well-known change in functional structure. The question arises, then, of how the missing information (past or passive?) is filled in. One solution, for a language like Italian, is to let morphology only generate fully specified past participles, which keep the argument structure of the original lexical verb, and to create the passive participle by a rule of derivational morphology, which turns past participles into passive participles by changing their mapping from argument structure to grammatical relations. This treatment has two advantages. It avoids the difficulties of a solution by underspecification (which only defers the question of where the necessary context information is to be found), and, by deriving the passive not from the lexical verb, as traditional analyses do, but from its past participle, it accounts for the fact that at the level of assembling morphological segments, there is just one participial form.

Auxiliaries are another case of apparent functional ambiguity at the level of morphology. In fact, in languages like Italian, French, English or German (but not Spanish) auxiliary verbs, at the level of morphological shape and agreement features, are not different from their non-auxiliary counterparts: It. *avere* "to have" and *essere* "to be" have the same inflection regardless of whether they are used as ordinary verbs or as auxiliaries. But they differ functionally: unlike ordinary verbs, auxiliaries do not represent predicates (Schwarze 1996) and, consequently, have no argument structure. Furthermore, the tense features assigned to temporal auxiliaries by morphology are not passed on to the sentence: the syntactic verb *hanno* "have" in both (25) and in (26) is present tense:

(25) *I ragazzi hanno un pallone*
"the boys have a ball"

(26) *I ragazzi hanno giocato a pallone*
"the boys played soccer"

But at the level of the sentence, (25) and (26) do not have the same tense: (25) is present tense, whereas (26) is compound past.

Therefore, these auxiliaries and their non-auxiliary counterparts are not only homonyms at the level of lexical semantics, but behave differently regarding the flow of their tense features at the morphology-syntax interface.[15]

1.4.2 *Defining c-structures.* In the tradition of morphological analysis, from classical structural morphology to current generative approaches, morphological segments and c-structures have been defined primarily on the basis of distributional facts. A feature-based morphology, however, must define c-structures mainly with respect to the flow of features from morphological segments into complex words. This may have consequences for the definition of c-structures. I will discuss two examples, the imperfect and future forms of the Italian verb.

Consider the following imperfect forms: *cantavo* "I sang", *cantavi* "you sang", etc. These forms can be segmented into the verb stem *cant-* "to sing", a thematic vowel *-a-*, a tense and mode suffix *-v-*, and a person and number suffix {*-o*, *-i*, etc.}. From the perspective of distribution, it is not obvious where the tense and mode suffix *-v-* belongs. Assuming that the imperfect forms of the Italian verb consist of a stem and an inflectional ending, that is, that they are generated by c-rule (27), the question arises whether *-v-* is part of the stem (v) or of the inflectional ending (Vinfl).

(27) V →   v   Vinfl
          $\uparrow = \downarrow$ $\uparrow = \downarrow$

Or, more generally, do we want to say that the Italian verb may have complex inflectional endings? The perspective of feature flow provides two arguments against this. The first one follows from the general criterion of simplicity: if all inflectional suffixes are simple segments, then category Vinfl in c-structure rule (27) is not split up into subcategories, and the rule directly finds all segments belonging to this category in the lexicon.

The second argument results from the observation that Italian verb stems are complex in large areas of their paradigms. In fact, many verb forms have a thematic vowel, which, given that it also occurs in word formation (cf. *pag-a-re*

---

[15] In Schwarze (1996) I proposed the following solution to this problem: There are two different tense attributes: TENSE and MORPHOLOGICAL_TENSE. Morphology creates the attribute MORPHOLOGICAL_TENSE and its values (PRESENT, FUTURE etc.). TENSE appears at the sentence level. By default, it takes value specified for MORPHOLOGICAL_TENSE. But when the verb is a temporal auxiliary, TENSE is assigned its value by the annotation of the c-structure rule which generates the compound tense construction.

LEXICAL-FUNCTIONAL MORPHOLOGY

"to pay" vs. *pag-a-mento* "payment"), is not an inflectional suffix and may reasonably be considered as an extension to the stem. Furthermore, in one inflectional class, there is an affix, *-sc-*, cf. *fin-i-sc-o* "I finish", *fin-i-sc-i* "you finish", etc. vs. *fin-i-te* "you (PL) finish", *fin-i-v-o* "I finished", *fin-i-v-i* "you finished" etc., which, appearing in several cells of the paradigm, does not contribute any feature to the syntactic level. Rather than analyzing it as a part of the inflectional suffix, I will consider it as a stem extension. It is true that, unlike this kind of stem extension, the tense and mode suffix does pass features to the syntactic word. But this is not an argument against categorizing it as a stem extension. As has been shown above, inflectional features are encoded in the "strong", i.e. irregular, perfect forms. We see now that inner stem inflection is not restricted to irregular verbs.

Consider now the morphology of the future tense, e.g. regular forms like *canterò* "I will sing", *finirò* "I will finish", *leggerò* "I will read", and irregular forms like *verrò* "I will come", *andrò* "I will go", *sarò* "I will be". The regular forms can be segmented into a stem {*cant-, fin-, legg-*}, a thematic vowel {*-e-* (an allomorph of *-a-*), *-i-, -e-*}, an affix *-r-*, which also appears in the infinitive (*cant-a-r-e, fin-i-r-e, legg-e-r-e*) and in the conditional (*cant-e-r-ei* "I would sing", *fin-i-r-ei* "I would finish", *legg-e-r-ei* "I would read"), and a person-and-number suffix, specific to the future, {*-ò, -ai, -à,* etc.}. Notice that none of these segments carries the feature (↑ TENSE) = FUTURE. This also holds for the person and number suffix, which is restricted to the future and can distinguish the future from the conditional, but cannot turn just any randomly chosen verb stem into a future form. This situation can be summarized by saying that the future forms are composed of a future stem (which is present also in the conditional) and a person and number suffix, which is restricted to the future, and that the future stem is complex in the regular forms, but (synchronically) unanalyzable in the irregular ones. (28a) and (28b) show the c-structures of *canterò* and *verrò* respectively:

(28a)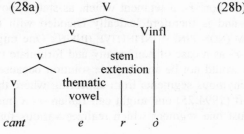

(28b)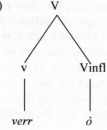

In order to see how the feature flow is organized in the future forms, let us first consider the irregular forms *verrò* "I will come" and *verrei* "I would come" In order to define the lexical entry for the future-and-conditional stem *verr-*, the value of the TENSE attribute can be expressed by, roughly speaking, a disjunction, represented by the following entries:

(29) *verr-*, v, ($\uparrow$ PRED) = VENIRE (SUBJ), ($\uparrow$ TENSE) = FUTURE

(30) *verr-*, v, ($\uparrow$ PRED) = VENIRE (SUBJ), ($\uparrow$ TENSE) = CONDITIONAL

As examples for person and number suffixes let us take those of the first person singular, *-ò* for the future, and *-ei* for the conditional. Here are the respective entries:

(31) *-ò*, Vinfl, ($\uparrow$ PERS) = 1, ($\uparrow$ NUM) = SG, ($\uparrow$ TENSE) =c FUTURE

(32) *-ei*, Vinfl, ($\uparrow$ PERS) = 1, ($\uparrow$ NUM) = SG, ($\uparrow$ TENSE) =c CONDITIONAL

These entries contain constraining equations, symbolized by '=c'. A constraining equation not only specifies a value for an attribute, but also expresses the requirement that this attribute must be present elsewhere in the f-structure. This means, in (31) and (32), that the tense value of a syntactic verb containing the suffix *-ò* is FUTURE if the stem is described as a FUTURE stem and it is CONDITIONAL, if the suffix is *-ei*, and the stem is described as a CONDITIONAL stem. In negative terms, these entries stipulate that the person-and-number suffixes specific to the future and the conditional (*-ò*, *-ei*, etc.) do not accept stems unless they are described as future or conditional stems respectively.

Our next step will be to inquire how the equations ($\uparrow$ TENSE) = FUTURE and ($\uparrow$ TENSE) = CONDITIONAL, which are lexically encoded in the irregular future stems, are introduced into the regular complex future-and-conditional stems. Consider first, not the *canterò* type with its allomorphous thematic vowel (the thematic vowel *cantare* is *-a-* in the other areas of the paradigm), but rather forms like *finirò*, where the thematic vowel does not show allomorphy. Since the thematic vowel does not carry inflectional features, the information we need can only come from the stem extension *-r-*, a segment which, as stated above, also characterizes the infinitive and is therefore lexically encoded with the equation NON_FINITE VERB FORM (NON_FIN) = INFINITIVE (INFIN). One might think of this double function of *-r-* as a case of homonymy and formulate two different lexical entries. But this would not be an adequate solution because it would not prevent the two homonymous segments from appearing where they do not belong. Following Aronoff (1994:25) one might call Italian *-r-* a 'morphome', meaning that there is just one segment which realizes various functions.

But in the LFG framework there is no need to postulate a 'morphomic' level. A lexically-encoded feature may be replaced by another feature by annotations in c-structure rules. This is made possible by the metavariables ↑ and ↓, which control the flow of features along c-structure trees and build up functional descriptions (Kaplan & Bresnan 1982). Intuitively speaking, the 'down' arrow makes sure that a given feature is present, but does not pass it on to a higher node. It is the 'up' arrow which makes the features flow from the lexicon to complex words, phrases and sentences. The 'up' arrow may move the features found by the 'down' arrow, as in the equation ↑ = ↓. It may also create features by itself. This is what happens in equations of the form (↑ ATTRIBUTE) = VALUE, which appear in all lexical entries and in some rule annotations. We use this property of the theory to formulate rules (33) and (34):

(33)   v   →   v   stem_extension
              ↑ = ↓   (↓ NON_FIN) = INFIN
                            (↑ TENSE) = FUTURE

(34)   v   →   v   stem_extension
              ↑ = ↓   (↓ NON_FIN) = INFIN
                            (↑ TENSE) = CONDITIONAL

These rules build up regular future-and-conditional stems. The annotation (↓ NON_FIN) = INFIN guarantees that the stem extension is -r- (the It. verb has more stem extensions), but does not pass on the feature (NON_FIN) = INFIN, encoded in the lexical entry of -r- (35):

(35)   -r-, stem_extension, (↑ NON_FIN) = INFIN

The additional annotations, (↑ TENSE) = FUTURE, and (↑ TENSE) = CONDITIONAL, then assign the regular future-and-conditional stems those tense features which are lexically encoded with the irregular stems.

This treatment shows how 'morphomes' can be accounted for by operations on feature structures. More generally, it shows that LFG, although commonly described as a unification formalism, actually provides a way of building up feature structures in a non-monotonic way.

1.4.3 *Global representation and diachronic change.* In order to justify the claim, formulated above, that there are complex words which are globally stored, but also accessible via morphological rules, empirical psycholinguistic evidence would be useful. But there is also strictly linguistic evidence. Certain processes of diachronic change, in fact, presuppose global access and representation of formally transparent items. To give just one example: It. *so* "I know"

(as opposed to the stem *sap-*, cf. *sapere* "to know") can be said to have originated by three successive processes:

(36) the last syllable is dropped (*sape*[16] > *sa* "knows"), as in other verb
forms (*ave* > *ha* "has", **vade* > *va* "goes", *puote* > *può* "can", 3rd
person, *face* > *fa* "does");

(37) the remaining sequence is reanalyzed as the stress-bearing stem of the
present indicative; accordingly the first person singular is *sao*,[17]

(38) the two syllables of *sao* are merged into one;

(39) the branching nucleus is simplified, yielding [sɔ].

Change (36) operates on syllables, ignoring morphological constituency.[18]
This can only happen if the original form is represented in the lexicon as an
unanalyzed unit. Change (38) dispenses with the (newly obtained) segmentation
of the form into stem and inflectional affix. Again, this can only happen if *sao*
is represented as a whole.

A large amount of morphological change can be explained along these
lines, e.g. the origin of the 3rd person singular perfect suffix -*ò*, which goes
back to -*a-u-it*, or the feminine plural suffix -*e*, which originated from -*a-s*. It is
interesting to see that unanalyzed representation of complex units also occurs in
syntax and may have similar consequences; cf., for instance, the origin of the
so-called 'articulated prepositions' of Italian, such as *al* < *ad illu*, *del* < *de illu*,
nel < *in illu*, etc. Changes of this kind can plausibly be explained by assuming
that the loss of structure has been preceded by global storage and processing.

---

[16] The untruncated forms, except **vade*, are attested in medieval Tuscan; (Rohlfs 1968:272ff.).
[17] It. *so* "I know" is usually explained by analogy with *do* "I give" and *sto* "I stand" (Rohlfs
[1968:272], Tekavčić [1980:338]), but Rohlfs (1968:276) thinks that It. *sto* is not the direct
continuation of Lat. *sto*, but has developed from **stao*, an opinion which Tekavčić (1980:337)
mentions without comment. If Rohlfs is right, my account of the origin of *so* may be looked
upon as an abbreviated version of Rohlfs' analysis. The hypothesis of a reanalysis of *sa-* as a
stem of the present tense is also confirmed by the 3rd person plural forms *fanno, sanno, vanno*
etc.: these forms are easily explained if we concur with Politzer (1958), Tekavčić (1980:285)
and Maiden (1995:131) that the suffix for 3rd plural was -*no* at an earlier stage of the language:
fa-, *sa-* and *va-* are stems which trigger 'raddoppiamento', as is shown by right-hand attached
clitics (e.g., *fammi vedere* "let me see", *fallo* "do it").
[18] It might be objected that the [p] of *sapere* disappears by final consonant deletion of the verb
stem. This would not explain, however, why the [p] has been preserved in other forms of the
paradigm (*sappiamo, sapete, sapevo, saprò, sapere* etc. (Samek-Lodovici, p.c.). The final syllable deletion analysis which I propose can explain this: it is restricted to weak, final syllables
of words which are not assigned stress.

1.5 *LFG for inflectional morphology?*

In order to express this conception of inflectional morphology, no more formal power than term unification, as represented in a language like Prolog, is required. The more sophisticated formalism of LFG may of course be used as a method of representation, but it is not really required by the linguistic facts. More specifically, there are no reasons in inflectional morphology to postulate anything resembling grammatical functions or wellformedness conditions like coherence and consistency conditions. There is no recursivity, no control and no long distance dependency. Inflectional morphology is much simpler than syntax.

2. *Derivational morphology*

As stated above, derivational morphology generates lexical words. It typically operates on lexical words, but it may also take other inputs: syntactic words (It. *lava-stoviglie* "dish-washing machine", where *stoviglie* "dishes" is a plural noun, whereas the compound is not specified for number), lexicalized phrases (It. *mille-piedi* "mille-pede"), and even sentences (It. *menefreghismo* "the attitude of one who refuses commitment", derived from *me ne frego* "I don't give a damn about it").

Just as in inflectional morphology, a rule of derivational morphology may leave word-internal constituent structure unchanged. In other words, no zero affix is needed to account for conversion, or, as Spencer (1991:432) puts it, "conversion is derivation with no affixation".

2.1 *Category-changing rules*

Unlike inflectional rules, rules of derivational morphology may change the lexical category of their input. This has consequences at the functional level: a change of lexical category may require a change of argument structure, and it may be associated with feature addition or deletion.

Regarding changes of argument structure, I will only mention a few well-known facts. When verbs are derived from nouns or from adjectives, an appropriate argument structure must be available. On the other hand, when verbs become nouns or adjectives, the expression of their argument structure must be adapted to the syntax of nouns and noun phrases.

As to feature addition associated with changes of lexical category, the most obvious case is gender: when verbs or adjectives are turned into nouns, they must be given a gender feature. Again, this feature may be inherited from a suffix or introduced by a c-structure rule annotation.

For the lexical representation of category-changing affixes, I will use the following conventional representation: the c-structure classification of category-changing suffixes will be expressed by terms of the form c_1/c_2, where c_1 is the category they operate on, and c_2 the category they bring about: v/n would thus represent an affix turning verbs into nouns.

As an example of feature addition, consider It. *-aggio*, a suffix that turns verbs of the *are*-class into masculine nouns, as in *lav-aggio* "(a) washing", derived from *lavare* "to wash". (40) is the lexical representation of that suffix:

(40)   *-aggi-*, v/n, ($\uparrow$ GEN) = MAS, ($\uparrow$ CLASS) = ARE[19]

The morphological rule that joins the affix to verbs will look roughly like this:

(41)   n $\rightarrow$ v   v/n
                     $\uparrow = \downarrow$ $\uparrow = \downarrow$

Notice, however, that rule (41) is not quite adequate. The arrow notation means that the lexically encoded functional properties of the verb and the suffix remain unchanged; they must merely unify. Neither the predicate nor the grammatical functions associated with the underlying verb are affected. It may well be the case that in the present example the conceptual meaning and the argument structure of the verb remain untouched. But there is one aspect of the functional properties of the underlying verb which is necessarily changed by the change of category, namely the grammatical functions it governs. In fact, in (42), the subject argument of *lavare* has no counterpart in *lavaggio* but it is existentially bound, whereas the direct object argument of the verb (*lavare la lana*) corresponds to an optional modifier of the derived noun:

(42) *il lavaggio della lana*
     "the washing of the wool"

In order to correctly interpret this modifier, the semantic structure of the underlying verb, namely **lavare (e,x,y)** $\wedge$ **agent (e,x)** $\wedge$ **theme (e,y)**,[20] must be available for semantic elaboration. What we need, then, is a function which

a.   stores the semantic argument and role structure of the verb with the derived noun for later use in semantics,

---

[19] The feature ($\uparrow$ CLASS) = ARE makes sure that *-aggio* is affixed only to verbs of the *are*-class: a word like *spedire* 'to send', which belongs to the *ire*-class, does not take this suffix; **spedaggio* is clearly ungrammatical.

[20] This semantic structure contains an event predicate (**lavare**) and an event argument (**e**), two role predicates (**agent** and **theme**) and two role arguments (**x** and **y**).

b.   deletes the grammatical functions governed by the verb, and replaces the attribute PRED(ICATE) with a provisional attribute BARE_PRED(ICATE).

Applied to the lexical form and semantic representation of *lavare* (43), this function (which I will not try to elaborate formally) will yield (44), the functional and semantic representation of *lavaggio*:

(43)   *lav*, v, ($\uparrow$ PRED) = 'LAVARE <(SUBJ), (OBJ)>'
          lavare (x,y) $\wedge$ agent (x) $\wedge$ theme (y)

(44)   *lav*, v, ($\uparrow$ BARE-PRED) = 'LAVARE'
          lavare (x,y) $\wedge$ agent (x) $\wedge$ theme (y)

We can now reformulate rule (41) more adequately. Rule (45) puts the verb stem *v* and the nominalization suffix *v/n* together and turns the provisional BARE_PREDICATE into an ordinary PREDICATE, as needed for the elaboration of (syntactic) f-structures:

(45)   n $\rightarrow$ v   v/n
                          ($\uparrow$ CLASS)= $\downarrow$ $\uparrow$ = $\downarrow$
                          ($\uparrow$ PRED)= ($\downarrow$ BARE_PRED)

The functional representation of the lexical word *lavaggi-* may then be formulated as (46):

(46) *lavaggi-*, n, ($\uparrow$ PRED) = 'LAVARE', ($\uparrow$ GEN) = MAS

In the case of conversion, as stated above, category change takes place without suffixation. When a conversion rule generates nouns, as in It. *rosso* (adjective) "red" vs. *il rosso* (noun) "the color red", the gender feature is introduced by the morphological c-structure rule:[21]

(47)   n $\rightarrow$ adj
                          $\uparrow$ = $\downarrow$
                          ($\uparrow$ GEN) = MAS

On the other hand, gender features are deleted when nouns are turned into verbs or adjectives, cf. *chiodo* (MAS) "(a) nail" vs. *in-chiod-are* (no gender) "to nail", *nuvola* (FEM) "cloud" vs. *nuvol-os-o* (no gender encoded in the stem) "cloudy".

As for the cases where syntactic words become parts of lexical words, such as when the plural *stoviglie* "dishes" appears in *lava-stoviglie* "a dishwasher", the inflectional suffix remains present at the c-structure level and blocks overt

---

[21] Masculine being the unmarked gender in Italian, one might think of a more general account of gender assignment, which would also apply to borrowings.

inflectional affixation (Samek-Lodovici, p.c.). The inflectional feature carried by the suffix is not passed on to the functional description of the compound. Thus, the *-e* in *stoviglie* "dishes" is plural, but the compound noun *lava-stoviglie* "dish-washing machine" does not specify a number.[22] This is another case of non-monotonic building-up of feature structures, which can be expressed by the 'down' function, cf. 1.4.2 above.

2.2 *Category-preserving rules*

Other rules of derivational morphology conserve lexical categories, but bring about changes at the functional level. They usually modify predicates, and they may also add or change other features. For a language like Italian, various types of processes can be distinguished:

(48) Morphological noun modification: a nominal suffix with an adjective-like semantics determines the inflectional class and may determine the gender of the derived noun, such as *-in-* in *testina* (FEM) "little head", derived from *testa* (FEM) "head", or *-ott-* as in *leprotto* (MAS) "young hare", derived from *lepre* (FEM) "hare".

(49) Morphological predicate embedding: a nominal suffix changes the gender value of its base and embeds the underlying predicate into some unspecified superordinate predicate, such as *-aio* in *vespaio* "wasp nest", cf. *vespa* "wasp", or in *benzinaio* "gas station attendant", cf. *benzina* "gas".

(50) Reversative or repetitive verb formation by prefixation: e.g. *ri-*, as in *rivenire* "to come back", cf. *venire* "to come".

(51) Motion, i.e., a process in which no derivational affix is involved and which simultaneously changes the gender and the meaning of nouns, cf. the relationship between *amico* (MAS) "a male friend" and *amica* (FEM) "a female friend", *mela* (FEM) "apple" and *melo* (MAS) "apple-tree".

(52) Nominal compounding, e.g. *piazza duomo* (FEM) "cathedral square", compounded from *piazza* (FEM) "square" and *duomo* (MAS) "cathedral".

As this sketchy typology of category conserving processes shows, lexical functional morphology has to deal, in addition to changes at the level of con-

---

[22] A curious fact about submerged plurals of this sort is that they have no impact on the value of the NUMBER feature of the compound but they are processed at the semantic level. In fact, the plural is felt to be justified by the fact that the machine washes dishes, not just one dish.

stituent structure, with a wide range of functional changes, including the predicate features which represent lexical meaning. In other words: derivational morphology may create new predicates.

2.3 Lexical semantics

There are many semantic processes by which derivational morphology generates new lexical meanings, many of them still waiting for systematic investigation. In this section, I will briefly look at the semantic and functional aspects of just one derivational process, dubbed *reversal* by Marchand (1953). Here are the facts: in Italian, there is a productive prefix *s-*, which may be compared to Engl. *un-*. An example is *slegare* "to untie", derived from *legare* "to tie". Unlike other affixes which just add something to a predicate in the way the diminutive does to a noun, the prefix *s-*, in order to apply, must look inside the lexical semantics of the predicate. In other words, in order to do its work, *s-* requires that the predicate be decomposed, as has been shown by Mayo et al. (1995:901-903, 924) and Schepping (1996). Both predicates, the underlying predicate **legare (e,x,y)** "to tie up", and the derived predicate **slegare (e,x,y)**[23] "to untie", describe the action of bringing about a change from a state s_1 to a state s_2. In the case of **legare (e,x,y)**, in s_1, **y** is not tied up, while in s_2, it is; whereas **slegare (e,x,y)** implies that in s_1, **y** is tied up, and in s_2 it isn't; schematically:

(53)   legare (e,x,y) $\Rightarrow$ bring_about (x, change (s_1, s_2) $\wedge$ s1 = $\neg$tied_up (y) $\wedge$ s_2 = tied_up (y)

(54)   slegare (e,x,y) $\Rightarrow$ bring_about (x, change (s_1, s_2) $\wedge$ s_1 = tied_up (y) $\wedge$ s_2 = $\neg$ tied_up (y)

Hence, the semantics of the prefix *s-* is a function which, so to speak, dislocates negation from one of the implied states to the other. Mayo et al. (1995:933) propose that functions of this kind are represented by an attribute D_PRED (derived predicate), the values of which are second order predicates, taking first order predicates as their arguments. In the case of reversative *s-*, the value of D_PRED is 'S- ($\uparrow$ ARG)'. (54) is the lexical entry for *s-*, and (55) is the rule which adjoins verb prefixes to verb stems:

(55)   s-, Vprefix, ($\uparrow$ D_PRED) = 'S- ($\uparrow$ ARG)'

(56)   v $\rightarrow$ Vprefix   v
         $\uparrow = \downarrow$ ($\uparrow$ ARG) = ($\downarrow$ PRED)

[23] For the variable **e**, cf. note 20.

The annotation to the right-hand side in rule (55) is necessary to make sure that the D_PRED contained in the lexical entry (54) finds its argument. Regarding *s-* and *legare*, the lexical entry for which is (57), this rule creates the new entry (57) simply by substituting LEGARE<($\uparrow$ SUBJ), ($\uparrow$ OBJ)> for ARG in S- ($\uparrow$ ARG):

(57) *leg-*, v, ($\uparrow$ PRED) = 'LEGARE <($\uparrow$ SUBJ), ($\uparrow$ OBJ)>', ($\uparrow$ CLASS) = ARE

(58) *sleg-*, v, ($\uparrow$ D_PRED) = 'S- (LEGARE <($\uparrow$ SUBJ), ($\uparrow$ OBJ)>)', ($\uparrow$ CLASS) = ARE

Now, the D_PRED function with its argument, as illustrated by (57), is not a lexical meaning. Formally speaking, lexical meanings are PREDICATEs, but 'S- (LEGARE <($\uparrow$ SUBJ), ($\uparrow$ OBJ)>)' is not a PREDICATE. Hence the D_PRED function must be resolved, creating a new PREDICATE, which may be represented by SLEGARE. The idea behind this formal account is that a complex word differs from a syntactic phrase in terms of semantics as well. In fact, if the lexical integrity principle is correct, and if derivational rules not only generate complex word forms but also derived meanings, then these meanings must be created before lexical insertion.[24] It is likely that the cognitive point of view confirms this hypothesis. It does not sound plausible, at least for speech production, that a complex word is generated and put into a sentence without a previously created lexical semantics. Therefore, it has been postulated by Mayo et al. (1995:934ff.) that possible words to which a D_PRED is associated are put into a temporary lexicon or lexical buffer, where their lexical semantics is elaborated and from which they may be pulled to be used in a sentence, and, after repeated use, copied to the permanent lexicon.[25]

Coming back now to the distinction I made at the beginning between lexical and syntactic words and drawing conclusions from the above D_PRED analysis, we must revise the notion of the syntactic word. The syntactic word can now be defined at both the c-structure and the f-structure level: it is a lexical item which has a c-structure category, N, V, ADJ, P, ADV, D, or C, and, at the f-structure level, does not contain a D_PRED.

Morphology then, can be characterized as a generative component of grammar which creates syntactic and new lexical words. And its interface to

---

[24] One might object, however, that semantic processing of lexical meaning may well take place after lexical insertion, at the levels of sentence and text. The resolution of lexical ambiguity or reinterpretations triggered by hedges like *sort of* or *so to speak*, are good examples of this kind of process. But it is a safe guess to say that semantic elaboration after lexical insertion is always triggered by contexts which are distinct from and outside the word, whereas a suffix is part of the word, and D_PRED is part of its functional description.

[25] It should be noticed that the temporal dimension introduced into a model of lexical memory might also turn out to be a starting point for an explicit treatment of lexical change.

syntax is defined, not only in terms of the objects accepted by lexical insertion, but also by a temporal lexicon which has access to lexical semantics.[26]

3. *A model of the lexicon*

In addition to the claim that morphology is a set of operations on feature structures below the level of the sentence, assumptions about the overall structure of the lexicon are central to the present conception of lexical functional morphology. It will be useful to resume this conception of the lexicon.[27]

The lexicon is thought to have two parts: the main and the temporary lexicon. The main lexicon contains those items, simple or complex, which are permanently stored in memory. The temporary lexicon is the locus of items of two classes. The first comprises words which have been derived and actually been used but are not accepted by the Lexical Immigration Authority. Examples might be, for inflection, regular *uomi* "men" instead of irregular *uomini*, and, for derivation, *arrivata* "arrival" regularly derived from *arrivat-*, the past participle stem, instead of *arrivo*, derived from *arriv-*, the default stem of the verb *arrivare* "to arrive". It also comprises, for some time after their use, infrequent verb forms such as It. *illustrassero* "they illustrated (PAST SUBJUNCTIVE)". The items belonging to the second class are complex words which contain an unresolved D_PRED. Such words are recognized as well-formed at the c-structure level, but will not be used because they have no meaning proper. A form like ?*marginaio*, from *margine* "margin" and *-aio* (cf. 2.2) might be an example.

Morphology feeds the temporary lexicon, and from there, via the diachronic process of lexicalization, the main lexicon. It also provides optional analytical access to those regularly built words which are stored in the main lexicon, thus supporting learnability. Syntax takes syntactic words from both the main and the temporary lexicon. It looks at the c-categories and at the feature structures, but never parses word-internal c-structures.

---

[26] Reversive *s-*, which I chose as an example, is one of the simpler cases. Things may be rather more complex, as for example in the so-called derivations in *-ata*, as illustrated by *badile* "a spade" – *badilata* "the action of using a spade", "a quantity of material constituted by using a spade", *bambino* "child" – *bambinata* "the action of behaving like a child" (Mayo et al. 1995, Schwarze 1994b and 1995). In these examples, the resolution of D_PRED does not only require semantic restructuring. It creates a predicate variable which can only be bound by constants like 'action' or 'quantity' after a search in (not specifically linguistic) conceptual structure. This type of derivation is a complex one also at the c-structure level: there are reasons to believe that denominal nouns in *-ata* are derived from nouns via denominal verbs; cf. Samek-Lodovici (1997). It. *-aio*: *vespa* "wasp" - *vespaio* "wasp nest", *libro* "book" - *libraio* "book seller" (and also Spanish *-ero*, French *-ier*) seem to require similar processes.

[27] Similar conceptions have already been proposed by Schwarze (1994a), Mayo et al. (1995), and Mayo (1996).

REFERENCES

Aronoff, Mark. 1994. *Morphology by Itself: Stems and inflectional classes*. Cambridge, Mass.: MIT Press.

Booij, Geert. 1997. "Allomorphy and the Autonomy of Morphology". *Folia Linguistica* 31.25-56.

Börjars, Kersti, Nigel Vincent & Carol Chapman. 1996. "Paradigms, Periphrases and Pronominal Inflection: A feature-based account". *Yearbook of Morphology* 1996. ed. by Geert Booij & Jaap van Marle, 155-180. Dordrecht: Kluwer.

Bresnan, Joan, ed. 1982. *The Mental Representation of Grammatical Relations*. Cambridge, Mass.: MIT Press.

——. 1996. *Morphology Competes with Syntax: Explaining typological variation in weak crossover effects*. Unpublished Manuscript, Stanford.

—— & Jonni Kanerva. 1989. "Locative Inversion in Chichewa: A case study of factorization in grammar." *Linguistic Inquiry* 20.1-50.

—— & Sam A. Mchombo. 1995. "The Lexical Integrity. Principle: Evidence from Bantu". *Natural Language and Linguistic Theory* 13.181-254.

—— & Lioba Moshi. 1990. "Object Asymmetries in Comparative Bantu Syntax." *Linguistic Inquiry* 21.147-185.

Butt, Miriam, Tracy Holloway King, María Eugenia Niño & Fréderique Segond. 1998. *A Grammar Writer's Handbook*. To appear 1999, Stanford, CA: CSLI Publications.

De Mauro, Tullio, Federico Mancini, Massimo Vedovelli & Miriam Voghera. 1993. *Lessico di Frequenza dell'Italiano Parlato*. Fondazione IBM Italia, ETAS.

Di Sciullo, Anna-Maria & Edwin Williams. 1987. *On the Definition of Word*. Cambridge, Mass.: MIT Press.

Kaplan, Ronald M. & Joan Bresnan. 1982. "Lexical Functional Grammar: A formal system for grammatical representation". Bresnan 1982.173-281.

Maiden, Martin. 1995. *A Linguistic History of Italian*, London & New York: Longman.

Marchand, Hans. 1953. "The Question of Derivative Relevancy and the Prefix *s-* in Italian". *Studia Linguistica* 7.104-114.

Mayo, Bruce. 1996. "Die Konstanzer LFG-Umgebung". *LDV-Forum* 13:1/2.31-53.

——. 1997. *Derivational Morphology in the Konstanz LFG-Workbench*. Universität Konstanz, Fachgruppe Sprachwissenschaft, Arbeitspapier Nr. 86, 80 pp.

——, Marie-Theres Schepping, Christoph Schwarze & Angela Zaffanella. 1995. "Semantics in the Derivational Morphology of Italian: Implications for the structure of the lexicon". *Linguistics* 33.883-938.

Politzer, R. L. 1958 "On the History of the Third Person Ending in Italian". *Italica* 35.192-197.

Rohlfs, Gerhard. 1968. *Grammatica Storica della Lingua Italiana e dei suoi Dialetti: Morfologia*. Torino: Einaudi.

Samek-Lodovici, Vieri. 1997. *A Unified Analysis of Noun- and Verb-based Italian Nominalizations in -ata*. Universität Konstanz, Fachgruppe Sprachwissenschaft, Arbeits-papier Nr. 80, 34 pp.

Schepping, Marie-Theres. 1996 "Zur Semantik von Derivaten: Wörter mit dem Präfix *s*-im Italienischen". *Lexical Structures and Language Use* ed. by Edda Weigand & Franz Hundsnurscher, vol. II, 113-125. Tübingen: Niemeyer.

Schwarze, Christoph. 1994a. "Struttura Grammaticale e Uso del Lessico". *Come Parlano gli Italiani* ed. by Tullio De Mauro, 71-81. Scandicci (Firenze): La Nuova Italia.

———. 1994b. "Ein Fall strukturell bedingter Wissensabhängigkeit der Übersetzung: die Wiedergabe einer Klasse italienischer *nomina vicis* im Deutschen". *Kognitive Grundlagen für die interlinguabasierte Übersetzung* ed. by Peter Bosch & Christopher Habel, Working Paper 3.135-154. IBM Deutschland.

———. 1995. "Semantic and Conceptual Structures in Word Formation". *Semantic and Conceptual Knowledge* ed. by Manfred Bierwisch & Peter Bosch, Sonderforschungbereich 340 "Sprachtheoretische Grundlagen für die Computerlinguistik", Arbeitspapier Nr. 71, Universität Stuttgart, Universität Tübingen, IBM Deutschland, 211-221.

———. 1996. "The Syntax of Romance Auxiliaries". *Lexical Functional Grammar Workshop: Proceedings of the First Lexical Functional Grammar Conference. Rank Xerox Research Centre, Grenoble, 26-28 August, 1996* ed. by Miriam Butt & Tracy Holloway, 418-433.

———. 1997. "Strutture Semantiche e Concettuali nella Formazione delle Parole". *Grammatica e Lessico: Teorie linguistiche e applicazioni lessicografiche.* Atti del convegno interannuale della Società Linguistica Italiana, Madrid, 21-25 February, 1995 ed. by Tullio De Mauro & Vincenzo Lo Cascio, 311-329. Roma: Bulzoni.

Spencer, Andrew. 1991. *Morphological Theory: An introduction to word structure in generative grammar.* Oxford: Blackwell.

Tekavčić, Pavao. 1980. *Grammatica Storica dell'Italiano: II. Morfosintassi.* Bologna: Il Mulino.

SOMALI AS A POLYSYNTHETIC LANGUAGE*

MARCO SVOLACCHIA & ANNARITA PUGLIELLI
Università degli Studi di Roma Tre

0. *Introduction*

In recent years considerable work has been carried out on non-configurational aspects of syntax in an attempt to integrate problematic structures into Universal Grammar (UG). A case in point is 'incorporation', such as is found in many Amerindian languages, a notion previously confined into a sort of a theoretical limbo, in spite of a long tradition of description dating back at least to Sapir's times. Baker (1988) has shown that incorporation structures of the kind found in various 'exotic' languages simply involve head-movement, and can therefore be derived and constrained on a principled basis. A refinement and extension of these ideas has recently been attempted by the same author with a proposal for a Morphological Visibility Condition, or 'Polysynthesis Parameter' – in fact a 'macroparameter' (Baker 1996).[1]

The aim of this paper is to provide evidence that Somali is a polysynthetic language in the technical sense as defined in Baker (1996). Interestingly, Somali seems to be a polysynthetic language of a particular subtype. We informally call it a 'Clitic Polysynthetic Language', since it does not seem to fit neatly with Baker's formulation. We will therefore argue for a refinement of the Polysynthesis Parameter, since it appears to be both too strong and too weak at the same time.

The paper is organised as follows: Sections 1-2 introduce the theoretical background and some non-configurational features of Somali; Section 3-5 explore the analysis of VP and its non-configurationality; Section 6 analyses the

* We wish to thank Professors Cabdalla Cumar Mansuur and Axmed Cabdullaahi Axmed for their invaluable help and patience with our questions. Many thanks to David Hart, for his help with our English. Special thanks to Lunella Mereu and Mara Frascarelli for all their work for the Colloquium and the Proceedings.

[1] 'Macroparameter' is defined in Baker (1996) as a primary, pervasive parameter ofUG whose particular settings entail a corollary of properties for each specific language.

subject argument and the functional projections above VP; Section 7 discusses
the problem of the precise location of Somali among non-configurational languages and examines some consequences for the Polysynthesis Parameter.

1.   *The Polysynthesis Parameter and Incorporation*

1.1   *Polysynthesis*

Following Baker, we will refer to the relevant parameter both as 'The
Polysynthesis Parameter' and, more appropriately, as the 'Morphological Visibility Condition' (MVC), as defined in (1) (Baker 1996:17):

> (1)   Morphological Visibility Condition (= 'Polysynthesis Parameter')
> A phrase X is visible for Θ-role assignment from a head Y only if it is coin-
> dexed with a morpheme in the word containing Y via:
> (i) an agreement relationship, or (ii) a movement relationship.

According to (1), in a language in which the MVC holds, a thematic role
(Θ-role) cannot be assigned directly by a lexical head to its argument Determiner Phrase (DP), but through the mediation of a morpheme which is coindexed with that DP and occurs in its governing head. Two kinds of morphemes are of relevance here: either agreement morphemes (co-indexed with
their antecedents DPs) or heads incorporated into the Θ-assigning lexical head
(coindexed via movement with their trace). Most notably, the MVC parameter is
in fact composed of two separate subparameters: one that states that *agreement*
makes the phrase visible for Θ-role assignment, and the other that states that *incorporation* makes a phrase visible to Θ-role assignment. Clearly, Baker's
claim bears considerably both on UG theory and on typologically-oriented
studies. As a consequence of the MVC, four possible language types are so defined *in principle* (Baker 1996:17-18):

> (i)   A language type in which both conditions of the MVC are met and are in a
> complementary distribution. These languages are referred to as *Polysynthetic* in the
> technical sense (e.g. some Iroquoian languages, such as Mohawk; some Gunwin-
> jguan languages, such as Mayali, etc.).
> (ii)   A language type in which condition (i) applies (the agreement relationship) but
> not condition (ii). In these languages the verb agrees with each of its arguments.
> They were referred to in Nichols (1986) as 'Non-configurational head-marking lan-
> guages'. Let us call them *Poly-agreeing* languages (e.g. Warlpiri, Navaho, etc.).
> (iii)   A language type in which neither part of the MVC holds. These are *Configura-
> tional* languages, such as English and other familiar languages.
> (iv)   The fourth type of language, one in which only condition (ii) holds, let us call
> it *Poly-incorporating* language, is excluded on general principles, because subject
> arguments cannot be incorporated without violating the properties of head-
> movement (because they are not c-commanded by the verb).

The MVC entails a set of important consequences. The most notable one is 'Case Absorption', which is formulated by Baker (1996:86) as in (2) below:

(2) An agreement morpheme adjoined to a head·X receives that head's Case at S-structure/PF.[2]

The statement in (2) means that an agreeing morpheme, which is, we may recall, obligatory in non-configurational languages in order to permit Θ-role assignment, absorbs the case assigned by the relevant head. Parallels to this phenomenon are found in the Romance and Semitic languages, among others, where, under standard analyses, clitics absorb the case of their head (Borer 1984). A crucial consequence of (2), given the Case Filter, is that *no phonetically realised DP can be in argument position*, i.e. *all DPs must be generated as adjuncts*. This is the main source of non-configurationality, apparent free word order in particular.[3]

1.2 *Incorporation*

We now review the essential elements of Incorporation, as reference will be made to it during the discussion. Incorporation, as understood here, is not an element of UG but a descriptive term for a cluster of independently existing elements in the theory. The basic mechanism underlying Incorporation is head-movement, which has a number of properties, most of which are well known and reasonably well established. The first one, the Head Movement Constraint (Travis 1984), entails the definition of 'locality' and 'directionality', and is formulated in (3) below:

(3) The Head Movement Constraint (HMC)
An X^0 category Y can only adjoin to the head of the phrase that immediately dominates the maximal projection of Y.[4]

Head-movement in terms of (3) entails a couple of important consequences for Incorporation. One is the formation of 'complexes', which are identical in category to the host head. (4) below illustrates:

---

[2] 'Agreement morpheme' must be understood here in a broader sense, comprising either coindexation via a binding relation, or via a movement relation.

[3] This idea owes a lot to Jelinek (1984) in spite of the differences between the two approaches.

[4] It is clear that the HMC is not an element of UG in its own turn. It has been derived variously from ECP, the Relativized Minimality Condition or the Economy Condition (Shortest Movement). Whatever the assumption, this issue is of no relevance here.

(4)
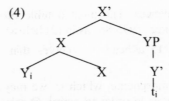

The complex [X [Y$_i$ X]] is a compound, a syntactic and, typically, a prosodic unit, which undergoes movement as a single constituent.[5] Cyclic movement is the source of large complexes, such as 'Verbal Complexes' (VC), in the traditional sense made familiar by descriptive work in non-configurational languages.[6]

Another basic property of head-movement has to do with *order* relations, which can be stated as in (5) (Baker 1996:29):

(5)   If X and Y are X^0 categories and X is adjoined to Y in the syntax, then X precedes Y in linear order.[7]

A consequence of head-movement as stated above is the 'Mirror Effect' ('Mirror Principle' in Baker 1985, 1988), whereby the order of elements in a Complex is the mirror image of the order of elements in the structure.[8]

2.   *Main Properties of Somali*

Now that the general framework is set, we can turn to Somali. We will now review some of its most significant characteristics which have proved a serious challenge to previous analyses and we will show how they can be handled in the light of the MVC and Incorporation.

---

[5] For potential counterexamples see Roberts (1991).

[6] Strictly speaking, VCs are, in fact, very rarely 'verbal', since the verb normally incorporates into higher functional categories, generating 'inflectional' complexes. The sense in which this term can be retained is that the verb is the highest lexical category in these complexes.

[7] This statement is directly related to Kayne's (1994) Antisymmetry Hypothesis. The formation of VCs is a much more general process than might appear from Baker's discussion. In fact, there seems to be no sense in which one would still distinguish between movements via substitution and movements via adjunction, at least as far as head movement is concerned, as more or less tacitly assumed in the Minimalist Framework (cf. Chomsky [1995:174-75], in particular).

[8] 'Mirror Principle' is a misnomer, since no independent principle at all is involved in it. The reversed order of heads in complexes is a result of the way in which movement applies.

2.1 *Free word order and obligatory clitics*

Free word order and obligatory pronominal clitics are key features of Somali and will be of great relevance in subsequent discussion. The examples in (6) illustrate (capitalised phrase = Focus):[9]

(6) a. *(Aniga)* *shalay* *baa* *la-*(y)* *dilay*
      me   yesterday FM   ARB.S-OCL beat-PAST
      "Someone beat me YESTERDAY"

    b. *Shalay* *baa* *(aniga)* *la-*(y)* *dilay*
      yesterday FM   me   ARB.S-OCL   beat-PAST
      "Someone beat me YESTERDAY"

    c. *Shalay* *baa* *la-*(y)* *dilay* *(aniga)*
      yesterday FM ARB.S-OCL beat-PAST   me
      "Someone beat me YESTERDAY"

    d. *Aniga* *baa* *shalay* *la-*(y)* *dilay*
      me   FM   yesterday ARB.S-OCL beat-PAST
      "Someone beat ME yesterday"

The above sentences do not exhaust all possible orders. At first glance, however, not many restrictions seem to hold. One main constraint is that the focus DP must be left adjacent to the FM *baa,* and must precede the clitic subject and the verbal cluster. Apart from this case, a DP is apparently not restricted in position.

Object clitics are obligatory in every configuration. As (6) shows, object clitics must always occur, no matter if or where a coindexed full DP occurs (an

---

[9] The Somali examples in the text, when not otherwise indicated, are drawn from our own database. Abbreviations in the text and in glosses are the following:

ARB.S	=	arbitrary subject	OCL	=	object clitic
CL	=	clitic	PAST	=	past tense
CLASS	=	classifier	PF	=	Phonetic Form
CLLD	=	Clitic Left Dislocation	PL	=	plural
COMP	=	complementizer	PP	=	Past Participle
ECP	=	Empty Category Principle	PRES	=	present tense
F	=	feminine	PROG	=	progressive
FM	=	Focus Marker	SCL	=	subject clitic
HAB	=	habitual	SG	=	singular
HMC	=	Head Movement Constraint	Spec	=	Specifier
LF	=	Logical Form	S-structure	=	Syntactic structure
M	=	masculine	SUBJ	=	subjunctive
MVC	=	Morphological Visibility Condition	UG	=	Universal Grammar
			VC	=	Verbal Complex

independent pronoun in the above examples). In (6d) an independent pronoun is the focus of the sentence and thus occupies the related position (Spec-CP, under standard analyses), but the coreferential object clitic is still obligatory. A slight complication arises with 3rd person DPs as (7a) below shows:

(7) a. *Cali   baa   dil-ay*
        Ali   FM   beat-PAST
        "ALI beat it/him/her/them"

    b. *Cali   baa* [vp *dil-ay* pro]

The 3rd person object clitics, both genders and numbers, have no phonetic realisation. The sentence in (7a) can thus have all the readings shown in the English translation. The empty category is interpreted as a pro, (7a) would thus be represented as in (7b). Notice that the object pro invariably has a referential reading; it can never have a generic, arbitrary interpretation, as in the pseudo-intransitive use in other languages. As a consequence it is always recoverable, no matter if or where a coindexed DP occurs, as shown in (8):

(8) *(Yaxaas) Cali baa (yaxaas)* [vp *dil-ay*   pro] *(yaxaas)*
     crocodile Ali   FM   crocodile   beat-PAST (it) crocodile
     "ALI beat (a crocodile)"

Subject clitics basically have the same properties, even if their syntax shows additional intricacies.[10] Consider the following examples:

(9) a. *Cali   adiga   b-uu   / *baa ku   dil-ay*
        Ali   you   FM-SCL /FM   OCL beat-PAST
        "Ali beat YOU"

    b. *Adiga   b-uu   / *baa ku dil-ay   Cali*
        you   FM-SCL / FM   OCL beat-PAST Ali
        "Ali beat YOU"

    c. *Adiga   b-uu   / *baa Cali   ku   dil-ay*[11]
        you   FM-SCL / FM   Ali   OCL beat-PAST
        "Ali beat YOU"

---

[10] Owing to their peculiar behaviour, subject clitics will be dealt with in detail in later discussion.

[11] Both versions of a sentence like this, in which the coreferential DP is positioned after *baa* and before the VC, would be judged as grammatical by many informants (for a previous analysis of these sentences cf. Svolacchia et al. 1995).

As (9) shows, the absence of the subject clitic pronoun rules out the sentences. A different case is illustrated in (10), which shows that the subject clitic pronoun cannot occur when the coindexed DP is subject to Wh-movement:

(10) *Cali   baa /*b-uu   adiga   ku   dil-ay*
     Ali   FM / FM- SCL   you   OCL   beat-PAST
     "ALI beat you"

To sum up, subject clitics are obligatory in any of the above configurations, except when the coindexed DP is in the Spec of Comp (or a Comp-like category) as a consequence of Wh-movement.[12]

2.2 *Discontinuous constituency*

In addition to free word order and obligatory clitics, *discontinuous constituency* in the VP is another remarkable property of Somali. There is no such thing as a 'prepositional (or postpositional) phrase' in Somali, as in more familiar languages. The closest approximation to a PP is a clitic cluster incorporated into the verb, formed by a clitic pronoun, coindexed with a coreferential DP, and the preposition which heads it. (11) is an example of this :

(11) *(Aniga_i)   b-uu   *(i_i)-la   hadl-ay-aa*
     me   FM-he   OCL-with   speak-PROG-PRES.3SGM
     "He is speaking with ME"

As with object clitics directly related to the verb, the full DP, here *aniga* "me", needs not occur. The coreferential clitic pronoun, on the other hand, is obligatory, as underlined by the notation.

2.3 *Verbal Complex*

As in other polysynthetic languages described in the literature, Somali has a VC. This contains many elements which in other languages are independent maximal categories, such as agreement, modals, negation, adverbials and deictics, predicate adjectives, some bare nouns and, most notably, prepositions and pronominal elements, that we have already discussed above. On the other hand, no DP can occur in the VC. In traditional descriptive work on Somali the VC was considered 'a microstructure of the whole sentence', in which all elements of the predication are represented (Puglielli 1981). What follows is an example (VC in square brackets):

---

[12] This is part of a more general anti-agreement phenomenon in Somali, for which see, among others, Frascarelli (this volume) and Mereu (this volume).

(12) *Annaga baa la*   [*-yno-o   soo   ord-ay-ay*]
     Us   FM   ARB.S   -OCL-to   DEICTIC run-PROG-PAST.3SGM
     "Someone was running towards US"

Apart from inflectional elements, which follow the verb, the VC in the above example is formed, from left to right, by an object clitic, a preposition and a deictic adverb-like particle.

3. *The analysis of VP*

The picture that emerges from the above facts recalls the sort of phenomena which justified the introduction of the MVC. A natural interpretation of the data is that object clitics are arguments, while coreferential DPs are adjuncts. If we assume this, free word order begins to make sense. More evidence for the interpretation of DPs as adjuncts will be brought in the next section. Let us remember, however, that the MVC requires that the coindexed morpheme be contained in the Θ-assigning head, here the verb. Indeed, there is evidence that object clitics are incorporated into the verb, thus providing direct evidence in favour if the MVC. To see this, let us look at the example in (9a), here repeated as (13):

(13) *Cali adiga   b-uu   ku   dil-ay*
     Ali   you   FM-SCL OCL   beat-PAST
     "Ali beat YOU"

According to our hypothesis clitics must be in their argument position in order to receive and transmit Θ-roles because they are assigned under minimal m-command.[13] The first head c-commanding the object clitic is the verb; the clitic can thus move to adjoin to the left of the verb without any violation of the HMC, as represented in (14):

(14) $[_{v'} \: dilay \: [_{DP} \: \underline{ku}]]$ → $[_{v'} \: [_v \: \underline{ku}_i \: dilay] \: [_{DP} \: t_i]]$[14]

This predicts the facts exactly. There is nothing special about the way in which object clitics are positioned in the VC. It is just head-movement. This seems to provide strong evidence in favour of the analysis in terms of the MVC.

---

[13] We stick here, for simplicity, to the traditional assumption about Θ-role assignment, even though a hypothesis in the lines of the Uniformity of Theta-role Assignment (Baker 1988) seems preferable, as a variety of considerations converge to suggest. This problem, however, has no bearing on the analysis at issue. By the same token, we will abstract from the agreement projection of VP and from the 'light vp' of the 'VP-shell hypothesis' (Larson 1988).

[14] For more evidence that Somali is a head-first language see discussion in Section 5.

We now wish to extend this argument further, showing that the process of incorporation of a clitic (coreferential with an argument DP) to the category that heads it is a general process in Somali. Let us then re-examine again the Somali version of a Prepositional Phrase. The relevant example is (11), repeated below as (15):

(15) *Aniga$_i$*   *b-uu*   [*i$_i$-la*   *hadl-ay-aa*]
     Me   FM-SCL OCL-with speak-PROG-PRES.3SGM
     "He is speaking with ME"

The DP, *aniga* "me", an independent pronoun, is in A' position, as it is the focus; the coreferential 1st person clitic pronoun and the preposition that heads it are in the VC, in a fashion reminiscent of the head-final order. (16) shows how this structure can be derived by means of Incorporation:

(16) a.   [$_{V'}$ *hadlayaa* [$_{P''}$ [$_{P'}$ *la* [$_{DP}$ *i*]]]]

     b. → [$_{V'}$ *hadlayaa* [$_{P''}$[$_{P'}$ [$_{P}$ [$_{P}$ *i$_i$ la*]] [$_{DP}$ t$_i$]]]]

     c. → [$_{V'}$[$_{V}$ [$_{P}$ *i$_i$ la*]$_j$ *hadlayaa*] [$_{P''}$[$_{P'}$[$_{P}$ [$_{P}$ t$_j$] [$_{DP}$ t$_i$]]]]

(16a) is the base component after Merge,[15] in which Θ-role assignment takes place and each head precedes its complement. As a first step, the object clitic adjoins to the left of its head, P, forming a Prepositional Complex (16b); the compound P then adjoins to the left of its head, V, yielding a VC in the proper sense (16c). Again, nothing at all needs to be stipulated in order to derive the correct structure. The derivation is absolutely straightforward. The obligatoriness of the object clitic results from the MVC. The preposition cannot assign its Θ-role directly to the argument DP, so the mediation of the clitic pronoun, contained in the P-Complex, is required. In the successive cycle of head-movement, the P-Complex incorporates into the verb, which heads it.[16] In this way, the remarkable feature of 'discontinuity' of the PP finds a natural explanation.[17]

4. *DPs as adjuncts: further evidence*

We will now consolidate the analysis based on the MVC by bringing further and more direct evidence that all DPs are adjuncts. This is the central element of

---

[15] For the notion of Merge see Chomsky (1995:226).

[16] And which, presumably, assigns a Θ-role to the PP as a whole.

[17] A further piece of evidence in favour of the configurational analysis of PP in Somali comes from the contrast between structural vs. inherent case assignment for direct objects vs. objects of prepositions in long-movement structures, as argued in Frascarelli (1998). This contrast makes sense if a normal X' structure is assumed for PP in Somali.

our analysis. We will make use of some standard diagnostics in generative
syntax and of some established generalisations about polysynthetic languages.
The argument will primarily relate to complement DPs.

4.1 *Disjoint Reference Effects*

One piece of evidence comes from the 'Disjoint Reference Effects', i.e. the
conditions in which two DPs cannot be coreferential. Condition (C) of Binding
Theory states as in (17):

(17) The Binding Principles: Condition (C)
  An R-expression must be A-free.
  (A-free = not coindexed with a c-commanding category in an A-position)

Condition (C) accounts for subject-object asymmetries such as those found in
the well-known English examples given below:

(18) a.   John$_i$'s knife helped him$_i$.
   b.   *He$_i$ broke John$_i$'s knife.

In (18a) *John*, the R-expression, can be coreferential with *him* because *him*, the
object, does not c-command the subject, *John's knife*. On the other hand, the
only possible relation between *he* and *John* in (18b) is one of disjoint reference
because the subject, *he*, does c-command the object, *John*, so they cannot be
coreferential. Let us look at some Somali parallels in (19) below:

(19) a.   *Shalay*   *b-ay$_i$*   *Maryan$_i$*   *mindi-deed$_i$*   *jabisay.*
      Yesterday   FM-SCL   Maryam   knife-her   break-PAST

   b.   *Shalay*   *b-ay$_i$*   *jabisay*   *Maryan$_i$*   *mindi-deed$_i$.*
      Yesterday   FM-SCL   break-PAST   Maryam   knife-her
      "She$_i$ broke Maryan$_i$'s knife YESTERDAY"

In both sentences in (19) a coreferential reading is possible, although they are
equivalent to the English example (18b) (where only the disjoint reference is
possible), since the R-expression, *Maryan*, follows the subject pronoun, either
immediately or not. Thus, an obvious deduction is that the subject pronoun, *ay*,
"she", does not c-command the object, *Maryan*. Why not? The answer must be
that a full DP, such as *Maryan* in our example, is never in its A-position, hence
must be an adjunct. [18]

---

[18] Here and below, we use the term 'A-position' in the sense of 'Lexical (L)-related position' of
Chomsky (1995:64).

4.2 Comp-trace effect

The phenomenon we will use to test the position of DPs is the familiar 'Complementizer-trace' effect, which is another instance of complement/non-complement asymmetry. The cross-linguistic generalisation is that a filled Comp position gives minimality effects, i.e. blocks Antecedent Government of a trace by a moved phrase. So, in order for a trace to be licensed, it must be L-marked, i.e. governed by a lexical head hence the subject/object asymmetry, as the following standard English examples in (20a-c) illustrate:

(20) a. Who$_i$ did you say **that** Phil admires t$_i$?

    b. *Who$_i$ did you say **that** t$_i$ wrote this song?

    c. Who$_i$ did you say t$_i$ wrote this song?

If in Somali object DPs could occur in argument position, no Comp-trace effect should take place, since the trace of a Wh-moved object would not need to be antecedent-governed in order to be properly governed. But in fact Somali data show no subject/object asymmetry, as can be seen in examples (21)-(22):

(21) a. *Cali$_i$ b-aan   sheegay   [in   buug   t$_i$ qoray]

         Ali   FM-SCL   say-PAS   that   book   write-PAST

         "CALI I said that wrote a book"

    b. Cali$_i$ b-aan   sheegay   [in-uu$_i$ buug   t$_i$ qoray]

         Ali   FM-SCL   say-PAST   that-SCL   book   write-PAST

         "CALI I said that wrote a book"

(22) a. *Aniga$_i$ b-aad   sheegtay   [in-uu$_j$ Cali$_j$ sugay   t$_i$]

         me   FM-SCL   say-PAST   that-SCL Ali   wait-PAST

         "You said that Ali waited for ME"

    b. Aniga$_i$ b-aad   sheegtay   [in-uu$_j$ Cali$_j$ i$_i$ sugay   t$_i$]

         book   FM-SCL   say-PAST   that-SCL Ali   OCL   wait-PAST

         "You said that Ali waited for ME"

While the ungrammaticality of (21a) is expected, the ungrammaticality of (22a) comes as a surprise since the Comp-trace effect should not affect the trace of the focused object, which has been moved to the Spec, CP of the upper clause, because it is supposed to be L-marked. But in fact it is not, nor can it be antecedent-governed because of the Minimality Effect induced by the overt Comp *in*. Here then is another piece of evidence that DPs are never in argument position.

Notice, however, that both in the case of the long-moved subject and in the case of the long-moved object the presence of a coreferential clitic, an agreement element, makes the sentences grammatical. This is, again, in line with the MVC, by which agreement forms mediate between the DPs and their head, here the verb. The thematic relation between a full DP and its Θ-governor can be recovered through the intervention of the coreferential clitic, with which the DP is in a binding relation. Then the DP is fully interpreted and the derivation converges at LF.

4.3 *Absence of DP anaphors*

A further piece of evidence is related to a typological generalisation about polysynthetic languages, i.e. they lack true DP anaphors, possibly because of the conflicting requirements of Binding Theory which arise.[19] In polysynthetic languages DP anaphors are replaced by a reflexive morpheme in the verb. This is precisely the situation that holds in Somali. Consider the following examples:[20]

> (23) W-*aan*$_i$ [*is*$_i$ dhaq-ay]
> CLASS-SCL self wash-PAST
> "I washed myself"

> (24) W-*ay*$_i$ [*is*$_i$ nabdaadiy-een]
> CLASS-SCL   self say goodbye-PAST
> "They said goodbye to each other"

The anaphoric element, both reflexive and reciprocal, is not a full DP and hence is not an adjunct, but is part of the VC. The subject clitic, in its A-position, c-commands the anaphoric clitic *is*, thus being in the desired configuration for Condition (A) of Binding to apply. The derivation thus converges at LF. The derivation of *is* parallels that of ordinary object clitics, being incorporated into the verb by head-movement, as (25) shows:

> (25) W-*aan*$_i$ [$_V$· dhaqay [$_{DP}$ *is*$_i$]] → W-*aan*$_i$ [$_V$· [$_V$ *is*$_i$ dhaqay] [$_{DP}$ t$_i$]]

4.4 *Absence of non-finite clauses*

Another well-established generalisation about polysynthetic languages is that they have fewer types of embedded clauses than in configurational languages. In particular, there are no non-finite clauses such as infinitivals, gerundives and participials (Mithun 1984, Nichols 1992). This generalisation seems to be directly related to the fact that non-finite clauses do not license subject agreement, which is necessary in polysynthetic languages, given the MVC

---

[19] For a principled account of the absence of DP anaphors along these lines, see Baker (1996:49). Whatever the reason, the generalisation is that DP anaphors are ruled out in polysynthetic languages because DPs are always adjuncts in these languages and adjuncts cannot function as anaphors.

[20] CLASS stands for Classifier, a functional head presumably related to Modality. Other terms common in Cushitic studies are 'Indicator Particle' and 'Selector'. In other work (Puglielli 1981, among others) *waa* has been considered a *verb focus particle*.

(Baker 1996:472). Somali shows exactly the expected absence of non-finite embedded clauses and a remarkable limitation of clausal types.[21] As a matter of fact, only two types of embedded clauses occur in Somali, relative and complement clauses; both of these are finite. A few examples are given in (26)-(28):

(26) *Wax-ay   doonaysaa*   [CP *in-ay   bish-a   dambe   tagto*]
Thing-SCL want-PRES.3SGF that-SCL month-the next   go-SUBJ.3SG
"She wants to leave next month"

(27) *Wax-aan   Xasan   u   diray* [CP *in-uu   seexdo*]
Thing-SCL Hasan to sent   that-SCL sleep-SUBJ.3SG
"I sent Hasan to sleep"

(28) *Isaga* [CP *oo   isbitaalka   ku   jira*], *ay-uu   dhintay.*
He   COMP hospital   in   stay   FM-SCL die-PAST
"He died while he was in hospital"

(26)-(27) are tensed complement clauses introduced by the finite Comp *in*; (28) is a relative non-restrictive clause, introduced by *oo*, which often translates circumstantial non-finite clauses.

4.5 *No Wh-questions or focuses in situ*

A remarkable characteristic of Somali is the impossibility of realising Wh-questions or focuses in situ. This characteristic of polysynthetic languages is a consequence of the impossibility for DPs to be licensed in argument position.[22] Again, the MVC plays a role in forcing Wh-movement to take place, ruling out Focuses and Wh-questions in situ. By the same token, multiple Wh-questions (or focuses) are banned in Somali, since at least one element should be realised in situ.[23]

(29) a.   *(*Yaa)   goor-m-uu   (*yaa)   yimid   (*yaa)?*
Who   time-which-SCL who   come-PAST who
"When who came?"

    b.   *(*Goor-ma)   yaa   (*goor-ma)   yimid   (*goor-ma)?*
Time-which who   time-which come-PAST time-which
"Who when came?"

---

[21] This property has not gone unnoticed by some scholars of Somali (cf. Antinucci 1981:227).

[22] For an account based on a proposal by Rizzi (1991) of why they cannot be licensed as adjuncts either, see Baker (1996:67). The issue is more wide-ranging than is suggested here and has to do with the impossibility of licensing quantifiers in general as adjuncts.

[23] Obviously, a focus and a Wh-question are also reciprocally exclusive. One way of permitting multiple Wh-questions/focuses would be to admit Wh-movement of all operators. But while this option is available in a few languages, polysynthetic or non-polysynthetic, it is not permitted in Somali.

4.6 *Discourse Configurationality, Focus Prominence*

Another informal typological feature of Somali, often recognised in the literature,[24] is its propensity to be 'discourse configurational',[25] or 'pragmatically oriented' (Mithun 1987). Even if it may be difficult to make this notion more explicit, there is a sense in which it captures a clear property of Somali, i.e. the frequency with which multiple topics occur in common sentences and the alleged obligatoriness of focus in matrix clauses.[26] Both features derive more or less directly from the Polysynthesis Parameter. The intuition is that since DPs are only licensed as adjuncts in the base component, thus being free from the burden of argumentality so to speak, full DPs have more license to assume discourse roles. The situation is very similar in this regard to that of Clitic Left Dislocation (CLLD) in Romance languages, among others.[27]

As for 'Focus Prominence', the explanation is straightforward. Because of the MVC, focus is not permitted in situ; a focus DP is therefore forced to move to clause initial position (Spec, CP under standard analyses). As a consequence, there is no such thing in Somali as the familiar distinctions between 'broad' (or 'presentational') and 'narrow' (or 'contrastive') focus constructions, in which the former tends to be unmarked in content and form, i.e. without resorting to marked syntactic resources such as movement, and the latter is marked in form and meaning.[28] Consider, for example, the following Italian sentences:

(30) a.   *(Gianni) è*   *andato* [pp *a casa*]
        John   be-PRES.3SG   go-PP   to home
        "John went home"

    b.   [pp *A CASA*] *è*   *andato (Gianni)*
        to home be-PRES.3SG   go-PP   John
        "John went HOME"

In (30a), the focus element is in situ and takes prominence by default. (30b), on the other hand, in which the focus DP has moved into Spec, CP (or a Comp-like category), takes prominence in its domain by rule. Sentences such as (30b) have

[24] Cf. Livnat (1984), Lecarme (1991), Svolacchia et al. (1995), among others.

[25] For an illustration of this and related notions, see Kiss (1995).

[26] There is good reason to think that the conventional notion of obligatoriness of focus in matrix clauses for Somali is in fact inaccurate, and derives from the interpretation of the classifier *waa* as a 'verbal focus marker'. For more information on this subject, see Saeed (1984), Svolacchia et al. (1995).

[27] For which see Cinque (1990). This parallelism between CLLD and polysynthetic languages is explicitly and extensively recognised in Baker (1996).

[28] For more of this, see Frascarelli (1997).

more restricted use in general. So, while the sentence in (30a) could be used in
reply to a question such as "Where did John go?", the sentence in (30b) sounds
rather odd in the same context. Let us look now at a Somali equivalent of (30):

(31) *Cali*   *guri-ga*   *b-uu*   *tegay*
       Ali   house-the   FM-SCL   go-PAST
       "John went home/HOME"

In (31) *guriga*, "home", has undergone movement, being in a Spec-Head relation with the FM *baa,* and is prosodically prominent, much like the Italian example in (30b). Yet its semantics and use differ from the analogous case in
Italian, in that it does not normally share the same narrowness of scope and
contextual specialisation. In fact, sentences like (31) above are the most common in the language. As the translation suggests, (31) is ambiguous, as the narrow focus reading is also possible. The conclusion that can be drawn from the
contrast between Italian and Somali is that while Italian normally resorts to the
more economical type of focalisation, the in situ one, Somali cannot do so because it is forced by the MVC to move the focus DP in Spec, CP to perform operator checking. Thus the parallelism shown in Italian between syntactic
markedness and semantic markedness does not work in Somali. This seems to
be what lies behind the notion of focus prominence, and this again results directly from the Polysynthesis Parameter.

5.   *Somali and the Head Parameter*

The analysis we have been developing so far relies heavily on the assumption that complements follow their heads in Somali. The fact that this assumption in association with incorporation yields the correct results seems to be
strong evidence in its favour.[29] There is independent evidence to support it. As
is well known, in 'true and tough' head-final languages such as Japanese, Korean or Turkish, clausal complements precede their heads, and their Comp follows the rest of the sentence, as expected. In Somali, on the contrary, clausal
complements follow their heads and the Comp precedes the rest of the sentence, as examples (26)-(28) show. This evidence is particularly compelling as

---

[29] Not to mention the fact that, as recent research has shown, there is good reason to assume it *a
priori,* at least as a working, *prima ratio* hypothesis (cf. Kayne 1994, in particular). Incorporation seems to provide further evidence in support of Kayne's claim that there is no head parameter. The point is that, given head-final languages it seems reasonable to expect to find mirror image structures at the right side of a host head. But, as far as we know, there are no clear
cases of such a language. The Mirror Effect as stated by Baker only makes sense with right to
left movement. In what follows, we will refer to *head-final* languages in an informal, epiphe-
nomenical sense.

there is general agreement that clausal complements need not or even cannot check case.[30] Since case is the main cause of DP-movement, this removes the need for embedded clauses to undergo movement and makes them a more reliable clue to word order.[31]

6. *The subject argument and the MVC* [32]

The data array shown above indicates that Somali does not licence complement DPs in argument position. We now turn our attention to subject arguments. The analysis of subject clitics (SCLs) highlights a number of problems. In general, there is good evidence that they count as arguments. This is shown by the fact that they are obligatory in many configurations, as shown in the example of *baa* sentences in (9). By contrast, SCLs can optionally be omitted in *non baa sentences*:[33]

(32) a. *Cali w-<u>uu</u>   / waa   yimid*
         Ali   CLASS-SCL/CLASS come-PAST
         "Ali came"

     b. *Walaal-kay w-<u>uu</u>   / waa   weyn yahay*
         brother-my CLASS-SCL/CLASS big   be-PRES.3SG
         "My brother is big"

Clearly, since Somali is hypothesised as polysynthetic and is therefore required to have subject agreement forms, the above cases are problematic. Let us consider the possible alternatives. One would be to state that the subject DP can occupy its argument position. The contrast between the sentences in which the clitic occurs, such as (9a-b), and the sentences in which it does not, such as (10) above, would be derived in much the same way as in Romance languages, in which the clitic (or a pro) is present in CLLD structures where the subject DP is an adjunct; but not present when the subject DP is in A-position or in a position coindexed with its trace via movement.[34] *Prima facie*, this analysis seems practicable. However, there are conceptual and empirical problems with this kind of solution. From a general, theoretical point of view, it is not clear how this result

---

[30] A case in point is Stowell (1981), who argued for a 'Case Resistance Principle'.

[31] For further evidence related to the formation of Complexes above VP, see Section 6.1.

[32] It goes beyond the limits of this paper to give a full fledged analysis of the issue. For this, we refer the interested reader to Svolacchia & Puglielli (1998). Here we summarize the main lines of the argument.

[33] Our informants have clear intuitions that the forms with the clitic subject are better in some way. The subject clitic tends to be omitted with 3rd person coreferential DP's.

[34] For a previous analysis of Somali along these lines see Svolacchia et al. (1995).

could be integrated into a general analysis of Somali, since there is little doubt that the MVC holds for complement arguments. Of course it would be possible *in principle* to stipulate that the MVC holds in Somali only as far as internal arguments are concerned. The external argument, on the other hand, would be assigned by a head, say a verb, directly to the argument DP. In this vein, Somali would be a 'semi-polysynthetic language'. This, however, is clearly not a promising line of inquiry.

On top of that there is substantial, independent evidence that subject DPs are never in A-position. The evidence is related to the *non baa sentences*, as in (32) above. A fact about this type of sentence is that a SCL, when it occurs, invariably occurs immediately after the Classifier and immediately before the VC, as can be seen in the following example:

(33) _Waa_ (*DP) _ay_[35] (*DP) [i sug-ay-s-aa]
    CLASS   SCL   me   wait-PROG-3SGF-PRES
    "She is waiting for me"

The same holds for the arbitrary subject clitic *la*, as (34) shows:

(34) _W-(*uu)_ (*DP) _la_ (*DP) [qabtay]
    CLASS-SCL   ARB.S   take-PAST
    "Someone took it/him/her/them"

Arbitrary *la* and the referential subject clitics behave exactly in the same way.[36] As expected, *la* cannot occur with a referential SCL in (34), on the assumption that both, when they occur, are in A-position. The fact that SCLs must be left adjacent to the VC is naturally explained in terms of the familiar notion of Spec-Head Agreement. So the SCL is in the Spec of a functional projection, whatever that might be. This analysis assumes that the SCL is not a head, but a maximal category. There is good reason to believe that this is so. As mentioned above, SCLs apart from *la* are not strictly speaking clitics at all as a number of properties show. First, they are invariably bimoraic, which is not typical of clitics;[37] second, they can occur alone, where no classifier occurs, as in relative clauses:

---

[35] In actual realisations the SCL cliticises onto the Classifier, here *waa,* and a contraction takes place, yielding *way*. Note that this process has nothing to do with Incorporation.
[36] This is a sharp departure from previous analyses, which assumed that 'impersonal *la*' was part of the VC (see Puglielli 1981, in particular).
[37] In more formal terms, this means that clitics, in the strict sense ('weak clitics' in the terms of Cardinaletti & Starke forthcoming) are not expected to comply with minimal word requirements (for which see McCarthy & Prince 1986).

(35) *Akhri buug-ag-gii [aan   ku-u   keenay]*
    read   book-PL-the SCL1SG SCL-to bring-PAST
    "Read the books I brought you"

The conclusion seems thus to be that SCLs are 'weak pronouns' (in the sense of Cardinaletti & Starke forthcoming), much like those of Germanic languages among others. The fact that they are semi-autonomous words seems to be in line with the idea of a maximal category.

Let us consider the possible alternative, that they are the head of a functional category of agreement, say AgrS. This possibility has to be discarded on account of the fact that the head of AgrS is in the VC, and can be shown to be derived via movement. To show this, we will examine Incorporation above VP.

6.1 *Incorporation above VP*

There is good evidence that in Somali the verb, i.e. the VC, moves to higher functional projections, as in most languages. (36) below is an example of a sentence with a modal:

(36) *Anigu   w-aan   cuni lah-aa*
    I   CLASS- SCL   eat have-PRES.HAB
    "I would eat it"

The modal immediately follows the verb it governs, apparently being part of a head-final pattern. In (37) this structure is reanalysed in terms of Verb to Auxiliary Incorporation (where the auxiliary is assumed to be the head of a Mood projection):

(37) a. *Anigu waan*   [$_\text{MOOD'}$ *lah-aa*   [$_\text{V'}$ *cuni* pro]]
       I   CLASS- SCL   have-PRES.HAB eat   it

    b. → *Anigu waan* [$_\text{MOOD'}$ [$_\text{MOOD}$ *cuni lah-aa*][$_\text{V'}$ t$_i$ pro]]

By the same token, there is evidence that the VC raises to Aspect, then to AgrS, and then to Tense, as mirrored by the linear order of elements in the VC. This is shown in (38):

(38) *W-ay*   [*i   sug-ay-s-aa*]
    CLASS-SCL me wait-PROG-3SGF-PRES
    "She is waiting for me"

in which the order of the head morphemes is

(39) VERB – ASPECT – AGRS – TENSE

which corresponds to the following representation:

(40)[38]

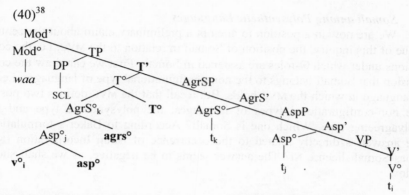

The order of functional heads is the one expected, in accordance with current research.[39] This seems good evidence for incorporation. The conclusion is therefore that the VC raises at least as far as Tense, through AgrS.

We can now make sense of the generalisation that SCLs are immediately right-adjacent to Classifiers and left adjacent to the VC. The VC moves cyclically from head to head to perform checking of features, in particular through AgrS, being in a Spec-Head relation with the SCL, and then moves to Tense, in whose Spec the SCL moves, again in Spec-Head agreement relation, presumably to check case. The Modality head, *waa* in the relevant example, blocks the raising of the VC, since the VC does not incorporate into it and the VC cannot jump over the head of Modality, given the HMC. This explains why there is strict adjacency between the modality classifier, the SCL and the VC.

Now the question of the subject DP arises. If subject DPs can occupy A-positions by hypothesis, why is it that they do not occur to the left of the VC in order to perform Spec-Head agreement? The answer must be that they cannot, given the MVC. This analysis assumes that whenever the highest L-related subject position is not overtly filled with a SCL that position be occupied by a pro.[40] In conclusion, this seems to be strong evidence that subject DPs, like non subject DPs, are always adjuncts.[41]

---

[38] The tree diagram has been simplified to some extents. In particular, it abstracts away from functional projections between VP and AspP, MoodP, for instance.

[39] For evidence that Tense precedes AgrS and Aspect, see Ouhalla (1994) for Arabic. This is also consistent with the generalisations in Cinque (1998), based on a wide sample of languages.

[40] It goes beyond the scope of this research to investigate the precise conditions under which pro is licensed in Somali. But our impression is that they could be quite intricate.

[41] In theory, there may be another hypothesis about the subject argument: it is verb agreement that counts as argument. But, if subject agreement on the verb counts for the MVC, what are the

7. *Somali among Polysynthetic Languages*

We are now in a position to attempt a preliminary claim about the central issue of this inquiry, the position of Somali in relation to the MVC, i.e. the conditions under which Θ-roles are assigned in Somali. First we can draw the conclusion that Somali belongs to the non-configurational type of languages, i.e. is a language in which the MVC holds. But recall that the MVC defines two possible non-configurational types of languages: the polysynthetic type and the Polyagreeing type. Which one is Somali? According to Baker's formulation, the answer is directly related to the occurrence of Noun Incorporation (NI). Does Somali license NI? The answer seems to be negative, as we shall show below.

7.1 *Noun Incorporation*

Among a number of diagnostics for testing whether a language has proper NI, Baker proposes two conditions that are relevant for this discussion. One is, not surprisingly, that NI must be 'productive', though it is sometimes restricted to specific classes of nouns; the second is that an incorporated noun can be 'referential'. Neither of these conditions are met in Somali, where NI is clearly a matter of lexicalization. This is shown by the tendency to develop idiom chunks, and, most importantly, because incorporated nouns are never referential. Let us look at some typical examples of NI in Somali:

(41) a. *W-uu*   *i*   [*fara   saaray*]
         CLASS-SCL   me   fingers put on
         "He beat me"

     b. *W-aan*   [*xoog   badn-ahay*]
         CLASS-SCL strength much-be-PRES.1SG
         "I am very strong"

The incorporated object nouns, *fara* "fingers" in (41a) and *xoog* "strenght" in (41b), cannot have a referential reading. They can never refer to a specific set of objects, nor can they assume a discourse role, say "the fingers we were talking about", or something like that. As a consequence, we conclude that *Somali does not license NI* in the strict sense.[42]

SCLs? Why should a language systematically duplicate its agreement features in order to absolve the MVC? There is therefore good reason to reject this hypothesis.

[42] Sasse (1984), who investigated NI in Eastern Cushitic languages in some detail, has reached the same conclusion, though based on somewhat different theoretical assumptions. NI in Somali is more complex than the forgoing discussion may suggest, as there is evidence that it has some productivity with some restricted classes of nouns. This does not however alter the basic facts.

One possible hypothesis is that Somali, in spite of all its similarities with polysynthetic languages, is a *Poly-agreeing* language. Nonetheless, there is good reason to reject this hypothesis. Agreement forms in Somali are indeed not affixes at all but clitics, which are incorporated into the governing, Θ-assignor head via head-movement, as shown above. Thus, the correct conclusion seems to be that Somali does in fact exploit NI but in the particular form of *Clitic Incorporation*.

This proposal clearly has some bearing on the MVC itself. From a descriptive point of view, Somali seems to fall between Poly-agreeing languages and polysynthetic languages since it *incorporates agreement forms*. But in fact what the Somali facts strongly suggest is that there may be no reason to distinguish between the two classes of argumental morphemes in non-configurational languages. Rather, they should be unified under the notion of 'incorporated element' in line with what has been proposed by Anderson (1982) for agreement in Breton.[43] As a consequence, there are no longer two sub-types of non-configurational languages. According to this hypothesis, the MVC would be formulated as in (42):

(42) Morphological Visibility Condition (MVC) (revised)
A phrase X is visible for Θ-role assignment from a head Y only if it is coindexed with a morpheme in the word containing Y via a movement relationship.

However, there is still a sense in which one would like to distinguish between two types of languages, as far as internal arguments are concerned. In one type the MVC is absolved by direct incorporation of the argument noun into its Θ-assignor; in the second the MVC is absolved by incorporation of a head pronominal form, coindexed with the argument DP. So, the first type would realise the MVC in a direct way and the second indirectly, through the mediation of an agreement form. Notice, however, that since external arguments cannot be incorporated into the verb, given the HMC, both language types behave uniformly in relation to subjects, for which invariably the MVC is invariably absolved by means of agreement forms. In the same way, this holds in many cases for indirect objects as well. These cannot be incorporated directly into the verb

---

[43] Interestingly, Baker recognises this possibility but he discards it on account of the problems arising from a unification, the main one being that agreement morphemes can or cannot count as arguments in different languages (cf. Baker & Hale 1990). There is no doubt, however, that pronominal clitics in Somali count as arguments.

because it would yield a violation of the HMC, since a preposition or a preposition-like element interposes.[44]

8. Conclusions

There is sound evidence that most of the apparent idiosyncrasies of Somali – such as scrambling, discontinuous constituency, obligatoriness of clitics, 'verbal complexes', discourse configurationality, absence of true anaphors, absence of non-finite clauses and multiple Wh-questions – can be ultimately derived from Baker's Morphological Visibility Condition. This condition of UG entails *Incorporation* of argument heads and the fact that full DP's are never arguments.

More specific evidence for the non-argumentality of full object DP's is derived from the Disjoint Reference and the Comp-trace effects. As for subject DPs, less direct evidence has shown that they too are never in argument position.

In relation to Somali's place among non-configurational languages, in a technical sense, we have advocated a simplification of Baker's MVC, on account of the fact that Somali, which does not incorporate nouns but clitics, seems to span the two subclasses of non-configurational languages proposed in Baker (1996). More generally, Somali displays some interesting properties which promise to enrich and deepen our understanding of non-configurational, polysynthetic languages.

REFERENCES

Anderson, Stephen. 1982. "Where's Morphology?". *Linguistic Inquiry* 13.571-612.

Antinucci, Francesco. 1981. "Tipi di Frase". *Studi Somali 2: Sintassi della lingua somala* ed. by Annarita Puglielli, 219-300. Roma: Ministero degli Affari Esteri.

Baker, Mark. 1985. "The Mirror Principle and Morphosyntactic Explanation". *Linguistic Inquiry* 16.373-417.

---

[44] Note that, since the MVC is expected to work in every domain in which Θ-role assignment is involved, the above conclusion is further supported by evidence that the MVC operates in DP as well. The case in point is the Genitive Construction (recently analysed in Lecarme 1996), an example of which is given below:

    (i)   *Maryan*$_i$ *buug-g-eed$_i$-a*
        M.   book-the(M)-her-the
        "Merriam's book"

The main features of this peculiar structure are: (i) the argument DP lacks genitive case and is to the left of its head; (ii) the head is obligatorily followed by a possessive clitic pronoun, which is coindexed with the argument DP. For an analysis of this structure on the basis of the MVC and Incorporation, see Svolacchia & Puglielli (1998).

——. 1988. *Incorporation: A theory of grammatical function changing.* Chicago: University of Chicago Press.

——. 1996. *The Polysynthesis Parameter.* New York & Oxford: Oxford University Press.

—— & Kenneth Hale. 1990. "Relativized Minimality and Pronoun Incorporation". *Linguistic Inquiry* 21.289-298.

Borer, Hagit. 1984. *Parametric Syntax: Case studies in Semitic and Romance languages.* Dordrecht: Foris.

Cardinaletti, Anna &. Michal Starke (forthcoming). "The Typology of Structural Deficiency: On the three grammatical classes". *Clitics in the Languages of Europe, vol. VIII of Language Typology* ed. by Hank van Riemsdijk. Berlin: Mouton de Gruyter.

Chomsky, Noam. 1995. *The Minimalist Program.* Cambridge, Mass.: MIT Press.

Cinque, Guglielmo. 1990. *Types of A'-Dependencies.* Cambridge, Mass.: MIT Press.

——. 1998. *Adverbs and Functional Heads: A cross-linguistic perspective.* Oxford: Oxford University Press.

Frascarelli, Mara. 1997. *L'Interfaccia Sintassi-Fonologia nelle Costruzioni di Focalizzazione e Topicalizzazione dell'Italiano.* PhD. Dissertation, Università di Roma Tre.

——. 1998. "Long movement, That-trace Effects and Anti-agreement in Somali". Paper presented at the 4th Conference on Afro-asiatic Languages, School of Oriental and African Studies, London, 25-27 June 1998.

Jelinek, Eloise. 1984. "Empty categories, case, and configurationality. *Natural Language and Linguistic Theory* 2:29-76.

Kayne, Richard. 1994. *The Antisymmetry of Syntax.* Cambridge, Mass.: MIT Press.

Kiss, É. Katalin. 1995. "Introduction". *Discourse Configurational Languages* ed. by Katalin É. Kiss, 3-27. New York & Oxford: Oxford University Press.

Larson, Richard. 1988. "On the Double Object Construction". *Linguistic Inquiry* 19.335-391.

Lecarme, Jacqueline. 1991. "Focus en Somali: Syntaxe et interprétation". *Linguistique Africaine* 7.33-65.

——. 1996. "Tense in the Nominal System: The Somali DP". *Studies in Afroasiatic Grammar: Papers from the second Conference on Afroasiatic languages, Sophia Antipolis, 16-18 June 1994* ed. by Jacqueline Lecarme, Jean Lowenstamm & Ur Shlonsky, 159-178. The Hague: Holland Academic Graphics.

Livnat, Michal Allon 1984. *Focus Constructions in Somali.* PhD. Dissertation, University of Illinois at Urbana-Champaign.

McCarthy, John & Alan Prince. 1986. *Prosodic Morphology.* Unpublished Manuscript, Waltham, Mass.: Brandeis University.

Mithun, Marianne. 1984. "How to Avoid Subordination". *Proceedings of the 10th Annual Meeting of the Berkeley Linguistic Society,* 493-509. Berkeley Linguistic Society, University of California, Berkeley.

——— . 1987. "Is Basic Word Order Universal?". *Coherence and Grounding in Discourse* ed. by Russell S. Tomlin, 281-328. Amsterdam & Philadelphia: John Benjamins.

Nichols, Johanna. 1986. "Head-marking and Dependent-marking Grammar". *Language* 62:1.56-119.

——— . 1992. *Linguistic Diversity in Space and Time.* Chicago: University of Chicago Press.

Ouhalla, Jamal. 1994. "Verb Movement and Word Order in Arabic". *Verb Movement* ed. by David Lightfoot & Norbert Hornstein, 41-72. Cambridge: Cambridge University Press.

Puglielli, Annarita. 1981. "Frase Dichiarativa Semplice". *Studi Somali 2: Sintassi della lingua somala* ed. by Annarita Puglielli, 1-44. Roma: Ministero Affari Esteri.

Rizzi, Luigi. 1991. "Residual Verb Second and the Wh-Criterion". *Technical Reports in Formal and Computational Linguistics* 2, Université de Genève. (Reprinted in *Parameters and Functional Heads: Essays in comparative syntax* ed. by Adriana Belletti & Luigi Rizzi. Oxford Studies in Comparative Syntax. New York & Oxford: Oxford University Press.).

Roberts, Ian. 1991. "Excorporation and Minimality". *Linguistic Inquiry* 22.209-218.

Saeed, John Ibrahim. 1984. *The Syntax of Focus and Topic in Somali.* Hamburg: Helmut Buske.

Sasse, Hans-Jürgen. 1984. "The Pragmatics of Noun Incorporation in Eastern Cushitic Languages". *Objects: Towards a theory of grammatical relations* ed. by Franz Plank, 243:268. London & Orlando: Academic Press.

Stowell, Timothy. 1981. *Origins of Phrase Structure.* PhD. Dissertation, Cambridge, Mass.

Svolacchia Marco & Annarita Puglielli. 1998. "Polysynthesis in East Cushitic". Paper presented at the 4th Conference on Afro-asiatic Languages, School of Oriental and African Studies, London, 25-27 June 1998.

——— , Lunella Mereu & Annarita Puglielli. 1995. "Aspects of Discourse Configurationality in Somali". *Discourse Configurational Languages* ed. by Katalin É. Kiss, 65-98. New York & Oxford: Oxford University Press.

Travis, Lisa. 1984. *Parameters and Effects of Word Order Variation.* PhD. Dissertation, Cambridge, Mass.

DUTCH VERBAL PREFIXES
MEANING AND FORM, GRAMMATICALIZATION AND LEXICALIZATION

JOHAN VAN DER AUWERA
University of Antwerp

0. *Introduction*

One of the phenomena that crucially concerns the interface between syntax and morphology is grammaticalization. The concept of grammaticalization and sometimes also the term itself have been used in the diachronic study of the development of verbal prefixes (e.g., Krahe & Meid [1967:42-43] for the concept but not the term; De La Cruz [1975:75-78] for both concept and term). Conversely, verbal prefixes have been on the agenda of grammaticalization theory ever since Lehmann (1982 [1995:97-104]). Lehmann's work has been highly instrumental in reviving interest in grammaticalization and has led to further theorizing in works such as Heine et al. (1991), Traugott & Heine eds. (1991), Bybee et al. (1994), and Hopper & Traugott (1993). This paper is set within that tradition and is an attempt to get verbal prefixes *off* the agenda, and back *into* research (for an independent attempt, see Kiefer 1997).

Verbal prefixes rightly belong to the subject matter of grammaticalization theory. They often have functions – or perhaps homonyms – as adverbs or prepositions: as adverbs and prepositions they seem to be in syntax, but as verbal prefixes, they belong to morphology. And here, as elsewhere, it seems that in general "today's morphology is yesterday's syntax". In languages such as Dutch and German the situation is a bit more complicated, for under certain circumstances the verbal prefix may be separated from the verb. This is illustrated with Dutch *terug-* and German *zurück-* "back", which are separated from their verbal base in (1) and connected in (2).

(1) DUT *Ik   stuur   het   boek   terug.*
    GER *Ich   schicke   das   Buch   zurück.*
        I   send   the   book   back
    "I am sending the book back."

(2) DUT *Ik*   *wil*   *het*   *boekte 'rug-sturen.*[1]
     GER *Ich*   *will*   *das*   *Buch*   *zu 'rück-schicken.*
     I   want   the   book   back-send
     "I want to send the book back."

Not all verbal prefixes are separable. Dutch and German *ver-*, for example, never separates.

(3) DUT *Anna*   *ver-'oordeelt*   *het.*
     GER *Anna*   *ver-'urteilt*   *es.*
     Anna   PRE[2]-judges   it
     "Anna condemns it."

(4) DUT *Anna*   *wil*   *het*   *ver-'oordelen.*
     GER *Anna*   *will*   *es*   *ver-'urteilen.*
     Anna   wants   it   PRE-judge
     "Ann wants to condemn it."

And both languages have a third class of verbal prefixes, whose separability depends on meaning. Dutch *door-* and German *durch-* "through" when combined with "run" verbs separate depending on whether the resulting verbs mean "continue" or "cross".

(5) DUT *De*   *paginering*   *van deze*   *delen*   *loopt*   *door.*
     GER *Die Paginierung*   *dieser*   *Bände*   *läuft*   *durch.*
     the pagination   of.these   volumes runs   through
     "The page numbering of these volumes continues throughout."

(6) DUT *De*   *paginering*   *kan*   *'door-lopen.*
     GER *Die Paginierung*   *kann*   *'durch-laufen.*
     the pagination   can   through-run
     "The page numbering can be continued throughout."

(7) DUT *Ik*   *door-'liep*   *het*   *park.*
     GER *Ich durch-'lief*   *den*   *Park.*
     I   through-ran   the   park
     "I crossed the park."

---

[1] In the verbal forms stress marks and hyphens are added when relevant.

[2] 'PRE' for 'prefix' is used whenever English does not allow a good semantic gloss. Thus I resort to 'PRE' in (3) and (4), but in, e.g., (1)-(2) I can be more specific and use the semantic gloss 'back'. The only other grammatical label used in the glosses is 'INFL' for 'inflectional element'.

(8) DUT *Ik kan het park door-'lopen.*
    GER *Ich kann den Park durch-'laufen.*
    I can the park through-run
    "I can cross the park."

Thus Dutch and German have three types of verbal prefixes:

(9)

separable	in some uses separable in other uses inseparable	inseparable
more syntactic		morphological

This paper is the third in a series of studies on Germanic verbal prefixes. In earlier work (van der Auwera 1995, in press), I assumed that the inseparable Dutch and German verbal prefix is more grammaticalized than the one that is sometimes or always separable. This is correct in the sense that morphology is the grammaticalization of syntax, but less so when we observe that the insepa-rable prefix may be partially (e.g., Dutch *ver-*) or completely (e.g., Dutch *ont-*) restricted to a fixed list of lexemes; in other words, they may be fully or par-tially non-productive. In that case, the process could be called 'lexicalization' rather than 'grammaticalization'. And interestingly, lexicalization does not only apply to inseparable prefixes, but also to separable ones. There has not been much work that focuses on lexicalization and its relation to grammaticalization, Lehmann (1989) being the exception. In this paper, I will distinguish between lexicalized and grammaticalized uses of prefixes.

Two further differences with the earlier work are that here I will only ana-lyze Dutch, rather than Dutch and German, and I will examine both meaning and form, rather than form only. Like the previous studies, however, the present is solely a synchronic study and solely based on the modern language.[3]

In Section 1, I report on the form of Dutch verbal prefixes, in Section 2, I analyze the meaning, and in Section 3, I relate form and meaning.

---

[3] The synchronic data can be found in De Haas & Trommelen (1993), Geerts et al. (1984) and Haeseryn et al. (1997). As to diachrony, a comprehensive study remains to be undertaken. Though the history of Dutch prefix verbs supports the general idea that inseparability develops out of partial separability which in turn comes from full separability, there is an interesting issue about some prefixes possibly having returned from partial separability to full separability, which would amount to degrammaticalization (see Van Loey 1976, Duinhoven 1997:106-134).

1. *Form*

To say that a Dutch prefix is separable, inseparable or that it can be both is rather simplistic. One has to make clear what it is that conditions the separation. So far I have only illustrated the 'V-2' subtype: in Dutch declarative main clauses the finite verb takes up the second position, the prefix – as well as any non-finite verb forms – is placed towards the end. One could say that the separator is the so-called 'middle field'.

(1')	*Ik*	*stuur*	*het boek*	*terug.*
		V-2 position	Middle field	V-late position

A second separator is the inflectional prefix *ge-*, used in the formation of past particles.

(10)	*Ik*	*heb*	*het boek*	*terug-*	*ge-*	*stuur-d.*
	I	have	the book	back	INFL	send-INFL

"I have sent back the book."

A third is the infinitival particle *te* 'to'.

(11)	*Ik*	*vergat*	*het boek*	*terug*	*te*	*sturen.*
	I	forgot	the book	back	to	send

"I forgot to send back the book."

Finally, the separator may be a finite verb and/or an infinitive preceding the base in a verb cluster.

(12)	*Ik*	*wil*	*het boek*	*terug*	*kunnen*	*sturen.*
	I	want	the book	back	can	send

"I want to be able to send back the book."

(13)	*... dat ik*	*het boek*	*terug*	*kon*	*sturen.*
	that I	the book	back	could	send

"... that I could send back the book."

In (12) the separator is the infinitive *kunnen* and in (13) the finite verb *kon*.[4]

---

[4] Note that in this respect the separability is higher in Dutch than in German, for in German verbal clusters cannot separate.

(12')   a.   *Ich   will   das   Buch   zurück-schicken   können.*
             I   want the book   back-give   can
             "I want to be able to send back the book."

        b.   **Ich will das Buch zurück können schicken.*

The separability of the prefix is also associated with four additional formal properties. First of all, past participles are formed in a different way. (10) has already shown that separable prefixes employ the usual inflectional prefix *ge-*. When a prefix is inseparable, however, the inflectional prefix *ge-* cannot be used.

(14)   *Anna   heeft   het ver-'oordeel-d.*
         Anna   has   it PRE-judge-INFL
         "Anna has condemned it."

Second, inseparable prefixes do not carry main stress, whereas separable ones do. This is shown in all of the preceding examples. Third, inseparable prefixes have no other function than that of prefix, whereas separable ones may or may not have other functions. Thus inseparable *ver-* in (1) is *only* a verbal prefix, as is separable *tegemoet-* in (15).

(15)   *Ik   liep hem tegemoet.*
         I   ran him towards
         "I ran towards him."

Separable *door* in (5-6), however, can also function as a preposition, as illustrated in (16).

(16)   *Ik liep door   het park.*
         I ran through the park
         "I ran through the park."

Fourth, inseparable prefixes can combine with non-verbs, whereas separable ones may lack this capacity. An illustration of the verbalizing character of inseparable *ver-* is shown in (17).

(17)   *Ik   heb   het ver-as-t   /ver-donkere-maan-d.*
         I   have   it PRE-ash-INFL/PRE-dark-moon-INFL
         "I have incinerated/embezzled it."

A separable prefix that combines with non-verbs is illustrated in (18).

(18)   *Hij heeft   mij na-ge-aap-t.*
         he has   me after-INFL-ape-INFL
         "He has imitated me."

(13')   a.   ... *daß   ich   das   Buch zurück-schicken konnte.*
               that   I   the   book back-send   could
               "... that I could send back the book."
         b.   * ... *daß ich das Buch zurück konnte schicken.*

dooreen-, illustrated in (19), is an example of a separable prefix that only combines with verbs.

(19)   *Hij   heeft   alles   door-een-ge-gooi-d.*
       he   has   all   through-one-INFL-throw-INFL
       "He has thrown everything together."

The inseparable and separable verbal prefixes of Dutch can thus be characterized (with four types of separability and four associated properties), as in (20). (20) does not mention the prefixes that have both separable and inseparable uses, but these would simply join either group depending on use.

(20)

properties	+ separable	− separable
verb base separated by middle field	+	−
verb base separated by *ge-*	+	−
verb base separated by *te*	+	−
verb base separated by finite or infinitival verb in verb cluster	+	−
past participle uses *ge-*	+	−
prefix carries main stress	+	−
prefix has non-prefix uses	±	−
prefix cannot combine with non-verbs	±	−

A detailed study of the entire set of prefixes, however, reveals that not all prefixes have *all* of the expected properties. For example, inseparable prefixes of Latinate stock lack one of the eight expected properties: they use *ge-* with past participles.

(21)   *re-organi'seren*   *ge-re-organi'seer-d*
       re-organize   INFL-re-organized-INFL
       "reorganize"   "reorganize"

Moreover, though prefixes usually react in the same way to the four types of separators, there are exceptions, the most conspicuous one being *her-*.

(22) a.   fully inseparable:
         her-'overen   **her te overen*   **her-ge'overd*
         "reconquer"   *te her-overen*   *her-'overd*

    b.   separable by *te*:
          'her-bebossen   *her te be'bossen*   *her-be'bost*
          "reforest"   *te 'her-bebossen*   **her-ge-be'bost*

    c.   separable by *te* and *ge-*:
          'her-formuleren   *her te formuleren*   *'her-ge- formuleerd*
          "reformulate"   *te 'her-formuleren*   *ge-'her-formuleerd*

In the charts in (23) we can see the actual clustering of the eight properties. The right pole of each chart is that of inseparability and associated properties (n=8), and the left pole that of the absence of these properties (n=0). The left chart is computed on the basis of prefix uses, such as the ones shown in (22) for *her-*. The right chart is computed on the basis of single values for each prefix; e.g., one value for *her-*, which generalizes over its various uses.

(23)   Properties of prefix uses   Properties of prefixes

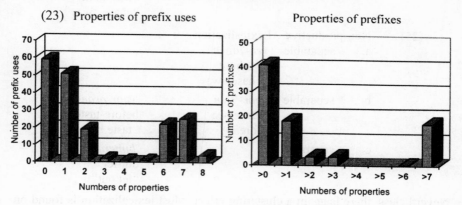

The tables show that prefixes and their uses tend to have either many of the eight properties or few. There are for example around 60 prefix uses that have none of the inseparability properties, there are only two prefix uses with 4 properties, but when the number of properties goes up to 7, there is again a higher number of prefix uses, viz. some 25.

There is one more formal feature that should be discussed here, viz. 'productivity'. As hinted at in Section 0, productivity is a graded phenomenon. Here, however, we will simplify matters and work with a binary opposition, saying that non-productive prefixes partake in lexicalization and only productive ones in grammaticalization proper. Productive and non-productive prefixes are found at either end of the property scales shown in (23). In (24) and (25) I

supply examples of productive and non-productive prefix uses for fully inseparable prefixes, for those that have both inseparable and separable uses, and for
fully separable ones.

(24)   Productive – Grammaticalization
        a.   – separable   *ver-'branden*
                              PRE-burn
                              "burn down"

        b.   ± separable   *om-'groeien*   *'om-rijden*
                              around-grow   around-ride
                              "grow around"   "make a detour"

        c.   + separable   *'weg-jagen*
                                                      away-hunt
                                                      "chase away"

(25)   Non-productive – Lexicalization
        a.   – separable   *ver-'jagen*
                              PRE-hunt
                              "chase away"

        b.   ± separable   *voor-'zien*   *'voor-proeven*
                              before-see   before-taste
                              "foresee"   "taste beforehand"

        c.   + separable   *'buiten-laten*
                                                      out-let
                                                      "let out"

Nevertheless, there is again a clustering effect. Most lexicalization is found on
the right hand side of the charts of (23). I cannot, however, quantify this in abstraction from meaning, for a prefix may be productive in one meaning, but
non-productive in another.

The clustering nicely illustrates that for those prefixes that have both separable and inseparable uses the inseparable ones are predominantly non-
productive and the separable ones are predominantly productive. Some examples are given in (26).

(26)   Inseparable   Separable
                            Non-productive   Productive
        a.   *onder-*   *onder-'gaan*   *'onder-gaan*
             under-   under-go   under-go
                            "undergo"   "go down"

    b.   *voor-*   *voor-'spellen*   *'voor-spellen*
          for   for-spell   for-spell
                  "predict"   "show how to spell"

In (27) I provide an overview of the formal properties of Dutch verbal prefixes. The terms 'separable[+]' and 'inseparable[+]' refer to the four (in)separability properties and to the four associated properties.

(27)

more separable[+]	more separable[+] in some uses more inseparable[+] in other uses	more inseparable[+]
more syntactic		morphological
less grammaticalized		more grammaticalized
less lexicalized		more lexicalized

2. *Meaning*

Dutch verbal prefixes convey a variety of meanings. Most types of prefixes partake in the meaning of the complex verb in a compositional way. Though a comprehensive analysis remains to be undertaken, I propose distinguishing them between five groups. For each group, I give examples of inseparable[+] prefixes, of those that have both inseparable[+] and separable[+] uses, and of fully separable[+] ones.

The first two groups of meanings concern space and time.

(28)   Space
       a.   – separable[+] *ver-'jagen*
                          PRE-hunt
                          "chase away"
       b. ± separable[+] *om-'groeien*   *'om-rijden*
                          around-grow   around-ride
                          "grow around"   "make a detour"
       c. + separable[+] *'weg-jagen*
                          away-hunt
                          "chase away"
(29)   Time
       a. – separable[+] Ø
       b. ± separable[+] *voor-'zien*   *'voor-proeven*
                          before-see   before-taste
                          "foresee"   "taste beforehand"

        c.   + separable$^+$ *'na-zenden*
                                                  after-send
                                                  "send on, forward"

The third and fourth groups concern aspect. I follow Dik (1989:204; 1997:225) in distinguishing between 'external aspect', which quantifies over states of affairs or relates them to an external reference point, and 'inner aspect', which concerns the internal dynamics of states of affairs. Outer aspect includes meanings like habit, frequency and continuity, and inner aspect includes phasal notions like 'ingressive' or 'egressive' as well as the perfective vs. imperfective contrast.

(30)   Outer aspect
        a.   – separable$^+$ Ø
        b.   ± separable$^+$ Ø   *'over-lezen*
                                                 over-read
                                                 "reread"
        c.   + separable$^+$ *'voort-bewegen*
                                               on-move
                                                 "move on"

(31)   Inner aspect
        a.   – separable$^+$ *ver-'branden*
                                    PRE-burn
                                    "burn up"
        b.   ± separable$^+$ *vol-'groeien*   *'vol-lopen*
                                    full-grow   full-run
                                    "mature"   "fill up"
        c.   + separable$^+$ *'uit-lezen*
                                               out-read
                                                 "finish reading"

Finally, the semantic contribution of the prefix may be non-compositional. The meaning of the prefix itself may still be more or less transparent,[5] but the meaning resulting from combining the prefix with the base is idiosyncratic.

(32)   Non-compositional meaning
        a.   – separable$^+$ *ver-'dwijnen*
                                    PRE-?
                                    "disappear"

---

[5] Yet another semantic dimension, to be included in a more exhaustive study, and different from both transparency and compositionality is the polysemy or even homonymy of the prefix.

b. ± separable[+] *voor-'komen* Ø
before-come
"prevent"

c. + separable[+] *'op-rotten*
up-rot
"get lost"

It can be observed that for most meanings examples could be found for each of the three formally distinguished prefix types. The exact relation between meaning and form will concern us in the next section. For the present purpose, one should explore whether the five types of meanings distinguished above can be related to each other in a sensible way and on purely semantic grounds. My proposal is that they can be placed on a cline of relevance in the sense of Bybee (1985:15): "A category is *relevant* to the verb to the extent that *the meaning of the category directly affects the lexical content of the verb stem*".

(33)

Space	Time	Outer aspect	Inner aspect	Non-compositional meaning
Less relevant				More relevant

That the non-compositional meaning is most relevant is obvious. That aspect is more relevant than time is argued convincingly by Bybee (1985), and within aspect, it makes sense to assume that inner aspect is more relevant than outer aspect. That space is least relevant is plausible too – witness, for example, the fact that Bybee does not even mention this category in her 1985 book.

3. *Form and meaning*

Both the formal and the semantic analysis have left us with a cline. We can thus ask whether the two clines, repeated together in (34), are related. If there is a strong relation, then we could simply conflate the two clines.

(34)

more separable⁺	more separable⁺ in some uses more inseparable⁺ in other uses	more inseparable⁺
more syntactic		morphological
less grammaticalized		more grammaticalized
less lexicalized		more lexicalized

Space	Time	Outer aspect	Inner aspect	Non-compositional meaning
Less relevant				More relevant

As far as the relation between meaning and form in grammaticalization is concerned, the literature contains three hypotheses. I will describe each and spell out what they imply for Dutch verbal prefixes.

The first hypothesis on the relation between meaning and form in grammaticalization says that meaning and form 'go hand in hand' (Lehmann 1995 [1982]; Croft 1990; Bybee et al. 1994:6-7,19-21). This hypothesis predicts that prefixes and prefix uses with the same degree of semantic relevance have the same degree of separability⁺. It makes sense to distinguish between lexicalization and grammaticalization proper, i.e., non-productive and productive cases, and between different prefixes and different uses of identical prefixes. This way we can distinguish between four kinds of situations. In (35) it is shown that the 'hand in hand' hypothesis is falsified in three of the four situations. In the examples below I use '=' for 'identical type of meaning', '>' for 'more relevant meaning', '»' for 'more inseparable⁺', and '«' for 'less inseparable⁺'.

(35) a. Different prefixes, non-productive
   ver-'jagen   =   *'achter-blijven*
   PRE-hunt   »   behind-stay
   "chase away"   "stay behind"

  b. Different prefixes, productive
   ver-'branden   =   *'uit-lezen*
   PRE-branden   »   out-read
   "burn up"   "finish reading"

  c. Identical prefixes, non-productive
   achter-'volgen   =   *'achter-blijven*
   behind-follow   »   behind-stay
   "follow, pursue"   "stay behind"

In each case, the meanings are equally relevant, but the inseparability[+] is different (inseparable[+] for the first verb or use, and separable[+] for the second). The one situation to which the 'hand in hand' hypothesis does apply is that of the different productive uses of an identical prefix. This is found only with the prefix *over-* and *door-*.

(36)   Identical prefixes, productive
      over-'laden   >   *'over-laden*
      over-load   »   over-load
      "overload"   "transfer (a load)", "load again"

"overload" is an inner aspect meaning, whereas "transfer (a load)" is spatial and "load again" has an outer aspect meaning. The inner aspect meaning is the more relevant one and it is inseparable[+], hence more inseparable[+] than the separable[+] space and outer aspect meanings.

The second hypothesis takes semantics to be prior (Givón 1975:86; Heine, Claudi & Hünnemeyer 1991:175; Haspelmath 1997; van der Auwera & Plungian 1998). Following van der Auwera & Plungian's (1998) work on modality, the priority of semantics could be taken to mean that when two prefixes occupy different positions on the semantic cline: (a) they will either occupy the same position on the formal cline, or (b) the semantically more relevant prefix is more inseparable[+·] and (c) it is ruled out that the semantically more relevant prefix is less inseparable[+]. This hypothesis fares better than the 'hand in hand' hypothesis. I can falsify it only when different prefixes are considered.

(37) a.   Different prefixes, non-productive
      'op-rotten   >   *ver-'jagen*
      up-rot   «   PRE-hunt
      "get lost"   "chase away"

    b.   Different prefixes, productive
      'uit-lezen   >   *her-'trouwen*
      out-read   «   re-marry
      "finish reading"   "remarry"

In both cases the verbs on the left are separable[+] and those on the right are inseparable[+], yet the former are more relevant than the latter (with non-compositional *'oprotten* vs. spatial *ver'jagen* and inner aspect *'uitlezen* vs. outer aspect *her'trouwen*).

When the prefixes are identical, however, the hypothesis of the priority of semantics holds true. (36) already illustrates the case of productive uses. (38) illustrates the non-productive uses.

(38)   Identical prefixes, non-productive

     a.   *aan-'horen*   >   *'aan-snijden*
           on-hear   »   on-cut
           "hear, grant"   "cut into"

     b.   *weer-'leggen*   >   *weer-'spiegelen*
           again(st)-lay   =   again(st)-mirror
           "rebut"   "reflect"

In (38.a) we get a non-compositional *aan'horen,* which is more relevant than an inchoative inner aspect *'aansnijden,* and the former is also more inseparable[+]. In (38.b) we get a non-compositional *weer'leggen,* which is more relevant than the arguably inner aspect *weer'spiegelen,* both are equally inseparable[+], but that is allowed by the hypothesis.

The third hypothesis amounts to a weakening of the first one. Though meaning and form do not always go hand in hand, they at least *tend* to go hand in hand. More often than not, relevant meanings are more grammaticalized and more lexicalized, and *vice versa.* A version of this hypothesis can be found in the literature, whenever defenders of the first hypothesis admit that the hand in hand hypothesis might not hold 100 % (see Lehmann 1995 [1982]:169-171; Croft 1990:243-244; Kiefer 1997:332). As for Dutch verbal prefixes, a complete, quantified analysis remains to be undertaken, but one can be optimistic about the result. First, lexicalization is associated with inseparability[+] and since lexicalization by definition instantiates the highest rung of relevance, we also get an association between inseparability[+] and relevance. Conversely, space and less so time, at the other end of the semantic cline, are strongly associated with separable[+] uses, particularly, with a group of complex prefixes, a small selection of which is shown in (39).

(39) a.   *achter-'aan-komen*
           behind-on-come
           "come at the end"

     b.   *voor-'op-gaan*
           for-on-go
           "walk in front"

     c.   *om-'hoog-vliegen*
           around-high-fly
           "fly up"

     d.   *voor-'bij-gaan*
           for-by-go
           "pass by"

e. *achter-'over-vallen*
behind-over-fall
"fall over backwards"

If this hypothesis is true, it amounts to the claim that the relevance of meaning participates in the clustering shown in (27). In other words, it is not so much that the relevance of meaning correlates with separability[+] and its associated clustering properties. Rather, relevance of meaning *is* one of these clustering properties.

4. *Conclusions*

In this paper I have analyzed the form and the meaning of Dutch verbal prefixes from the point of view of grammaticalization theory. Formal properties were argued to cluster around two poles of a formal cline. Meanings were ordered on a cline of semantic relevance, and I investigated the relation between the two clines. Three hypotheses were evaluated: (i) form and meaning go hand in hand, (ii) semantics is prior, and (iii) formal and semantic properties cluster. The preliminary conclusion is that the third hypothesis holds better than the second, and the second better than the first.

REFERENCES

Bybee, Joan. 1985. *Morphology: A study of the relation between meaning and form.* Amsterdam & Philadelphia: John Benjamins.
——, Revere Perkins & William Pagliuca. 1994. *The Evolution of Grammar: Tense, aspect and modality in the languages of the world.* Chicago: University of Chicago Press.
Claudi, Ulrike, Bernd Heine, & Frederike Hünnemeyer 1991. *Grammaticalization. A conceptual framework.* Chicago: University of Chicago Press.
Croft, William. 1990. *Typology and Universals.* Cambridge: Cambridge University Press.
De Haas, Wim & Mieke Trommelen. 1993. *Morfologisch handboek van het Nederlands: Een overzicht van de woordvorming.* The Hague: SDU Uitgeverij.
De la Cruz, Juan M. 1975. "Old English Pure Prefixes: Structure and function". *Linguistics* 145.47-81.
Dik, Simon C. 1989. *The Theory of Functional Grammar: The structure of the clause.* Dordrecht: Foris. (2nd, revised ed., Berlin: Mouton de Gruyter 1997.)
Duinhoven, A. M. 1997. *Middelnederlandse Syntaxis: Synchroon en diachroon. Vol. II: De werkwoordgroep.* Groningen: Martinus Nijhoff.
Geerts, G., W. Haeseryn, J. De Rooij & M. C. Van den Toorn. 1984. *Algemene Nederlandse spraakkunst.* Groningen: Wolters.

Givón, Talmy. 1975. "Serial Verbs and Syntactic Change: Niger-Congo". *Word Order and Word Order Change* ed. by Charles N. Li, 47-112. Austin: University of Texas Press.

Haeseryn, W., K. Romijn, G. Geerts, J. de Rooij & M.C. van den Toorn. 1997. *Algemene Nederlandse spraakkunst.* 2nd ed. Groningen: Martinus Nijhoff.

Haspelmath, Martin. 1997. "Why is the Change from Lexical to Functional Categories Irreversible?". Paper read at the 13th International Conference of Historical Linguistics, Düsseldorf, August 1997.

Heine, Bernd, Ulrike Claudi & Frederike Hünnemeyer. 1991. "From Cognition to Grammar: Evidence from African languages". Traugott & Heine 1991, vol. II, 149-187.

Hopper, Paul J. & Elizabeth Closs Traugott. 1993. *Grammaticalization.* Cambridge: Cambridge University Press.

Kiefer, Ferenc. 1997. "Verbal Prefixation in the Ugric Languages from a Typological-Areal Perspective". *Language and Its Ecology: Essays in memory of Einar Haugen* ed. by Stig Eliasson & Ernst Håkon Jahr, 323-341. Berlin: Mouton de Gruyter.

Krahe, Hans & Wolfgang Meid. 1967. *Germanische Spachwissenschaft. Vol. III: Wortbildungslehre.* Berlin: Walter de Gruyter.

Lehmann, Christian. 1982. *Thoughts on Grammaticalization: A programmatic sketch.* (=Arbeiten des Kölner Universalien-Projekts, 48.) Köln: Universität. (Revised ed. as *Thoughts on Grammaticalization,* München: LINCOM EUROPA 1995.)

――――. 1989. "Grammatikalisierung und Lexikalisierung". *Zeitschrift für Phonetik, Sprachwissenschaft und Kommunikationsforschung* 42.11-19.

Traugott, Elizabeth Closs & Bernd Heine, eds. 1991. *Approaches to Grammaticalization.* 2 vols. Amsterdam & Philadelphia: John Benjamins.

van der Auwera, Johan. 1995. "Les préverbes du Néerlandais – Une comparaison avec l'Allemand". *Les Préverbes dans les Langues d'Europe: Introduction à l'étude de la préverbation* ed. by André Rousseau, 77-94. Lille: Presses Universitè du Septentrion.

――――. 1998. "Verbal Prefixes in Dutch and German". *Germanistische Linguistik* 141-142.102-127.

――――. & Vladimir Plungian. 1998. "Modality's Semantic Map". *Linguistic Typology* 2.79-124.

Van Loey, A. 1976. *Scheidbare en onscheidbare Werkwoorden Hoofdzakelijk in het Middelnederlands: Analytische studiën.* Gent: Koninklijke Academie voor Nederlandse Taal en Letterkunde.

THE IRREALIS IN THE POLISH LANGUAGE
A QUESTION OF VERBAL MOODS, CONJUNCTIONS OR THE MODAL PARTICLE *BY?*[*]

MARIA ZAŁĘSKA
University of Warsaw

0. *Introduction*

In this paper I investigate one of the most controversial problems in Polish grammar, namely the 'modus realis'/'modus irrealis' distinction marking within Polish inflected verb forms. Given the way the 'modus irrealis' is realized, this paper may also be regarded as an essay on the evolution of the verb *być* "to be".

In modern Polish, *być* "to be" functions as a full verb and as the future tense auxiliary of imperfective verbs. Diachronically, the verb *być* has also been used as an auxiliary of compound verb forms of the past tense (preterite and pluperfect) and of the modus irrealis. In all these analytical paradigms the auxiliary *być* has undergone a process of decategorialization and desemanticization, becoming a clitic ending (e.g. in the case of the preterite) and giving rise to the modal particle *by* (as in the case of the modus irrealis). The evolution of the verb *być* in the paradigms relevant to this paper is as follows:[1]

---

[*] I am indebted to Lucyna Gebert, Jadwiga Linde-Usiekniewicz and Lunella Mereu for their helpful comments on an earlier draft of this paper. Needless to say, I am the only one responsible for the views presented above and for all errors of interpretation.

[1] In order to understand the evolution of the forms discussed in the paper, some general information concerning Polish verb paradigms is needed.

The analytical forms were based on the auxiliary *być* "to be" and on the past active participle (PAP), which is called 'historical', because it no longer functions as an autonomous participle in modern Polish. For the verb *robić* "to do", the forms of PAP are: SGM *robił*, F *robiła*, neuter *robiło*; PL: [+masc] *robili*, [-masc] *robiły*. Within the paradigms that concern us in this paper (i.e., the indicative preterite and modus irrealis), a synthetization of the post-posed auxiliary *być* with the PAP occurred. The synthetization of the preterite indicative occurred in the 15th century, cf.: 1SGM *robił jeśm* > *robiłem* (where *–e* remained, in order to allow an easy pronunciation), 1SGF *robiła jeśm* > *robiłam*, etc.; the indicative preterite endings are clitic.

138 MARIA ZAŁĘSKA

(1) PRETERITE INDICATIVE[2]
   robił jeśm   > (since 15th cent.) robiłem
   PAP   1SG.PRES.AUX
   "I (M) was doing"

(2) MODUS IRREALIS
   (12th cent.)   bych   robił > (modern Polish) bym robił
                      be-1SG.AOR.AUX PAP

   (till 16th cent.) robił   bych   > (since 16th cent.) robiłbym
                      PAP   1SG.AOR.AUX
   "I would be doing"

It is the contemporary status of the former modus irrealis auxiliary (i.e. the modern forms issuing from the aorist of the verb być) that concerns us in this paper. Irrealis is here intended as a broad semantic category, dealing with hypothetical, possible, uncertain states or events that have not yet occurred (cf. Givón 1984:285; Mithun 1995:367).

The paper is organized as follows. In the first Section I will briefly overview the current proposals for describing the modern Polish verbal system, with special regard to the modus irrealis marking. Next, operating within gram-

---

Importantly, in the 3SG/PL, the auxiliary entirely disappeared at the end of the 16th century (e.g., for the M, 3SG: robił jest / jeść / je > robił, for the 3PL: robili są > robili). Due to this phenomenon, the 3SG/PL of the modern preterite indicative is formally identical to the historical PAP. The synthetization also meant a decategorialization of the elements involved: to use Gebert's (1989) terms, a 'deverbalization' of the auxiliary być and a parallel 'verbalization' of the PAP occurred. Indeed, for the modern Polish period, the historical PAP is referred to as the verbal stem (this convention is also followed in this paper).

Under the influence of the synthetized indicative preterite, the synthetization of the modus irrealis occurred (in the 16th century), involving adoption of the preterital endings (robił bych > robiłbym "I would be doing"). Consequently, the 3SG/PL ending in the modus irrealisis also –0, thus the forms end with a mere –by (e.g. 3SGM robiłby "he would be doing"). For convenience of description I will use the term 'modal marker by', since by is a common element of all the forms discussed.

[2] Abbreviations in the text and in glosses are the following:

ACC	=	accusative	M	=	masculine
AUX	=	auxiliary	PAP	=	past active participle
GEN	=	genitive	PART	=	participle
COND	=	conditional	PL	=	plural
EMPH	=	emphasis	PRET	=	preterite indicative
F	=	feminine	SG	=	singular
INF	=	infinitive	TAM	=	Tense-Aspect-Mood

maticalization theory, I will adopt the Verb-to-TAM (i.e. Tense-Aspect-Mood) chain as an explanatory device likely to clarify the formal and functional changes within the Polish modal marking. In Sections 3 and 4 I will present arguments in favour of the existence of two irrealis moods (meant as functional categories), i.e. the conditional and the subjunctive. The imperative – which could also be regarded as an instance of irrealis – is outside the range of our investigation since it is not marked by *by*.

1. Descriptions of modus realis : modus irrealis marking in the modern Polish verbal system

The terms of discussion among Polish linguists on modal marking are summarized in the title of this paper. Leaving aside the imperative mood, the existence and formal identity of which are not in question, some scholars present the opposition between modus realis and modus irrealis as a question of verbal moods (i.e. indicative vs. conditional and subjunctive, cf. Section 1.1). Others maintain that the opposition exists only between the indicative and the conditional, further irrealis distinctions being carried out by a special class of conjunctions, agglutinated to the verb form (Section 1.2). According to a third proposal, the modern Polish modal marking is alien to the system of verbal moods, since it is conveyed by the modal particle *by*, which does not belong to the verbal system (Section 1.3).

1.1 The four moods theory

As regards the first proposal four verbal moods are recognised: indicative, imperative, conditional and subjunctive (cf. Puzynina 1969, Wierzbicka 1988, Maldzieva 1992). It has been maintained that in spite of the identity of morphological marking by *by*, the functional difference between the conditional and the subjunctive has been grammaticalized due to the distinct patterns of *by* distribution. Indeed, both analytic and synthetic forms are admitted in the conditional (e.g. *robiłbym – bym robił* "I would be doing") whereas the subjunctive only allows discontinuous forms, in which the markers of syntactic dependence, modality, grammatical person and number (i.e. *-bym, -byś, -by // byśmy, - byście, -by* endings) are preposed with respect to the verbal stem (for instance *abym robił* "in order that I do", *żebym robił* "in order that I do").

1.2. The three moods and modal conjunctions theory

The most widespread opinion is that Polish has three inflected moods: the indicative, the imperative and the conditional, the conditional being marked by the *-bym, -byś, -by // -byśmy, -byście, -by* morphemes. Within the conditional, most scholars distinguish a particular class of applications, signalled by special modal conjunctions. In Polish one can delineate two series of conjunctions whose formal differentiating element is *by*, for instance *że* "that" vs. *żeby* "so that, in order that"; *gdy* "when" vs. *gdyby* "if", "when if"; *jak* "how" vs. *jakby* "as if". An identifying mark of these "particular uses of the conditional" (as opposed to their normal use) is the agglutination of person and number markers to the conjunctions. The main point of scholarly discussions is whether these conjunctions (in inflected constructions such as *żebym robił* "so that I do") should be described as *że+bym* (i.e. as a conjunction, agglutinated to a verbal morpheme of the conditional which carries modal values) or rather as *żeby+m* (i.e. as a conjunction modalized by *by* and agglutinated to a verbal morpheme of the preterite). The first solution has been adopted by Gołąb (1964) who refers to a 'subjunctive function' of the conditional; Tokarski (1951) labels the construction 'entangled conditional mood' and Pisarkowa (1972) refers to it as 'spoiled' or 'syntactic conditional mood'. The second interpretation has been put forward by Puzynina (1971), who describes the verb form involved as the indicative preterite, attached to a conjunction modalized by *by*.

1.3 The two moods and the modal particle 'by' theory

Using Puzynina's (1971) framework as a starting point, Czarnecki (1973, 1977) claims that an appropriate description of the contemporary Polish verbal system must recognize the existence of only two verbal moods: the indicative and the imperative. According to Czarnecki, since the formal marker of what was traditionally called conditional mood (i.e. *by*) does not synchronically belong to the verbal system at all, it cannot form an inflectional paradigm. The author points out that the conjunctions with *by* and *by* used autonomously are also compatible with non-inflectional and even with non-verb forms (the English translation of Polish examples requires, however, an inflected form):

(3) *Żeby   tak   gdzieś   pójść!*
     so-that   EMPH   somewhere   go-INF
     "I wish I could go somewhere!"

(4) *Herbaty   by!*
     tea-GEN
     "I wish I could have a cup of tea!"

The occurrence of *by* outside the system of inflected verbal paradigms as well is a basis for Czarnecki's claim that *by* should be excluded from the inflected verbal mood markers.

In sum, the main question addressed in scholarly discussions is: should the system of modern Polish modal marking within inflected forms be described in terms of patterns of distribution of the modus irrealis endings –*bym, -byś, -by...* etc., in terms of modalized subordinating conjunctions followed by the preterite indicative or in terms of individuation of a modal particle *by*?

2. Emergence of the neo-Slavic modal marking

2.1 Verb-to-TAM chain: from the verb 'być' to the modal particle 'by'

As is clear from the above overview descriptions of modus irrealis marking in modern Polish are far from consistent.

Since a synchronic description of modality phenomena in a language is unclear without access to the relevant diachrony, the notion of grammaticalization can be adopted. The process of grammaticalization is referred to in Meillet's (1912:132) classical definition as "the attribution of a grammatical character to a formerly independent word". Kuryłowicz (1965:52) pointed out its gradual nature, stressing that "grammaticalization consists in the increase of the range of a morpheme advancing from a lexical to a grammatical or from a less grammatical to a more grammatical status [...]". The gradualness of grammaticalization has been aptly captured in Hopper's (1987) concept of 'emergent grammar', which accounts for ongoing rearrangements of the sub-systems of a language (in this case, the sub-system of modal marking in Polish).

The notion of a grammaticalization chain (i.e. a predictable sequence of both a conceptual and a formal evolution of a linguistic form) has been elaborated upon within the theory of grammaticalization (cf. Heine et al. 1991, Bybee et al. 1994).

The evolution of the modern Polish modal marker *by*, issued (as the majority of studies admit) from the verb *być* "to be" will now be outlined. It should be noted that the analysis is somewhat obscured by the fact that in numerous historical examples one finds the third grammatical person. This is important, since the 3SG/3PL in compound forms have lost their specific person/number endings (see note 1) and in modus irrealis it therefore ends with *by*. The ending *by* of the 3SG/3PL is thus identical with what is described as the modern Polish modal particle *by* and with the conjunction *by* (cf. Section 4.1). If one assumes (as claimed in some studies, discussed in Rittel [1975:125-132]) that in Old Polish there already existed an autonomous particle and conjunction *by*, one could hypothesise that in constructions with conjunctions, referred to as subjunctive (cf. Section 4) a contamination of this particle/conjunction *by* with the forms of the verb *być* occurred.

Below we will investigate the explanatory power of the Verb-to-TAM chain, applied to the description of modal marking in Polish. The label 'Verb-to-TAM' was proposed by Heine (1993), but the phenomenon itself had already been observed in previous studies on grammaticalization (cf. for instance Givón [1984:271]). What particularly interests us here is the Verb-to-modal marker shift.

2.2 *Emergence of a new modal construction (PAP + AUX aorist)*

In the pre-Polish stage inflected verb forms were organized into numerous verbal patterns. Nevertheless, the first Old Polish written documents show only a few cases of the imperfect and aorist forms, not to mention the optative which had already disappeared in the Slavic period. Since the Polish language had no other modus irrealis paradigms available, the disappeared optative was supplanted by a new device allowing modal values to be expressed within the system of inflected verb forms. Indeed, a neo-Slavic construction emerged. The construction involved the aorist form of the Slavic verb *byti* (Pol. *być* "to be") which had the function of an auxiliary, and the past active participle (henceforth glossed PAP) in *-l* (in Polish *-ł*). The construction has been widely used in Slavic languages since the 12th century (Rittel 1975:107).

2.3 *Conceptual shift from the temporal to the modal value*

It is interesting to analyze a conceptual shift from the temporal to the modal interpretation of the aorist form of *być* in the construction being analysed. The theory of grammaticalization predicts such a change: it has been discovered on the basis of typological research that past markers show a tendency to develop into irrealis or nonactuality markers (cf. Fleischman 1989).

There are two main hypothesies explaining this conceptual change: one is based on semantic-conceptual arguments, another points out the importance of syntax and context in shaping the meaning of a verb form.

Explanations in terms of semantics suggest that the ability of past tense forms to be put to modal uses stems from the very 'irrealis nature' of all events which do not belong to the immediate present time of the speaker (cf. Antinucci & Miller 1976). As a number of studies on this conceptual shift show, in the languages in which the interrelation between the past and the irrealis occurs, "the morphological element involved should best be regarded as having at its basic meaning not 'past tense', but rather 'distant from present reality' " (James 1982:375).

Dahl (1997) argues against this widespread view, pointing out the importance of syntax. Indeed, not in all syntactical environments may a past tense form be appropriately used to convey modal meanings. Dahl (1997:100) concludes that marking of irreality is as a rule done by "the combination of a past tense with something else": the modal value of a past tense starts out with the counterfactuals having past time reference.

It seems that both semantic and syntactic factors are responsible for the conceptual shift from the temporal to modal value of the construction involving the aorist forms of the verb *być*. The influence of semantics might be attributed to the above-mentioned meaning 'distant from present reality'. The semantic notion of metaphorical distance from the moment of speaking (which could refer both to anteriority or posteriority) would not suffice, however, to account for the emergence of the grammatical category 'conditional'. As observed in a number of studies, the conditional, as a rule, is connected with posteriority marking (see Fleischman 1982:59-66). From the semantic-conceptual point of view, the irreality of posteriority is connected with such notions as expectation, intentionality, hypotheticity. The posteriority marking in the past may be grammaticalized as a future-in-the-past paradigm. Its emergence is possible in texts with past time reference, in which it signals posteriority relations. The combination of two conceptual notions: 'past' and 'posteriority', in specific syntactic contexts, gives rise to the emergence of a primarily modal paradigm of the conditional, which may or may not preserve its temporal value of the future-in-the-past. This line of conceptual and functional evolution is postulated for the Polish construction being analysed. Gołąb (1964:32-35) argues that the paradigm issuing from the Common Slavic construction is a future-in-the-past, reanalyzed next as the conditional.[3] In his explanations of this change, Gołąb (1964:33) points out the importance of syntax:

> As in other cases of a functional evolution of the meaningful units of language – the basic condition is the use of a given unit in a given syntactic construction (context). For the development of the 'future in the past' into the 'conditional' the decisive constructions are: the irreal conditional period and the adversative couple of clauses [...]. When the 'future in the past' is situated in the apodosis of the former or in the

---

[3] As far as the evolution of the Common Slavic conditional is concerned, Gołąb (1964: 35) writes: "[...] we can start from the Common Slavic type of the future tense *bodo* + *l*-participle and treat e.g. the **byxb xodilb* construction as a kind of 'future in the past' derived from the normal future **bodo xodilb* (the use of the perfective aorist *byxb* is understandable here in face of the perfective present *bodo*!). Then we would have in Slavic two historically separated processes of the developement: *future in the past > conditional*, the first one already prehistorical and based upon the original Slavic construction of the future tense, namely: *bodo xodilb > byxb xodilb* (future in the past) > *byxb xodilb* (conditional) and the second one historical, restricted to South Slavic languages [...]". The Polish conditional after the reanalysis does not function as a future-in-the-past.

first clause of the latter construction it undergoes secondarily a functional variation conditioned by the syntactic environment: after the protasis denoting a contrary-to-fact condition it must denote an unreal process, etc. [...] If we realize further that in connection with different transformations of the primary irreal conditional period there is possibility to replace the protasis-apodosis construction by a simple sentence in which the contrary-to-fact condition would be expressed only lexically – we will understand the release (liberation) of the conditional function of the original 'future in the past' from the conditioning framework of the above syntactic constructions [...].

It seems, therefore, that a combination of notional categories 'past' and 'posteriority', modelled in specific syntactic contexts, is responsible for a conceptual and functional shift from the temporal to the modal value of the construction with the aorist form of the verb *być.*

3. *Modal marking: the Polish conditional*

3.1 *Analytic form*

In contemporary descriptions of the Polish language a peculiarity of the conditional with respect to other verbal paradigms is emphasised: namely, the modern conditional markers (i.e. *-bym, -byś, -by // -byśmy, - byście, -by*) may be both preposed or postposed with respect to the verbal stem (i.e., historical PAP, e.g. *robiłbym – bym robił* "I would be doing"). In the analytical (i.e. preposed) form it is possible to insert other elements between *bym* and *robił.*

The original construction with the auxiliary *być* in the aorist form has been exclusively analytical up to the beginnings of the 16th century (Rittel 1975:111). The auxiliary has been preposed with respect to the PAP (e.g. *bych robił* "I would be doing", i.e. AUX PART), accordingly to the predictions concerning languages with predominant VSO order (cf. Gebert 1977, 1989; Comrie 1980).

3.2 *Synthetic form*

The expansion of the synthetized forms of the conditional began from the 16th century onwards. The synthetized forms have been prevalent since the 19th century (although both analytical and synthetical forms are still in use). The change from the AUX PART sequence into the PART AUX is attributed to the change in Polish word order from VSO to the SVO (cf. Gebert 1977, 1989). In modern Polish both sequences of elements (i.e. *robiłbym – bym robił* "I would be doing") are still allowed (though with a preference for the synthetized forms since the 19th century).

The synthetization of the conditional forms occurred under the influence of the already synthetized (in the 15th century) preterital forms (as in *robił jeśm* > *robiłem* "I was doing", cf. note 1). During the process of synthetization the aorist endings were substituted by the preterital ones (i.e. *-m, -ś, -0 // -śmy, -ście, -0*, e.g. *robiłbch* > *robiłbym* "I would be doing"; cf. Decaux 1955). This means that the former auxiliary of the preterite (i.e. the verb *być* "to be" in the present tense form, e.g. O.Pol. *jeśm* "I am" > *-m*) has been completely desemanticized and decategorialized, since, during synthetization of the conditional paradigm, it was possible to treat it simply as an ending and to agglutinate elements stemming from two inflected forms of the same verb (i.e. − for the 1SG − the present tense form *jeśm* > *-m* and the aorist *bych*). As mentioned before, the synthetized form is the only one in use as far as the preterite is concerned, while for the conditional both analytical and synthetical forms are still possible.

The adoption of the preterital endings has led to a striking similarity of form between the preterite indicative and the conditional paradigms, the only difference being *by* (cf. the preterite: 1SGM *robił+em*, 1SGF *robiła+m* "I was doing", as compared to the conditional: 1SGM *robił+by+m*, 1SGF *robiła+by+m* "I would be doing"). This formal parallelism has led Puzynina (1971) and Czarnecki (1973, 1977; cf. Section 1.3) to reduce the system of the Polish inflected moods to the indicative and imperative paradigms and to treat the form traditionally called conditional as a variant of the preterite indicative modalized by *by*.

Synthetization marks a further stage in the Verb-to-TAM chain, namely the cliticization of the auxiliary *być* "to be", and signals the next step in its desemanticization and decategorialization. The full verb *być* "to be" has passed through the stage of auxiliarity (i.e., for the 1SG, the aorist form *bych* preceding the PAP *robił*) and has achieved the status of a clitical ending of the modus irrealis paradigm. This last stage is characterized by a preferred post-position of the auxiliary with respect to the PAP (i.e., *bych robił* supplanted by *robił bych*), by adoption of the preterital endings by the auxiliary (i.e, for the 1SG, *bych* > *bym*) and by a subsequent synthetization of the PAP and of the auxiliary, recategorized as a clitical ending (i.e., for the 1SGM, *robił+bym*). The synthetization, signalling at the conceptual level that the two elements involved are conceived as one unit of meaning, is correlated with another important parameter of grammaticalization − a phonetic shift. With the loss of autonomy of the verb *być* within the construction (due to its fusion with the PAP), it also loses its ability to carry distinctive tone or stress (cf. Heine 1993:56).

4. *Further differentiation: the emergence of a hybrid conjunction + verb construction*

Apart from the purely verbal construction which gave rise to the contemporary synthetized conditional, there is a special group of mixed discontinuous constructions marked by *by* and functionally correspondent to the inflected subjunctive of the Romance languages. Their heterogeneity is caused by agglutination of a verbal morpheme to a conjunction (e.g. *żebym robił* "so that I do"). The second element of the construction is the historical PAP (*robił*). *Żebym*, as mentioned in section 1.2, is given three descriptions: as *że+bym* (i.e. a conjunction *że* "that", agglutinated to a morpheme of the 1SG of the modus irrealis), as *żeby+m* (i.e. a modalized conjunction *żeby* "so that", "in order that", agglutinated to the morpheme of the 1SG of the preterite indicative) or as *że+by+m* (i.e. a conjunction, agglutinated to an invariant modalizing particle *by*, followed by the morpheme of the 1SG of the preterite indicative). These constructions are labelled, according to the framework adopted, 'subjunctive', 'entangled conditional mood' or 'indicative preterite modalized by *by*'.

4.1 *Origin of the element 'by' in constructions with conjunctions*

The origin of the element *by* within the conjunctions being analyzed has not been clarified. As mentioned above, some scholars view *by* as a part of the conditional mood (i.e. of the former auxiliary *być* "to be"). According to others, the element *by* does not have a verbal origin since from the outset it has constituted part of this class of conjunctions or at least of some of them (cf. ex. (6)-(7)). In some historical examples, the conjunction and *by* are not agglutinated (see, for instance, ex. (8) below: O.Pol. *gdi by* > modern Polish *gdyby* "if", "when if").[4]

The status of the *by* itself, which may function as a conjunction when used autonomously, is particularly problematic:

(5) *Chcę,*   *byś*   *to*   *zrobił*
     want-1SG   by-2SG   it   do-PAP
     "I want you to do it".

The descriptions available are of little help in definitely clearing up the question. I will limit myself here to a discussion of two interrelated problems concerning the verb forms accompanying the conjunctions. The first problem is the use of the modal marker *by*. The examples presented below illustrate two main strategies: a single marking by *by*, appearing only within the conjunction

---

[4] For the main lines of debate and further references, cf. Rittel (1975: 125-132).

(ex (6) and (9)), and a double marking by *by*. In the latter case, *by* appeared not only within or near the conjunction (as in ex. (8): *gdi by* "if", "when if"), but also preceded the PAP (ex. (7)), followed the PAP (ex. (8)) or was synthetized with the PAP (ex. (9)); in the case of the synthetized form, it is glossed as conditional, in the case of analytical forms the componential glosses are used (i.e., PAP and *by*+a corresponding personal morpheme). The second problem to be analysed is the choice of the verb form which follows the conjunctions. As shown by the examples below, the single marking by *by* was correlated with the preterite indicative (ex. (6)). The double marking by *by* was correlated with analytic (ex. (7) and (8)) or synthetic (ex. (9)) verbal constructions involving PAP and *by*. As noted above (cf. Section 1), an appropriate description of these constructions with *by* gave rise to considerable discussion. Numerous historical examples available refer to the third grammatical person, which has lost its specific personal endings; therefore, the 3SG/3PL of the preterite indicative is identical with PAP (see note 1). This gives at least two possible interpretations of the constructions in which the 3SG/3PL appears (cf. ex. (7) and (8)). On formal grounds, they could be interpreted as: (i) the preterite indicative modalized by a modal marker *by* of a non-verbal origin, or (ii) as analytical forms of modus irrealis (made up of the PAP and the forms of the auxiliary *byĉ* "to be"). If one follows the latter interpretation, which has been adopted by most scholars, the patterns of occurrence of *by* (identified with the auxiliary of the 3SG/3PL and therefore lacking specific personal endings), which might otherwise seem random, clearly illustrate the word order changes: the pre-position (as in the ex. (7): *by były wysłuchany* "they would be fulfilled") illustrates the AUX PART word order, while the post-position (as in: (8) *przegygrał by...* "he would lost...") demonstrates the PART AUX word order (cf. Section 3). The hybrid construction in examples (6)–(9) fulfils the function of the subjunctive and is translated correspondingly; in the discussion of the examples, if only the verbal part of the construction is referred to, it is translated by the English conditional.

The example below illustrates the first case discussed above, i.e. the conjunctions with *by* followed by the indicative preterite:

(6) *proszę was   aby   jedząc byliście   weseli*
    ask-1SG you(PL)-ACC so-that eating be-2PL.PRET good-humoured
    "I am asking you to be good-humoured while you are eating".
              (*Historia Aleksandra* 1510, quoted in Rittel 1975:113)

As mentioned above, the use of the preterite indicative after the conjunctions marked by *by* was not an established norm of this period. Even in the

same text (as *Historia Aleksandra* 1510 quoted here) one can find constructions illustrating both types of the verb complements discussed above. In the
ex. (6) *aby byliście* "so that you be" one has the preterite indicative and only
one *by* within the conjunction *aby* "so that". Ex. (7) below illustrates the strategy of a double marking by *by*, which appears both within the conjunction
iżeby "so that" and autonomously, preceding the PAP (here appearing in a
passive construction): *by były wysłuchany* "they would be fulfilled". In accordance with the observations formulated above, *by* appearing twice co-occurs
with a verb form identifiable as an analytical paradigm of the modus irrealis
(cf. Section 3.1):

(7) *iżeby   by   były   wysłuchany   twoje   prośby*
    so-that   be-PL.PAP fulfilled   your   prayers
    "so that your prayers be fulfilled".
                       (*Historia Aleksandra* 1510, quoted in Rittel 1975:113)

The next example illustrates two phenomena. First of all, it shows the
stage of Polish language evolution in which not all subordinating conjunctions
were agglutinated with *by* (O.Pol. *gdi by* > modern Pol. *gdyby*). Second, ex. (8)
illustrates the newer PART AUX word order, but still without the synthetization
of the PAP and the auxiliary (*przegygrał by...* "he would lost"):

(8) *ysz gdi   by   cziy   syn,   oboyga   porodzyczela   sdrowa*
    that when   somebody's   son   both   parents   healthy

będąc   przegygrał by
being   lose-PAP
"that if somebody's son lost [at play], both his parents being healthy..."
                       (*Kodeks Świętosławów* 1450, quoted in Rittel 1975:114)

The next example (9) illustrates the pattern of a double marking by *by*:
within the conjunction (*aby* "so that") and within the verb form of the conditional which, importantly, has been already synthetized:

(9) *aby   czcilibyśmy*
    so-that   worship-1PL.COND
    "so that we worship"
                       (*Modlitwy Wacława*, 15th century, quoted in Rittel 1975:114)

This double modal marking (i.e. *by* repeated twice) has never constituted a
norm in the Polish language; it should rather be interpreted as a search for new
patterns of expression of modal meanings (cf. Rittel 1975:115-117). The modern norm of modal marking (i.e. only one *by*), established since the 19th century, follows "a general principle in complementation that information tends

neither to be repeated nor lost" (Noonan 1990:100). According to this predicted information structure of the utterance, in contemporary standard Polish the modalizing *by* appears only once, within the conjunction.

4.2 *Information structure of the construction*

The fact that among the different possibilities of modal complementation available in the language (cf. ex. (6)-(9)) the pattern 'conjunction+ *by*/number/person marker followed by the verbal stem (i.e., historical PAP)' begins to constitute a linguistic norm in expressing the meanings associated with the subjunctive is very significant. The above principle of the economy of language leads to an avoidance of redundancy of modal marking. However, although the principle accounts only for the quantitative reduction of the modality markers (i.e. *by* appearing only once), it does not explain the pattern of distribution of all the elements involved.

According to one hypothesis, *by* has been always a part of at least some of the conjunctions concerned (e.g. *aby+m* "so that I...", *aby+ś* "so that you...", etc.). According to another hypothesis, the former simple conjunctions merged with grammatical morphemes of the modus irrealis (e.g. *że+bym* "so that I...", *że+byś* "so that you...", etc.). The data available does not allow for a conclusive answer to this question (cf. Section 4.1). There is no doubt that the parameter of merger of the conjunction and a verb morpheme accounts for a functional difference between bounded and free *by* forms in modern Polish. The modus irrealis forms specialized in the functions of the conditional admit two patterns of distribution of the element *by*: (i) pre-posed with respect to the verbal stem (i.e., to the historical PAP, cf. note 1), e.g. *bym robił* "I would do"; (ii) post-posed and synthetized with the verbal stem, e.g. *robiłbym* "I would do". What is more, the element *by* involved in the conditional never merges with the conjunction (cf. below, ex. (10): *że by... zrobił* equivalent to *że zrobiłby* "that he would do"). On the other hand, the modus irrealis forms fulfilling the functions of the subjunctive allow for only one order of elements, with *by* obligatorily preceding the historical PAP and obligatorily bounded with the conjunction (cf. ex. (11): *żeby zrobił* "so that he do"). The difference in meaning is illustrated by the following contrastive pair:

(10) *Mówi, że by to zrobił* = *Mówi, że zrobiłby to.*
     say-3SG that   it do-PAP = say-3SG that do-3SG.COND it
     "He is saying that he would do it".

(11) *Mówi,   żeby   to   zrobił.*
     say-3SG so-that it   do-PAP
     "He is telling him to do it".

As pointed out above, a characteristic feature of the hybrid construction fulfilling the functions of the subjunctive is an obligatory agglutination of the verbal person/number markers with the conjunction. Whichever theory concerning the contemporary morphological division of elements is adopted, it is clear that a part of the grammatical information relevant to the verb is agglutinated to the conjunction, while all the lexical information and the grammatical gender and number markers are conveyed by the verbal stem (i.e., the historical PAP). A construction such as *żebym robił* "so that I do" is given three morphological descriptions. The sequence presented in (12a) refers to descriptions according to which *by* within the conjunctions issues from the modus irrealis ending (i.e. from the former auxiliary *być*), and the whole construction, labelled 'subjunctive' or 'entangled/spoiled/syntactic conditional mood', is conceived of in terms of the distribution of modus irrealis endings. Two other morphological divisions shown below suggest that, for the convenience of the grammatical description of modern Polish, the verbal element involved is best described as the preterite indicative. Ex. (12b) shows the agglutination of a clitical preterital ending to a modalized subordinating conjunction (cf. Puzynina 1971), while ex. (12c) illustrates the individuation of the modalizing marker *by* (Czarnecki 1973, 1977):

(12a) *że*   + *bym*   *robił*
       conjunction   + 1SG-COND   PAP-SGM
(12b) *żeby*   + *-m*   *robił*
       modalized conjunction   + 1SG   PAP-SGM
(12c) *że*   + *by*   + *-m*   *robił*
       conjunction   + modal *by*   + 1SG   PAP-SGM
       "so that I do"

The fact that the grammatical person marker appears within the conjunction and not within the verbal stem (i.e., former PAP) leads one to interpret this hybrid, discontinuous construction as one unit of meaning; otherwise it would be impossible to complete all the grammatical information relevant to the predicate. The position of the modality marker *by* itself can be explained by Wackernagel's law, according to which clitics tend to occupy the second place in the sentence after the first accented word, especially if it is a conjunction or particle (e.g., in ex. (8), *by* comes immediately after the conjunction O.Pol. *gdi*> modern Polish *gdy* "when"; this position has led to their subsequent agglutination in a modern Polish form *gdyby* < *gdi by* "when if"; for a detailed discussion, cf. Gebert 1989).

The question which now arises is what was the use of this peculiar way of distributing grammatical information relevant to the verb. Indeed, the linguistic strategy used apparently violates the main principle of iconic coding, according to which "what belongs together (in a mentalistic sense) is placed together" (Behagel 1932, quoted in Campbell 1993:53). As far as verbs are concerned, this principle seems to account for such phenomena as, for instance, the vicinity of linguistic items in compound verb paradigms. This vicinity (as predicted by the theory of grammaticalization) leads in many cases to a fusion of the elements. This is an unequivocable sign that they have been conceived as a mental unity. One may ask, therefore, what was to be gained by the obligatory dispersion of grammatical information relevant to verb inflection (i.e., by collocation of the grammatical person marker, ex. (12b) and (12c) or, according to other theories, of the grammatical mode marker *by* (cf. 12a)), outside the lexical verb.

First, according to the predictions of grammaticalization theory, differentiation within the modus irrealis could be expected. The Verb-to-TAM chain predicts a sequence: "lexical/verbal > TAM (one concept) > various kinds of grammatical functions" (Heine 1993:67). Since there was only one modal marker (i.e. *by*) within the Polish verb paradigms, the predicted differentiation occurred through morphosyntactic procedures, such as word order, agglutination, and distribution in different types of clauses. In this way, two functional variants emerged within the Polish modus irrealis: one identifiable with a general category 'conditional' in the universal grammar and the other, identifiable with the category 'subjunctive'. From the point of view of syntactic distribution, a characteristic feature of the universal category 'conditional' is its occurrence in types of clauses in which the indicative could also appear (i.e. independent clauses and dependent object clauses, cf. Tekavčić 1972:661), and, for the conditional only, in the apodosis of the conditional periods of possibility and irreality. A defining feature of the cross-linguistic category 'subjunctive', sometimes defined as 'subordinating mood' (cf. Bybee *et al.* 1994:212-214), is its function as a syntactic dependence marker in certain types of subordinate clause in which neither the indicative nor the conditional could appear. In this way the subjunctive also marks a conceptual link between the matrix and the subordinate clause. Although the available evidence does not allow for absolute certainty (cf. Section 4.1), one may hypothesise that the linguistic way of encoding this conceptual differentiation within the modus irrealis between the functions of the conditional and the subjunctive has been, in the case of the subjunctive, a unification of a verb morpheme with markers of connection between clauses, i.e. with conjunctions. The collocation of a part of the grammatical information relevant to the verb within the conjunction seems to indicate that the two elements involved – the conjunction and the verb – constitute one (albeit discontinuous) unit of meaning, marking syntactic dependence and scope relations.

4.3 Grammatical classification of the construction

The question that now arises is how to describe these constructions. As outlined above (Section 1), different suggestions have been put forward. They may be divided into two main approaches. One is based on formal grounds and tries to offer a unified description accounting for the invariant irrealis meaning of the by; another is based on semantic-functional grounds.

4.3.1 *Surface-based approaches*. The formal identity of endings that are typical of the indicative preterite and the construction with conjunctions has led to descriptions of it as a variant of indicative, modalized by by, treated as a modal particle (cf. Puzynina 1971, Czarnecki 1973, 1977). Another solution in the same vein is based on the formal identity of modal marking by by, both in the conditional (e.g. *robił+bym* or *bym robił* "I would be doing") and in the hybrid form with conjunction (e.g. *że+bym robił* "so that I do"), which leads to treat the latter construction as particular instance of the conditional (cf. Tokarski 1951 or Pisarkowa 1972).

4.3.2 *Functional approach*. Looking at the hybrid construction with by from the point of view of its function and semantics, the 'subjunctive' label proposed in Section 4.2 seems the most appropriate. Relating occurrences of these constructions to the general category 'subjunctive', one obtains a unified and predictable pattern of distribution which would otherwise seem random (cf. Załęska, in press). The subjunctive category is not meant here strictly as a verbal mood paradigm but, to use Gołąb's (1964:14) wording, as a 'functional value'.

Major predictabilities connected with the typological category of the 'subjunctive' concern (i) its semantics, (ii) grammatical environments, and (iii) scope relations (cf. Givón 1984, chapter 8, and Givón 1995:112-155).

From the semantic point of view, the subjunctive is associated primarily with deontic modality, optative meanings and counterfactuals. The examples quoted above (cf. ex. (5) and (6) for volitive meanings, (3) and (4) for the optative and (8) for the hypothetical) are thus consistent with the types of clauses where the category 'subjunctive' is to be expected.

Since semantic and pragmatic meanings affect syntactic forms, they account for the range of grammatical contexts in which the subjunctive is most likely to grammaticalize. The agglutination of the conjunctions with the inflected verb forms in subordinated clauses governed by 'verba voluntatis' (cf. ex. (5)) or 'verba dicendi' (used in volitive meaning, cf. ex. (11)), i.e. clearly linked to deontic modality, is an example of these predictable semantics and syntax interactions.

Finally, from the point of view of scope relations, the union of the conjunction with a part of an inflected verb form explicitly signals a connection of the subordinate clause predicate with the matrix clause. The construction is thus one of the clause-linking devices, clearly relating the subordinate clause predicate to the higher predicate and changing the modal-propositional scope of the subjunctive as compared to the scope of the conditional (see in particular ex. (11) illustrating the use of the subjunctive with the (10) showing the use of the conditional).

5. *Conclusions*

I have tried to show that the evolution of the modal marking within Polish inflected forms has followed the Verb-to-TAM grammaticalization chain. As a result of desemanticization, decategorialization, cliticization and phonetic erosion, the forms of the former full verb *być* "to be" have become a grammatical modalizing marker of its former complement (i.e. the historical PAP), recategorized in modern Polish as the verbal stem. I believe that this description is correct as far as the forms of the conditional are concerned. Nevertheless, as I have pointed out above, it cannot be claimed with absolute certainty that in all conjunctions concerned the element *by* stems from the verb *być* "to be".

Returning to the problem posed in the title of this paper, it seems that the answer depends on what level of language is being considered. From the formal point of view, *by* in modern Polish is a general marker of irrealis meanings. If we take this position, it should be admitted that the mood system has almost disappeared in Polish and that non-inflectional ways of expression (such as the particle *by* and syntactic devices) are used instead of moods to mark irrealis meanings.

At the functional level, however, the universal grammar categories 'conditional' and 'subjunctive' are very useful for grammatical description. They allow patterns of *by* distribution to be related to a universally predictable range of meanings grammaticalized within irrealis as functionally different paradigms.

The evolution of modal marking in Polish is a good example of a boundary phenomenon between morphology and syntax: the above reanalysis of 'free lexical morphemes' into bound ones whose order is determined by the syntax of a language confirms Givón's (1971:413) claim that "today's morphology is yesterday's syntax". A further search for semantic and morphosyntactic regularities within Polish irrealis marking should help to better understand patterns of conceptual relationships which are mapped onto language.

REREFENCES

Antinucci, Francesco & Ruth Miller. 1976. "How Children Talk about What Happened". *Journal of Child Language* 3.167-190.
Behagel, Otto. 1923-32. *Deutsche Syntax: Eine gesichtliche Darstellung* (4 volumes). Heidelberg: Carl Winters Universitätsbuchhandlung.
Bybee, Joan, Revere Perkins & William Pagliuca. 1994. *The Evolution of Grammar: Tense, aspect and modality in the languages of the world.* Chicago and London: University of Chicago Press.
Campbell, Lyle. 1993. "The Explanation of Syntactic Change: A historical perspective". *Historical Linguistics 1991. Papers from the Tenth International Conference on Historical Linguistics, Amsterdam, 12-16 August 1991* ed. by Jaap van Marle, 49-69. Amsterdam & Philadelphia: John Benjamins.
Comrie, Bernard. 1980. "Morphology and Word Order Reconstruction: Problems and prospects". *Historical Morphology* ed. by Jacek Fisiak, 71-82. The Hague: Mouton.
Czarnecki, Tomasz. 1973. "O Formie Tzw. Trybu Przypuszczającego we Współczesnym Języku Polskim" [On the Form of the So-called Conditional Mood in Modern Polish Language]. *Język polski* 5.337-344.
——. 1977. *Der Konjunktiv im Deutschen und Polnischen: Versuch einer Konfrontation.* Wrocław: Zakład Narodowy im. Ossolińskich.
Dahl, Östen. 1997. "The Relation Between Past Time Reference and Counterfactuality: A new look". *On Conditionals Again* ed. by Angeliki Athanasiadou & René Dirven, 97-114. Amsterdam & Philadelphia: John Benjamins.
Decaux, Etienne. 1955. *Morphologie des Enclitiques Polonais.* Paris: Institut d'Etudes Slaves.
Fleischman, Suzanne. 1982. *The Future in Thought and Language.* Cambridge & London: Cambridge University Press.
——. 1989. "Temporal Distance: A basic linguistic metaphor". *Studies in Language* 13.1.1-50.
Gebert, Lucyna. 1977. "L'Ordine delle Parole in Polacco". *Rivista di Grammatica Generativa*, 2:2.181-239.
——. 1989. "La Particule Russe *by*: Un problème d'ordre des éléments dans la phrase". *La Licorne. Etudes de linguistique.* 15.301-311.

Givón, Talmy. 1971. "Historical Syntax and Synchronic Morphology". *Papers from the Seventh Regional Meeting: Chicago Linguistic Society.* Chicago: CLS, 394-415.
——. 1984. *Syntax*, vol. I, Amsterdam & Philadelphia: John Benjamins.
——. 1995. *Functionalism and Grammar.* Amsterdam & Philadelphia: John Benjamins.
Gołąb, Zbigniew. 1964. "The Problem of Verbal Moods in Slavic Languages". *International Journal of Slavic Linguistics and Poetics* 8.1-36.
Heine, Bernd. 1993. *Auxiliaries. Cognitive Forces and Grammaticalization*, New York & Oxford: Oxford University Press.
——, Ulrike Claudi & Friederike Hünnemeyer. 1991. *Grammaticalization: A conceptual framework.* Chicago: University of Chicago Press.
Hopper, Paul. 1987. "Emergent Grammar". *Berkeley Linguistic Society* 13.139-157.
James, Deborah, 1982. "Past Tense and Hypothetical: A cross-linguistic study", *Studies in Language* 4:3.375-403.
Kuryłowicz, Jerzy. 1965. "The Evolution of Grammatical Categories". *Esquisses Linguistiques II.* ed. by Jerzy Kuryłowicz, 38-54. Munich: Fink.
Maldzieva, Vjara. 1992. "Osobennosti Konjunktiva Slavianskogo Tipa" [Peculiarities of the Slavic Type Subjunctive]. *Etudes de Linguistique Romane et Slave* ed. by Wiesław Banyś, Leszek Bednarczuk & Krzysztof Bogacki, 395-404. Kraków: Wyższa Szkoła Pedagogiczna.
Meillet, André. 1912. "L'Evolution des Formes Grammaticales". *Scientia 12/26* [reprinted 1951 in *Linguistique Historique et Linguistique Générale.* 138-148. Paris: C. Klincksieck].
Mithun, Marianne. 1995. "On the Relativity of Irreality". *Modality in Grammar and Discourse* ed. by Joan Bybee & Suzanne Fleischman, 367-388, Amsterdam & Philadelphia: John Benjamins.
Noonan, Michael. 1990. "Complementation". *Language Typology and Syntactic Description* ed. by Timothy Shopen, *Complex Constructions*, vol. II, 42-140. Cambridge: Cambridge University Press [I ed. 1985].
Pisarkowa, Krystyna. 1972. "Tryb Przypuszczający i Czas Zaprzeszły w Polszczyźnie Współczesnej (Formy i Funkcje)" [The Conditional and the Pluperfect in Modern Polish (Forms and Functions)]. *Język Polski* 52.183-189.
Puzynina, Jadwiga. 1969. *Nazwy Czynności we Współczesnym Języku Polskim: Słowotwórstwo, semantyka, składnia* [Names of Action in Modern Polish: Word formation, semantics, syntax]. Warszawa: Państwowe Wydawnictwo Naukowe.
——. 1971. "Jeden Tryb czy Dwa Tryby. (Problem form trybu przypuszczającego w języku polskim)" [One mood or Two Moods. (The problem of the conditional mood forms in modern Polish)]. *Biuletyn Polskiego Towarzystwa Językoznawczego* 29.131-139.
Rittel, Teodozja. 1975. *Szyk Członów w Obrębie Form Czasu Przeszłego i Trybu Przypuszczającego* [The Order of Elements within the Preterite Tense and Conditional Mood Forms]. Wrocław: Zakład Narodowy im. Ossolińskich.

156 MARIA ZAŁĘSKA

Tekavčić, Pavao. 1972. *Grammatica Storica dell'Italiano*, vol. II, *Morfosintassi*. Bologna: Il Mulino.
Tokarski, Jan. 1951. *Czasowniki Polskie: Formy, typy, wyjątki* [*Polish Verbs: Forms, types, exceptions*]. Warszawa: Wydawnictwo S. Arcta.
Wierzbicka, Anna. 1988. *The Semantics of Grammar*. Amsterdam & Philadelphia: John Benjamins.
Załęska, Maria. 1997. "Grammaticalizzazione della Categoria del Congiuntivo in Polacco". *Ricerche Slavistiche* XLIV.185-207.

II
MORPHO-SYNTAX AND PRAGMATICS

MORPHOLOGICAL AND SYNTACTICAL COMPLEXITY IN FRENCH INTERROGATIVE PREDICATES

CLAIRE BLANCHE-BENVENISTE
Université de Provence

0. *Introduction*

Morphological complexity in basic grammatical domains like interrogativity raises an interesting problem. It is usually interpreted as a merely formal accident, produced by historical evolution and without any connection to a syntactic or semantic counterpart (Grevisse & Goosse 1986). Few explanations were given for the most complex forms in French interrogative pronouns (cf. Le Goffic 1994), as for example the seven distinct morphemes in (1):

(1) *Qu'est-ce que c'est que la grammaire?*
  1 2   3   4   5   6   7
  "What is grammar?"

When explained (Agard 1984), morphological complexity is generally linked to some phonemic peculiarity or to some pragmatic influence. Is there a particular weakening of the French interrogative form *que*, preventing the more simple use of its Spanish or Italian equivalents (Coveney 1990)? Is there a special French trend for 'expressivity', a move towards heavy topicalisations (Le Goffic 1994, Caffarel 1995)? In this paper I propose to follow a syntactic and semantic explanation, in the perspective of Riegel (1985) and Givón (1990).

Before analyzing the forms of interrogative predicates, as in (1), I will recall some morphological complexities of interrogative subjects and complements. I will then describe the two main interrogative predicates, one questioning on meaning and the other on naming, the distinction between both types being a possible explanation for morphological complexity (Chisholm 1984).

1. *Interrogative subjects and complements*

It is a well-known fact that, in the morphological system of French interrogative pronouns, questions on [+Human] and [-Human] are not on the same
level. There is a simple morpheme, *qui*, for questioning on [+Human] subjects,
whereas no simple morpheme can question on a [-Human] one, the specific
[-Human] forms *que* and *quoi* being non-grammatical:

(2) *Qui bouge?*
     "Who is moving?"

(3) **Que bouge?/*Quoi bouge?*
     "What is moving?"

The only morphological solution in this case is given by the so-called 'reinforced form' *qu'est-ce que*:

(4) *Qu'est-ce qui bouge?*
     "What is moving?"

The 'reinforced form' can be used for [+Human] too:

(5) *Qui est-ce qui bouge?*
     "Who is moving"

as an alternative choice (although less normative) for questioning on [+Human]
subjects. Figure 1 shows what is missing for [-Human]:

	pronoun	verb
[+Hum]	*qui*	*bouge*
[-Hum]	....	
	re-inforced forms	verb
[+Hum]	*qui est-ce qui*	*bouge*
[-Hum]	*qu'est-ce qui*	*bouge*

Fig. 1: *Interrogative forms for the subject*

According to standard morphological devices (Tranel 1978, Eynde &
Blanche-Benveniste 1987), the five items of the 'reinforced' forms can be analyzed into three composants:

(6) a. *qui est-ce qu- i:*
       1   2   3   4 5

     b. *qu' est-ce qu- i:*
        1   2   3   4 5

Initial *qui/qu'* (henceforth written in bold italics), here labelled as 1, stands for the interrogative pronoun. ***Qui***, semantically marked as [+Human], can stand alone in front of the verb (***qui bouge?***), whereas ***qu'***, semantically marked as [-Human] and never standing alone in front of a tensed verb without a subject, requires the addition of the reinforcement.

Reinforcement *est-ce qu-*, labelled as 2,3,4, originates from a set expression for topicalization, *c'est...qu-...*, with inverted subject: *est-ce... qu-* (cf. Marchello-Nizia 1997:217). This expression must now be taken as a whole. Evidence for its non-analyzability comes from old writings (XIV-XV century), in which the sequence *est + ce* is written in one word, without any trace of a verbal component, *esse que.*

Part 5, the final *-i*, is the mark for the subject, whether human or not, as is the case for relative pronouns (Tranel 1978). Figure 2 shows the whole set of interrogative subjects:

	pro	reinforcement	function: subject	verb
[+Hum]	*qui*			*bouge*
[- Hum]	**que*			*bouge*
[+Hum]	*qui*	*est-ce qu-*	*-i*	*bouge*
[- Hum]	*qu'*	*est-ce qu-*	*-i*	*bouge*

Fig. 2: *Interrogative forms for the subject*

Interrogative complement pronouns do not show this kind of asymmetry. Both [+Human] and [-Human] have simple forms, ***qui*** and ***que*** or ***quoi*** respectively. Used as fronted interrogatives, in front of the verb, ***qui*** and ***que*** normally entail the post-position of the subject, be it a pronoun or a lexical form, as shown in Figure 3:

	interr. Compl.	verb	Subject
[+Hum]	***qui***	*veut*	*-il*
	qui	*veut*	*le monstre*
[-Hum]	***que***	*veut*	*-il*
	que	*veut*	*le monstre*

Fig. 3: *Simple forms for interrogative complements*

(7)   a.   *Qui veut-il?*
           "Who does he want?"
      b.   *Qui veut le monstre?*
           "Who does the monster want?"

    c.   *Que veut-il?*
        "What does he want?"
    d.   *Que veut le monstre?*
        "What does the monster want?"

When reinforcement *est-ce qu-* is used, which is optional, for both [+Human] and [-Human], the complement function is marked by vowel *-e* (deleted before another vowel). Simple interrogative forms remain the same but there is usually no post-position of the subject (cf. Figure 4):

	interr. pron.	reinforcement	compl. function	subject	verb
[+Hum]	*qui*	est- ce qu-	*(e)*	*il*	*veut*
[-Hum]	*qu'*	est-ce qu-	*(e)*	*il.*	*veut*
[+Hum]	*qui*	est-ce qu-	*e*	*le monstre*	*veut*
[-Hum]	*qu'*	est-ce que-	*e*	*le monstre*	*veut*

Fig. 4: *Interrogative complements with reinforcement*

(8) a.   **qui** *est- ce qu' il veut?*
        "Who does he want?"
    b.   **qu'**est-ce qu' il veut?
        "What does he want?"
    c.   **qui** *est-ce qu-e le monstre veut?*
        "Who does the monster want?"
    d.   **qu'**est-ce que le monstre veut?
        "What does the monster want?"

The [-Human] interrogative pronoun, **que**, is a clitic form, only used in front of the verb. A non-clitic allomorph, **quoi**, stands for the pronoun when postponed; it is used alone or with a preposition:

(9) a.   **Que** *voulez-vous?*   (more normative)
        "What do you want?"
    b.   *Vous voulez* **quoi**?   (less normative)
        "What do you want?"
    c.   **Quoi** *de neuf?*   (the only possible form)
        "What new?"
    d.   *A* **quoi** *pense le monstre?*   (the only possible form)
        "What is the monster thinking about?"

Figure 5 summarizes the various morphological solutions for [-Human] interrogative complements, equivalent to **what** *does he want?*:

	clitic pron.	reinforc.	function	subject	verb	subject	non-clitic pron.
[-Hum]	que				veut	-il	
				il	veut		quoi
	qu'	est-ce qu-	(e)	il	veut		

Fig. 5: *Three realizations for [-Human] interrogative complements*

Interrogation on [-Human] predicates shows a different and more complex morphology.

2. *First type of interrogative predicate pronoun*

By 'predicate' I mean the special complements of *to be* or other similar verbs (they are called 'attributs' in French grammars). I will focus on the very frequent interrogative predicates used for questioning on the definitions.

A first striking difference from the ordinary complements should be noted: we find here almost the same morphological forms as those shown in figure 5, *que, quoi, qu'est-ce que*, but with a number of acceptability problems. They all tend to be supplanted by more complicated form involving syntactic dislocation devices.

2.1 *Interrogative pronoun que*

Que is sometimes used in literary texts to question the identity of a term but is never used in informal style or in ordinary oral conversation:

(10) *Qu'est la vieille langue?* (Littré)
"What is the old language?"

(11) *Qu'est le plaisir?* (Courteline)
"What is pleasure?"

(12) *Qu'était cela? De l'amour* (Maupassant)
"What was that? Love"

Togeby (1982.1:469) has described it as a rather rare and old-fashioned form. Grevisse & Goosse's 'bon usage' (1986:388) considers it unclear: "Lors-qu'on interroge sur l'attribut, la langue littéraire emploie parfois avec le verbe être le tour [que attribut + copule + sujet], *Qu'est un héros*. Mais ce tour reste rare: il est senti comme peu clair".

This acceptability problem highlights an interesting difference between the use of *que* as a complement and the use of *que* as a predicate. The former is a

---

very easy morphological solution whereas the latter sounds so strange as to be non-grammatical:

(13) a.   *Que veut le snark?*
         "What does the snark want?"

     b.   **Qu'est un snark?*
         "What is a snark?"

2.2 *Que and lexical subject dislocation*

Contemporary French never uses the typical **que** complement construction **que** + Verb + subject when asking for a definition, as in (13b). Such a question requires a more complicated morpho-syntactic scheme based on a special status for the subject. The only subject which can be linked directly to the verb is the demonstrative clitic *ce*:

(14) ***Qu'est-ce?***

A lexical subject can only appear apart from the grammatical subject *ce* in a dislocated position:

(15) ***Qu'est-ce, un snark?***

Left dislocation (16) and right dislocation (17) are regularly used:

(16) *Mais, un baiser, à tout prendre, **qu'est-ce?*** (written French, Rostand)
     "But a kiss, on the whole, what is it?"

(17) ***Qu'est-ce, au juste, le benjoin?***   (spoken French, Cl-r, 2,97)
     "What is it, exactly, benzoin?"

In these examples, *est-ce* does not stand for the reinforcement mentioned before. It is the main governing verb *est* and its inverted subject *ce*.

A more familiar version of the same construction would use the allomorph **quoi** after the verb: *c'est **quoi?***, as in (18) and (19):

(18) *C'est **quoi**, un hayon élévateur?*   (spoken French, Alf 15,2)
     "It is what, a fork-lift truck?"

(19) *Alors, c'est **quoi**, le ketchup?*   (spoken French, Law 10,10)
     "Then, it is what, ketchup?"

These examples have right rather than left dislocation. This use of **quoi** and dislocation, considered very colloquial, appears in ordinary conversations but not usually in formal speech or in written texts (cf. Figure 6 below).

lexical subject	left disl.	pron.	verb grammatical subject	right disl.	lexical subject
un snark,	/	***qu'***	*est- ce,*	/	*un snark*

lexical subject	left disl.	grammatical subject	verb pron.	right disl.	lexical subject
un snark,	/	*c'*	*est* ***quoi,***	/	*un snark*

Fig. 6: *Lexical subject dislocation*

2.3 *Que with dislocation and reinforcement*

This same construction, with interrogative **que**, grammatical subject *ce*, main verb *est* and dislocation of the lexical subject, is often reinforced with the special particle *est-ce que*:

(20) *Qu'est-ce que c'est, un snark?*
"What is it, a snark?"

Morphological decomposition for (20) would be (20'):

(20')   pron. + particle + gram. subject + main verb + disl. + lex. subject
          que   *est-ce que c'*   *est,*   /   *un snark*

The reinforcement particle *est-ce que* comes just after the interrogative pronoun. In this case, the grammatical subject of the main verb *est* is not inverted: *c'est*. The lexical subject appears in left dislocations as in (21) as well as in right dislocations (22)-(23) (cf. Figure 7 below):

(21) *Alors, le fielas,* ***qu'****est-ce que c'est?*   (spoken French, Gorilla, 1, 22)
"Then, the fielas, what is it?"

(22) ***Qu'****est-ce que c'est, le yoga?*   (spoken French, Law 28,14)
"What is it, yoga?"

(23) *Alors,* ***qu'****est-ce que c'est, un wagon-lit?* (spoken French, Law 25,12)
"Then, what is it, a sleeping car?"

The reinforcement particle does not change the status of the grammatical subject, which, as in the preceding cases, cannot be linked directly to the main verb (24):

(24) **Qu'est-ce qu' est un snark?*

It has to be dislocated, either on the right or on the left, and the grammatical subject *ce* is obligatory (cf. Figure 7 below):

(25) *Un snark, qu'est-ce que c'est?*

(26) *Qu'est-ce que c'est, un snark?*

lexical subject	left disl.	pro.	reinforcement	grammat. subject	verb	right disl.	lexical subject
un snark,	/	*qu'*	*est-ce que*	*c'*	*est,*	/	*un snark*

Fig.7: *Dislocation + reinforcement*

As dislocation has been considered colloquial by purist French grammarians, many people try to avoid it when writing. However, it is widely used in all types of speech.

As will be shown below, however, the main specific feature of the interrogative predicate is the obligatory separation of the lexical subject and the grammatical subject *ce*. The dislocative device is only one of the possibilities given for realizing this separation, the other being what I call the 'anti-dislocative *que*'.

The next pattern shows a special morphological item *que*.

2.4 *Anti-dislocative que*

A very specific *que* (henceforth written *que*) appears in these interrogative predicates:

(27) ***Qu'est-ce qu'un tyran?***   (Camus, in Grevisse & Goosse 1986)
"What is a tyrant?"

(28) ***Qu'est-ce, hélas! que le génie?*** (Hugo)
"What, alas! is genius?"

No special connotation is associated with the turn, frequently used in spoken language as well as in written texts:

(29) ***Qu'est-ce que le socialisme français, aujourd'hui?***

(written French, Bredin)

"What is it French socialism, today?"

(30) ***Qu'est-ce qu'un colissimo?***   (spoken French, Alf 26,10)
"What is it a colissimo?"

It is a very common formulation when asking for a definition:

(31) ***Qu'est-ce qu'un pédiatre?***   (textbook)
"What is it a pediatrician?"

(32) ***Qu'est-ce <u>qu</u>'une arme blanche?***   (textbook)
     "What is it a blade?"

This special <u>*que*</u> puzzled many grammarians and was very often compared to the *que* found in a well-known predicate clause in a non-interrogative context (Grevisse & Goosse [1986:646]):

(33) *C'est une belle fleur <u>que</u> la rose*
     "It is a nice flower [that] the rose"

(34) *C'est imiter quelqu'un <u>que</u> de planter des choux*
                         (Musset, in Grevisse & Goosse 1986:1337)
     "It is to imitate someone [that] to plant cabbage"

(35) *Quelle triste histoire <u>que</u> cette histoire!*
     "What a sad story [that] this story"

This special <u>*que*</u> occurs when a predicate (rhematic element) is put in first position and the topic (which can be called the thematic element) is given afterwards (Rothenberg 1989:157). It has been explained as both a 'disjunctive' and 'junctive' morpheme between a rhematic element and a subsequent thematic one. In my view, <u>*que*</u>, in both types, acts as a marker for a kind of 'anti-dislocation device'. A very strict parallel can be drawn between dislocations (symbolized here by a slash) and this special <u>*que*</u>. The parallel applies to interrogative constructions (33)-(34):

(36) ***Qu'est-ce,***   / *un tyran?*

(37) ***Qu'est-ce***   *qu' un tyran*

It is also very striking in the non-interrogative predicates: .

(38) *C'est une belle fleur,*   /   *la rose*

(39) *C'est une belle fleur <u>que</u>*   *la rose*

Verheugd-Daatzelaar (1990:220) analyzed this <u>*que*</u> as a marker for 'extraposition': "The presence of *que* before the subject may be taken to indicate that it is in extraposed position".

Extraposition implies a position on the right of the main verb, never on the left.[1] Lexical and grammatical subjects are distinct. There is no prosodic dislocation and yet the lexical subject is somehow ejected from the main construc-

---

[1] Mine differs from the frequent description, given for instance by Martinon (1929), Agard (1985) and Le Goffic (1994), according to which the first sequence, *c'est*, or *est-ce* is a presentative form and the main verb *est* is deleted: "*Qu'est-ce qu'[est] la science? C'est une belle fleur que la rose [est]*" (Martinon 1929:210, 134). I agree with the analysis of Grevisse & Goosse (1986).

tion. I call this special *que* 'anti-dislocative' to indicate that, occurring in the same syntactic frame as standard right dislocative devices, it does not trigger any prosodic disjunction. On the contrary, this *que* brings in a cohesive element, prosodically different from the dislocation, though syntactically analogous. Figure 8 below shows the comparison between interrogative complement *que* and *que* as an interrogative predicate anti-dislocative *que*. The specificity of the interrogative predicate does not lie in the morphological use of the pronoun *que* but in the syntactic distinction between grammatical and lexical subject, either with a dislocative construction or with a special extraposing *que*:

	interrogative predicate		interrogative complement
Que	**Qu'est un snark?*		*Que veut le snark?*
Que + *ce* + *dislocation*	*Qu'est-ce,*	/	*un snark?*
Que + *ce* + *que*	*Qu'est-ce*		*qu' un snark?*

Fig. 8: *Pronoun* **que**: *predicate and complement*

2.5 *Interrogative* **que**, *extraposing* que *and reinforcement*

The occurrence of the reinforcement particle *est-ce que* applies as for all fronted interrogative pronouns. The only difficulty here is to distinguish correctly between *est-ce* pertaining to the particle and *c'est* pertaining to the main verb. There is no difficulty in ordinary uses. The construction occurs in literary language (40)-(41) as well as in conversational speech (42)-(44):

(40) *Ô nuit, qu'est-ce que c'est que ces guerriers livides?*
(Hugo, in Grevisse & Goosse 1986:651)
"O night, what is it that these livid warriors?"

(41) *Qu'est-ce que c'est que ce supplice?* (Verlaine, ibid.)
"What is it that this torture?"

(42) *Qu'est-ce que c'est que la grammaire, la syntaxe, etc.?*
(spoken French, Prof. 1, 24)
"What is it that grammar, syntax, etc.?"

(43) *Et qu'est-ce que c'est que la schizophrénie réellement?*
(spoken French, Inform. 2,7)
"And what is it that schizophrenia, really?"

(44) *Qu'est-ce que c'est que la vente pure?* (spoken French, Ch. 4, 11)
"What is it that pure sale?"

The analytical decomposition in (45) shows the different elements:

(45) Interrog. pron.	reinforc. particle	gram. subject	main verb	extraposition *que*	lexical subject
Qu'	*est-ce que*	*c'*	*est*	*que*	*la schizophrénie*

2.6 Conclusion for the first type interrogative predicates
Going back to the example given in (1):

(1) *Qu'est-ce que c'est que la grammaire?*
    1   2   3   4   5   6   7

we can now account for the seven items involved in the interrogative predicate. As well as the apparent morphological complexity of pronoun *que*, as stated in many grammatical descriptions, we noted a syntactic complexity compelling any non-clitic subject to shift to an extraposed position (either dislocated or not, either reinforced or not).

In this perspective, interrogative pronoun *que* could be interpreted as one and the same morpheme, independently of its grammatical functions. The different functions would bring no special form for the interrogative pronoun itself but special requirements for the expression of the subject involved in [-Human] interrogatives:

a) obligatory reinforcement *est-ce qu-i*, when [-Human] interrogation bears on the subject, as in *Qu'est-ce qu-i bouge?*. Such a requirement could be functionally explained by the obligatory marking of the subject in French.

b) obligatory extraposition of the non-clitic subject, such as *la grammaire* in (1) when [-Human] interrogation bears on a particular type of predicate. This requirement could be semantically explained by referring to the meaning of the question in all the examples we have seen until now. Examination of the second type interrogative predicates grounded on different semantic bases will facilitate a semantic hypothesis.

3. Second type interrogative predicates

3.1 Two semantic types for [que + est + subject]
Interrogative predicates are involved in the well-known ambiguity of constructions of the type [X is Y] and [Y is X] (cf. Moreau 1976, Verheugd-Daatzelaar 1990, Boone 1991, Rey-Debove 1997).

Rey-Debove (1997: 185-187) proposes a clear-cut distinction: one interpretation is about meaning (46), the other (47) about naming:

(46) *Une librairie est un magasin où l'on vend des livres*
     "A book-shop is a shop where books are sold"

(47) *Un magasin où l'on vend des livres est une librairie*
"A shop were books are sold is a book-shop"

For (46), the paraphrase could be

(46') "[the meaning of the word] *librairie* is..."

Whereas for (47) the paraphrase would be:

(47') "[The name of] a shop where books are sold is..."

The ambiguity existing in the affirmative sentence also exists in the interrogative formulation. The questions for (46) could be formulated on the same five models that we have already mentioned:

(48) a.   *Qu'est-ce, une librairie?*
     b.   *C'est quoi, une librairie?*
     c.   *Qu'est-ce que c'est, une librairie?*
     d.   *Qu'est-ce qu'une librairie?*
     e.   *Qu'est-ce que c'est qu'une librairie?*

The questions for (47) could have almost the same forms (49), though far less natural:

(49) a.   *Qu'est-ce, un magasin où l'on vend des livres?*
     b.   *C'est quoi, un magasin où l'on vend des livres?*
     c.   *Qu'est-ce que c'est, un magasin où l'on vend des livres?*
     d.   *Qu'est-ce qu'un magasin où l'on vend des livres?*
     e.   *Qu'est-ce que c'est qu'un magasin où l'on vend des livres?*

But the second type, questioning the naming, also has a simpler form, which appears in special conditions.

3.2 *Second type interrogative predicates*

The second type allows direct formulations of the subject, without extraposition:

(50) **Que** serait Paris sans la Seine?   (touristic brochure)
"What would Paris be without River Seine?"

(51) **Qu'**était en fait la féodalité en ce temps-là   (newspaper)
"What was in fact feudalism in those times?"

Lexical subjects *Paris* in (50) and *la féodalité* in (51) are not placed in extraposion but directly placed after the main verb; yet acceptability in sentences (50) and (51) is very good. The syntactic construction is thus different from the first type, which prevents direct formulation of the subject. Semantic interpretation is different too. The questions in (50) and (51) do not ask for any definition of *Paris* or *la féodalité* but for a particular quality of the subject that could affect its naming. How would you name Paris in this case? How would you name this special kind of feudalism? As Rey-Debove states (1997:187), the naming device can be used in a rhetorical orientation meaning "would the subject deserve such a name?":

> *S'appeler* possède un emploi rhétorique où il prend le sens de 'mériter le nom de X', qui implique 'être véritablement un X, être un vrai X'.
> [To be named X has a rhetorical use in which it means 'to deserve such X name', which implies the meaning of 'being a real X']

3.3 *Semantic characteristics of the subjects in the second·type*

In many examples, the verb has a conditional tense (French 'conditionnel') and the formulation of the subject suggests a hypothetical property which could change its name:

(52) *Que serais-je sans toi?*   (Chanson de J. Ferran)
    "What would I be without you?"

(53) *Que serait un cormoran qui aurait cassé son bec?*
                                  (spoken French, Cl-r, 76,5)
    "What would a cormorant be with a broken beak?"

(54) *Que serait l'audace sans la grâce?*   (advertisement)
    "What would audacity be without grace?"

(55) *Que serait la France sans ses poulets pourris? Ses chauffeurs de taxi grincheux?*   (Canard Enchaîné, 1309975)
    "What would France be without its rotten cobs and grumpy taxi-drivers?"

When the subject is a personal pronoun as in (52), the question clearly means no interrogation on the person but a rhetorical way of asking *would I be the same person?*

When formulated with a past or a future tense, the question bears on the qualities of the subject:

(56) *Qu'a été jusqu'ici l'histoire de l'Europe?*   (newspaper)
    "What was until now the history of Europe?"

(57) *Qu'étiez-vous pour lui?*   (newspaper)
    "What were you for him?"

(58) *Que sera l'Europe de demain?*   (newspaper)
    "What will Europe be tomorrow?"

(59) *Que sera, ensuite, son avenir?*

(De Gaule, in Grevisse & Goosse 1986)

"What will later be his future?"

3.4 *Conclusion for the second type interrogative predicates*

The second type of interrogative predicates question on the naming, not on the meaning. This semantic difference allows for the presence of a non-extraposed subject which is impossible for the first type. This interrogative type has a much simpler morpho-syntactic form. It seems possible to link the simplicity or the complexity of the interrogative type to the semantic difference of the questioning.

4. *Conclusions*

Interrogation on [-Human] predicates appears in some very complex forms. At first sight, the complexity seems to involve the morphological part of the interrogative turn, particularly the interrogative clitic pronoun *que*. In fact, the only morphological complexity brought by the pronoun *que* is that of the competing form *quoi* and the existence of the reinforcement particle *est-ce que*.

The complexity of interrogative utterances in type 1 can be described more accurately as a syntactic complexity concerning the subject. The hypothesis for explaining this kind of ambiguity depends on the relation between syntactic forms and semantics.

Type 1 questions on the meaning of the subject; a syntactic constraint forces this subject to appear in an extraposed position, which implies more morphological material and a more complex syntactic organization.

Type 2 questions on the naming of the subject. This subject has no syntactic constraint similar to type 1. It can be linked directly to the main verb without obligatory extraposition.

Following Riegel's (1985:201) discussion of the difference between identifying and descriptive predicates, a pronominal representation of the difference between the two types would read as follows:

(60) Type 1: *Qu'est-ce que c'est que cela?*

(61) Type 2: *Que serait-il, dans ces conditions?*

Within French diachrony, a particular change in the meaning of another interrogative form, the adjective *quel*, could be explained by the dissociation of two such meanings. Until the end of XIXth century, [*quel* + N] could question on the identity or on the description of the subject. Littré's dictionary, published in 1869, explained the different meanings of a sentence such as (62):

(62) *De Paris à Lyon, quelle est ma route?*
   "From Paris to Lyon, what is my road?"

It could question on the identity of the road, passing through such and such places or it could question on the descriptive qualities of the road: pleasant or not, longer or shorter. Present use of *quel* can only question on the identity.

Within Romance languages, Portuguese and French are the only languages showing reinforcement particles for interrogative pronouns (Agard [1984:91]).

> Para dar maior ênfase à pergunta, em lugar de *que* pronome substantivo, usase *o que* [...] Tanto uma como outra forma pode ser reforçada por *é que: O que é que eu vejo, nestas tardes tristes?* (Cunha-Cintrea 1987:353).
>
> [In order to give more emphasis to a question, *que* is used in place of the pronoun *que*. Both forms may be reinforced by *è que*: what is it that I see, during these sad evenings?]

It would be interesting to know how many similar complexities can be explained in the same way.

In these kinds of problem, morphological complexity is often the most evident phenomenon. Morphological facts can be explained as a consequence of a more fundamental syntactic complexity, which can be explained by some fundamental semantic distinctions.

REFERENCES

Agard, Frederick B. 1984. *A Course in Romance Linguistics: A synchronic view. vol. I* . Washington: Georgetown University Press.

Blanche-Benveniste, Claire. 1988. "Eléments pour une Analyse du mot *quel*". *Hommage à la mémoire de Jean Stéfanini* ed. by Claire Blanche-Benveniste, A. Chervel & M. Gross, 59-75. Aix-en-Provence: Publication de l'Université de Provence.

——— . 1997. "A propos de *Qu'est-ce que c'est* et *C'est quoi*". *Recherches Sur le Français Parlé* 14.127-146.

Boone, Annie. 1991. "Remarques sur les Phrases Copulatives". *Actes du XVIIIe Congrès International de Linguistique et de Philologie Romanes*, 127-141. Tübingen: Niemeyer,.

Burston, J. & M. Monville-Burston. 1981. "The Use of Demonstrative and Personal Pronouns as Anaphoric Subjects of the Verb *être*". *Lingvisticae Investigationes* 5:2.2231-2257.

Caffarel, Alice. 1995. "Approaching the French Clause as a Move in Dialogue: Interpersonal organisation". *On Subject and Theme: A discourse functional perspective* ed. by R. Hasan & P.H Fries, 1-49. Amsterdam & Philadelphia: John Benjamins.

Chisholm, William. 1984. *Interrogativity: A colloquium on the grammar, typology and pragmatics of questions in seven diverse languages*. Amsterdam & Philadelphia: John Benjamins.

Coveney, Aidan. 1990. "Variation in Interrogatives in Spoken French: A preliminary report". *Variation and Change in French: Essays presented to Rebecca Posner on her sixtieth birthday* ed. by J. N. Green & W. Ayres-Bennett. New York: Routledge.

Cunha, Celso & Cintra, Lindley. 1987. *Nova Gramática do Português contemporâneo*. Lisboa: Edições João Sá da Costa.

Eynde, Karel van den & Claire Blanche-Benveniste. 1987, *Analyse Morphologique et Syntaxique des Formes QUI, QUE, QUOI*. Preprint 114, K.U. Leuven: Department Linguistiek.

Givón, Talmy. 1990. *Syntax: A functional and typological approach*. Vol. II. Amsterdam & Philadelphia: John Benjamins.

Grevisse, Maurice & André Goosse. 1986. *Le Bon Usage: Grammaire française*. Douzième éd. Louvain: Duculot.

Harris, Martin. 1978. *The Evolution of French Syntax: A comparative approach*. London: Longman.

Kupferman, Lucien. 1979. "Les constructions *Il est médecin/C'est un médecin*: Essai de solution". *Cahiers de Linguistique* 9.131-164.

Le Goffic, Pierre. 1994. *Grammaire de la Phrase Française*. Paris: Hachette.

Marchello-Nizia, Christiane. 1997. *La Langue Française aux XIVème et XVème Siècles*. Paris: Nathan (Série Linguistique).

Martinon, Philippe. 1929. *Comment on Parle en Français*. Paris: Larousse.

Molinier, Charles. 1996. "Constructions en 'c'est': Une classification générale". *Cahiers de Grammaire* 21.75-94.

Moreau, M. L. 1976. *C'est: Étude de syntaxe transformationnelle*. Mons.

Pollock, Jean-Yves. 1983. "Sur Quelques Propriétés des Phrases Copulatives en Français". *Langue française* 58.89-125.

Rey-Debove, Josette. 1997. *Le Métalangage*. Paris: Armand Colin.

Renzi, Lorenzo. 1985. *Nuova Introduzione alla filologia romanza*. Bologna: Il Mulino.

Riegel, Martin, J. C. Pellat & R. Rioul. 1994. *Grammaire Méthodique du Français*. Paris: Presse Universitaire Française.

Riegel, Martin. 1985. *L'Adjectif Attribut*. Paris: Presse Universitaire Française.

Rothenberg, Mira. 1989. "Quelques Moyens Syntaxiques de Rhématisation et de Thématisation en Français". *Bulletin de la Société de Linguistique de Paris* LXXXIV:1.143-161.

Ruwet, Nicolas. 1975. "Les Phrases Copulatives en Français". *Recherches Linguistiques* 3.143-191.

Togeby, Knud. 1982. *Grammaire Française* vol. I: Le Nom ed. by Magnus Berg, Ghani Merad & Ebbe Spang-Hassen, Copenhague: Etudes Romanes de l'Université de Copenhague.

Tranel, Bernard. 1978. "On the Elision of /i/ in French *qui*". *Studies in French Linguistics* 1:1.53-75.

Verheugd-Daatzelaar, Els. 1990. *Subject Arguments and Predicate Nominals: a study of French copular sentences with two NPs*. Amsterdam & Atlanta: Rodopi.

Wilmet, Marc. 1986. *La Détermination Nominale: quantification et caractérisation*. Paris: Presse Universitaire Française.

INTEGRATING PRAGMATICS INTO THE GRAMMAR[*]

ELISABET ENGDAHL
Göteborg University

0. *Introduction*

In recent years, the number of linguists who refer to notions like 'focus' and 'ground' has grown rapidly.[1] Many interesting articles have appeared which show that we cannot give a complete syntactic, morphological or prosodic analysis without taking such notions into account. By the 'focus of an utterance' I mean the new information that the speaker wants to convey. The 'ground of an utterance' corresponds to material that is assumed to be already known to the hearer. Focus and ground are thus defined in terms of what the speaker and hearer of an utterance know and want to achieve with their utterances. In this respect, they are clearly pragmatic notions since they refer to users of language and particular contexts of use.

In this paper I will discuss three types of phenomena which illustrate the need for integrating the pragmatic notions 'focus/ground' with other components of the grammar. I will look at intonation, word order and morphology. However, the point of the paper is not just to argue once more that a proper treatment of these different aspects of the grammar requires access to pragmatic notions. My aim is rather to discuss what principled ways there are to account for the interaction between the 'core' components of grammar such as syntax, morphology and intonation and pragmatic notions such as focus and ground. In order to make the discussion fairly concrete, I will compare two distinct ways

[*] Some of the ideas in this article derive from joint work with Enric Valldují, see e.g. Valldují & Engdahl (1996) and Engdahl & Valldují (1996). I have benefitted from comments and questions from participants at the Colloquium on the Boundaries of Morphology and Syntax. I thank Anna Cooper, Robin Cooper, Mara Frascarelli and Åsa Wengelin for formatting assistance and Lunella Mereu for helpful comments. This work was supported by a grant from the Bank of Sweden Tercentenary Foundation.
[1] An overview of recent studies can be found in Valldují & Engdahl (1996) which also contains an analysis of the terminology used in different traditions.

of accounting for the grammar-pragmatics interface; one is the derivational approach taken in Government-Binding theory and the Minimalist Program and the other is a constraint-based approach, illustrated by Head-driven Phrase Structure Grammar (HPSG).

1. *Three types of phenomena*

1.1 *Focus and link accents in English*

It is well known that English to a large extent uses intonation to distinguish the focus, i.e. the new, informative part of an utterance, from the ground, the part that is assumed to be known in the given context. Consider the two dialogues below. I use small capitals to indicate the main stress of the utterance. % indicates that the utterance is inappropriate in the given context.

(1) a.   What does John PLAY?
    b.   He plays RUGBY
    c.   %He PLAYS rugby

(2) a.   Does John LIKE rugby?
    b.   No, he HATES rugby
    c.   %No, he hates RUGBY

(1b) and (2b) are both plausible and coherent answers to the questions in (1a) and (2a) respectively. But (1c) and (2c) are clearly not possible answers to these questions. They do not form a coherent discourse with the given questions, although they may very well be appropriate in other contexts. Why, then, are (1c) and (2c) inappropriate answers? The reason, I argue, is that they do not fit in with the 'focus/ground' partitioning indicated by the question. By asking the question in (1a), the speaker indicates to the hearer that s/he wants to know what game a person called *John* plays. The new information conveyed by the answer in (1b) is that the relevant game is *rugby*. I will use the term 'focus' to refer to the part of an utterance that conveys new information. Note that what is new information will be determined with respect to the speaker's assumptions about what the hearer already knows (ground) and wants to find out (focus). I will refer to the mental states of the dialogue participants as 'information states'.[2]

In English, the informational focus of an utterance is normally marked by an accent (nuclear stress), as is the case with the accented phrase *rugby* in (1b). The remainder of the utterance, *He plays*, will be ground, given that it has al-

---

[2] In the pragmatic and computational literature, it is also common to refer to the hearer's attentional state, see Grosz (1981) and Sidner (1981).

ready been introduced in the question in (1a). Given the two informationally defined notions 'focus' and 'ground', we can now explain why (1c) is an inappropriate answer. Accenting the verb *plays* in (1c) signals that this is the new information, contrary to the fact that playing has already been introduced in the question in (1a). (2a) is a polarity question, whether John likes rugby. This question is appropriately answered in (2b), where additional information about John's attitude to rugby is given. Similarly, the reason (2c) is an inappropriate answer to (2a) is that by not accenting the new information *hates* and accenting the ground element *rugby*, (2c) is not a coherent reaction to the utterance in (2a).

I assume that all utterances contain a focus.[3] The ground is often not expressed when it can be inferred. An equally felicitous answer to (1a) would have been the single phrase *rugby*. Within the ground, we need to make a further distinction, as can be seen in the following dialogues. From now on I will enclose the focus of an utterance in brackets labelled F.

(3) a. What do the boys DO?
    b. **John** [F plays RUGBY], **Bill** [F goes SAILING], and ...

(4) a. What do the boys PLAY?
    b. **John** [TAIL plays] [F RUGBY], **Bill** (plays) [F HOCKEY], and ....

The question in (3a) uses the definite description *the boys* to refer to a set of boys which is presumably known to the hearer, who answers the question by mentioning individual boys from this set and, for each boy, provides information about what he does. The initial NP, *John* in (3b) is also accented, but the accent is distinct from the one on *rugby*. The accent that goes with focus interpretation is a high pitch accent (indicated by H* in Pierrehumbert 1980), whereas the accent on *John* is a complex fall-rise pitch accent (L+H*), often perceived as a wavy tune. Jackendoff (1972) referred to the focus accent as the A-accent and to the accent on *John* as the B-accent and I will use his terminology here. In the examples, the A-accent is rendered with small capitals, the B-accent with boldface. The B-accented words in (3b) and (4b) serve to anchor the answer to the set of boys mentioned in the question. Vallduví (1992) introduces the term 'link' for this function. A link is part of the ground of an utter-

---

[3] Disregarding metalinguistic uses of language and certain perlocutionary utterances such as uttering *There, there ...* soothingly.

ance; it latches on to some referent or set of referents already mentioned in or inferred from the previous utterance.[4]

The notion 'link' allows us to make a distinction between (3b) where the ground only consists of the link *John*, and (4b) where there is additional ground material besides the link, viz. *plays*. We also need a term to refer to that part of the ground which is not a link, and we will adopt Vallduví's term 'tail' for this, as shown in (4b). Tail material is never accented and is often left out, as shown in (4b). In this answer, the focus consists of a single word *rugby*. This is an instance of what is usually called 'narrow focus'. In (3b), where the focus corresponds to the entire VP *plays rugby* we have an instance of 'wide focus'.

In English, the two accents are not interchangeable. Each accent goes with a special informational function and one could also talk about focus accent and link accent. Consequently, it would be totally inappropriate to answer the question in (3a) with the informational focus realised with a B accent. Since all utterances have a focus, all utterances must have an A-accented constituent. Link accents are sometimes optional, but when a link picks out some member of a set (a contrastive link) as in (4b), it is often realised with a B-accent.

We have seen that in order to account for the intonational realisation of utterances in English, we need to refer to notions like focus, link and tail. These notions are not inherent properties of the sentence but rather reflect the use of the utterance by the speaker who takes into account the hearer's information state.

1.2 *Dislocation in Catalan*

We next turn to the Romance languages where the informational status of a constituent is normally signalled by its position. I will assume, together with Vallduví (1992), Zubizarreta (1994), Frascarelli (this volume) and others, that when the subject is part of the informational focus in Catalan, it appears in postverbal position where it receives stress.

---

[4] Links, especially B-accented links are sometimes called 'topics' or 'contrastive topics' by other writers. But since the term 'topic' is often used for other phenomena as well, I will stick to the term 'link'.

(5)   *Ahir*   [F *va tornar   a Barcelona   el PRESIDENT*]
        yesterday   return-3SG-PAST to Barcelona the president
        "Yesterday the president returned to Barcelona"[5]

(5) is an example of an utterance with an all-focus interpretation. If some part of the utterance is ground, then that part cannot occur inside the core clause but must be dislocated. According to Vallduví (1992), links are obligatorily left-dislocated and tails are right-dislocated in Catalan, as shown in (6). The dislocated elements correspond to clitics inside the core clause, which are marked by coindexing.

(6)   a.   [L *A Barcelona₁*] [F *hi₁ va tornar el PRESIDENT*]
      b.   [F *Hi₁ va tornar el PRESIDENT*] [T *a Barcelona₁*]

As can be seen from these examples, the stress is placed on the final element of the focal part. A constituent following the stressed constituent will thus be interpreted as tail, i.e. as part of the ground.

The pattern we see in (6) also applies when the subject is part of the ground. If it is a link, it has to be left-dislocated as in (7a) and if it is a tail, it appears right-dislocated as in (7b).

(7)   a.   [L *El president*] [F *va tornar a BARCELONA*]
      b.   [F *Va tornar a BARCELONA*] [T *el president*]

There are no subject clitics in Catalan which would prove that link subjects are really dislocated,[6] but this seems highly plausible given the general pattern in (6) and the contrast between (5) and (7a).

In order to explain when the different utterances in (5)-(7) can be used in Catalan, we therefore need to have a way of connecting syntactic position with informational interpretation.

---

[5] Abbreviations in the text and in glosses are the following:

ACC	=	Accusative case	IS	=	Information Status
CI	=	Conceptual-Intentional	L	='	link
DEC	=	declarative	LinkP	=	Link Phrase
F	=	focus	LP	=	Linear Precedence
FIN	=	finite tense	NOM	=	nominative case
FocP	=	Focus Phrase	PAST	=	past tense
GEN	=	Genitive case	PRES	=	present tense
HON	=	honorific form	SG	=	singular
HPSG	=	Head-driven Phrase Structure Grammar	T	=	tail
ID	=	Immediate Domain	TailP	=	Tail Phrase

[6] Frascarelli (this volume) mentions some Italian dialects which have subject clitics.

1.3 *Honorific marking in Korean*

There are many languages in which the morphological form of lexical
items is sensitive to pragmatic notions such as the relative standing of the
speaker with respect to the hearer. I will here look at some data from Korean
discussed in Lee (1996). Honorification is widespread in Korean and shows up
both in the case marking system for nouns and in the verbal inflection system.
Given an utterance such as (8a), the hearer can infer that the speaker of (8a)
honours the subject of the sentence, viz. *John's father*.

(8) a.   *John-uy   apeci-kkeyse   mayil   sanchaykha-si-e*
          John-GEN father-NOM.HON   every day   take a walk-HON-DEC
          "John's father takes a walk every day"

     b. %*John-uy   apeci-kkeyse   mayil   sanchaykha-n-ta*
          John-GEN father-NOM.HON   every day   take a walk-PRES-DEC

In (8a) the speaker has chosen the honorific form of the nominative subject
NP as well as a honorific verb form. (8b) is judged to be inconsistent since the
honorific marking on the verb is absent. This may lead one to think that honorific marking in Korean involves some kind of agreement between the subject
and the verb in honorific status. However, the matter is not so simple, as Lee
argues. In (9) the honorific marking is on the possessive NP inside the subject
NP, but still the predicate is marked with the honorific infix *si*.

(9) *Ku pwun-uy   son-i   cham   potulawu-si-e*
     the man-GEN.HON   hand-NOM   very   soft-HON-DEC
     "The man's hands are very soft"

Lee shows that similar honorific marking may be used to indicate that the
speaker honours the object of the sentence, provided that the object then is
more socially prominent than the subject. (10) provides another interesting type
of example.

(10) *Minsoo-ka   mayil   sanchaykha-yeyo*
     Minsoo-NOM every day   take a walk-DEC.HON
     "Minsoo takes a walk every day"

The absence of any honorific marking on the subject NP indicates that the
speaker and the subject are of equal social standing. Nevertheless there is honorific marking on the verb which is taken as an indication that the speaker honours the addressee.

The Korean examples differ from the English and Catalan examples in that
they do not involve the way focus and ground material is realised. Instead they
illustrate how the relative social standing between speaker, hearer and the peo-

ple referred to in the sentence can be reflected in the case marking system of a language. In languages like Korean, these pragmatic conditions interact systematically with inflectional morphology and the relative prominence of grammatical functions in the language.

The three types of phenomena surveyed in this Section show that pragmatic notions systematically affect the prosodic, syntactic and morphological realisation of utterances. Mastering the language particular realisation of these pragmatic notions is clearly part of a native speaker's competence.

We next turn to the question of how this competence can be accounted for in two current theories of grammar.

2.   *A derivational approach: Minimalism*

A central idea in transformational grammar is that the connection between form (or Phonetic Form, PF) and meaning (or Logical Form, LF) is mediated through syntactic structure. The syntactic or, more generally, the computational component generates a structure which then provides input to both phonetic and semantic interpretation. In recent work, Chomsky (1995) has emphasised the role of PF and LF as 'interface levels', i.e. levels which provide the interface between the grammatical system and other systems such as articulatory and conceptual systems. The embedding of the grammatical system in other cognitive systems can be represented as in Figure 1:

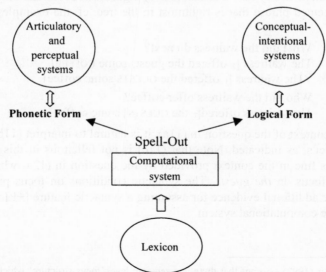

Fig.1: *The organisation of the grammar in the Minimalist Program*

Where do pragmatic notions such as context of use fit in with this model? It seems to me that the only way the context of use can interact with the language system is via the Conceptual-Intentional systems (CI-systems). I will thus assume that the focus/ground distinction is relevant at the interface level between the CI systems and LF. At LF, then, one needs to distinguish what part of the structure should be interpreted as focus, link and tail, respectively.

Let us now look at how the three phenomena surveyed in Section 1 can be accounted for. We saw in Section 1.1 that the choice of accent in English reflects the speaker's assumptions about the hearer's information state. A speaker of English must realise the focal part of an utterance with the A-accent. At the same time, the focal part must be identified as such at LF in order for the correct form-meaning pairing to obtain. Since both PF and LF operate on the Spell-Out from the computational system, it seems clear that that structure[7] must contain the relevant information. The way the information is normally expressed is as a syntactic feature, e.g. [+F]. Such a feature has been used by many linguists, including Jackendoff (1972) and Selkirk (1984), who assume that a word marked [+F] must be realised with the A-accent.

The feature [+F] also plays a role in accounts of so called 'focus projection', i.e. the process that gives rise to wide focus interpretations as in (3). As is well-known, focus projection in English displays an interesting interaction between intonation and syntax. Bresnan (1971) argued that focus can only project from an accented phrase that is rightmost in the tree, cf. the examples in (11) and (12).

(11) a. What did the waitress do next?
     b. The waitress [F offered the guests some COFFEE]
     c. %The waitress [F offered the GUESTS some coffee]

(12) a. Who did the waitress offer coffee?
     b. The waitress offered[F the GUESTS] some coffee

In the context of the question in (11a), it is natural to interpret (11b) with a wide VP focus, as indicated. Note that (11c) is not felicitous in this context, whereas it is fine in the context provided by the question in (12a) which calls for narrow focus on *the guests*. The syntactic conditions on focus projection then provide additional evidence for assuming a syntactic feature [+F] which is visible in the computational system.

---

[7] Erteschik-Shir (1997) assumes that there is a separate level 'focus-structure' which provides the input to PF and LF.

Given that English distinguishes A-accented focal material, B-accented links and obligatorily deaccented tails, it is clearly not sufficient to assume a single feature [+F]. We would also need features for links and tails say, [+L] and [+T].[8] Let us refer to these features as 'Information Status' features (IS-features), since their raison d'être is precisely to encode the correlation between a particular accent and the information status of the word. Let us next consider the question of where IS-features appear in the grammar. One possibility would be to assume that they are part of lexical entries, i.e. that each lexical entry comes with a specification of its informational contribution. This is not a very plausible solution since the IS-features do not reflect a property of the word itself, or of its appearance in a particular syntactic context. Rather the IS-features reflect properties of the utterance. Note furthermore that enriching lexical items with IS-features will lead to a huge duplication of lexical items. I do not think that this is the right approach and I will outline an alternative in Section 3. For now, I will just assume that the computational system has access to IS-features.

Within the Minimalist Program, a natural way to handle these features is to assume that each IS-feature corresponds to a functional projection, i.e. a Focus Phrase (FocP), a Link Phrase (LinkP) and a Tail Phrase (TailP), which presumably would be part of the universal inventory of functional categories. The existence of a FocP has already been suggested for languages like Hungarian where the focus constituent necessarily moves to a designated position before the verb (cf. Horvath 1995, Brody 1990, Uriagereka 1995). In these languages, [+F] would be a strong feature and the movement to FocP would be overt, i.e. take place before Spell-Out. In Catalan, the movement to LinkP and TailP is (presumably) overt since it affects the actual word order. Given that the tail material is realised in final position, this entails that movement to FocP is also overt in Catalan, on the assumption that all movement is leftward.

Accounting for the correlation between accents and informational status in English turns out to be somewhat more problematic. Intonation in English is very flexible. When a wide focus is intended, the nuclear stress normally falls

---

[8] We will also need an account of link projection, which is similar to focus projection, but involves the B-accent. There are several interesting constraints involving movement and accent in English. For instance, fronted constituents have to be accented. A fronted constituent with the A-accent is interpreted as a preposed focus, as in (i) from Prince (1981) whereas a B-accented fronted constituent is interpreted as a contrastive link, as in (ii). See Vallduví & Engdahl (1996) for discussion.

(i)   [F MACADAMIA nuts] I think they are called.
(ii) [L **Tacos**] I LIKE, but [L**beans**] I HATE.

on the rightmost constituent, but in the case of narrow focus, almost any word
can be accented in situ. Consider the examples in (13).

(13) a.   He drove to LONDON,   not to OXFORD.
     b.   He DROVE to London,   he didn't FLY.
     c.   He drove TO London,   not FROM London
     d.   HE drove to London,   I didn't.

It seems most plausible to assume that movement to FocP in English is
covert, i.e. it only happens after Spell-Out given that almost all words can be
realised with focal accent regardless of their position.[9] If movement of [+F]-
marked constituents to FocP does not happen until after Spell-Out, there must
be a way of ensuring that a [+F] constituent is realised with the A-accent in PF
which does not require that the constituent be in [Spec, FocP] at Spell-Out.
This consequence clearly complicates the interplay between syntactic features
and functional projections. The nice correlation between overt movement and
PF-effects and covert movement and lack of PF-effects can no longer be up-
held.

So far we have seen that we need to assume syntactic features corresponding
to the information status notions focus, link and tail. This can presumably be
justified given the prosodic and positional correlates of these notions in the languages we have looked at. But what features would we need in order to account
for Korean in a similar fashion? It would seem that we would need features that
encode the sociolinguistic system of the Korean society given that the morphological form of the words used in a particular utterance reflects the speaker's
attitudes and relative social standing. This can presumably be done in terms of
features, but I seriously doubt that it could be done within the syntax. It seems
desirable to be able to express the connection between morphology and context
of use directly, without assuming that there is a functional projection for honorification where the appropriateness of a particular form is checked. In the
next Section we will look at a multidimensional constraint-based grammar
which allows these types of constraints to be expressed directly, without being
mediated by some syntactic feature or projection.

3.   *A multidimensional approach: HPSG*

HPSG is a lexically based theory which has elaborated the Saussurian idea
that all linguistic expressions are units of information, simultaneously specified

---

[9] A more detailed discussion of prosodically marked informational foci in English can be found
in Vallduví & Engdahl (1996:Section 5.3.1).

in various dimensions.[10] In this respect HPSG differs from the main conception of grammar in the transformational tradition, in which different aspects of a sentence are factored out into separate levels of representation which are related by derivation. The multidimensional units in HPSG are called 'signs'. A basic sign for a word may be structured as in (14).

$$(14) \quad \begin{bmatrix} \text{PHONOLOGY} & : & [\quad] \\ \text{CATEGORY} & : & [\quad] \\ \text{CONTENT} : & & [\quad] \\ \text{CONTEXT} : & & [\quad] \end{bmatrix}$$
sign

Signs in HPSG are represented as feature structures with features (or attributes) and values. The value of a feature may be an atomic symbol or another feature structure. In (14) we see a skeletal sign which has the features PHONOLOGY, CATEGORY, CONTENT and CONTEXT. The value for the PHONOLOGY feature should contain the relevant phonological information pertaining to the sign. How this information is presented, e.g. whether it is an orthographic rendition of a word form or a detailed phonological structure, will depend on the purpose to which the grammar will be put. The CATEGORY feature will contain all information that is relevant to the syntactic behaviour of the sign, i.e. its syntactic category and what kinds of words or phrases it may or needs to combine with. Valency information can be expressed as a single feature SUBCAT, which takes an ordered list of arguments as value, or as distinct valency features, e.g. Subject (SUBJ), Complements (COMPS), and SPECIFIER. The relevant semantic information is encoded in the CONTENT field which provides an interpretation of the sign in some logical language which can be evaluated in a particular context of use. The CATEGORY and CONTENT fields are linked through 'structure sharing', i.e. the referential index of a NP-sign that occurs as a value of a valency feature in CATEGORY may be shared (or 'unified') with the index of an argument in CONTENT.

One of the most innovative aspects of HPSG is that it includes an explicit connection to the context of use of a sign. Each sign contains a feature CONTEXT in which information about relevant use conditions for the sign is encoded. The context field will typically look like (15).

---

[10] See Pollard & Sag (1994) and Sag & Wasow (in prep.) for a general introduction to HPSG. A more detailed presentation of how information structure can be integrated with HPSG can be found in Engdahl & Vallduví (1996).

(15)

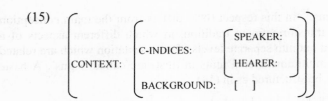

The value of the feature C-INDICES, an abbreviation for CONTEXTUAL-INDICES, will be a feature structure with features like SPEAKER and HEARER (or ADDRESSEE), whose values in turn will be anchored to the actual speaker and hearer of the utterance. The field BACKGROUND will contain relevant contextual information which may play a role in resolving potential ambiguities, establishing reference and interpreting elliptical utterances.

Basic lexical signs are put together according to general principles. When two signs are combined, their information is said to 'unify'. Two signs can only combine if their information is unifiable, i.e. if all feature specifications are compatible. It is customary within HPSG to distinguish Immediate Dominance (ID) relations, i.e. the vertical relations between a mother category and its daughter categories, and Linear Precedence (LP) relations, i.e. the horizontal ordering relations between daughters.

Where in this model of grammar do the notions focus and ground fit in? Given that I consider focus/ground to be an inherently pragmatic phenomenon, it seems that the most natural strategy would be to enrich the CONTEXT field with a feature INFORMATION-STRUCTURE (INFO-STRUCT), which takes focus and ground as values, as shown in (16).

(16)

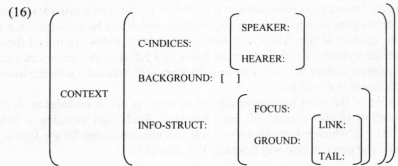

The values of the features FOCUS, LINK and TAIL will be structure-shared with the CONTENTS of the words or phrases that realise the focus, link and tail material respectively.[11] Given that the focus/ground partitioning of an utterance has to be consistent with the INFO-STRUCT of the previous utterance, I assume that this is available, presumably as part of BACKGROUND of the current utterance.

3.1 *English*

We will now look at how we can establish the connection between accent and information status in English within this multidimensional model. The basic idea is that the prosodic realisation of a word or phrase constrains its informational contribution, and vice versa. I assume that the PHONOLOGY (PHON) field of a lexical sign should contain only the idiosyncratic phonological properties of that word, but no specification of whether the word is realised with a particular accent. In order to capture the connection between the *use* of a word, its pronunciation and its information status, I assume that there are general lexical rules which add information about accenting and information status. For English we would need the three schematic rules in (17).

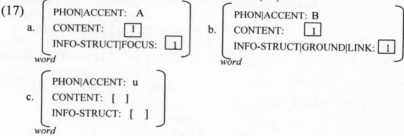

(17)

a.
```
⎡ PHON|ACCENT:  A        ⎤
⎢ CONTENT:      [1]       ⎥
⎣ INFO-STRUCT|FOCUS: [1]  ⎦
   word
```

b.
```
⎡ PHON|ACCENT:  B              ⎤
⎢ CONTENT:      [1]            ⎥
⎣ INFO-STRUCT|GROUND|LINK: [1] ⎦
   word
```

c.
```
⎡ PHON|ACCENT:  u   ⎤
⎢ CONTENT:     [ ]  ⎥
⎣ INFO-STRUCT:  [ ] ⎦
   word
```

These lexical rules act as conditions on lexical insertion. According to the template in (17a), a sign may be specified as being realised with accent A whenever its CONTENT is structure-shared with the value of FOCUS. The template in (17b) allows the CONTENT of a sign to act as a LINK whenever its PHONOLOGY field is specified to have the value 'B' for the attribute ACCENT. In addition to (17a,b), where the accent information determines the information status, we need the template in (17c) for an unaccented word which by itself cannot be interpreted as having a particular information status. Rather the information status of an unaccented word depends on the over-all focus/ground

---

[11] Given that there are pointers to the speaker and the hearer within C-INDICES, it would actually be possible to encode explicitly that the focus and ground are understood in relation to the information states of a particular speaker and hearer. But for ease of exposition I will adopt the simpler representation in (16).

structure of the utterance, as shown in Section 1.1. In (4b), the unaccented word *plays* is tail, whereas in (3b), it is part of a wide focus. Let us look at how these two focus/ground partitionings are expressed in HPSG. I am here using a schematic tree representation showing how signs are combined.

(18) *Narrow object focus:*

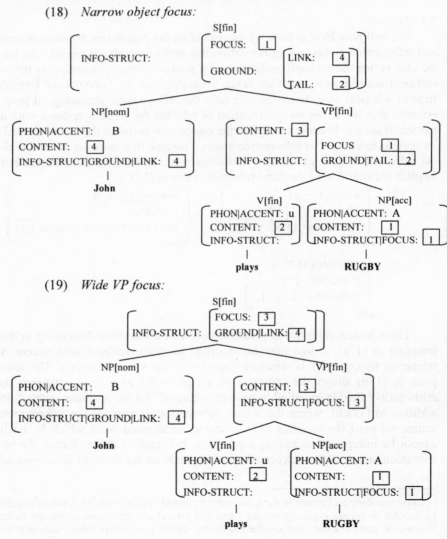

(19) *Wide VP focus:*

In Engdahl & Vallduví (1996), we propose that the general composition rules (or ID-schemata) for English should be enriched by instantiation principles for the INFO-STRUCT features. In the case of narrow foci and links, we assume that the mother inherits the specified value of the daughters, as shown in (18). If a daughter's INFO-STRUCT is not instantiated, as in the sign for *plays* in (18), the INFO-STRUCT|GROUND|TAIL of the mother may be set to the CONTENT of the unaccented word. In the case of wide focus, we assume that the focus of e.g. a VP may be the content of the whole VP, as shown in (19).

The interesting question now is how one can constrain focus projection so that it only happens when the rightmost daughter's information status is focus, as shown in (5). Given that ID-schemata do not refer to left-right order, we cannot state this restriction directly in terms of linear order. Instead we will make use of Pollard & Sag's obliqueness hierarchy for English (cf Pollard & Sag 1987, 1994). The value of the feature SUBCAT is a list of arguments, ordered according to relative obliqueness, in which the least oblique argument is the argument that is most accessible to syntactic processes. The least oblique argument, i.e. the argument that is highest on the list, normally corresponds to the subject. In some languages, the obliqueness hierarchy also constrains the word order, as for instance in English where the less oblique arguments precede more oblique ones. We can then formulate the relevant instantiation principle as in (20).

(20) *Wide focus:*
      If the FOCUS of the most oblique COMP-DAUGHTER is instantiated, then the value of the FOCUS of the mother is structure-shared with the value of the CONTENT of the mother.

Accounting for focus projection in terms of relative obliqueness instead of left-right position has the advantage that it also accounts for the examples in (21)-(22).

(21) a.   [F Your MOTHER] phoned
     b.   [F Your MOTHER phoned]

(22) a.   Your mother [F PHONED]
     b.   %[F Your mother PHONED]

If the subject is realised with the A-accent as in (21), the utterance can either be interpreted as a narrow subject focus or as a wide focus, i.e. an *all focus*, utterance. (21b) is thus a case of focus projection, despite the fact that the projecting phrase is not rightmost. Nevertheless, the subject will be the only element on the SUBCAT list, and hence the most oblique daughter, and focus pro-

jection is allowed according to (20). Note that focus only projects from arguments (COMP-DAUGHTERS in the terminology used in (20)) and not from heads.
This correctly predicts that (22) only has a narrow verb focus interpretation, i.e.
your mother must be ground.[12]

We see that the multidimensional model allows syntactic properties of a
phrase such as whether it is a head or a complement and its relative obliqueness
to constrain focus projection in the desirable way. Given that the linguistic representation, the sign, contains both CATEGORY and INFO-STRUCT, and that these
can constrain each other, it is possible to state the conditions on focus instantiation and projection directly without relying on mediating features like [+F] in
the syntax. Simultaneous access to the various dimensions thus obviates the
need for using syntactic features as carriers of information in the way they are
used in the derivational model.

3.2 *Catalan*

Turning now to Catalan, we recall that in this language there is a correlation between the position in the sentence and the information status. Link material is left-dislocated and tail material is right-dislocated. What remains inside
the core clause is interpreted as focal. There is no contrastive use of accents.
The sentence accent falls on the final constituent inside the core clause. We assume that there is general focus projection in Catalan so that focus projects
from the accented word to the core clause.

We account for the correlation between position and information status by
assuming that the ID-schemata that license dislocations also constrain the informational status of the daughters, as outlined in (23).

(23) a.   *Link ID-schema for Catalan:*

	S	→	NP,		S	
	FOCUS	[1]	CONTENT	[2]	CONTENT	[1]
	LINK	[2]			FOCUS	[1]

   b.   *Tail ID-schema for Catalan:*

	S	→	NP,		S	
	FOCUS	[1]	CONTENT	[2]	CONTENT	[1]
	TAIL	[2]			FOCUS	[1]

(23a) says that a sentence in Catalan may consist of a NP and a S whenever the
CONTENT of the NP is structure-shared with the mother's LINK value. The FOCUS

---

[12] Non-contrastive links in subject position are often realised without the characteristic B-
accent, see Vallduví & Engdahl (1996).

of the mother is structure-shared with the FOCUS of the S-daughter, which is structure-shared with its CONTENT. (23b) is similar, but here the information status of the NP is constrained to be TAIL.

In addition to the ID-schemata, we need to constrain the ordering so that a constituent whose LINK value is instantiated must precede the FOCUS, which in turn precedes a TAIL, if there is one. We can express this schematically as in (24).

(24)   *LP-statement for Catalan:*
         link < focus < tail

In our analysis of Catalan we thus exploit the fact that the ID-schemata in HPSG may refer not just to the CATEGORY features of the daughters but also to features within the CONTEXT field, in particular the features that encode the information status of the constituent.

3.3 *Korean*

The interesting aspect of Korean morphology that we are looking at here is the way in which the relative social standing of the speaker and hearer come into play. We saw in (15) that a sign may contain explicit anchors to the speaker and the hearer. In addition we need some way to encode the sociolinguistic conventions in the language in the feature structure. I will here outline the analysis proposed in Lee (1996) which is an extension and further development of the treatment of honorification in Pollard & Sag (1994:chapter 2.5.3).

Lee assumes that the BACKGROUND field in the CONTEXT contains facts that must hold for a particular form of a noun or a verb to be used. Consider the example in (25) which is a partial sign for a honorific noun form, as used for instance in (8a).

(25)
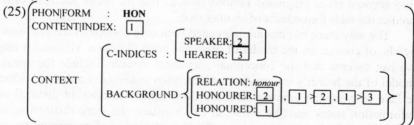

According to the information in BACKGROUND, the 'honour' relation must hold between two referents, where the referential index of the HONOURER [2] is structure-shared with the SPEAKER of the utterance and the referential index of the HONOURED [1] is structure-shared with the index of the CONTENT, i.e. with the referent of the word. In addition, the background is constrained to meet the condition that the referents stand in some relation, represented by '>', whose intended meaning is 'to be more socially prominent'. According to Lee, the honorific noun form can only be used if the referent of the noun is more socially prominent than both the speaker and the addressee.[13]

How do signs like (25) come into the grammar? Recall the idea proposed for English that the accent information be introduced by a lexical rule which simultaneously instantiates INFO-STRUCT features. We can take a similar approach to Korean morphology and assume that (25) arises as the result of a lexical rule which simultaneously specifies a particular morphological form and adds the constraints that must be satisfied in the context when that form is used.[14] Again, the viability of this analysis depends on the basic assumption in HPSG that the relevant linguistic structure, the sign, can be simultaneously specified in terms of phonological or morphological features and according to contextual constraints.

4. *Conclusions*

There are many areas in grammar where we need to refer to the information status of a constituent. I have tried to show in this paper that it is not sufficient to assume a single syntactic feature [+F]. Rather we need to have a proper theory of information status and of how informational distinctions are expressed by grammatical means. Continuing the line of research initiated in Vallduví (1992), I have discussed a three-way distinction in information status, using the terms focus, link and tail. I have also outlined what these notions amount to in a theory of information update. The widespread use of honorific forms in the world's languages further shows that the grammar needs to take into account other pragmatic notions such as relative social status in order to predict the well-formedness of an utterance.

The way these notions are integrated with core notions of the grammar depends, of course, on the model of grammar used. Within a Minimalist model, we can assume that the conceptual-intentional systems include the speaker's model of the hearer's information and attention states. Given that LF is the interface between the grammar and the CI-systems, the relevant distinctions in information status must be visible at LF. Similarly the same distinctions must be visible at PF in order to achieve the correct pairing of pronunciation, word

---

[13] See Lee's article for additional examples of the interaction between participants in the utterance situation and the referents mentioned in the utterance and their grammatical relations.

[14] Sag & Wasow use lexical rules for both inflectional and derivational morphology.

order, morphology and LF. I discussed a proposal to use specific information status features in the syntax and came to the conclusion that it involved replicating all the distinctions that are relevant to information status in the computational system. This, to my mind, leads to undesirable redundancy in the system.

Multidimensional constraint-based grammars offer an alternative which does not run into the problem of replicating information status distinctions in the syntax. In this model of grammar, the correlation between a particular realisation, be it accent, position or morphological form, and its information status can be established directly, using structure sharing and simultaneous specifications of different dimensions of the sign.

REFERENCES

Bresnan, Joan. 1971. "Sentence Stress and Syntactic Transformations". *Language* 47.257-281.

Brody, Michael. 1990. "Some Remarks on the Focus Field in Hungarian". *University College London Working Papers in Linguistics* 2. 201-226.

Chomsky, Noam. 1995. *The Minimalist Program*. Cambridge, Mass.: MIT Press.

Engdahl, Elisabet & Enric Vallduví. 1996. "Information Packaging in HPSG". *Studies in HPSG*. Grover & Vallduví 1996. 1-31.

Erteschik-Shir, Nomi. 1997. *The Dynamics of Focus Structure*. Cambridge: Cambridge University Press.

Grover, Claire & Enric Vallduví, eds. 1996. *Studies in HPSG*. Edinburgh Working Papers in Cognitive Science. Vol 12.

Grosz, Barbara. 1981. "Focusing and Description in Natural Dialogues". *Elements of Discourse Understanding* ed. by Aravind K. Joshi, Bonnie L. Webber & Ivan Sag, 84-105. Cambridge: Cambridge University Press.

Jackendoff, Ray. 1972. *Semantic Interpretation in Generative Grammar*. Cambridge, Mass.: MIT Press.

Horvath, Julia. 1995. "Structural Focus, Structural Case and the Notion of Feature Assignment". *Discourse-Configurational Languages* ed. by Katalin É. Kiss, 176-206. Oxford: Oxford University Press.

Kiss, Katalin É., ed. 1995. *Discourse Configurational Languages*. Oxford: Oxford University Press.

Lee, Dong-Young. 1996. "An HPSG Account of the Korean Honorification system". Grover & Vallduví 1996. 165-190.

Pierrehumbert, Janet. 1980. *The Phonology and Phonetics of English Intonation*. Ph.D. Dissertation, Cambridge, Mass.

Pollard, Carl & Ivan Sag. 1987. *Information-based Syntax and Semantics*. (Center for the Study of Language and Information Lecture Notes 13) Stanford.

——. 1994. *Head-driven Phrase Structure Grammar*. Chicago: Chicago University Press.

Prince, Ellen. 1981. "Towards a Taxonomy of Given-new Information". *Radical Pragmatics* ed. by Peter Cole, 223-255. New York: Academic Press.

Sag, Ivan & Tom Wasow. in prep. *Syntactic Theory: A formal introduction.* Stanford: CSLI Publications.

Selkirk, Elisabeth. 1984. *Phonology and Syntax: The relation between sound and structure.* Cambridge, Mass.: MIT Press.

Sidner, Candace L. 1981. "Focusing for Interpretation of Pronouns". *American Journal for Computational Linguistics* 7.217-231.

Uriagereka, Juan. 1995. "An F Position in Western Romance". Kiss 1995. 153-175.

Vallduví, Enric. 1992. *The Informational Component.* New York: Garland.

—— & Elisabet Engdahl. 1996. "The Linguistic Realization of Information Packaging". *Linguistics* 34.459-519.

Zubizarreta, Maria Luisa. 1994. "On Some Prosodically Governed Syntactic Operations". *Paths Towards Universal Grammar* ed. by Guglielmo Cinque, Jan Koster, Jean-Yves Pollock, Luigi Rizzi & Raffaella Zanuttini, 473-485. Georgetown University Press.

SUBJECT, NOMINATIVE CASE, AGREEMENT AND FOCUS*

MARA FRASCARELLI
Università degli Studi di Roma Tre

0. *Introduction*

This paper can be divided in two main parts examining two distinct but related phenomena. First, I analyse narrow Focus constructions, that is, sentences where new information is represented by only one constituent which carries the main prominence, whatever location it occupies in the sentence; this section also looks briefly at the realization of Focus for different levels of the grammar (syntax, phonology, pragmatics). In the second part of the paper the analysis concentrates on a set of peculiar phenomena occurring in some languages when a Subject (henceforth, SUBJ) is the Focus of the sentence; these are the absence of morphological Nominative (NOM) case (if available in the language) and the presence of 'anti-agreement effects',[1] i.e. the presence of an invariable (or reduced) form of verb Agreement (henceforth, AGR), irrespective of the features of the SUBJ.

The paper is organized as follows: Sections 1 introduces the notion of Focus and provides a general background on recent analyses while Section 2 investigates the formal characteristics of Focus. On the basis of the data discussed Section 3 argues for an analysis of Focus as a functional feature, whose interpretation is the consequence of a feature-checking process, a core mechanism in

* I wish to thank Annarita Puglielli, Lunella Mereu, Marco Svolacchia and Axmed Cabdullaahi Axmed for helpful comments and discussion. I have also benefited from suggestions and criticism from members of the European Colloquium on "The Boundaries of Morphology and Syntax".

[1] I take the term 'anti-agreement' from Ouhalla (1993). It must be said that anti-agreement effects can be found in a wider range of cases (when the SUBJ is wh-questioned, in negative sentences, in the presence of a preverbal QP, etc.) and it shows alternating effects according to the type of SUBJ movement (short vs. long; cf. Mereu this volume). The discussion of the entire range of cases, however, goes beyond the purposes of this paper (wh-questions are briefly addressed in Section 5.2). A more extensive application of the theory proposed on anti-agreement phenomena will be the subject of further work.

Chomksy's (1995) Minimalism.[2] Section 4 analyses NOM case and AGR in the light of feature-checking and anti-agreement (henceforth, AA) is illustrated using data from Selayarese, Trentino, Fiorentino and Somali. In Section 5 I will maintain that AA originates from a feature-checking 'conflict', that is to say a structure in which the SUBJ is in configuration with different heads for different checkings. This problematic situation is rescued by a repair strategy, illustrated in Section 6. Section 7 presents conclusive remarks.

The fundamental tenets for the present work are taken from the Minimalist framework of grammar (Chomsky 1995), especially the theory of feature-checking (see note 2). The aim of this paper is to provide a unified treatment of Focus and the interaction between AA, lack of (morphological) NOM Case and the role of the SUBJ.

1. *The notion of Focus*

Focus is generally associated with 'new information', although there is no general agreement on how this should be defined in a grammatical analysis. Two main types of Focus can be distinguished: broad (or presentational) Focus and narrow Focus. Broad Focus sentences carry 'all new' information, while in narrow Focus structures the informative content is restricted to a part of the constituents. The present study is concerned with narrow Focus (henceforth, simply Focus).

The literature on Focus provides several possible interpretations,[3] but they all appear problematic. Some scholars consider Focus on the basis of the opposition between new and old information. Rochmont (1986) defines Focus as the element which is not 'c-construable', i.e. which is not in the conversational context. This proposal is, however, hardly tenable since the Focus of an answer may also be presupposed:[4]

---

[2] Within the Minimalist Program, lexical items are assumed to be inserted in the numeration 'fully inflected' but, at a certain point of the derivation, all features must be checked in the relevant functional projections in order to be 'visible' (i.e., interpretable) at the interface levels of Phonetic Form and Logical Form (henceforth <PF, LF>). This operation is called 'feature-checking'. Given the basic principle of Economy, feature-checking preferably occurs in the covert component of LF. Nonetheless, if all costless options do not meet the principle of Full Interpretation (FI), feature-checking is realized in overt syntax. For this reason movement is considered a 'morphologic necessity': "move raises α only if morphological properties of α itself would not otherwise be satisfied in the derivation" (Chomsky 1995:261).

[3] In the following outline of Focus I will only consider generative literature. For other approaches to Focus, cf. Engdhal (this volume) and references therein cited.

[4] The Focus constituent is in small capitals.

(1) A: *La sorella di Carlo è partita da sola, vero?*
          "Carlo's sister left alone, didn't she?"

     B: *Ti sbagli, CARLO è andato con lei!*
          "You are wrong, CARLO went with her!"

CARLO is the Focus of the answer, but it cannot be considered 'new' in Rochemont's sense. It is not a new element, yet it carries new information because of its contrastive force.

Calabrese (1992) proposes that Focus be distinguished by the property of non-referentiality, so that it cannot form anaphoric chains in the Universe of Discourse (UD):

(2) a.   **The woman he$_i$ loved betrayed someone$_i$*
     b.   **The woman he$_i$ loved betrayed JOHN$_i$*

But, as Zubizarreta (1994) has shown, generic NPs, though they are not part of UD, can form binding relations:

(3) *When he$_i$ is hungry a tiger$_i$ may be dangerous*

Other scholars have based their analysis of Focus on the analogy with quantifiers. Brody (1990) for example proposes the well-known 'Focus criterion':

(4) a.   At S-structure and LF the Spec of an FP must contain a +f-phrase;
     b.   At LF all +f-phrases must be in an FP.[5]

The apparent simpleness of this criterion, however, is endangered by two orders of facts, whose importance is fundamental. First, Brody presents condition (4a) as a specific parameter of 'Focus-prominent' languages. However, this does not take into account the existence of some languages belonging to that typology, whose Focus must be obligatorily realized postverbally (from Tuller 1992):

---

[5] The 'Focus Phrase' (FP) is the functional projection which immediately dominates the sentential node (i.e., IP in pre- 'split-INFL hypothesis' terms, cf. Pollock 1989), whose Specifier (Spec) position contains the Operator-Focus constituent in case of syntactic (i.e., preverbal) Focus. The '+f feature' indicates, in Brody's (1990) terms, "identificational interpretation, i.e. focushood" (p. 208). As can be seen, this analysis proposes a perfect analogy between Focus and wh-constructions (cf. Rizzi's 1991 'wh-criterion').

(5) a.   *A wupə-(ro)   landai   GƏN SHIRE*   (Kanakuru)
           he sell-PAST-CL dress-the with her
           "He sold the dress TO HER"
     b.   *GƏN SHIRE a wupə -(ro) landai*[6]

Thus, Brody's Criterion makes wrong predictions cross-linguistically. Secondly, condition (4b) is proposed as the principle of UG governing Focus interpretation. However, it does not take the interpretation of in situ Focus into account. Let us consider (6):

(6) *I saw LUIGI at the cinema (not Mario)*

LUIGI is an in situ Focus but it is not the rightmost constituent of the sentence, so it cannot receive the main prominence by default. Nonetheless, it is correctly assigned the main prominence and interpreted as the Focus of the sentence. Now, if an in situ Focus must wait for LF operations to be interpreted as such, how can PF operate on the relevant structure? Since there is no contact between the two interface levels after Spell-Out,[7] it is difficult to obtain the correct output on Brody's terms.

The interpretation of in situ Focus has always been a problem and a free, non syntactic assignment has usually been proposed for it (cf. Horvath 1995). Such proposals make syntax fundamental for the interpretation of initial Focus,

---

[6] Abbreviations in the text and in glosses are the following:

AA	=	Anti-agreement	NOM	=	Nominative case
ACC	=	Accusative case	OBJ	=	object
AGR	=	agreement	OCL	=	object clitic
AgrOP	=	Object Agreement Phrase	PF	=	Phonetic Form
AgrSP	=	Subject Agreement Phrase	PL	=	plural
CL	=	clitic	PP	=	past participial
F	=	feminine	PRES	=	present tense
FI	=	Full Interpretation	PROG	=	progressive
FM	=	Focus Marker	(R)	=	restricted paradigm
FP	=	Focus Phrase	SCL	=	subject clitic
IMP	=	impersonal	SG	=	singular
INFL		inflection	Spec	=	Specifier
INT		intransitivizer prefix	S-structure	=	syntactic structure
LF		Logical Form	SUBJ	=	subject
M	=	masculine	XP,YP	=	the maximal projection level of a category X,Y
PAST	=	past tense			

[7] Within the Minimimalist framework, Spell-Out is the operation that "switches [the derivation] to the PF component" (Chomsky 1995:189). In other words, the point of Spell-Out marks the end of the computational process.

whereas in situ Focus rests on pragmatic interpretation. However, this dichotomy cannot be accepted in a grammar whose principles are based on economy.[8]

2.   *The formal characteristics of Focus*

Even though Focus shows various realizations cross-linguistically, it has some common features which must be taken into account.

2.1   *Prosodic data*

Within the framework of Prosodic Phonology (Nespor & Vogel 1986), prosodic constituents are the phonological translation of syntactic structure (after the 'mapping rules'). The argument structure is entirely included in an Intonational Phrase (I), while any extrasentential constituent forms an independent I. As for Focus constituents, several scholars have studied the interaction between Focus and prosodic constituency (cf. Inkelas & Zec, ed. 1990, Kenesei & Vogel 1990 among many others). Taking cross-linguistic studies as a starting point, a personal investigation on the prosody of Focus has provided evidence for the phrasal organization given in Table 1:[9]

a. [YP]$_I$ [**XP**$_{[+F]}$ verb]$_I$	Initial Focus marks the left boundary of its I.
b. [verb **XP**$_{[+F]}$]$_I$ [YP]$_I$	In situ Focus marks the right boundary of its I.
c. [verb]$_I$ [YP]$_I$ [**XP**$_{[+F]}$]$_I$	When Focus is not adjacent to the verb, the YP which is present between the Focus and the verb is included in a separate I.

Table 1: *Prosodic constituency in the presence of a narrow Focus*

This data sheds new light on Focus analysis. It shows that any element, except the verb, is excluded from the sentential I in the presence of a Focus. This leads to the conclusion that *Focus always marks one of the two boundaries of the sentential I.* Consequently, Focus always marks one of the two boundaries

---

[8] Reinhart (1995) radically eliminates this problem by proceeding in the pragmatic direction. She claims that the computational system derives only a "set of possible foci" (p. 75) and that marked Focus operations are always governed by discourse appropriateness. However, as the author herself observes, this seems to be too permissive a system and the problem is how and where to restrict it.

[9] To provide examples and discussion for the relevant data would take too long here. The interested reader may refer to Frascarelli (1997a,c and forthcoming).

of the syntactic argumental structure before Spell-Out.[10] In other words, in a narrow Focus structure, prosodic analysis provides evidence that any constituent which is not included in the Focus is extrasentential, i.e. a Topic.[11]

2.2 Word Order

Cross-linguistic data on linear order shows that there is a tight, obligatory relation between Focus and the verb. This relation has been noticed by many scholars, but it has been generally considered a property of Operator Focus (see note 5) or a characteristic of Focus-prominent languages. Our counterclaim is that this is a property shared by all kinds of foci: in any kind of language Focus must be adjacent to the verb, both in initial (cf. (7)-(8)) and in situ (cf. (9)-(10)) position:[12]

(7) a. *LUIGI ho   visto   al   cinema, non Mario*
        L.   have-1SG see-PP   at-the   cinema, not M.
        "I saw LUIGI at the cinema, not Mario"

    b. *[?]LUIGI al cinema ho visto, non Mario*

(8) a. *KITAAB-AN   qara?at   Zaynab-u*   (Ouhalla 1992)
        book-ACC   read-PAST.3SGF Z.-NOM
        "It was a book that Zaynab read"

    b. **KITAAB-AN Zaynab-u qara?at*

(9) a. *Ho visto LUIGI al cinema, non Mario*   (= (7))

    b. **[?]Ho visto al cinema LUIGI, non Mario*

(10) a. *Into the room walked JOHN*   (Lasnik & Saito 1992)

     b. *Into the room nude walked JOHN*

     c. **Into the room walked nude JOHN*

---

[10] Data shows that the behaviour of Focus does not change according to its particular 'degree of newness', since the focused XP and the verb always form one of the configurations shown in Table 1. Consequently, the contrast between different foci must be considered a pragmatic inference, while the interpretation of Focus is always a syntactic concern.

[11] Prosodic data seems thus to confirm and give new shape to Antinucci & Cinque's (1977) 'marginalization of the presupposed constituent'.

[12] There are languages like Italian that seem to allow a certain degree of toleration in this, so that Focus is not always adjacent to the verb. Nonetheless, it is important to keep in mind the possibility of inserting linguistic material between pauses in these languages, that is, the possibility of realizing virtually any kind of linear order adding parenthetical or topicalized constituents and forming marked intonational breaks. Prosodic structure (c) in Table 1 above represents exactly the case in point. Consequently, this cannot be considered a counterexample to grammatical rules and judgements must always be based on unmarked intonational melodies.

2.3 *Main Prominence*

A third formal element attested across languages is main prominence assignment. The Focus constituent carries the main prominence of the sentence, independently of its position.

This fact has been widely demonstrated for different languages and will not be treated further in the present work (the reader can refer to Chomsky 1971, Jackendoff 1972, Gussenhoven 1992, among many others).

3. *Focus and feature-checking*

Prosodic evidence and, in particular, verb adjacency lead to the following hypothesis for Focus:

(11) a.   Focus information is encoded in a strong feature [+F];
    b.   [+F] checking category is the verb.

This hypothesis represents a complete reversal of Brody's Criterion (4) since the crucial point for Focus interpretation is not the (overt/covert) substitution of the relevant XP in [Spec FP], but *verbal movement to F°* to check the [+F] feature and make it visible to interfaces. This movement must occur in overt syntax because [+F] provides instructions for both the conceptual-intentional level of LF and the articulatory-perceptual level of PF. For this reason [+F] is said to be 'strong' (cf. (11a)): it must be checked before Spell-Out in order to make its information interpretable at <PF, LF>. The movement of a focused XP to [Spec FP], on the other hand, is due to parametric variation and is not a crucial element in Focus interpretation.[13]

Following the feature-checking mechanism, [+F] checking requires a specific checking configuration between the checking category (the verb) and the relevant constituent. This is obtained through a local relation: Spec-Head (for syntactic Focus) or Head-Complement (for in situ Focus), respectively shown in (12a) and (12b):

(12a)
```
          FP
         /  \
       XP_i   F'
        |    /  \
        | V    AgrSP
      [+F]    /\
            ... t_i ...
```

(12b)
```
          FP
          |
          F'
         /  \
        V    AgrSP
        |    /\
        |  ...XP...
      [+F]
```

---

[13] Given this hypothesis, broad and narrow Focus sentences may be distinguished by the position of the verb inside IP (that is, in one of the many functional projections of INFL; refer to Pollock 1989, Chomsky 1991 and subsequent work) and in F° respectively.

Prosodic data shows that what is not included in the Focus is a Topic. This is a straightforward consequence of the Head-Complement configuration for [+F] checking in case of in situ Focus. As shown in (12b), only one XP can be realized within Subject Agreement Phrase (AgrSP) and focused in its argument position. All presupposed, non-Focus constituents must be realized in extrasentential position so as not to interfere with the relevant [+F] checking.[14] So, in situ and syntactic Focus constructions are *perfectly symmetrical*: there must be an exclusive relation between an in situ Focus and the verb just as in syntactic Focus there can be only one XP in Spec position. There is not 'free assignment', in situ Focus is visible at <PF, LF> because it is the only phonetically realized constituent inside AgrSP (which is the Complement of the verb in F°). We can assume that [+F] percolates[15] inside AgrSP and it needs to find one XP in order to be successfully realized (a feature can be checked only once).

As for word order, the strict adjacency between the Focus and the verb can be interpreted in the light of the relation existing between a Head and its Spec or its Complement.

Finally, main prominence assignment can be explained since in situ Focus reproduces the same formal conditions of a broad Focus sentence: the [+F] constituent is always the element marking the right boundary of AgrSP and is thus visible to PF.

Focus is therefore treated as a uniform phenomenon, in which the same conditions for interpretation hold both for initial and in situ realizations.[16] The

---

[14] If more than one XP were dominated by AgrSP, the verb in F° would assign [+F] to all of them, giving rise to a multiple Focus construction, which is barred by the grammar.

[15] Percolation is a standard device of all current theories to represent the idea that maximal projections project their properties to their heads and vice versa. Following Manzini (1994), we generalise this mechanism to the extent that an index (a feature, in this case) percolates "freely until it is blocked by an incompatible index" (p. 495). Since none of the maximal projections (AgrSP, VP, etc.) which dominate the Focus XP is Focus- or Case-marked, we conclude that none of them can block [+F] percolation.

[16] Chomsky (1995) actually reduces all checking operations to the Spec-Head relation, so that the Head-Complement option is abandoned in favour of Spec-Head checking in LF for in situ Focus. Though this problem needs further investigation, I think we can conform with this without confuting the theory. Since there are no contacts between the two interface levels and the (right-)boundary position of the Focus is necessary for main prominence facts (cf. Section 2.1), we can assume that both configurations are crucial for interpretation, but *not for both* interface levels. In other words, we can assume a 'split' in their range of activity so that PF interpretation relies on both configurations, while LF has access only to the Spec-Head relation. Consequently, in case of an in situ Focus, the constituent inside AgrSP must be submitted to LF substitution in [Spec FP] for the purposes of semantic/pragmatic interpretation, but its syntactic location is fundamental for PF visibility. I thank Nigel Vincent for posing this problem.

computational system operates in order to make [+F] visible to interfaces and this operation must occur in overt syntax since [+F] carries particular instructions to both PF and LF.[17]

To conclude, the arguments presented in the previous sections provide evidence for a theory of Focus as a feature-checking mechanism, which can be summarized as follows (for further details, cf. Frascarelli 1997a,b):

(13) a. Focus information is encoded in [+F] feature, generated in F°;
  b. [+F] is a strong feature to be checked before Spell-Out;
  c. the [+F] checking category is the verb;
  d. Focus visibility is obtained through the realization of a checking configuration between the verb and the relevant XP;
  e. all the linguistic material which is not included in the Focus must be extrasentential.

4. *Focus, nominative case and subject agreement*

Since Focus interpretation is part of the computational system, we expect it to interact and interfere with other syntactic operations. The aim of the second part of this paper is to illustrate this interaction. In particular, I will show that in the feature-checking mechanism, one syntactic operation can inhibit another so that only one can be performed in overt syntax and emerge in PF.

---

[17] This unified theory of Focus allows, among other things, an alternative approach to the analysis of postverbal SUBJs, whose role and structure have been widely investigated in recent literature (cf. Burzio 1986, Rizzi 1991, Zubizarreta 1994, among others). Although different, the various proposals agree that the postverbal SUBJ is located in a lower position than the 'canonical' one. Given the present proposal on Focus, the postverbal SUBJ is *not* a construction marked by a lower position of the SUBJ, but by a higher position of the verb, which raises to F° to check the [+F] feature with the SUBJ *in its canonical position*. Thus, in a sentence like Burzio's (1986):

(i)   *Giovanni*$_i$ *viene*   *lui*$_i$
      G.   come-PRES.3SG him

there are not 'two SUBJs' in the sentence, but a topicalized SUBJ (*Giovanni*) and a focused one (*lui*), in which the former is generated extrasententially, while the latter is in [Spec AgrSP]:

(ii) [$_{TopP}$ *Giovanni*$_k$ [$_{FP}$ [$_{F'}$ *viene*$_v$ [$_{AgrSP}$ *LUI*$_k$ [$_{AgrS'}$ t'$_v$ [$_{VP}$ t$_k$ t$_v$]]]]]]

The fact that *LUI* is a Focus can be immediately shown by a syntactic device. It is the only constituent which can be marked by the focusing adverb *solo* "only" (for critical discussion and details, cf. Frascarelli 1997a,b):

(iii) a.   *Giovanni viene*   *solo lui alla riunione*
           G.   come-PRES.3SG only him to-the meeting
      b.   **Solo Giovanni viene*   *lui alla riunione*
           Only G.   come-PRES.3SG him to-the meeting

4.1 *Focus, NOM and AGR as features*

In current Case Theory, a distinction is made between inherent case and structural case. The former is semantic, realized prepositionally or morphologically; the latter is grammatical, assigned to NPs according to their position in a structural configuration. NOM case is a typical structural case, a manifestation of a Spec-Head relation in AgrSP.

The Spec-Head configuration in AgrSP also realizes another feature, namely SUBJ AGR (in overt syntax for languages with a 'strong AGR', in LF in case of 'weak AGR'[18]):

(14) $[_{TopP} [_{FP} [_{AgrSP}$ SUBJ$_i$ $[_{AgrS'}$ verb $[_{VP}$ t$_i$ t$_V$]]]]]
     |___[AGR] / [NOM]___|

The lexical Head involved in both checkings is the verb, which raises to AgrS° where it checks the relevant features and makes them visible to <PF, LF>.

When a SUBJ is focused, the checking category involved in [+F] checking is once again the verb. Moreover, it seems plausible to claim that, like NOM, even Focus assignment is structural, since "[Focus assignment] never seems to be a lexically or thematically governed process" (Horvath 1995:35). In other words, Focus and NOM/AGR checkings share the same formal properties. Given these premises, let us consider some cross-linguistic data in which these structural operations seem to interact.

5.   *Cross-linguistic data*

5.1 *Selayarese*[19]

Selayarese is a VOS language, with both SUBJ and Object (OBJ) clitics, the former of which generally occurs as a verbal prefix (SCL = SUBJ clitic, OCL = OBJ clitic). As Finer (1994) considers SCLs and OCLs to be expressions of case and AGR features, we infer that they are located in AgrS° and AgrO° respectively (the latter being the head of the functional projection immediately dominating VP, cf. Chomsky 1995:173). (15) shows the locations of SCLs and OCLs with a transitive verb:

(15) *la$_i$-alle-i$_k$*   *doe$_k$ iñjo i Baso$_i$*
     SCL-take.PAST-OCL   money   the Baso
     "Baso took the money"

---

[18] The meaning of strong vs. weak features has been widely debated in recent literature and will not be treated here.

[19] Selayarese is an Austronesian language of the Makassar group, from Selayar Island, South Sulawesi Indonesia. The grammatical information and examples given in this section are taken from Finer (1994).

When the OBJ is indefinite, the OCL cannot be present, while the SCL is realized as a suffix of the verb, which also shows an 'intransitivizer' (INT) prefix, (a)ng:

(16) (a)ng-alle-kang   doe
     INT-take.PAST-SCL1PL money
     "We took some money"

Despite the fact that Selayarese is a VOS language, it allows arguments to appear in preverbal position, although in this case there are consequences for SUBJ interpretation, depending on the type of verb:

a) when the verb is transitive, the SUBJ can be placed before the verb without triggering either formal or pragmatic changes in the sentence:

(17) a. SVO i $Baso_i$ la_i-alle-i_k doe_k $iñjo$ (= (15))
     b. OSV doe_k $iñjo$ i $Baso_i$ la_i-alle-i_k (= (15))

b) with verbs bearing the INT marker, the initial position of the SUBJ necessarily triggers a specific pragmatic interpretation of the SUBJ itself: it will be either a Topic or the Focus of the sentence. In the latter case, the SCL cannot appear:

(18) i $BASO_i$ (a)ng-alle   (*-i_i)   doe
     B.   INT-take.PAST SCL   money
     "It was BASO who took some money"

(19) i $Baso_i$ (a)ng-alle-*(i_i)   doe
     B.   INT-take.PAST-SCL   money
     "As for Baso, he took some money"

We thus conclude that Selayarese preverbal SUBJs cannot be in their unmarked position (i.e., [Spec AgrSP]) in which NOM and AGR are checked, but in a higher location, triggering special pragmatic information. The question is, then, why do only Focus constituents interfere with the position and presence of the SCL?

5.2 Northern Italian Vernaculars[20]

Fiorentino (F) and Trentino (T) are two Northern vernaculars of Italian, in which SCLs are available. When the linear order of the sentence is unmarked (SVO), the SCL cannot be omitted (cf. (20)), while the case of the 'inverted SUBJ' shows some peculiarities (cf. (21)-(22)):

---

[20] The examples given in this section are taken from Brandi & Cordin (1989).

(20) a.   *Gianni e   parla   /   e   parla   F
             *El Gianni el parla   /   el   parla   T
             the G.   SCL speak-PROG.3SG / SCL speak-PROG.3SG
             "Gianni is speaking" / "(he) is speaking"
     b.   *Gianni parla /*El Gianni parla

(21) a.   gl'   ha   telefonato   le   tu'   sorelle   F
     b.   Ø   ha   telefonà   le   to'   sorelle   T
             SCL.IMP have-3SG telephone-PP the your   sisters
             "YOUR SISTERS telephoned"

(22) a.   gl'   ha   portato la torta le mi' amiche   F
     b.   Ø   ha   portà   la torta le m'   compagne T
             SCL.IMP have-3SG bring-PP the cake the my   friends
             "MY FRIENDS brought the cake"

As (21)-(22) show, in SUBJ inversion structures the verb shows an invariable third person singular and the SCL, when present, is the impersonal one,
both with intransitive and transitive verbs. Since in Italian a postverbal SUBJ is
typically interpreted as new information (see note 17), we can conclude that
these effects are triggered by the presence of a Focus (as in Selayarese).

Remarkably, the same morpho-syntactic behaviour is present when a preverbal SUBJ has the Operator function of contrastive Focus:

(23) a.   La MARIA gl'   /*l' ha   parlato, non la Carla   F
     b.   La MARIA Ø   /*l' ha   parlà,   no la Carla   T
             the M.   SCL.IMP/SCL have-3SG speak-PP, not the C.
             "MARIA spoke, not Carla"

Therefore, both contrastive and non contrastive Focus trigger the same effects,
providing further evidence in favour of a homogeneous approach to Focus.

Interestingly, AA effects can also be found when the SUBJ is wh-
questioned:[21]

(24) a.   Chi gl'   è venuto   con te?   F
     b.   Chi Ø   è vegnù   con ti?   T
             who SCL.IMP is come-PP   with you?
             "Who came with you?"

---

[21] AA in T and F can be also found in SUBJ (restrictive) relative clauses (see Mereu this volume). AA effects in F and T have been examined by several authors with different results (cf.
Brandi & Cordin 1989, Suñer 1992, Mereu this volume, among others). Mereu (1995) proposes
a 'mixed role' for clitics in these and other languages, so that they can act both as AGR morphemes and as arguments.

5.3 *Somali*[22]

Somali is a very interesting case, since the absence of NOM case and AA effects are combined.

The case system in Somali shows the opposition between an unmarked ACC form[23] (the quotation form) and a NOM case which marks the NP in [Spec AgrSP]. Somali is typically considered a Focus-prominent language, so that in a main declarative sentence one constituent must be overtly realized as the Focus of the sentence. Nominal Focus occurs obligatorily in preverbal position and it is marked by the Focus Marker (FM) *baa*, which follows it. The FM is a part of verb inflection, as shown in recent studies (cf. Svolacchia et al. 1995). Let us consider (25):

(25) *Nimankaas-u*$_i$ *hilib bay*$_i$ *(baa + ay)*   *cunayaan*
     men-those-NOM   meat FM-SCL   eat-PROG
     "Those men are eating MEAT"

In (25), the FM *baa* focuses the noun on its left (*hilib*), while the SUBJ *nimankaasu* is marked by NOM case (the suffix *-u*) and is coindexed with the SCL *ay* cliticized on the FM. However, when the SUBJ is the Focus of the sentence, a number of consequences arise. Let us consider (26) and the ungrammatical sentences in (27):

(26) *Hilib nimankaas baa cunayá*
     meat men-those FM eat-PROG (R)
     "THOSE MEN are eating meat"

(27) a.   **Hilib nimankaasu baa cunayá*
    b.   **Hilib nimankaas bay cunayá*
    c.   **Hilib nimankaas baa cunayaan*

Comparison between (26) and (27) shows that in Somali: a focused SUBJ cannot show NOM case (but it does show the unmarked ACC case); the SCL cannot appear (while it is obligatory in all other cases); there is not full agreement of the verb, but a form of the so-called 'restricted paradigm' instead.

---

[22] The grammatical information about Somali and the examples given in this section are taken from Svolacchia et al. (1995). For further details and discussion of the Somali phenomena at issue in this paper, cf. Lecarme (1995), Svolacchia & Puglielli (this volume), Mereu (this volume).

[23] It would perhaps be more correct to say that it is a 'non-NOM' form however, given the familiarity of the NOM/ACC opposition, the 'ACC' label is preferred.

Once again, SUBJ focusing seems to inhibit certain morpho-syntactic operations that are connected with the realization of features checked in Spec-Head relation in AgrSP.

6.   *The feature-checking conflict and the criterion of visibility*

The question is, why does Focus interfere with the realization of NOM case, SUBJ AGR and SCLs? A straightforward and unified solution can be provided by analysing the complementarity between NOM/AGR, on the one hand, and Focus, on the other, in the light of a *feature-checking conflict*. If correct, this explanation has important consequences for the theory of grammar.

The proposed conflict concerns the application of various checking operations which involve the same lexical categories *in different syntactic positions.* Such conflicts must be repaired in order to avoid a violation of FI requirements.[24] Let us consider this violation in detail.

As proposed in Section 4.1, Focus is a syntactic operation, a structural assignment, analogous to NOM case. Consequently, Focus interpretation is subject to the conditions operating on chains. So, when a SUBJ is the Focus, it forms a checking configuration with the verb in FP (cf. (12a,b)) and this relation gives rise to a chain which is interpreted in LF for [+F] information. According to the Chain Condition (Chomsky 1986), a chain can only have one position marked for case and one thematic position. For this reason, a focused SUBJ cannot form another chain with the verb in AgrSP to check NOM case: this 'double chain' would create a conflict and the structure would 'crash' at LF:

(28) * [$_{TopP}$ [$_{FP}$ SUBJ [$_{F'}$ V [$_{AgrSP}$ t'$_{SUBJ}$ [$_{AgrS'}$ t'$_V$ [$_{VP}$ t$_{SUBJ}$ t$_V$]]]]]]
               |___[+F]___| |__[AGR]/[NOM]__|

Therefore, even though the verb and a focused SUBJ form a Spec-Head relation in AgrSP, this relation cannot serve for the purposes of NOM feature-checking. We can assume that the computational system 'cancels' (this will be explained later) this checking relation for the sake of Focus checking and interpretation. This 'cancellation' has obvious consequences on AGR checking, too. Analysis of the data below highlights this conflict and suggests a possible solution.

6.1 *Selayarese*

In order to understand the syntactic reasons underlying the Selayarese phenomena, attention must be paid to the position of SCLs.

---

[24] The notion of FI requires that representations (and derivations) be 'minimal', so that no 'superfluous elements' be present in them (cf. Chomsky 1995:130).

Following Baker's (1985) 'Mirror Principle', the order of inflectional morphemes of the verb is the mirror of the syntactic operations which have produced it; in other words, it gives us information about the type and the extent of verb movement up the functional projections. On this basis, we can conclude that Selayarese verbs are located in different positions according to their type.

A transitive verb incorporates the OCL in AgrO° and adjoins the SCL in AgrS°.[25] Consequently, (15) has the structure represented in (29):

(29) $[_{FP}[_{F'}[_{AgrSP}pro_i[_{AgrS'}la_{SCL}\text{-}alle_V\text{-}i_{OCL}[_{TP}[_{T'}t'_{V+OCL}[_{AgrOP}[_{AgrO'}t_{V+OCL}[_{VP}t_V\ldots$

Since *la* is an expression of case and AGR, we assume an empty pronoun in SUBJ position, licensed by the verb in Spec-Head relation.

On the other hand, an intransitive use of the verb shows the presence of the INT prefix *(a)ng* and the SCL changes position, becoming a suffix of the verb. This can be interpreted as proof that the intransitive verb has incorporated the SCL (showing now on its right), rising to a higher node where it adjoins the prefix *(a)ng*. In other words, the contrast between verb morphology in transitive vs. intransitive structures provides evidence that an intransitive verb is not in AgrSP, but in F°. Sentence (16) can be thus analysed as follows:

(30) $[_{FP}\ [_{F'}\ (a)ng_{INTR}\text{-}alle_V\text{-}kang_{SUBJ}\ [_{AgrSP}\ pro_i\ [_{AgrS'}\ t_{V+SUBJ}[_{TP}\ t'_V\ [_{VP}\ t_V\ldots$

If our reasoning is correct, we can provide a plausible explanation for the data presented in Section 5.1.

In transitive sentences, the SUBJ can be in either periphery without triggering particular pragmatic interpretations because the verb is in AgrS°; consequently, the SUBJ can never be a Focus since [+F] has not been checked and it is invisible to interfaces. AGR and case checkings can thus freely occur between the verb and the SUBJ position.

In intransitive sentences, on the other hand, the verb has moved to F° (cf. (30)) and this is the reason why a preverbal SUBJ cannot be the grammatical SUBJ of an intransitive verb (cf. (18)-(19)). Since the verb is in F°, the SUBJ can only be in [Spec FP] or higher, in [Spec TopP], either as a Focus or as a Topic:

(31) $[_{FP}\ i\ BASO_i\ [_{F'}\ (a)ng\text{-}alle_V\ [_{AgrSP}\ t'_i\ \ [_{AgrS'}\ \ t_V\ [_{VP}\ t_i\ t_V\ doe\ ]]]]]$
    |_____[+F]_____| |_[AGR]/[NOM]_|

(32) $[_{TopP}\ i\ Baso_i\ [_{FP}\ [_{F'}(a)ng\text{-}alle_V\text{-}i_i\ [_{AgrSP}\ pro_i\ [_{AgrS'}\ \ t'_V\ [_{VP}\ t_V\ doe\ ]]]]]]$
                  |_[AGR]/[NOM]_|

---

[25] As for the order of elements, I use the notion of 'adjunction' in a 'loose way' with respect to the general principles stated in the recent literature (cf. in particular Baker 1985). The nature of the 'right adjunctions' of Selayarese verbs will be the subject of future research.

In (31), the SUBJ is in Spec-Head relation with the verb in FP to check [+F]. Consequently, the same two constituents cannot form another checking relation in AgrsP for NOM/AGR features. The latter relation is thus cancelled by the computational system in order to avoid a FI violation and allow Focus interpretation at <PF, LF>. No checking relation is therefore formed in AgrSP and the SCL, which is an expression of NOM and AGR features, is not licensed.

In (32), on the other hand, the SUBJ is a Topic, generated in TopP and is not in a checking configuration with the verb (cf. Frascarelli 1997a). For this reason, the verb can mantain the Spec-Head relation (through its trace) with the pro in [Spec AgrSP]. The SCL i is thus licensed and can emerge in PF.

6.2 *Northern Italian Vernaculars*

In the case of Italian vernaculars, the appearance of the SCL is similarly dependent on the presence of the verb in AgrS°, forming a Spec-Head relation with the SUBJ (or a pro-drop SUBJ).

However, when a Focus is present, the verb cannot be found in AgrS°, since it rises to F° to check [+F] and assign it to the 'postverbal SUBJ', which is actually in its canonical position (cf. note 17), or to the preverbal SUBJ, which is in [Spec FP] (only Fiorentino is considered here for ease of exposition):

(33) $[_{FP}$ $[_{F'}$ *gl'ha telefonato*$_v$ $[_{AgrSP}$ *le tu sorelle*$_k$ $[_{AgrS'}$ t'$_v$ $[_{VP}$ t$_k$ t$_v$]]]]]
        |_____[+F]_____| |_[AGR]/[NOM]_|

(34) $[_{FP}$ *la Maria*$_k$ $[_{F'}$ *gl'ha parlato*$_v$ $[_{AgrSP}$ t'$_k$ $[_{AgrS'}$ t'$_v$ $[_{VP}$ t$_k$ t$_v$]]]]]
        |_____[+F]_____| |_[AGR]/[NOM]_|

As (33)-(34) show, no Spec-Head relation can be realized in AgrSP in the relevant structures for the above reasons. Consequently, the SCLs *le* (3PLF) and *la* (3SGF) cannot be licensed and the impersonal clitic *gli* appears in their place. As for the reduced form of AGR, this can be considered a 'default' form, that is to say a form which does not need any feature-checking mechanism. It is a repair strategy which is available in some languages in order to make up for the lack of AGR morphology when no other form is allowed, as in the case of the feature-checking contrast created by SUBJ focalization.

The wh-SUBJ in (24) corroborates the present analysis. Recent studies on the nature of wh-questions (including Chomsky 1995) have proposed that they are the realization of a [+wh] feature checked by the verb in a functional projection higher than AgrSP. So, in this case too, the verb cannot be in AgrS° to check AGR and NOM features and the 'reduced AGR' is present again.

6.3 *Somali*

In the case of Somali too, the three phenomena which occur in SUBJ focalization are all linked and dependent on the checking configuration assumed by the verb and the SUBJ on the one hand, and by the SUBJ and the FM on the other. Let us consider the structure in (35), corresponding to (25):[26]

(35) [TopP *nimankaasu*$_k$ [FP*hilib* [F' *baa* [AgrSP *ay*$_k$ [AgrS' *cunayaan*$_V$ [VP t$_V$...
                          |__[+F]__| |__[AGR]/[NOM]__|

The verb, which shows AGR and Tense morphology, moves to AgrS°, while the FM (generated in F°; cf. Lecarme 1991) checks [+F] with the OBJ *hilib* in [Spec FP]. The SCL in [Spec AgrSP] is in the appropriate checking configuration with the verb for AGR and NOM features and the latter is transmitted to the SUBJ-Topic *via* binding. This configuration thus allows the presence of AGR and NOM morphology in the sentence.

When the SUBJ is the Focus, the conditions for AGR and NOM feature-checkings can no longer be realized:[27]

(36) [TopP *hilib* [FP *nimankaas*$_k$ [F' *baa* [AgrSP t'$_k$ [AgrS' *cunayàv*$_V$ [VP t$_k$ t$_V$ ...
                   |____[+F]____| |
        |_____[AGR]/[NOM]__|

As we can see, the SUBJ forms two checking configurations in this structure: one with the FM *baa* in FP and the other with the verb in AgrSP (through its trace). This is not allowed by the grammar and, as in the other languages examined, the PF output shows that only Focus information is selected so that the SUBJ is not marked for NOM case and AGR is present in a reduced form.

7. *Conclusions*

This data seems to provide evidence that Focus interpretation is governed by feature-checking and that when different checking operations are in conflict, the computational system selects a 'winner' for overt syntax, while all other operations are procrastinated in LF and will not have an overt realization. This conclusion has various consequences for the theory of grammar.

---

[26] I will follow Svolacchia et al. (1995) in assuming an argument role for SCLs, generated in AgrSP, while the SUBJ-Topic is generated extrasententially.

[27] Following Svolacchia et al.'s (1995) analysis, I assume that SUBJ NPs have an argument role in so far as they show complementarity with SCLs, when they are not topicalized (cf. *Cali baa /*buu moos cunay* "CALI ate a banana" vs. *Cali moos *baa/buu cunay* "as for Cali, he ate a BANANA"). However, see Svolacchia & Puglielli (this volume) for a different analysis of SUBJ NPs in Somali, in which full NPs are always extrasentential and an empty pronoun (pro) is proposed in SUBJ position when no SCL is allowed.

7.1   The 'visibility principle'

Syntactic feature-checking seems to be subject to a 'priority principle'. As we have seen, NOM case and AGR checkings are procrastinated in favour of other checkings (i.e., [+F] and [+wh] feature-checkings). How is this selection operated? I propose the relevant criterion to be one of *visibility at interfaces*.

Within the Minimalist framework, the interface levels <PF, LF> are the only 'conceptually necessary' ones and UG must specify "the elements that constitute these levels and the computations by which they are constructed" (Chomsky 1995:169). The feature-checking mechanism may therefore be considered a formal device to represent the necessity and the process of making information visible at interfaces for interpretation.

On this basis, [+F] checking is a legitimate operation for both interface levels since it corresponds both to a specific phonological instruction (main prominence) and to a specific semantic notion (new/contrastive information). There is no way of recovering this information unless [+F] is checked in overt syntax. Its visibility would otherwise be lost. On the other hand, NOM case does not have a specific semantic content. It is more abstract and its information can be recovered in overt syntax. by other elements (word order, adjacency to the verb, context, etc.). SUBJ AGR is likewise generally recoverable. Moreover, NOM case and AGR may not have morphologic realizations cross-linguistically.

In conclusion, given a principle of 'visibility priority' at <PF, LF>, the [+F] feature shows obligatory (morpho-)phonological and semantic requirements which cannot be eluded. For this reason the computational system solves the feature-checking conflict by procrastinating those features whose interpretation can be otherwise recovered.

7.2   Consequences for Case Theory

Current Case Theory can be summarized as follows (cf. Chomsky 1995:110-124):

(37) a. every N in the numeration has a case;
     b. every case must be checked (the former 'Case Filter').

In a recent study, Longobardi (1997) has pointed out that this theory encounters several problems. In particular, the distribution of case to the right or to the left of a Head relevant for checking is unexplained. Moreover, the behaviour of NOM case in some languages (such as Dutch, Italian and Arabic) has led Koopman & Sportiche (1988), followed by many others, to propose that NOM case can be assigned under government as well (though a structural case). How and why some languages should allow such an option is unexplained.

The alternations shown by case marking in this paper cast additional doubt on the adequacy of present Case Theory. A possible solution could be that of eliminating the 'Case Filter' as a condition for overt syntax. If a checking conflict arises, (structural) case can be checked in LF.

Naturally, if case checking is procrastinated, the relevant NP cannot simply 'lack a case', but we may plausibly propose that a 'default' case assignment will be at work. Thus, the relevant SUBJ will show the case that a language provides as unmarked, i.e., the quotation form of a noun. Obviously, when NOM case is the default case of a language, no conflict is evident. This is the reason why we do not very often see any case consequence on Focus SUBJs. Somali, however, which has ACC as the unmarked case, seems to support this hypothesis.[28]

7.3 Consequences for SUBJ AGR analysis

As far as AGR is concerned, its alternations have generally been explained through the relative position of the SUBJ and the verb only. Greenberg's (1966) Universal 33 generalized that "when number agreement between the noun and the verb is suspended and the rule is based on order, the case is always one in which the verb precedes and the verb is in the singular" (p. 94).

On the basis of the present analysis, the lack of AGR with a postverbal SUBJ can be interpreted in the light of a higher position of the verb (higher than AgrSP), to which it moves in order to meet some specific morphological requirement whose visibility conditions overtake agreement. On the other hand, when the SUBJ is in preverbal position and AA effects are also present, our theory predicts that the SUBJ is not located in the canonical SUBJ position, but in a higher node (namely, FP), in Spec-head relation with the verb.

Further research will be extended to other languages where the relevant conflicts can be found, in order to verify the present proposals.

REFERENCES

Antinucci, Francesco & Guglielmo Cinque. 1977. "Sull'Ordine delle Parole in Italiano: L'emarginazione". *Studi di grammatica italiana* 6.121-146.
Baker, Mark. 1985. "The Mirror Principle and Morphosyntactic Explanation". *Linguistic Inquiry* 16.373-417.
Brandi, Luciana & Patrizia Cordin. 1989. "Two Italian Dialects and the Null Subject Parameter". *The Null Subject Parameter* ed. by Osvaldo Jaeggli & Ken J. Safir, 111-142. Dordrecht: Kluwer.

---

[28] The idea of a 'default Case' has already been supported in the literature; see Everaert (1990), among others.

Brody, Michael. 1990. "Some Remarks on the Focus Field in Hungarian". *University College London Working Papers in Linguistics* 2.201-225.

Burzio, Luigi. 1986. *Italian Syntax: A government-binding approach.* Dordrecht: Reidel.

Calabrese, Andrea. 1992. "Some Remarks on Focus and Logical Structure in Italian". *Harvard Working Papers in Linguistics* 1.91-127.

Chomsky, Noam. 1971. "Deep Structure, Surface Structure and Semantic Interpretation". *Semantics: An interdisciplinary reader in philosophy, linguistics and psychology* ed. by Danny D. Steinberg & Leon A. Jakobovits, 183-216. Cambridge: Cambridge University Press.

——. 1986. *Knowledge of Language: Its nature, origin and use.* New York: Praeger.

——. 1991. "Some Notes on Economy of Derivation and Representation". *Principles and Parameters in Comparative Grammar* ed. by Robert Freidin, 417-454. Cambridge, Mass.: MIT Press.

——. 1995. *The Minimalist Program.* Cambridge, Mass.: MIT Press.

Cinque, Guglielmo. 1990. *Types of A'-Dependencies.* Cambridge, Mass.: MIT Press

Everaert, Martin. 1990. "Nominative Anaphors in Icelandic: Morphology or syntax?". *Issues in Germanic Syntax* ed. by Werner Abraham, Wim Kosmejer & Eric Reuland, 277-307. Berlin: Mouton de Gruyter.

Finer, Daniel L. 1994. "On the Nature of Two A'-Positions in Selayarese". *Studies on Scrambling* ed. by Norbert Corver & Henk van Riemsdijk, 153-184. Berlin: Mouton de Gruyter.

Frascarelli, Mara. 1997a. *L'Interfaccia Sintassi-Fonologia nelle Costruzioni di Focalizzazione e Topicalizzazione dell'Italiano.* PhD. Dissertation, Università di Roma Tre.

——. 1997b. "Focus e 'Feature-checking': Un'ipotesi minimalista". *Lingua e Stile* 32:2.247-272.

——. 1997c. "The Phonology of Focus and Topic in Italian". *The Linguistic Review* 14.221-248.

——. forthcoming. "The Prosody of Focus in Italian (and the Syntax-Phonology Interface)". *Probus.* 12.3.

Greenberg, Joseph. H. 1966. "Some Universals of Grammar with Particular Reference to the Order of Meaningful Elements". *Universals of Language* ed. by Joseph H. Greenberg, 73-113. Cambridge, Mass.: MIT Press.

Gussenhoven, Carlos. 1992. "Sentence Accents and Argument Structure". *Thematic Structure: Its role in grammar* ed. by Iggy M. Roca, 79-106. Berlin & New York: Foris.

Horvath, Julia. 1995. "Structural Focus, Structural Case and the Notion of Feature Assignment". *Discourse-Configurational Languages* ed. by Katalin É. Kiss, 176-206. Oxford: Oxford University Press.

Inkelas, Sharon & Draga Zec, eds. 1990. *The Phonology-Syntax Connection.* Chicago: University of Chicago Press.

Jackendoff, Ray. 1972. *Semantic Interpretation in Generative Grammar*. Cambridge: Cambridge University Press.

Kenesei, Istvan & Irene Vogel. 1990. "Focus and Phonological Structure". Paper presented at the GLOW XIII meeting, Cambridge and London, 6-8 April 1990.

Koopman, Hilda & Dominique Sportiche. 1988. "The Position of Subjects". *Lingua* 85.211-258.

Lasnik, Howard & Mamoru Saito. 1992. *Move α*. Cambridge, Mass.: MIT Press.

Lecarme, Jacqueline. 1991. "Focus en Somali: Syntaxe et interprétation". *Liguistique Africaine* 7.33-65.

———.1995. "L'accord restrictif en Somali". *Langues Orientales Anciennes, Philologie et Linguistique* 5-6.133-152.

Longobardi, Giuseppe. 1997. "Case Theory and the Minimalist Program". Paper presented at the GLOW XX meeting, Rabat, 19-21 March 1990.

Manzini, Maria Rita. 1994. "Locality, Minimalism and Parasitic Gaps". *Linguistic Inquiry* 25:3.481-508.

Mereu, Lunella. 1995. "Verso una Tipologia dell'Accordo Verbo-Soggetto". *Rivista di Linguistica* 7:2.333-367.

Nespor, Marina & Irene Vogel. 1986. *Prosodic Phonology*. Dordrecht: Foris.

Ouhalla, Jamal. 1992. "Focus in Standard Arabic". Unpublished Manuscript, Queen Mary and Westfield College, London.

———. 1993. "Subject-Extraction, Negation and the Anti-agreement Effect". *Natural Language and Linguistic Theory* 11.477-518.

Pollock, Jean-Yves. 1989. "Verb Movement, Universal Grammar, and the Structure of IP. *Linguistic Inquiry* 20.365-425.

Reinhart, Tanya. 1995. "Interface Strategies". *Onderzoeksinstituut voor Taal en Spraak Working Papers,* Utrecht.

Rizzi, Luigi. 1991. "Residual Verb Second and the Wh-Criterion". *Technical Reports in Formal and Computational Linguistics* 2. Université de Genève. (Reprinted in *Parameters and Functional Heads: Essays in comparative syntax* ed. by Adriana Belletti & Luigi Rizzi. (Oxford Studies in Comparative Syntax) New York & Oxford: Oxford University Press.).

Rochemont, Michael. 1986. *Focus in Generative Grammar*. Amsterdam & Philadelphia: John Benjamins.

Suñer, Margarita. 1992. "Subject Clitics in the Northern Italian Vernaculars and the Matching Hypothesis". *Natural Language and Linguistic Theory* 10.641-672.

Svolacchia, Marco, Lunella Mereu & Annarita Puglielli. 1995. "Aspects of Discourse Configurationality in Somali". *Discourse-Configurational Languages* ed. by Katalin É. Kiss, 65-98. Oxford: Oxford University Press.

Tuller, Laurice. 1992. "The Syntax of Postverbal Focus Constructions in Chadic". *Natural Language and Linguistic Theory* 10.303-304.

Zubizarreta, María Luisa. 1994. "The Grammatical Representation of Topic and Focus: Implication for the structure of the clause". *University of Venice Working Papers in Linguistics* 4:1.97-126.

THE ENGLISH CLEFT CONSTRUCTION AS A FOCUS PHRASE

KATALIN. É. KISS
Hungarian Academy of Sciences

0. *Introduction*

This paper will argue that the English Cleft Construction, whose analysis and derivation raises various, so far unsolved, syntactic and semantic questions, is the realization of a Focus Projection (FP), with the cleft constituent occupying Spec,FP. Under this assumption, the so far problematic syntactic and semantic properties of the cleft construction all become predictable.

The theoretical assumptions and notions on which the proposal is built are those of the Principles and Parameters version of generative theory in the early nineties.

Section 1 of the paper will present the syntactic and semantic properties of the English cleft construction to be accounted for. Section 2 will survey previous analyses of the phenomenon, pointing out their inadequacies. Section 3 will present the new proposal, showing how the properties described in section 1 fall out from it.

1. *The English Cleft Construction*

The English cleft construction appears to consist of a relative clause headed by the cleft constituent preceded by the copula and the expletive *it*. However, the relation between the 'wh-clause' or 'that-clause' and the cleft constituent is different from the relation between a relative clause and its head in several respects. A relative clause analysis cannot predict the following cleft construction properties:

i. The cleft constituent shows so-called connectedness effects, i.e., it has properties which are licensed in a position inside the relative clause. For example, it can be bound by a constituent in the relative clause, as if it were c-commanded by it:

(1) a. It is each other$_i$ that they$_i$ trust the most.
    b. It was a picture of myself$_i$ that I$_i$ was looking for.

Certain connectedness effects are absent when the cleft constituent corresponds to the subject of the relative clause. Thus a cleft subject is in the accusative case in standard English:

(2) It is me/him who is responsible.

Furthermore, if the cleft subject is other than 3rd person, the embedded verb does not agree with it; the verb is always 3rd person:

(3) a.   It is me who is not satisfied with himself.
     b.   *It is me who am not satisfied with myself.

At the same time, as Akmajian (1970) points out, there is a dialect in which connectedness optionally extends to cleft subjects as well. In this dialect, (4a) is also an option, in addition to (4b). In (4a), connectedness extends to both case-marking and agreement with the Verb (V). In (4b), on the other hand, the cleft constituent and the embedded subject are not connected in either respect. (4c) and (4d), in which the cleft constituent is connected to the embedded subject only in one respect (agreement in (4c) and case-marking in (4d)) are ungrammatical.[1]

(4) a.   It is I who am responsible.
     b.   It is me who is responsible.
     c.   *It is me who am responsible.
     d.   *It is I who is responsible.

ii. As a different instantiation of the connectedness effects, a quantifier in the embedded clause of a cleft construction can have matrix scope – even though in other types of embedded sentences it cannot scope out of its clause. Compare:

(5) a.   It was some paper by Chomsky that everybody wanted to read for the exam.
     b.   I have some paper by Chomsky that everybody wanted to read.
     c.   He said about some paper by Chomsky that everybody wanted to read it.

In (5a) *everybody* can have scope over *some paper* (that is, the referent of *some paper* can covary with the entities in the domain of the universal quantifier), whereas in the regular complex sentences in (5b,c) the maximal scope of the universal quantifier is the embedded clause.

iii. If the cleft constituent is a PP, the embedded clause may lack an otherwise obligatory preposition. Whereas (6b) is ungrammatical with the preposition

---

[1] For some further details, see Akmajian (1970).

spelt out, in an ordinary relative clause we find the opposite situation: (7a), in which the preposition is missing, is out, and (7b) is in.

(6) a. It was to John that I spoke.
    b. *It was to John that I spoke to.
(7) a. *He gave the book to the man that I spoke.
    b. He gave the book to the man that I spoke to.

iv. The tense of the matrix *be* either agrees with the embedded tense, or is a default present tense (as observed by Meinunger 1996):

(8) a. It was John who was responsible.
    b. It is John who was responsible.

v. The cleft constituent cannot be a universal quantifier, or an 'even phrase', and it can be an 'also phrase' only in special contexts such as (9d):

(9) a. *It was everybody that John invited.
    b. *It was even Mary that John invited.
    c. A: "John invited almost everybody."
        B: *"Yes. It was also Mary that he invited."
    d. A: "John invited only Susan."
        B: "No. It was also Mary that he invited."

vi. As Emonds (1976) observed, basically only NPs and PPs can be clefted; APs, AdvPs, VPs, and most types of that-clauses cannot. Compare the following examples by Emonds (1976:133, 138-141):

(10) a. It was a tax break I counted on.
     b. It was to John that I spoke.
     c. It was because it was raining that I left.
     d. *It is quite unhappy that Bill is.
     e. *It was explicitly that he rejected our assumptions.
     f. *It was ask John for money that I heard you.
     g. *It was to buy a new house that I wanted.
     h. *It was that Mary came home early that John was happy about.
     i. It was buying a new hat that I enjoyed.

vii. The cleft constituent expresses exhaustive identification. That is, the meaning of (11a) can be paraphrased as (11b):

(11) a. It was John that invited Mary.
     b. "Of a set of relevant persons it is true of John and noone else that he invited Mary."

As the paraphrases make clear, the cleft constituent presupposes a set of relevant entities for which the predicate can potentially hold, and exhaustively identifies the proper subset of this set for which the predicate actually holds. The operation of exhaustive identification can also be pointed out by tests – see Szabolcsi (1981). One of Szabolcsi's tests is based on the comparison of a minimal pair one member of which contains a focused co-ordinate phrase (12a), and the other has one of the co-ordinate phrases dropped (12b). If the second sentence is not a logical consequence of the first sentence, but contradicts it, the focused phrases (in our case, the cleft constituents) express exhaustive identification.

> (12) a. It was JOHN and PETER that invited Mary.
>   b. It was JOHN that invited Mary.

In a situation in which (12a) is true, (12b) cannot also be true, which is evidence of the fact that the cleft constituent expresses exhaustive identification.

2. *Previous analyses*

The first analysis of the cleft construction in the generative framework was put forth by Akmajian (1970). He derived the cleft construction from the pseudo-cleft construction by extraposition. More precisely, he claimed that the underlying source of a cleft sentence is a pseudo-cleft sentence with a reduced initial relative clause, whose head is a dummy it - see (13a). The relative clause within the pseudo-cleft construction is subject to the Cleft Extraposition Rule, which results in the cleft construction in (13b):

> (13) a. [$_{NP}$ it [$_S$ who is sick]] is me →
>   b. it is me [$_S$ who is sick]

Akmajian's solution was designed primarily to account for the agreeement facts of standard English, in which the embedded V does not agree with a cleft subject in person but is always 3rd person – see (3a,b). In Akmajian's framework this fact falls out from the fact that the subject of the embedded sentence, with which the embedded V agrees, is the 3rd person relative pronoun. The agreement facts of the dialect in which the embedded V can agree with the cleft subject (examples (4a-d)), on the other hand, cannot be derived in a straightforward way. Nor do any of the other properties of the cleft construction enumerated in section 1 follow from the proposed analysis. For example, it remains a mystery what licenses the anaphor in (1a,b) it is not c-commanded by its antecedent at any step of the derivation.

Akmajian's theory was criticized in the seventies primarily because it could not derive sentences of the following type:

(14) It was to John that I spoke.

He had to assume the following unlikely deep structure:

(15) [$_{NP}$ it [$_S$ that I spoke]] was to John

The primary intention of the theory put forth in Emonds (1976) was to derive sentences of type (14). In Emond's theory, cleft constructions are derived from subject clauses, with the consecutive applications of the rules of focus placement, optional relativization, and cleft extraposition. The source of (14) is the structure in (16):

(16) [that I spoke to a friend] was

An NP or PP of the subject clause can undergo focus placement of the following kind:

(17) a.   [that I spoke t] was [$_{PP}$ to a friend]
    b.   [that I spoke to t] was [$_{NP}$ a friend]
    c.   [that I spoke to him] was [$_{NP}$ a friend]

In (17c) the place of the focus-moved NP is filled by a resumptive pronoun. If this option is chosen, the resumptive pronoun, or the PP dominating it, must be supplemented with a wh-feature, and must undergo wh-fronting:

(18) a.   [who I spoke to] was a friend
    b.   [to whom I spoke] was a friend

If the derivation proceeds via the intermediate structure in (17a) or (17b), the complementizer is optionally deleted:

(19) a.   (that) I spoke was to a friend
    b.   (that) I spoke to was a friend

Eventually, cleft extraposition takes place, and the empty subject position is filled by an expletive *it*. Depending on whether these operations are performed on the intermediate structures in (19a,b) or (18a,b), the following outputs may arise:

(20) a.   It was to a friend (that) I spoke.
    b.   It was a friend (that) I spoke to.
    c.   It was a friend to whom I spoke.
    d.   It was a friend who I spoke to.

Since in Emonds's derivation the cleft constituent originates in the relative clause, the connectedness facts fall out. It is less clear how the lack of connectedness effects in the case of cleft subjects can be explained. However, the main problem with Emonds's solution is that it is very stipulative. The initial structure is highly unlikely, and the focus placement rule assumed is not independently motivated. It also remains unclear why cleft extraposition is obligatory, when subject clause extraposition, generally, is optional.

Chomsky (1977) proposes an alternative solution to the problem represented by the cleft construction in (14). He claims that the underlying structure of all cleft sentences is of the following type:

(21) It is S''

S'' is a potential domain of Topicalization and Adverbial Preposing, both of which go together with wh-movement in the theory of Chomsky (1977). For example:

(22) a.   It was [$_{S''}$ this book [$_{S'}$ which/that I read t]]
    b. . It was [$_{S''}$ to a friend [$_{S'}$ 0/that I spoke t]]

The theory not only motivates structure (22b) by relating it to Adverbial Preposing, but also accounts for the connectedness effects; it also explains the Subjacency attested between the cleft constituent and the empty position in the embedded clause,[2] i.e., it explains the grammaticality difference between (23a) and (23b) (cf. Chomsky [1977:95]):

(23) a.   It is this book that I asked Bill to get his students to read.
    b.   *It is this book that I wonder who read.

The most obvious problem that Chomsky's theory raises is that if the cleft constituent is indeed moved out of the embedded clause, the wh-pronoun has no source. The analogy with Topicalization and Adverbial Proposing is not complete: whereas Topicalization and Adverbial Preposing involve neither an overt relative pronoun nor an overt complementizer, the cleft constituent can or, when represented by a subject, must be followed by one or the other. It also remains unexplained why the cleft constituent obligatorily expresses exhaustive identification and why it is associated with the distributional restrictions illustrated in (9).

3. *A new proposal*

It will be argued below that the cleft construction is the realization of a functional projection called focus phrase (FP), and the cleft constituent itself is

---

[2] The cleft constituent must be subjacent to the clause in which it binds an empty position or a wh-pronoun; i.e., no syntactic barrier can intervene between them. (23b) is ungrammatical because the object trace intended to be bound by the cleft constituent is in a wh-island, behind a barrier.

a type of focus operator occupying Spec,FP, expressing exhaustive identification.

The notion of focus projection adopted in this paper goes back to Brody (1990). He claims that in the type of language which has an invariant focus position, the focus occupies the Specifier of a functional projection which he calls focus phrase. In the language analyzed by Brody in detail, Hungarian, the focus position immediately precedes the inflected V, hence Brody (1990) assumes that FP immediately dominates VP. (The FP projection can be dominated by quantifier and topic projections, and eventually, a CP, which are irrelevant in the present context.)

The V, which normally follows the verbal prefix in Hungarian – see (24a), precedes it in the presence of a focus, which Brody derives from the assumption that the V undergoes V-to-F movement across the verbal prefix:

(24) a. [$_{VP}$ *meg ette János a levest*]
          up   ate John the soup
          "John ate the soup."

     b. [$_{FP}$ *A LEVEST$_i$ ette$_j$* [$_{VP}$ *meg* t$_j$ *János* t$_i$]]
          "It was the soup that John ate."

Brody (1990) concludes that the F head of the focus projection must be lexicalized by V movement into it, which he derives from the assumption that the source of the focus feature to be assigned to the constituent in Spec, FP is the V. Consider the structure of (24b):[3]

(25)

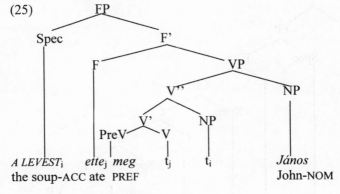

A LEVEST$_i$ ette$_j$ meg   t$_j$ t$_i$ János
the soup-ACC   ate PREF   John-NOM

---

[3] Abbreviations in the text and in glosses are the following:

ACC =	Accusative case	PREF=	verbal prefix
FP =	Focus Phrase	SG =	singular form
NOM=	Nominative case		

Brody (1990) assumes the following Focus Criterion:

(26) Focus Criterion
    a.   At S-structure and LF the Spec of an FP must contain a [+f]
        phrase.
    b.   At LF all [+f] phrases must be in an FP.

Whereas (26b), i.e., the requirement that constituents with an [identificational]
focus feature be located in FP in logical form, is claimed to hold universally,
(26a), i.e., the requirement that constituents with an [identificational] focus
feature be moved to Spec,FP visibly, at S-structure already, is assumed to be
parametrized. It is a feature of languages like Hungarian, but not of languages
like English, where the focus is assumed to occupy Spec,FP only at LF.

I will argue below that (26a) may be satisfied in English as well, i.e. English sentences with a focus expressing exhaustive identification can also contain a focus projection at S-structure. In English the realization of the FP projection is the cleft construction. If we complement Brody's theory with the assumption that an F head takes in some languages a CP complement instead of a
VP, then we can account for all the properties of the cleft construction enumerated in section 1. The structure to be assigned to example (1a) differs from
standard assumptions only in that the embedded CP is dominated by an FP
projection:

(27)

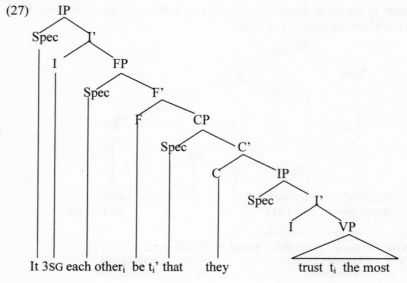

The cleft constituent originates in the embedded clause, and is preposed into Spec,FP via Spec,CP. (This transformation can also be referred to as focus movement.) The fact that the root of the chain headed by the phrase in Spec,FP (each other) is c-commanded by the embedded subject explains why it can be bound by the embedded subject. The head position of FP must be lexicalized by a verb, as in the case of Hungarian. However, the embedded verb is not available, and an embedded auxiliary would not be available either. In the case of (27) it is the intervening complementizer that blocks V movement into F. V movement and I movement cannot cross the CP boundary when the complementizer is covert. Apparently, an auxiliary adjoined to C cannot leave the CP; or an auxiliary adjoined to C is not an acceptable lexicalizer for F. Consequently, F is lexicalized by the dummy be. Be must combine with tense and agreement morphemes, hence it is raised to I. The Extended Projection Principle requires that Spec,IP always be filled, hence it is filled by the dummy it. By spec-head agreement, the V be will bear a 3rd person singular agreement marker. Its tense is either a copy of the embedded tense, or is a default simple present.

In cleft constructions in which the Spec,CP of the embedded clause is filled by a wh-pronoun, the cleft constituent is, in all probability, generated in Spec,FP, and it is associated with the wh-chain in the embedded clause by coindexing. That is, the cleft constructions containing a wh-pronoun are base-generated structures. The cleft construction containing a *that* complementizer, on the other hand, can be derived by focus movement. At the same time, the base-generated analysis cannot be excluded either because a 'that-clause' can also contain a covert relative wh-phrase. As is well-known from Cinque (1990), a chain derived by coindexation instead of movement can also display connectedness effects, e.g. with respect to binding.

When the cleft constituent is the understood subject of the embedded clause, the structure can only be derived with the focus base-generated in Spec,FP. Cf.

(28) a. It was me who did it.
     b. It was me that did it.
     c. *It was me did it.

In (28a), focus movement into Spec,FP is blocked by Subjacency: the relative pronoun in Spec,CP occupies the intermediate landing site. In (28b), on the other hand, focus movement is blocked by the ECP: the intervening complementizer in C would prevent the proper government of the subject trace by the trace in Spec,CP. (28c) is ruled out by the independent constraint that does not

license clauses with an empty subject and a covert complementizer, such as
*We talked about the man came in.

The fact that the cleft subject is base-generated in Spec,FP explains why it
does not have to bear nominative case. In present-day standard English the default form of personal pronouns is me, you, him, her, it, us, them; this is the
form that has to be used in non-case-marked positions, e.g. predicatively. Apparently, in certain dialects the nominative form is (or can be regarded as) the
default form; in these dialects the nominative form is used in Spec,FP, too (as
in (4a)). There still remains the question of what accounts for the dialectal facts
illustrated in (4a-d), rewritten here as (29a-d):

(29) a.   It is me who is responsible.
     b.   It is I who am responsible.
     c.   *It is me who am responsible.
     d.   *It is I who is responsible.

In (29a) me and who form a referential chain; who is referentially dependent on
me. Referential dependence is sufficient to licence connectedness effects with
respect to binding (cf. It is me$_i$ who$_i$ t$_i$ cut myself$_i$); however, since me and who
are distinct with respect to case, they cannot form an agreement chain. In this
dialect, apparently, non-distinctness with respect to case is sufficient to license
a chain which displays connectedness with respect to agreement as well as
happens in (29b).

In our approach, the PP occupying Spec,FP in cleft constructions like (6a), rewritten here as (30), is preposed there through Spec,CP by focus movement:

(30) It was [$_{FP}$ to Peter$_i$ [$_{CP}$ t$_i$ that [$_{IP}$ he spoke t$_i$]]]

The base-generated variant of (30) is (31a). (31b) is illegitimate because the
wh-pronoun, an NP, is categorially different from the IP-internal gap, a PP,
whereas (31c) is illegitimate because who is categorially different from the
head of the referential chain: to Peter.

(31) a.   It was [$_{FP}$ to Peter$_i$ [$_{CP}$ to whom$_i$ [$_{IP}$ he spoke t$_i$]]]
     b.   *It was [$_{FP}$ to Peter$_i$ [$_{CP}$ who$_i$ [$_{IP}$ he spoke t$_i$]]]
     c.   *It was [$_{FP}$ to Peter$_i$ [$_{CP}$ who$_i$ [$_{IP}$ he spoke to t$_i$]]]

A crucial property of the cleft constituent is that it expresses exhaustive identification, i.e., it represents the value of an operator which exclusively identifies
the proper subset of a set of relevant entities for which the predicate holds. É.
Kiss (1998) demonstrates on the basis of cross-linguistic evidence that in languages like Hungarian or Greek, which have both a structural focus position
and a focus in situ, only the structural focus, i.e., the constituent in Spec,FP,

expresses exhaustive identification; the focus in situ is a mere information focus. It is concluded that the semantic function 'exhaustive identification' is a
function associated with Spec, FP. In other words, the constituent in Spec,FP is
to be interpreted semantically as the value of a semantic operator expressing
exhaustive listing. This fact has various syntactic consequences as well, which
are at the same time diagnostic of the presence of identificational focus. For
example: since an identificational focus operator identifies a proper subset of a
relevant set, its value cannot be a quantifier whose value is other than the
proper subset of a relevant set. Thus it cannot be a universal quantifier, an
'even phrase' or an 'also phrase' (given that *also* X and *even* X mean
"everybody of a relevant set plus X"). This is what we find in Hungarian: the
preverbal focus position cannot host either a universal quantifier or an 'even
phrase' or an 'also phrase'. Cf.

> (32) a.   *János* [FP *MARIT*   *hívta*   *meg*]
>   John   MARY-ACC   invited   PREF
>   "It was Mary that John invited."
>
>   b.   **János* [FP *mindegyik   lányt hívta   meg*]
>   John   each   girl invited PREF
>   "It was each girl that John invited."
>
>   c.   **János* [FP *Marit   is   hívta   meg*]
>   John   Mary also   invited   PREF
>   "It was also Mary that John invited."
>
>   d.   **János* [FP *még   Marit is   hívta   meg*]
>   John   even   Mary also invited PREF
>   "It was even Mary that John invited."

Recall that the English cleft constituent has the so far unexplained property of not tolerating a universal quantifier, an 'even phrase' or an 'also
phrase'.

(33) *It was everybody/also Mary/even Mary that John invited.

More precisely, an 'also phrase' can also be acceptable – but only in a context
in which the cleft constituent clearly identifies a proper subset of a relevant set,
and the 'also phrase' adds an element to the subset identified – in such a way
that it still remains a proper subset of the relevant set. E.g.

> (34) A: John invited only Susan from among all his colleagues.
>   B: No, it was also Mary that John invited.

If we assume that the cleft constituent is a constituent in Spec,FP, the facts illustrated in (33)-(34) fall out.

The primary domain of an exhaustive identification operation is a set of individuals. According to Szabolcsi and Zwarts (1993), this is a consequence of the fact that a crucial element of the exhaustive identification operation is complement formation: whereas the focus phrase primarily identifies the proper subset of a relevant set for which the predicate holds, secondarily it also identifies the complementary subset for which the predicate does not hold. The Boolean operation of complement formation, however, can only be performed on an unordered set of discrete entities.[4] The par excellence syntactic realizations of individual-denoting entities are NPs; hence we predict that the primary targets of focus movement are also NPs. This was what we attested under (10) in connection with the English cleft construction as well: clefting is basically restricted, to NPs, PPs (which inherit the individual-denoting capability of the NP they dominate), and gerunds, which are also of the category NP. The question whether or not an embedded clause can be clefted clearly depends on whether what it denotes can be looked upon as an individual. This is what the following pair of sentences demonstrate:

(35) a.   It was what he said about his family that I did not believe.
     b.   *It is as you like that you can do.

Szabolcsi (1983) argues that non-individual denoting entities can also be 'individualized', i.e., represented as if they denoted distinct entities – e.g. by being listed or contrasted. Two contrasted predicative adjectives, for example, can be understood to represent a two-member set of distinct properties – in which case they are also potential targets of the identificational focus operator. This would explain the otherwise inexplicable grammaticality difference between (36a) and (36b):

(36) a.   *It was tired that he was.
     b.   It was not sick that he was but tired.

If *tired* is contrasted with *sick*, then they clearly denote two distinct properties. In (36b) exhaustive identification is performed on the set consisting of the properties 'sick' and 'tired'.

---

[4] É. Kiss (1998) modifies this claim (somewhat) by pointing out that scales are also potential domains of complement formation, hence elements ordered into scales are also potential domains of exhaustive identification.

4. Conclusions

It has been argued that the English cleft construction is the realization of a focus projection (FP), with the cleft constituent occupying Spec,FP. From this assumption, the following properties of the cleft construction can be derived:

i. The cleft constituent is interpreted as identificational focus.

ii. The cleft construction displays the distributional restrictions typical of identificational foci (the cleft constituent cannot be a universal quantifier or an 'even phrase').

iii. Given that exhaustive identification is an operation performed on a set of entities, a non-individual denoting expression cannot be clefted.

iv. Since the cleft constituent forms a chain with a corresponding empty category in the embedded clause, it displays connectedness effects. Whether it is a referential chain created by coindexation, or an A'-chain created by movement, it displays connectedness with respect to binding and scope. When the chain headed by the cleft constituent is created by movement, it also displays connectedness with respect to case and agreement.

v. Since the matrix V in the cleft construction is a dummy V which serves to lexicalize the F head of FP, it has no situationally anchored tense; it either inherits its tense from the embedded clause or it is a default present.

REFERENCES

Akmajian, Adrian. 1970. "On Deriving Cleft Sentences from Pseudo-Cleft Sentences." *Linguistic Inquiry* 1.147-168.

Brody, Michael. 1990. "Some Remarks on the Focus Field in Hungarian." *University College London Working Papers in Linguistics* 2. 201-225.

Chomsky, Noam. 1977. "On wh-movement." *Formal Syntax* ed. by Peter Culicover, Thomas Wasow & Adrian Akmajian, 71-132. New York: Academic Press.

Cinque, Guglielmo. 1990. *Types of A'-Dependencies*. Cambridge, Mass.: MIT Press.

Emonds, Joseph. 1976. *A Transformational Approach to English Syntax*. New York: Academic Press.

É. Kiss, Katalin. 1998. "Identificational Focus versus Information Focus." *Language* 74:2.

Meinunger, André. 1996. "Speculations on the Syntax of (Pseudo-)Clefts." Unpublished, Berlin, Zentrum für Allgemeine Sprachwissenschaft, Typologie und Universalienforschung.

Szabolcsi, Anna. 1981. "The Semantics of Topic-Focus Articulation." *Formal Methods in the Study of Language* ed. by Jan Groenendijk et al., 513-541. Amsterdam: Matematisch Centrum.

——. 1983. "Focusing Properties, or the Trap of First Order." *Theoretical Linguistics* 10:125-145.

—— & Frans Zwarts. 1993. "Weak Islands and an Algebraic Semantics for Scope-Taking." *Natural Language Semantics* 1.235-285.

AGREEMENT, PRONOMINALIZATION AND WORD ORDER IN PRAGMATICALLY-ORIENTED LANGUAGES[*]

LUNELLA MEREU
Università degli Studi di Roma Tre

0. *Introduction*

This paper is about some special cases of interaction between agreement, pronominalization and word order on the one hand, and pragmatic functions on the other, that is cases in which the pragmatic context affects the syntactic and morphological structure of the sentence. I am referring to the peculiar ways in which in some languages a subject marked as a constituent in focus or as a wh-element is signalled not only through its position but also through the lack of (or reduced) verbal agreement, the absence of clitic pronouns if the language obligatorily selects them in the unmarked sentence and the absence of morphological case on the subject if the language shows case marking. The following example from Somali illustrates the phenomenon: [1]

(1) *Adiga   baa moos   cunaya*
    you-nonNOM FM banana eat-PROG
    "YOU are eating a banana"

---

[*] I wish to thank Annarita Puglielli, Mara Frascarelli and Axmed Abdullahi Axmed for their comments on a previous version of this paper.

[1] Focused constituents are in capital letters.

Abbreviations in the text and in glosses are the following:

AA	=	anti-agreement	OCL	=	object clitic
AGR	=	agreement	PAST	=	past tense
CL	=	clitic	PL	=	plural
COMP	=	complementizer	PP	=	past participial
DCL	=	dative clitic	PRES	=	present tense
DEP	=	dependent mood	PROG	=	progressive
F	=	feminine	R	=	restricted paradigm
FM	=	focus marker	S	=	subject
IMP	=	impersonal	SCL	=	subject clitic
M	=	masculine	SG	=	singular
NOM	=	nominative case	SUBJ	=	subjunctive

In (1) the subject (S) is focused as it is signalled by the focus marker (FM) *baa,* which is right-adjacent to it, and also by its position before the verb (V); the subject clitic (SCL), which is normally attached to the FM when an argument other than the S is focused, does not occur and the V shows a reduced form. In addition, the S does not bear the nominative case (NOM).

This set of properties is realized in pragmatically marked contexts and concerns those languages closely related to the 'pragmatically-based type' (Mithun 1987) or described as 'discourse configurational' (Kiss 1995), that is languages that mark the pragmatic functions of the constituents in the sentence rather than (or in addition to) their syntactic functions.[2]

Languages vary according to the form the V takes in these contexts – a partial agreement paradigm as in Somali, an invariable third singular form as in Trentino, an Italian dialect, or a non-finite form as in Berber or Turkish.

Languages also vary according to the pragmatic contexts these morpho-syntactic peculiar rules are applied to; in some languages, such as Somali, these rules apply to S focus structures, wh-questions, relative clauses, and cleft sentences, in others, such as Trentino, to all these contexts except cleft sentences, and in Turkish to S relative clauses only.[3]

The phenomenon of lack of agreement between V and S has recently been analysed by Ouhalla (1993), who sees it as the manifestation of what he calls 'the anti-agreement effect', and by Lambrecht & Polinsky (1997), who use the term 'suspended subject-verb agreement'. I will maintain the term 'anti-agreement' to refer to the whole set of morphological and syntactic properties (relative to agreement, case marking, clitic behaviour, and position of the S) which may occur in pragmatically-marked contexts.

The aim of this paper is, therefore, to present and discuss anti-agreement (AA) exploring the relationship between its morpho-syntactic and pragmatic properties and to characterize the specific ways in which languages apply it.

I will present two linguistic systems which undergo AA, Somali and Trentino, and will focus on the similarities and differences between the two. It will emerge from the data that the two systems represent different ways of realizing AA. In the former the phenomenon is more syntactically based, while in the latter it is more sensitive to the semantic-pragmatic properites of specific contexts. Discussion will be at a pre-theoretic level. For reasons of space, I will re-

---

[2] See the introduction to this volume for a presentation of the kinds of languages Mithun (1987) and Kiss (1995) characterize.

[3] Negative structures are also interesting for the phenomena I am describing. However, for reasons of space, I will not discuss them here; see Antinucci (1981) and Lecarme (1991) for a presentation of these structures in Somali.

strict myself to present a correct interpretation of the data and only hint at the theoretical background which can best account for it.

1.   *Description of Somali*

1.1   *The data*

Somali is a SOV language. It distinguishes between NOM and nonNOM case; NOM is the marked case realized on Ss, while nonNOM is the unmarked case applied to all arguments other than the S.[4] The language realizes S agreement on the V and, in addition, it has two series of pronominal clitics, SCLs and OCLs (= non-S clitics), the former attached to the FM, the latter within the verbal complex, a cluster of clitic forms, prepositions,[5] and other particles on the left of the V:

(2) $(Axmed_i)$ $annaga_j$ buu $(baa+uu_i)/*baa$ [$_{vc}$ $nala_j$ / $*la$
       Axmed   us   FM-SCL/*FM   OCL-with/*with
       $ordayay]$[6]
       run-PAST.3SGM
       "Axmed was running with US" (As for Axmed, he was ...)

As (2) shows, while lexical arguments such as the S can be omitted, pronominal clitics cannot.

Somali is a topic and focus prominent language [7] (Svolacchia et al. 1995); topicalization is realized through the application of the resumptive pronoun strategy, that is through the presence of SCLs on the FM (or of OCLs within the verbal complex), coindexed with the topic constituent. No word order restrictions are associated with topicalization. As a matter of fact, (2) can also occur as (2)':

(2)' a   *Annaga buu Axmed nala ordayay*
      b   *Annaga buu nala ordayay Axmed*

---

[4] The genitive case, the only other morphological case marked in Somali, does not concern us here. As for the NOM case, it has to be pointed out that in some cases it is realized prosodically.

[5] As (2) shows, prepositions in Somali are not adjacent to the constituents they govern but are grouped together with the other particles within the verbal complex. See Puglielli & Svolacchia (this volume) for a full description of the verbal complex in Somali and for an explanation of the non–adjacency property of prepositions.

[6] The examples from Somali are from Livnat (1984), Puglielli (1981), Saeed (1984) and Svolacchia et al. (1995).

[7] Topic corresponds to the part of the sentence bearing given information and focus to the one bearing new or contrastively presented information.

Focalization obligatorily occurs in matrix sentences in Somali and it can be either nominal or verbal. The former is realised through word order, as the focused constituent must occur in a position before the V, and through its lexical marking by the right-adjacent F *baa*, as (1) and (2) above show; the latter is realised through the lexical marking of the verbal complex by the left-adjacent F *waa*:

(3) *Cali adiga wuu (waa+uu)*   *ku*   *dilay*
     C.   you   FM-SCL   OCL   hit-PAST.3SG
     "Cali HIT you"

As regards nominal focalization, we have already hinted in the introduction that S focus structures behave differently from non-subject focus structures in that the latter show AA. In other words, when S focalization applies in Somali, the V has a reduced inflection, a 'restricted paradigm' in Andrzejewsky's (1956, 1968) terms, which means that the V is inflected for tense and for a limited number of persons (the third singular feminine and the first plural), while all other persons are invariably realized as third singular masculine forms; no SCL forms can be attached to the FM and the S does not bear the NOM case (see also Lecarme 1995 and Svolacchia et al. 1995). As a matter of fact, (1) would be ungrammatical if no AA applied:

(1)' **Adigu*   *baad (baa+aad) moos*   *cunaysaa*
      you-NOM FM-SCL   banana eat-PROG.2SG

Instead, when arguments other than the S are focused, no such effect is present. In (2) above, the focused constituent is doubled by the OCL, and no special morpho-syntactic rules are applied; the V is fully inflected, the SCL on the F is present and the S is at the NOM case. Notice, however, that when the non-subject argument is third person, the OCL is not visible because third person OCLs are always Ø-forms:

(4) *Naagi*   *libaax bay (baa+ay) Ø*   *aragtay*
     woman-NOM lyon FM-SCL   OCL see-PAST.3SGF
     "A woman saw A LYON"

1.2 *Extension of the AA phenomenon in Somali*

AA does not apply only to S focalization but also to a number of other pragmatically-marked contexts. As expected, it applies to S wh-questions. In (5) the wh-constituent *yaa* behaves as a focused S; therefore it cannot occur with a SCL and is associated with a restricted form of the V (R):

(5) *Yaa   ku   toosiya?*
    who OCL wake-up(R)
    "Who wakes you up?"

In opposition to (5), the object wh-constituent in (6) cooccurs with a SCL and with a fully inflected V:

(6) *(Adigu)   yaad (yaa+aad)   Ø   aragtay?*
    You-NOM   who-SCL   OCL see-PAST.2SG
    "Who did you see?"

The same pattern applies to relative clauses, which are structures with no complementizer to introduce them:

(7) *Wiilasha [warshadda   sonkorta ka shaqueeyaa]   waa kuwaas*[8]
    boys-the   farm-the   sugar-the at work-(R).NOM FM those
    "The boys who work at the sugar farm are those".

(8) *Mooska$_i$ [(ay)$_j$ wiilashaasi$_j$ Ø$_i$ cunayaan]   waa ceeriin*
    banana-the SCL boys-those-NOM OCL eat-PROG.3PL FM unripe
    "The banana that those boys are eating is unripe"

In (7), which is a S relative clause, the V shows the restricted paradigm and no SCL coindexed with the head of the relative clause is present. In (8), which contains an object relative clause, AA does not apply; thus the OCL, although a non-visible form, is present, the V is fully inflected, the S is at the NOM case and can optionally be associated with a SCL.

Not surprisingly, the same asymmetry between subject and non-subject structures is related to cleft clauses, as they are built as relative clauses headed by the expletive NP *waxa*; once more there is AA when the head noun is a S:

(9) *Waxa$_i$ [$_i$ yimid]   waa tareen*
    thing-the   came(R) FM   train
    "What came was a train" / "It was a train which came"

(10) *Waxa [aan   Ø$_i$ doonayaa]   waa lacag*
     thing SCL   OCL want-PRES.1SG FM money
     "What I want is money" / "It is money that I want"

(9), which is an instance of a S cleft clause, shows AA in the embedded relative structure, whereas (10), an instance of an object cleft clause, does not undergo AA in the embedded structure.

---

[8] As regards complex NPs, if they are Ss, the NOM marker is attached to the end of the complex constituent and not to the head of the NP; since the end of the S constituent in (7) is given by the V, the marker is added to it (Antinucci 1981).

However, when the same structures appear in long-distance contexts, that is when focus structures, wh-questions, relative or cleft clauses are embedded within a complement clause, the asymmetry is not present, that is AA never applies. Therefore, as (11) shows, in order to be marked as focus an embedded S which occurs in the matrix sentence[9] must be associated with a SCL in the embedded structure while the V is fully inflected and at the dependent mood (DEP):

(11) *Nimankii$_i$ buu   Cali rumaysanayay   [inay$_i$ /*in*
      men-the   FM-SCL C.   think-PAST.3SGM COMP-SCL

      tageen]
      leave-PAST.3PL(DEP)
      "THE MEN Cali thought (that they) would leave"

The same pattern applies to long-distance wh-questions (12) and relative clauses (13):[10]

(12) *Maxaad (maxaa$_i$+aad) doonaysaa   [inay$_i$/*in*
      What-SCL   think-PROG.2SG   COMP-SCL

      dhacaan]?
      happen-PRES.3PL(DEP)
      "What do you think (that it) will happen?"

(13) *Naagta$_i$ [(uu$_j$) Cali$_j$ qabo   [inay$_i$/*in   ninka*
      woman-the SCL C.   think-PRES.3SG(DEP) COMP-SCL man-the

      buugga   siisay]]   waa Amina
      book-the give-PAST.3SGF   FM A.
      "The woman that Cali thinks (that she) gave the book to the man is Amina"

In both (12) and (13) the embedded sentence must have, attached to the complementizer, a SCL coindexed with either the wh-S or with the head of the relative in the matrix sentence.

---

[9] Focalization cannot apply to embedded structures in Somali. Therefore, to focus an embedded constituent, it must be obligatorily extracted and must occur in the main sentence, anywhere before the V; see Saeed (1984), Lecarme (1991) and Svolacchia & al. (1995) for a discussion of these complex structures.

[10] For lack of space, we will not give examples of non-S long-distance focus, wh- and relative constructions, nor will we give examples of long-distance cleft clauses, all contexts in which Vs are fully inflected and OCLs are present if phonetically realized.

Summarizing, Somali shows an asymmetry between S and non-S constituents in pragmatically-marked contexts, that is in focus structures, wh-questions, relative and cleft clauses. This is shown in (14):

(14) S structures: [- NOM] [- SAGR] [-SCL]
     Non-S structures: [- NOM] [+ SAGR] [+OCL]
     [+ AA]:   S focus, wh-, relative and cleft structures
     [- AA]:   in all long-distance contexts

2.   *Description of Trentino*

2.1 *The data*

Like Italian the Trentino dialect is SVO and its nominal constituents do not show morphological case distinctions. It realizes S agreement on the V and presents thrèe series of clitics, SCLs,[11] object clitics and oblique clitics, which can form a clitic cluster on the V:

(15) *La gh' ha magnà la torta al   Mario*[12]
     SCL DCL has eaten the cake to-the M.
     "She has eaten Mario's cake"

SCLs obligatorily occur in the sentence while the lexical S can be omitted, as (16) shows:

(16) a.   *La Maria *(la)   parla   troppo*
          the M.   SCL   speaks too much
          "Mary speaks too much"
     b.   *La parla troppo*

Trentino is also topic and focus prominent; as in Italian, topicalization is realized through the initial or final position of the topic constituent, that is through its right or left dislocation, and through the application of the resumptive pronoun strategy with clitics coindexed with the topic argument:

(17) *L$_i$' ho   encontrà, la Giovanna$_i$*
     OCL have-1SG met-PP   the G.
     "I have met her, Giovanna"

---

[11] The SCL paradigm in Trentino shows some gaps, as the first singular and the first and second plural persons are lacking.

[12] The examples in the text are from Brandi & Cordin (1981, 1989), Cordin (1993), and Suñer (1992).

Focalization is generally realized through word order, as the nominal focused constituent occurs in post-verbal position.[13] As in Somali, S focus structures in Trentino undergo AA, which is realized through an invariable third singular form of the V, the impersonal form and through the dropping of the SCL:

(18) a.   E'   vegnù   le so'   sorele
          be-3SG   come-PP   the his/her sisters
          HIS/HER SISTERS came

     b.   *Le son   venute   le so' sorele
          SCL be-3PL   come-PP.FPL ...

However, non-subject focus structures do not invariably behave as in Somali;
we must distinguish here between object and oblique focalization. Object focus
structures pattern with S focus structures, that is they undergo AA, as no object
clitic can cooccur with the object;[14] oblique focus structures, on the other hand,
do not show AA, as the oblique clitic must cooccur with the oblique argument:[15]

---

[13] The post-verbal position is not, however, the only position for focused constituents; contrastive focused subjects can occur pre-verbally:

(i) a.   La Maria è   vegnù,   no la Carla
          the M.   be-3SG come-PP   not the C.
          MARY came, not Carla

     b.   *La Maria la   è   vegnuda,   no la Carla
          the M.   SCL be-3SG   come-PP.FSG   not la Carla
          *"MARY she came, not Carla"

[14] This does not hold for first and second persons subject and object clitics, which must always
double their corresponding subject and object pronouns, as the following examples show:

(i) Te   vegni ti
     SCL come you
     "YOU come"

(ii) El *(me) vol   mi
     SCL OCL wants me
     "He wants ME"

This is not surprising; a number of languages show the same asymmetry, which can be explained in terms of the intrinsic emphatic properties of tonic pronouns. In other words, these
are highly marked forms, whose emphatic value in contexts in which they cooccur with clitics
or bound forms, can either determine a conflict (as in Semitic languages) or a reinforcement of
the marked pragmatic meaning (as in Trentino).

[15] The literature does not explicitly refer to the structures in the text as cases of object and
oblique focalization. However, as the cooccurrence of the object clitic and the lexical object is
possible only when the object is topicalized, it is easy to conclude that in (19) the object is the

(19) (*L') *ho   encontrà la Giovanna*
     OCL have-1SG   met-PP   the G.
     "I have met Giovanna"

(20) *(Ghe) dago   el regal al   Mario*
     DCL give-1SG   the present to-the M.
     "I'll give the present to Mario"

(19), which is an example of an object focus structure, would be ungrammatical if the object clitic occurred, while (20), which is a dative focus structure, would be ungrammatical without the dative clitic.

Thus the asymmetry in focus rules seems to work differently in Trentino and in Somali.

2.2 *Extension of the AA phenomenon in Trentino*
As in Somali, AA in Trentino applies to S wh-questions:

(21) a. *Quante   putele è   vegnù   con ti?*
         how many girls   be-3SG   come-PP with you
         "How many girls came with you?"

     b. **Quante putele le è   vegnude   con ti?*
         SCL be-3SG come-PP.FPL with you

In (21) the wh-constituent, which is the S, cannot cooccur with the SCL, and the V must be in the invariable impersonal form. As for object and oblique wh-questions, these behave as focus structures; again, the former apply AA (22) as they cannot be associated with the object clitic, while the latter do not (23):

(22) *Cosa hala   portà   la Maria?*
     what have-3SG-SCL   bring-PP the M.
     "What did Mary bring?"

(23) *A chi   no *(ghe) pias   sta musica?*
     to whom not DCL like-3SG this music
     "Who does not like this music?"

The same pattern applies to relative clauses. Therefore SCLs and a fully inflected V cannot occur in S relative structures (24) and object clitics cannot oc-

---

focused constituent. As for the oblique argument, as the example below shows, there is no doubt that oblique clitics and new information cooccur:

(i) *A chi_i   gh_i' honte   comprà na casa?*
     to whom DCL have-1SG buy-PP a house
     Who have I bought a house for?

cur in object relative clauses (25), while oblique clitics must occur in oblique relative structures (26):

(24) a. *Le putele che è   vegnù   algeri*
         the girls   that be-3SG come-PP yesterday
         "The girls who came yesterday"

     b. **Le putele che le   è   vegnude   algeri*
                           SCL be-3SG come-PP.FPL ...:

(25) *Le putele che te   hai   vist   algeri*
     the girls   that SCL have-2SG   see-PP   yesterday
     "The girls that you saw yesterday"

(26) *L' om che te gh' hai   dat   la me' roba*
     the man that SCL DCL have-2SG give-PP the my stuff
     "The man you gave my stuff to"

Unlike Somali, however, cleft clauses, although they are subordinate structures built as relative clauses, do not apply AA:

(27) *L'   è   stà   la Maria che l'   ha   fat   la torta*
     CL-IMP be-3SG be-PP the M.   COMP SCL have-3SG make-PP the cake
     It was Mary who made the cake

Even in long-distance contexts Trentino behaves differently from Somali, as in these structures AA applies.[16] This can be seen in (28) for focus structures and in (29) for wh-questions:

(28) a. *La Maria te   sai   che   è   vegnù,   no la Carla*
         the M. SCL know-2SG COMP be-3SG   come-PP, not the C.
         "MARY, you know that she came, not Carla"

     b. **La Maria te sai che la è   vegnuda,   no la Carla*
         ...   SCL be-3SG come-PP.FSG

(29) a. *Quante   putele te   pensi   che   abia   parlà?*
         how-many girls   SCL think-2SG COMP have-SUBJ.3SG speak-PP
         "How many girls do you think spoke?"

---

[16] However, in cases in which both subject and object are extracted out of contexts which are islands, AA does not apply; take, for example, long-distant relative clauses:

  (i) *Le putele che gh'è in giro la voze che   le è   rivade   algeri*
      ...   rumour has it COMP SCL be-3SG arrive-PP.FPL yesterday
      "The girls I heard say (they) arrived yesterday"

  (ii) *La putela che   no ghe credo   ala storia che te   l' hai   vista algeri*
      the girl   COMP not DCL believe.1SG to-the story COMP SCL OCL have-2SG see-PP .
      ?"The girl that I do not believe the tale that you saw her yesterday"

b. *Quante putele te pensi che le abia parlà?*
... SCL ..

The same holds for relative clauses (30), but not for cleft clauses (31):

(30) *Le putele che te pensi che sia vegnù con mi*
the girls COMP SCL think-2SG COMP be.SUBJ.3SG come with me
"The girls that you think (that) came with me"

(31) *L' è la to' amica$_i$ che tuti i pensa che la$_i$*
CL-IMP be-3SG the your friend COMP everybody SCL thinks that SCL
abia mandà i soldi en Svizzera
have.SUBJ-3SG sent-PP the money in S.
"It is your friend that everybody thinks (that she) sent the money to in Switzerland"

As expected, in (31) the long-distant cleft clause does not show AA, while the relative structure in (30) does.

Summarizing, in Trentino subject and object short and long-distant contexts pattern together, in that they show AA, although this does not hold for cleft clauses; AA does not apply to oblique structures:

(32) S structures: [-SAGR] [-SCL]
object structures: [+SAGR] [-OCL]
oblique structures: [+SAGR] [+DCL]

[+AA]: S and object short and long-distance focus structures, wh- and relative structures
[-AA]: S short and long-distance cleft clauses, oblique focus, wh- and relative structures

3. *Discussion of the data*

Given the set of data we have presented for Somali and Trentino above, we can now ask the following questions: a) what is the reason for the asymmetry in the behaviour of subject and non-subject constituents in focalization in the two languages?; b) why does the asymmetry extend to object constituents in Trentino as well?; c) why does AA apply to the contexts above? What is common to these contexts?; d) how can we explain the differences in the contexts to which Somali and Trentino apply AA?

Let us start with the first question, why Somali and Trentino show asymmetry between subject and non-subject focalization. Subject focalization is certainly a very marked process in languages, given the fact that in pragmatically unmarked contexts the S is generally the topic of the sentence, while the predicate or a non-subject argument or both are new information. Therefore, when the S comes to be the focus of the sentence, that is when it introduces new information or indicates a contrast, its grammatical properties may change.

Drawing on languages other than Somali and Trentino, Lambrecht & Polinsky (1997)[17] have interestingly proposed that when the S is not the topic of the sentence, in particular when both the S and the predicate are in focus, the former undergoes 'detopicalization'; this means that it is not coded with the prosodic and/or morphosyntactic features associated with the topic. The extreme case in this process is the total assimilation of the subject to the formal properties of the object, what the authors call 'objectivizing' the subject or 'subject-object neutralization'. This analysis is useful in explaining the data from Somali and Trentino. Somali seems to apply the weak strategy to detopicalize the subject. Remember that when focused, the S loses its case marking and does not trigger complete verbal agreement (third singular feminine and first plural Ss are the only agreement forms distinguished). In focalization, while Ss must drop SCLs, objects and non-subject arguments in general must cooccur with clitics. So differences in the formal properties of subjects and non-subject constituents remain in Somali, thus avoiding cases of ambiguity in the interpretation of the arguments in the sentence.[18] We might say that the loss of morphology on the S is made up for by the different behaviour associated with S and non-subject constituents, or that the partial loss of morphology creates a S by default.

Differently from Somali, Trentino seems to apply the strong strategy to detopicalize the S, that is, when focused, the S is objectivized. Remember that objects in Trentino are coded as post-verbal constituents, do not cooccur with clitics and do not trigger agreement; these are exactly the features of the focused subject: the post-verbal position, the lack of SCLs and the lack of agreement (or impersonal/invariable agreement).

A further question concerning asymmetry is why it extends to object constituents in Trentino but not in Somali. Somali and Trentino embody different

---

[17] For lack of space we cannot extensively discuss Lambrecht & Polinsky's (1997) theory. Briefly, it is based on a three-way distinction among focus structures: sentence focus (SF), predicate focus (PF) and argument focus (AF). Lambrecht and Polinsky show howSF structures are different from AF and PF structures and apply detopicalization and objectivization of Ss to SF structures only. Somali and Trentino weaken the theory somewhat, as detopicalization also applies to AF structures when Ss are involved.

[18] Remember that in Somali linear order does not help identify the different grammatical relations in the sentence; as long as they are in pre-verbal position, they can occur anywhere. Only when a constituent is a topic can this occur post-verbally.

ways of realizing the relationship between the formal (=morpho-syntactic) and semantic (=deep case) properties of the grammatical relations in the sentence. Somali opposes Ss to all other functions through case morphology in that only Ss are case-marked while all other functions, objects, obliques and adjuncts are unmarked. In addition, as already pointed out, there are two sets of clitics, subject and non-subject clitics, occurring in different positions. There are no word order restrictions between constituents and no adjacent markers to distinguish between non-S constituents, as the prepositions which govern some of them occur within the verbal complex. Trentino, on the other hand, grammatically realizes a three-way distinction, as S, object and oblique constituents are marked through linear order, adjacent prepositions for obliques, and are associated with three different sets of clitics.[19] An interesting way of accounting for the differences in the extension of AA in the two systems is by using Bresnan's (1982) distinction between semantically restricted and semantically unrestricted functions; the former are functions which have a limited number of semantic roles, while the latter are functions which are not limited as to the kind of semantic roles they can have. Normally Ss and objects are semantically unrestricted functions, while oblique constituents are semantically restricted. This gives rise to the different syntactic phenomena the two kinds of functions exhibit. Given the strict interrelation that languages show between semantic interpretation, syntactic functions and morphology, the different patterning that Somali and Trentino realize as to AA is to be expected. As a matter of fact, the morpho-syntactic rules in Somali only formally distinguish between S and non-subject functions, therefore objects pattern with oblique constituents and they are all classified as semantically restricted functions, not allowing AA. The morpho-syntactic rules of Trentino, on the other hand, distinguish between the three functions; objects like subjects are thus semantically unrestricted functions and have the same behaviour as subjects with regard to AA.

Let us now consider now the third question – what is common to the structures undergoing AA. They definitely do not share the same pragmatic function in all contexts. Whereas for focalization and wh-questions we can speak of the same mechanism of identification of new information in the sentence, the same cannot be said for the constituent heading a relative clause. As is well known, the head of a relative clause is the theme rather than the focus of the subordinate clause (Kuno 1976). The fact that AA applies to pragmatically

---

[19] Subject and object third person clitics, however, have the same form and can cause ambiguities in the interpretation of sentences with these forms. See Brandi & Cordin (1981) for a discussion of this set of data.

different structures might be interpreted as an argument against an explanation
of AA in terms of the relationship between the formal and pragmatic properties
of pragmatically-oriented languages. Therefore, in line with Ouhalla (1993),
we might be tempted to adopt a syntactic approach to AA, viewing all these
phenomena as effects of a S extraction rule. In other words we might analyse S
focus or wh-structures as cases of extraction. However, in languages undergoing AA, these would not simply be structures such as (33):

$$(33) \quad [_{CP} NP_i \ _{FOC/WH} [_{IP} t_i \ VP]]^{20}$$

in which a S NP is moved to CP, while in IP a trace, or the empty category left
by the movement of the S and coindexed with it, occurs in the position of the S.
According to Ouhalla (ibid.), languages undergoing AA are all languages with
rich verbal agreement; they are thus all null S languages which can license an
empty pronominal form, a pro, in S position. This means that a focus or wh-
structure in these languages has the following representation:

$$(34) \quad [_{CP} NP_i \ _{FOC/WH} [_{IP} pro_i \ S\text{-}AGR \ VP]]^{21}$$

(34), as it is, is ruled out in terms of the binding principles preventing a pronominal form from being bound to an antecedent such as the NP in CP in the same
local domain.[22] The only way to make (34) possible would be with a weak S-
AGR occurring in IP, unable to license a pro in subject position; this is just the

---

[20] CP and IP are the functional projections proposed by Chomsky (1986a), the former corresponding to S', the position in which extra-sentential constituents such as topic or wh-elements
occur, the latter to the sentence, containing both the S NP and the inflectional material associated with the sentence.

[21] We will not fully discuss Ouhalla's syntactic analysis of AA, partly for lack of space, and
partly because his theoretical explanations do not extend to all the data we present here.
This analysis is not totally clear as to the kind of rules focalization and wh-movement are: he
speaks of a resumptive pro as a pronominal trace left by the movement of a constituent to an A'
position, following a suggestion by Chomsky (1986b).

[22] Different formalizations of the binding principles and of locality have been proposed to account for the co-reference restrictions of pronouns, anaphors and lexical NPs since Chomsky
(1982). The ones Ouhalla refers to here concern the impossibility of a resumptive pronoun in
the subject position of the clause which contains the antecedent and he states that pronouns
must be "A'-disjoint from a closely located antecedent" (Ouhalla 1993:490); in other words
pronouns cannot be coreferent with a close antecedent in CP, an A' position. He adopts here
the theoretical framework proposed by Aoun & Li (1989).

structure we have when AA is involved.[23] Notice that Ouhalla bases his syntactic analysis of AA on two assumptions: 1) languages with AA are null S languages; 2) clitics are part of the agreement inflection of the V (they license an empty pro in subject position); of course the validity of both these assumptions has to be proved. However, even if these assumptions were correct, we would still have to explain why in other languages with rich S-Agr there is no AA in the same contexts; (35) shows an example from Italian:

(35) *Quali ragazzi sono /*è   venut-i/*-o?*
     which boys   be-3PL/be-3SG come-PP.MPL/-MSG
     "Which boys came?"

This solution would also leave unexplained why, at least in Somali, the extraction of an object does not exhibit the same phenomenon, that is the lack of resumptive pronouns when objects are focused or undergo wh-movement, since the same locality conditions hold both for Ss and objects. Of course we might try to add conditions or parameters in the way Ouhalla does to be able to represent correctly what is going on in each language in relation to AA and to focus rules. However, it would perhaps be more useful to try to understand what kind of pragmatic process the contexts undergoing AA share. Our intuition here is that AA is not a process concerning a specific pragmatic function such as the focus function but a mechanism for making subjects discourse-prominent. In these terms, S relative clauses in the two languages would apply AA not because they share the pragmatic function of focus and wh-questions, but because they share the same mechanism for making Ss pragmatically prominent.[24]

We can now start to address the fourth question concerning the differences between Somali and Trentino in the application of AA in some of the contexts discussed. As regards cleft clauses, which undergo AA in Somali but not in Trentino, we can notice that it is not completely true that Trentino does not ap-

---

[23] As Brandi & Cordin (1981, 1989) have pointed out, in Trentino the structure in (34) with a weak SAGR would depend on the post-verbal position of the focused S, with an expletive pro in S position, as in:

(i)   [CP [IP pro_expl S-AGR_weak VP] NP_subj]

This representation is not valid on the basis of cross-linguistic data, as the S does not occur post-verbally in all languages undergoing AA (see Somali, for example); however, as Suñer (1992) shows, the representation in (i) does not extend either to the full set of data from Trentino, as the S, when focused, is not necessarily always in post-verbal position (see the examples in (i), note 14.

[24] Discourse prominence extends to objects in Trentino as well, given the peculiar patterning of semantically restricted and unrestricted functions it shows.

ply AA in these contexts. There are cases in which AA applies, as in the following cleft question:

(36) *Chi è*   *(lo)*   *che è*   *vegnù?*
who be-3SG   (CL-IMP) that be-3SG come-PP
"Who was it who came?"

In (36) the cleft clause is embedded in the wh-question, i.e. in a context in which the cleft constituent cannot be identified. If we compare (36) to the example in (37):

(37) *Perché te ghe tegni el mus ala*   *Carla?*
why   SCL are cross   with-the C.
"Why are you cross with Carla?"

perché l'   *è*   *ela che la m' ha*   *rovinà i libri*
because CL-IMP be-3SG her COMP SCL DCL have-3SG destroy-PP the books
"Because it was her who destroyed the books"

we can conclude with Brandi & Cordin (1981) that Trentino is sensitive to the status of the cleft constituent: if it is given information, it does not undergo AA, if it is new information, it does. It therefore seems that in Trentino there is a stricter relationship between the semantics and the grammar of pragmatically-marked contexts than in Somali. This property of Trentino does not apply only to cleft clauses. If we take the structures normally undergoing AA and create contexts in which the S is given information, AA does not hold, as the following examples prove:

(38) *Quante dele putele hale*   *parlà con ti?*
how-many of-the girls have-3SG –SCL speak-PP with you
"How many of the girls spoke to you?"

(39) *La Maria, che l' ha*   *ciapà quatro de matematica*
the M.   COMP SCL have-3SG score-PP four of mathematics
"Mary, who got a low mark in mathematics"

The S in the wh-question in (38) and in the S relative clause, an appositive clause, in (39) corresponds to given information and so AA does not apply. We can conclude then with Suñer that in Trentino AA does not apply "whenever the speaker can identify the subject referent" (Suñer 1992:668).

As to the differences between long-distance contexts in Somali and Trentino, we do not have the space here to deal with these structures fully. We suggest a possible explanation based on the two assumptions used by Ouhalla, namely the status of the languages undergoing AA as null S languages and the status of SCLs as agreement forms. Remember that Somali does not undergo AA in long-distance contexts, whereas Trentino does. Let us now reconsider (11) whose incomplete syntactic representation is shown in (40) below:

(40) *Nimankii$_i$ buu   Cali rumaysanayay* [$_{CP}$ *inay$_i$/*in* e$_i$ *tageen*]
      men-the   FM-SCL C.   think-PAST   COMP-SCL leave-PAST(DEP)
      "THE MEN Cali thought (that they) would leave"

As shown in Svolacchia et al. (1995), the empty category in the embedded clause is not possible since, because of an intervening CP, it is too far away from the constituent it is coindexed with. Therefore constraints on movement would not allow AA in (40). Notice that this implies that SCLs in Somali behave as resumptive pronouns and not as agreement forms; remember also that SCLs must always be present when lexical Ss are dropped. Now, if they behave as pronouns, this means that they are Ss when lexical Ss are missing. Therefore the two assumptions by Ouhalla are not correct, at least as far as Somali is concerned.

As for Trentino, which applies AA in long-distance contexts, we see that SCLs behave as resumptive pronouns in some contexts here too:

(41) *Le putele$_i$ che gh'è in giro la voze che   le$_i$ è   rivade*
                  rumour has it   COMP SCL be-3SG arrive-PP.FPL
      algeri
      yesterday
      "The girls I heard say (they) arrived yesterday"

In (41), which is an island, that is a context which blocks movement of the S from the complex NP, the SCL must be interpreted as a resumptive pronoun and not as an agreement form. In addition, we notice that in Trentino too, when the lexical subject is dropped, the SCL must always be present. These two facts prove once more that Ouhalla's assumptions as to the status of this dialect as a null S language and of SCLs as agreement forms are at least weakened.[25] However, it is not totally incorrect to say that Trentino is a null S language. If we take the paradigm of a V in Trentino, we notice that with some persons there is no SCL:

---

[25] In Mereu (1994,1995) we view SCLs in Trentino and Somali as ambiguous forms, both as agreement markers and as clitic pronouns, on the basis of diagnostic tests which help detect the status of these forms. Undoubtedly, there is a mismatch in these languages between the morphology and syntax of clitic forms. Clitic forms behave as morphological markers of AGR in that they cannot be dropped whenever SAGR and the lexical argument they refer to occur, but they also behave syntactically as pronominal arguments, intervening as resumptive pronouns whenever the syntax requires them.

(42) 1SG   *parlo*
     2SG   *te parli*
     3SG   *el/la parla*
     1PL   *parlem*
     2PL   *parle*
     3PL   *i/le parla*

In this sense one might say that Trentino is partially a null S language since with some persons there is no SCL when the full S is dropped. Therefore (29), for example, is as bad as its Italian equivalents:

(43) *Quante   ragazze tu pensi   che (*loro) abbiano*
     how-many girls   you think-2SG that   they   have-SUBJ.3PL
     parlato   con te?
     speak-PP with you
     "How many of the girls do you think (that they) spoke with you?"

Now, in our opinion, the ungrammaticality of the example from Italian is due to the fact that real null S languages choose pro-drop instead of pronominal forms, either independent or clitic pronoun, in pragmatically-marked contexts. Given our interpretation of Trentino as a partially null S language and of its SCLs as pronominal forms (whenever they occur in contexts in which the full S is missing), we can say that the same explanation in terms of non-acceptance of pronominal forms is valid both for Italian and for Trentino.[26]

Therefore, contra Ouhalla (1993), we conclude that AA does not apply to languages which are totally null S and whose SCLs are always agreement forms; if our interpretation of the data is correct, AA applies to languages whose SCLs can be analysed as pronouns, and the difference in terms of occurrence versus non-occurrence of these forms in long-distance contexts is simply due to whether they show some evidence of being null S or not.

4. *Conclusions*

In this paper we have provided an analysis of the AA phenomenon and have tried to suggest a few explanations for the differences which languages cross-linguistically show in both syntactic and pragmatic behaviour in AA.

---

[26] After all it makes sense that Trentino be grouped closer to languages like Italian, which are null S or pro-drop, than to non-pro-drop ones. The same constraints to movement are applied to both. Take, for example, the behaviour of Italian with regard to island phenomena, which is the same as in Trentino (see (41) above):

(i)   *Le ragazze che c'è in giro la voce che le hanno mandate via*
       "The girls I heard say (that they) have been sent away"

We have reached the following conclusions regarding AA:
– since it is associated with pragmatically-oriented languages, it is the morpho-syntactic realization of discourse subject prominence;
– it is realized through an asymmetry of behaviour between either S and non-subject arguments as in Somali, or between S, object and oblique arguments as in Trentino, that is between the semantically-restricted and semantically unre-stricted functions the two languages formally distinguish;
– it is connected with languages whose clitics have a pronominal status, and the difference of behaviour AA gives rise to in long-distance contexts depends on whether there is evidence that the language is null S, since this kind of langua-ge only allows the presence of clitics as resumptive pronouns in highly con-strained contexts.

REFERENCES

Andrzejewski, Bogumił 0W. 1956. "Accentual Patterns in Verbal Forms in the Isaaq Dialect of Somali". *Bulletin of the School of Oriental and African Studies* 18.1.103-129.

——— . 1968. "Inflectional Characteristics of the So-called 'Weak Verbs' in Somali". *African Language Studies* 9.1-51.

Antinucci, Francesco. 1981. "Tipi di Frase". *Studi Somali 2. Sintassi della Lingua Somala* ed. by Annarita Puglielli, 219-300. Roma: Ministero degli Affari Esteri.

Aoun, Joseph & Audrey Li. 1989. "Two Cases of Logical Relations: Bound pronouns and anaphoric relations". Unpublished Manuscript, University of Southern California.

Brandi, Luciana & Patrizia Cordin. 1981. "Dialetti e Italiano: Un confronto sul para-metro del soggetto nullo". *Rivista di Grammatica Generativa* 6.3-32.

——— . 1989. "Two Italian Dialects and the Null Subject Parameter". *The Null Subject Parameter* ed. by Osvaldo Jaeggli & Ken J. Safir, 111-142. Dordrecht: Kluwer Aca-demic Publishers.

Bresnan, Joan. 1982. "Control and Complementation". *The Mental Representation of Grammatical Relations* ed. by Joan Bresnan, 282-390. Cambridge, Mass.: MIT Press.

Chomsky, Noam. 1982. *Some Concepts and Consequences of the Theory of Govern-ment and Binding.* Cambridge, Mass.: MIT Press.

——— . 1986a. *Barriers.* Cambridge, Mass.: MIT Press.

——— . 1986b. *Knowledge of Language: Its nature, origin and use.* New York: Praeger.

Cordin, Patrizia. 1993. "Dative Clitics and Doubling in Trentino". *Syntactic Theory and the Dialects of Italy* ed. by Adriana Belletti, 130-154. Torino: Rosenberg & Sellier.

Kiss, Katalin É., ed. 1995. *Discourse Configurational Languages.* Oxford: Oxford University Press.

250   LUNELLA MEREU

Kuno, Susumu. 1976. "Subject, Theme, and the Speaker's Empathy: A reexamination of relativization phenomena". *Subject and Topic* ed by. Charles N. Li, 417-444. New York: Academic Press.

Lambrecht, Knud. & Maria Polinsky. 1997. "Typological Variation in Sentence-Focus Constructions". *Proceedings of the Chicago Linguistic Society 33.* Chicago: Chicago University Press.

Lecarme, Jacqueline. 1991. "Focus en Somali: Syntaxe et Interpretation". *Linguistique Africaine* 7.33-65.

——. 1995. "L'accord restrictif en Somali". *Langues Orientales Anciennes, Philologie et Linguistique* 5-6.133-152.

Livnat, Michal A. 1984. *Focus Constructions in Somali.* Ph.D. Dissertation, University of Illinois at Urbana-Champaign.

Mereu, Lunella. 1994. "On the Status of Subject Clitics in Languages and the Null Subject Parameter". *Teoria del Linguaggio e Analisi Linguistica: XX Incontro di Grammatica Generativa, Padova, 17-19 February 1994* ed. by Gianluigi Borgato, 315-339. Padova: Unipress.

——. 1995. "Verso una Tipologia dell'Accordo Verbo-Soggetto". *Rivista di Linguistica* 7:2.333-367.

Mithun, Marianne 1987. "Is Basic Word Order Universal?". *Coherence and Grounding in Discourse* ed. by Russell S. Tomlin, 281-328. Amsterdam & Philadelphia: John Benjamins.

Ouhalla, Jamal. 1993. "Subject Extraction , Negation and the Antiagreement effect". *Natural Language and Linguistic Theory* 11.477-518.

Puglielli, Annarita. 1981. "Frase Dichiarativa Semplice". *Studi Somali 2. Sintassi della Lingua Somala* ed. by Annarita Puglielli, 1-44. Roma: Ministero degli Affari Esteri.

Saeed, John I. 1984. *The Syntax of Focus and Topic in Somali.* Hamburg: Helmut Buske.

Suñer, Margarita. 1992. "Subject Clitics in the Northern Italian Vernaculars and the Matching Hypothesis". *Natural Language and Linguistic Theory* 10.641-672.

Svolacchia, Marco, Lunella Mereu & Annarita Puglielli. 1995. "Aspects of Discourse Configurationality in Somali". Kiss 1995. 65-98.

III
MORPHO-SYNTAX AND SEMANTICS

THEMATIC-ROLE ASSIGNMENT
AND ASPECT IN ITALIAN PRONOMINAL VERBS
A LEXICOLOGICAL STUDY

VINCENZO LO CASCIO & ELISABETTA JEZEK
University of Amsterdam

0. *Introduction*

In this paper we analyse the class of Italian Pronominal Verbs (PRVs), i.e. those verbs that:

1) show at the surface the presence of the pronominal marker *si* (formal criterion);

2) show a lexicalised pronominal form (lexical criterion). Morphological constructions such as pronominal impersonals and passives are not taken into consideration here, even if, as we will see from the examples, the boundary between lexicalised and morphological uses is rather frayed at the edges.

We prefer to talk about 'pronominal marker' rather than 'reflexive marker', because, according to our criteria, we regard the term 'reflexive' as too restrictive and therefore misleading. Examples of PRVs are: *guardarsi allo specchio* "to look at oneself in the mirror", *asciugarsi le mani* "to dry one's hands", *prepararsi la cena* "to get dinner ready", *sedersi in prima fila* "to sit down in the front row" etc.

PRVs are interesting both from a quantitative and a qualitative point of view. From a quantitative perspective, they constitute a large lexical class. From a qualitative perspective, even though they share the same morphology, their nature is considerably different. Depending on the specific case, the *si* assumes different values, so that we can say that various functions correspond to one form. But even though there seems to be general agreement at all levels of the literature (lexicographic, descriptive and theoretical) regarding the multifunctional status of the pronominal marker, there is no agreement at all about the extension and internal structure of its functional domain and about which is/are the parameter(s) that are relevant to the distribution of its different functions. Indeed, the main difficulty one is confronted with when looking at the various classifications is the lack of a consistent terminology; this, in our opinion, reflects the still unclear theoretical status of the notions involved.

The current lexicographic classification, for example, both monolingual and bilingual, distinguishes generally among 'reflexives', 'intransitive pronominal' (or 'middle') and 'reciprocal verbs'. [1] But this classification is often not consistent, even within the same dictionary. 'Reciprocal' or 'intransitive pronominal' uses, for example, are often wrongly classified as 'reflexive' ones. Even Palazzi & Folena (1995), that seems to be the monolingual dictionary with the richest terminology regarding the *si*-verbs (see the labels 'indirect reflexive', 'intensifier reflexive', 'pronominal transitive' etc.) shows irregularities and frequently assigns similar uses to different classes.

At a theoretical level, most researchers put forward their own syntactic or semantic definition. This leads to a proliferation of labels defining similar structures: see for example the use of terms like 'derived intransitive', 'ergative', 'unaccusative', 'anticausative' to refer to similar phenomena. [2]

1. *Definition of the problem*

One of the main problems we are interested in regards the description of the intransitive pronominal use of transitive verbs. Consider (1b), (2b) and (3b) below:

TRV[3]	PRV
(1a) *il fumo ha riempito la stanza* "the smoke filled the room"	(1b) *la stanza si è riempita di fumo* "the room filled with smoke"
(2a) *Qualcuno ha incendiato il bosco* "Somebody set the wood on fire"	(2b) *il bosco si è incendiato* "the wood caught fire"
(3a) *Gianni ha aperto la porta all'improvviso* "G. opened the door suddenly"	(3b) *La porta si è aperta all'improvviso* "the door opened all of a sudden"

---

[1] Except for Dizionario Italiano Sabatini Coletti (1997), which employs a single label ('reflexive') for all uses.

[2] For these labels, see Halliday (1985), Burzio (1986), Perlmutter (1978), Siewierska (1984) respectively.

[3] Abbreviations in the text and in glosses are the following:

Aux	=	auxiliary	PRES	=	present tense
F	=	feminine	PRM	=	pronominal marker
GPT	=	Given Primary Time	PRV	=	Italian Pronominal Verb
IMP	=	imperfective tense	SG	=	singular
IN	=	intransitive	SoA	=	State of Affairs
INV	=	intransitive verb	SPP	=	simple past perfective
M	=	masculine	TR	=	transitive
PP	=	past participle form	TRV	=	transitive verb
PR	=	pronominal			

Verbs showing this alternation have often been called 'ergatives' or 'causative pairs' in the literature (see among others Levin & Rappaport 1995), because of the possibility of deriving the transitive from the intransitive use adding the element [Cause] to their semantic representation.[4] The intransitive use normally describes changes in the physical shape of appearance of some entity, and can be associated with the lexical template: [y become STATE].[5]

The analysis of the argument alternation between transitive verbs and their pronominal variant has led to the identification of two different patterns of verbal behaviour, shown in (4) and (5) below:

	TRV	INV	PRV
(4)	Gianni rompe il bicchiere	*il bicchiere rompe	il bicchiere si rompe
	G. break-3SG the glass	the glass break-3SG	the glass PRM break-3SG
	"G. breaks the glass"	"the glass breaks"	"the glass breaks"
(5)	Gianni brucia la carne	la carne brucia	la carne si brucia
	G. burn-3SG the meat	the meat burn-3SG	the meat PRM burn-3SG
	"G. burns the meat"	"the meat burns "	"the meat burns up"

The reason why some transitive verbs allow both an INV [-PR] and an INV [+PR] alternation as in (5); while other transitive verbs allow only the INV [+PR] use, as in (4), is not clear. In particular, it is not evident:

a)   according to which criterion the pronominal element is present or absent (in the surface structure);

b)   what is the function and semantic value of the *si* in the various cases (argument, morpheme, lexical idiosyncrasy?).

2.   *The aim of the analysis*

The aim of the analysis is to answer the issues in a)' and b) above. To do so, we will proceed in the following way:

1.   we will first show how a purely syntactic approach fails to account consistently for pronominal intransitive uses such as those in (1)-(5) above (Section 4) (cf. Jezek 1997). Because of the presence of two types of intransitivity ([+PR] and [-PR]) in (5), it is evident that the intransitive *si* can-

---

[4] The direction of the process of derivation (intransitive → transitive versus transitive → intransitive) is still a very controversial point. See for details Levin & Rappaport (1995).

[5] Cf. Levin & Rappaport (1995). In this respect, notice that change of state verbs can be further subdivided into two classes. The first class contains verbs that necessarily entail the achievement of an end state (different from the initial one) by the entity that undergoes the change (see *fermarsi* "to stop", *chiudersi* "to close"). The second class contains verbs that can entail the achievement of an end state or just a change in a particular direction (see *raffreddarsi* "to get cold", *allargarsi* "to become wide", "to widen out" etc.). We will refer to the latter subclass as the class containing the feature [+transformative].

not be a simple de-transitivizer, i.e. a marker of valency reduction, as suggested by Salvi (1988) among others.

2. we will then argue that only a multifactorial semantic approach, based on notions such as 'thematic relations', 'aktionsart', 'aspect' and 'time' will allow us to interpret the function of the *si* properly (Section 4 and 5);

3. in particular, we will put forth the hypothesis that the distribution of the *si* in intransitive predications is determined by the interplay among these features, with lexical and grammatical Aspect triggering it off (Section 6). We presume that in the presence of two types of intransitivity, i.e. [-PR] and [+PR] (see again (5) above), the difference can be explained in terms of an aspectual opposition;

4. on the basis of these assumptions, we will then analyse a selection of PRVs in order to verify whether the attempt to explain the behaviour of *si* in (4) and (5) from an aspectual point of view is a reasonable one to be followed (Section 7). In this respect, it will become increasingly clear that the *si*-marker assigns a [+eventive] aspectual function at the sentence level.

In this perspective, we believe that PRVs may serve to verify a number of theoretical assumptions regarding the nature and typology of 'states of affairs'(cf. Dik 1989:89) and their relevance to the definition of the possible thematic structures.

3. *The syntactic perspective of the Unaccusative Hypothesis*

We begin from a syntactic perspective. In this respect the Unaccusative Hypothesis is relevant to our study because it deals with types of intransitivity. As is widely known, this hypothesis was first formulated by Perlmutter within the context of Relational Grammar (Perlmutter 1978, 1989) and later adopted by Burzio within the Government-Binding framework (Burzio 1986). It is a syntactic hypothesis which argues that there are two kinds of intransitive verbs, the 'unaccusative' verbs and the 'unergative' verbs, each associated with a different underlying syntactic configuration as follows:

a) Unergative verbs   NP [$_{VP}$ V]   *lavorare* "to work"
b) Unaccusative verbs   ___[$_{VP}$ V NP]   *arrivare* "to arrive"

From a Government-Binding perspective, 'unergative' verbs take an underlying subject and no object, whereas 'unaccusative' verbs take an underlying object and no subject. In argument structure terms, 'unergative' verbs have an external argument but no direct internal argument, whereas 'unaccusative' verbs have a direct internal argument but no external argument.

Table 1 below shows to what extent the unaccusativity parameter is relevant to PRVs:

Verbs	TR	IN	PR	Formal properties	Aux IN[6]
rompere	X	-	X	unaccusative ergative[7]	essere
bruciare	X	X	X	unaccusative ergative	essere
cominciare	X	X	-	unaccusative ergative	essere
sedere	-	X	X	unaccusative not ergative	essere
pentirsi	-	-	X	unaccusative not ergative	essere
cadere	-	X	-	unaccusative not ergative	essere
telefonare	-	X	-	unergative	avere

Table 1: *Argument alternations and the unaccusativity parameter*

The syntactic parameter of split intransitivity does indeed seem to be relevant to PRVs. All PRVs fall within the unaccusative class. But the following issues arise:

1)   what makes all PRVs fall into the unaccusative and not the unergative class (see field Formal properties)?;

2)   which criterion determines the different behaviour of the *si* towards unaccusativity (see field PR)?

4.   *The semantic perspective of Thematic Roles*

The reason why the Unaccusative Hypothesis is not by itself able to answer these issues is that unaccusativity is *syntactically* represented but *semantically* determined (for this claim, see among others Levin & Rappaport 1992, Van Valin 1987). In order to answer the issues raised in 1) and 2) above, we therefore turn to the analysis of the semantics of PRVs. We start with the investigation of their thematic structure. In this respect, we notice that the intransitive *si* occurs only in predications which might be called 'Patient-oriented', i.e. predications in which an argument bearing the thematic role Theme is assigned grammatical primacy and chosen as the surface subject of the sentence (see again (1)-(5) above). Notice that in such constructions the surface subject does not have control over the 'State of Affairs' (SoA) expressed by the predication.

As regards the status of the *si*, research has often considered it a sort of 'trace' of a deleted Causer or Agent (cf. Cennamo 1993:22-23). This claim is supported by the observation that all PRVs found in the causative VTR/IN alternation would actually imply the underlying presence of an external Cause. This led many researchers to the conclusion that the *si* could represent a 'trace' of this external Causer that has been deleted. But even though the evidence from

---

[6] Auxiliary selected in the intransitive use.

[7] 'Unaccusative ergative' verbs show a TR/IN alternation, in which the subject of the IN use corresponds to the object of the TR one. 'Unaccusative not ergative' verbs do not show this alternation.

this specific subclass of PRVs supports this hypothesis, other subclasses of PRVs do not. See examples (6)-(9) below:

(6)   *la lava si è riversata sulle pendici del vulcano*
      "the lava flowed along the slopes of the volcano"

(7)   *il cielo si è coperto*
      "the sky became overcast"

(8)   *pregiudizi che si sono radicati nel tempo*
      "prejudices that have taken root over time"

(9)   *il tempo si è ristabilito*
      "the weather (has) cleared up"

Here in our opinion, the grammatical primacy assigned to the surface subject does not necessarily imply a backgrounded or defocused external Causer.

We therefore believe that the hypothesis that the pronominal marker is an argument or a semi-argument capable of bearing a thematic role should be abandoned, because of the difficulty in assigning a referent or a thematic role of any kind to it. In our opinion, the *si* can be better interpreted as due to a sort of 'passive-like' or 'middle' morphology, i.e. a morphology associated with a specific encoding of the lexical argument(s) of a predicate, in which the emphasis is placed on the action itself. The *si*-morphology is in contrast with the active morphology, whose emphasis is on the 'actor', and with the passive one, whose emphasis is on the 'undergoer', and where the 'actor' can be omitted. In the presence of this 'middle' morphology, the verbal meaning is to be interpreted with reference to the subject, which has no control over the SoA expressed by the verb. The hypothesis that the *si*-constructions represent a third voice, alongside the active and the passive ones, has recently been reproposed by Wehr (1995).

However, this hypothesis still does not solve the problem regarding the presence of two types of intransitivity ([+PR]/[-PR]) pointed out in (5).

5.   *The aspectual perspective*

The solution to this problem may lie in the lexical semantics of the predicates on the one hand and in the hypothesis that the *si* has an aspectual function on the other hand.

As a number of recent studies have pointed out (see among others Levin & Rappaport 1992, 1995, Van Valin 1987, Chierchia 1992), there is a strict correlation between the thematic and argument structure of verbs and their lexical semantics. The quantity of arguments a predicate selects and the type of thematic role it assigns to them is deeply influenced by its Aktionsart.

In the last 30 years, one of the main concerns of lexical semanticists dealing with verbs has been to produce a semantic typology of predications that could account for the correlation between lexical aspect, thematic structure and argument configurations (see the classifications of Vendler 1967, Borgato 1976, Mourelatos 1978, Dowty 1979, Van Valin 1987, Dik 1989, Bertinetto 1986). Vendler's classification ('state' verbs, 'activity' verbs, 'accomplishment' verbs, 'achievement' verbs), like many other classifications of Aktionsart, is based on a set of more abstract semantic (binary) oppositions. In fact, verbs can be grouped into classes according to features such as: [±dynamic], [±durative], [±transformative], [±resultative], [±iterative], etc.

In our view, these features are crucial not only because they determine the argument behaviour but also because in combination with grammatical forms (morphemes, periphrastic structures and morphological tenses) they take part in the definition of the aspectual features a predication acquires in a specific context. In this respect, following the compositional approach of Verkuyl (1972), we believe that the predication is assigned its final aspectual functions only at the sentence level, where all pieces of information, coming from Aktionsart, Time, Aspect and the lexicalisation of the internal argument selected by the predicate, merge. In order to identify the specific aspectual function covered by the *si* in intransitive predications, it is therefore essential to analyse the way Aktionsart, Aspect and Time interact. Aktionsart refers to the lexical Aspect. Aspect refers to the features assigned to the predication by grammatical forms (imperfective, perfective, inchoative etc.). The temporal information refers to the placement of the predication in the past, present or future.[8]

In Section 6 below we state our aspectual hypothesis and define the notion of Aspect within the theoretical framework we are going to adopt. In Section 7 we apply the above compositional approach to the analysis of a selection of PRVs.

6. *The aspectual hypothesis*

We assume that the morpheme *si* has an aspectual value. At the Phonetic Form level, we assume it to be the lexical output of the sentential aspectual function [+eventive], which is present at the Logical Form level and is dominated by the superior sentential node ASPECT.

---

[8] The claim that Aktionsart is a decisive factor is shown by the fact that while *parlava* and *stava parlando* are synonymous ("he was talking"), and they both differ from *stava perparlare* ("he was about to talk"), it seems that *moriva, stava morendo* ("he was dying") and *stava per morire* ("he was about to die") are all semantically close (see Lo Cascio 1995). This is due to the fact that the imperfective information is dynamic anddurative and is therefore not consistent with a momentaneous predication.

6.1 *Aspect in Lo Cascio's theory*

Aspectuality, according to Lo Cascio (1995), is the expression of a relation of inclusion between two time intervals: the time interval E, expressing the SoA in question, and the time interval L, which functions as localizer and which has the task to anchor the SoA E to a time axis. The time axis to which the E is anchored is indicated by the tense marking the SoA, and is controlled (dominated) by the time interval which functions as antecedent (called 'time binder') for the tense in question. This antecedent, or 'time binder', may be the speech point (in Lo Cascio's theory called Given Primary Time, GPT) or another time interval mentioned in the text.

In a sentence such as *yesterday he was ill* the temporal adverb *yesterday* delivers the localizer of the SoA *to be ill* which is placed in the past with respect to the moment of enunciation (GPT). The relation of inclusion between the L (*yesterday*) and the E (*to be ill*) in this case is such that E includes (is equal to or bigger than) L. The relation L⊆E expresses **imperfectivity**.

On the contrary, in a sentence as *yesterday he danced with Mary*, the L includes (and is bigger than) the E (*he danced*). E is a subpart of the time interval defined by *yesterday*. The relation L⊃E expresses **perfectivity**.

According to Lo Cascio's theory,[9] a SoA presented as imperfective cannot be quantified, while a SoA interpreted as perfective can be measured and quantified (cf. *he danced with her for two hours*). The SoA *he was ill* cannot be quantified because it is a time interval bigger than the localizer *yesterday* (cf. **he was ill for two hours*). The SoA *he danced*, on the contrary, is shorter than its localizer and therefore can be measured or quantified.

At the level of Aktionsart (lexical Aspect), achievement predicates cannot be quantified, since they are [-durative]. Achievement predicates therefore behave as imperfective SoA do.

Achievement SoA marked by a [+perfective] morpheme, or which must be interpreted as [+perfective], cannot be quantified either, since they still remain [-durative]. To sum up, SoA can only be quantified on condition that they are [+durative] and [+perfective].

---

[9] In languages whose morphology does not provide for aspectual marking at the Phonetic Form level, there is always need to have an aspectual interpretation at the discourse level in order to carry a story forward. Therefore, the presence of aspectual information at the level of the Logical Form (deep level) must be postulated. Accordingly, in Lo Cascio's theory, a L must always be postulated at the Logical Form level even if there is no lexicalization at the Phonetic Form level.

6.2 *The case of Italian*

As is widely known, Italian has a tense morphology which lexicalises both temporal and aspectual information at the same time. For example, the 'Imperfetto' (Simple Past Imperfective) indicates 'past + coincidence with the moment of enunciation + the fact that the SoA includes its reference time'. Therefore both semantic categories, Time and Aspect, must be taken into account in our analysis. Furthermore Italian is very strict with respect to the congruency of information between Aktionsart and Aspect. This is why, according to a 'congruency principle', for reasons of coherence an Italian perfective form (which indicates a closed time interval) in the past cannot combine with a progressive form (which indicates an open time interval), as the ungrammaticality of (10) shows:[10]

(10) * *la biblioteca stette chiudendo*
      the library be-SPP.3SG closing

In order to explain the behaviour of 'aspectual *si*-constructions', we will therefore take into account the tense combination, and consequently the congruency between the aspectual and temporal information carried by the tenses and the sentential aspectual value introduced by the *si*-marker. We will therefore distinguish among the present morpheme, the past morphemes ('Passato remoto', 'Imperfetto' and Present perfect) and the future morpheme.[11]

The Present form in Italian carries two types of information: temporal information and aspectual information, as shown in Table 2 below:

	Time	Aspect at VP level	Aspect at sentence level
Present: a.	[+coincidence][12]	[-perfective]+[-dynamic]	⇒ [+situation]
b.	[+coincidence]	[-perfective]+[+dynamic]	⇒ [+habitual]
c.	[+coincidence]	[-perfective]+[+dynamic]	⇒ [+progressive]
d.	[+future]	---???----	⇒ [+eventive]
e.	[atemporality]	-----------	⇒ [+characteristic]

Table 2: *'Present Tense'*

[+Coincidence]+[-perfectivity] can thus have three types of reading: [-perfective]+[-dynamic] which indicates a situation, or [-perfective]+ [+dynamic], which indicates a habit or an activity in progress.

Italian simple past distinguishes between two forms:

---

[10] This rule does not apply to other languages such as Spanish where (10) would be acceptable. The semantic reading of the Spanish progressive form would be different from the Italian one.

[11] Notice that the future morphemes are neutral with respect to the aspectual information, although a [+perfective] reading is more plausible.

[12] Coincidence with the moment of enunciation.

'Passato remoto'   [+past]+[+perfective]
'Imperfetto'   [+past]+[-perfective]
The [-perfective] form in turn can be combined with [-dynamic] or
[+dynamic].

Since the simple past 'Passato remoto' indicates perfectivity and it presents therefore an event and not a situation, habit or characteristic, this tense would be a candidate for a [+eventive] reading at the sentence level. The 'Imperfetto', on the contrary, will indicate a situation, an iteration or, if a [+dynamic] semantic feature is present, a SoA seen as an activity in progress.

So the following description holds:

	Time	Aspect at VP level	Aspect at sentence level
'Passato remoto':	[+past]	[+perfective]+[+dynamic] ⇒	[+eventive]
'Imperfetto':	[+past]	[-perfective] + [-dynamic] ⇒	[+situation]
	[+past]	[-perfective] + [+dynamic] ⇒	[+habitual]
	[+past]	[-perfective] + [+dynamic] ⇒	[+progressive]

Table 3: *'Passato remoto and Imperfetto'*

The 'Present perfect' in Italian can have the same reading as the 'Passato remoto' as regards its aspectual values [+perfective] and [+eventive], with the addition of aspectual value [+resultative] in some cases. The semantic feature [+resultative] shows here that the verb indicates the situation originating from the event. So the expression *è partito* can either mean that at some time in the past the event "he leaves" has occurred, or indicate the situation originating from the occurrence of the event "he leaves" and therefore indicate that "the person is not there at this very moment". The latter reading no longer involves the 'Present perfect' and is marked by the time [[+coincident] with the moment of enunciation], i.e. it has a present reading. In other words, the Present perfect morpheme carries the following possible information:

	Time	Aspect at VP level	Aspect at sentence level
Present perfect :	[+past]	[+perfective]+[+dynamic]	⇒ [+eventive]
	[+pres]	[+perfective]+[-dynamic]	⇒ [+situational]//[+resultative]

Table 4: *'Present perfect'*

7. *The analysis*

Let us now apply the three schemata shown in the tables in Section 6.2 to the analysis of a selection of '*si*-constructions', in order to see which aspectual role is covered by the morpheme *si* and to explain the differences in behaviour between verbs allowing the 'aspectual *si*-marker' and those refusing it.

7.1 The [-durative] verbs and the 'aspectual si-construction'

Let us first consider the verbs *chiudere, rompere, fermare.* These three verbs carry the semantic feature [-durative]. This explains why (11), (12), (13):

(11) *la biblioteca sta chiudendo*   "the library is closing"
(12) *il treno si sta fermando*   "the train is stopping"
(13) *il bicchiere si sta rompendo*   "the glass is breaking"

are semantically equal to (11a), (12a) and (13a) below respectively:

(11a) *la biblioteca sta per chiudere*   "the library is about to close"
(12a) *il treno si sta per fermare/??sta per fermare*   "the train is about to stop"
(13a) *il bicchiere si sta per rompere*   "the glass is about to break"

However, only *chiudere* and *rompere* also carry the semantic feature [+resultative]. This means that the past participles of *rompere* and *chiudere* can indicate a situation, while the past participle of *fermare* cannot. In order to indicate the situation originating from the event "to stop" we need to employ the adjective *fermo.* So if we have the structure shown in Table 5 below:

Chiudere	[-durative]	[+resultative]	[+habitual/iterative]
Rompere	[-durative]	[+resultative]	[-habitual]
Fermare	[-durative]	[-resultative]	[+habitual/iterative]

Table 5: *The [-durative] Verbs*

in the presence of the Present marker combined with a [-durative] feature, the combination according to the 'congruency principle' should assign a [+eventive] reading, lexicalise a 'future' time and consequently require the 'aspectual *si*-marker' in order to confirm the [+eventive] reading.[13]

As a matter of fact, the absence of the *si*-marker gives a [-eventive]+ [+habitual] reading to the verbal phrase. So we have:

(14a) [-eventive]+[+habitual]   (14b) [+eventive]
     La porta chiude male   *La porta si chiude male*
     the door close-PRES.3SG badly   the door PRM close-PRES.3SG well
     "the door closes badly"   "the door closes badly"

---

[13] Notice that the Present tense is a tense marked by a [-perfective] marker or by a [-perfective]+ [+progressive] markers combination. Therefore, since verbs such as *chiudere* or *fermare* are [-durative], when combined with a present morpheme they can take on the meaning of [-perfective]+[+progressive]; in that case, however, the action would focus on the situation leading to the moment of closing or stopping, and the predication would get a [+eventive] reading.

(15a) [-eventive]+[+habitual]

    Il treno ferma a Roma

    the train stop-PRES.3SG in Rome

    "the train stops in Rome"

(15b) [+eventive]

    Ecco, il treno si ferma

    Look, the train PRM stop-PRES.3SG

    "Look, the train is stopping"

In absence of the *si*-marker (as in (14a) and (15a)), the SoA has a [-eventive] reading and expresses habitual meaning.

Rompere has a [-habitual] reading. The SoA is marked by a [+unicity] semantic feature. *Rompere* therefore refuses the [+characteristic] or [+progressive] or [+habituality], and is only [+eventive]. In our view this explains why only a *si*-construction is allowed, and why *rompere* does not allow a non-*si* construction. The other two verbs, *chiudere* and *fermare*, allow a [+habitual] reading. Therefore they can show up in a construction with a [-eventive] reading, which is the counterpart of the *si*-construction. In order to acquire a [+eventive] reading they need the *si*-marker, which changes the aspectual value of the Present from [-perfective] into [+perfective].

The [+eventive] function of the aspectual *si*-construction will become clearer with the past tense morphemes, since Italian disposes of morphemes which lexicalise the opposition perfectivity [+eventive]/imperfectivity [-eventive]. See (16) to (19) below:

(16a) **La porta chiuse*

    the door close-SPP.3SG

(16b) *La porta si chiuse*

    the door PRM close-SPP.3SG

    "the door closed"

(17a) *La porta chiudeva*

    the door close-IMP.3SG

    "the door closed"

(17b) *La porta si chiudeva*

    the door PRM close-IMP.3SG

    "the door closed/was closing"

(18a) **Il bicchiere ruppe*

    the glass break-SPP.3SG

(18b) *Il bicchiere si ruppe*

    the glass PRM break-SPP.3SG

    "the glass broke"

(19a) **Il bicchiere rompeva*

    the glass break-IMP.3SG

(19b) *Il bicchiere si rompeva*

    the glass PRM break-IMP.3SG

    "the glass broke/was breaking"

(16a), (18a) and (19a) are not acceptable since the absence of the *si*-marker would allow the [-perfective] reading (and thus [-eventive] reading), while the use of the 'Passato remoto' requires the presence of [+perfective] value. The fact that *rompere* is only [+eventive] and [-habitual] also explains the ungrammaticality of (19a) and the reason why it cannot be assigned a structure [-eventive]+[+habitual], as in the case of absence of the *si*. Sentences (16b) and (18b) are [+eventive]. This is confirmed by the use of the *si*-marker. Consider further:

(20a) *?Il treno fermò*
the train stop-SPP.3SG

(20b) *Il treno si fermò*
the train PRM stop-SPP.3SG
"the train stopped"

(21a) *Il treno fermava*
he train stop-IMP.3SG
"the train used to stop"

(21b) *Il treno si fermava*
the train PRM stop-IMP.3SG
"the train stopped/used to stop"

In our view, in the b sentences there is a preference for a [+eventive] reading. The 'Passato remoto' again indicates perfectivity and therefore presents an event. The fact that the verb *fermare* requires the presence of the *si*-marker in combination with the 'Passato remoto' is explained by the fact that the construction without *si* would get a [-perfective] reading which would contradict the information of the 'Passato remoto'. Let us now take the Present perfect:

(22a) *La porta è chiusa*
the door is close-PP.3SGF
"the door is closed"

(22b) *La porta si è chiusa*
the door PRM is close-PP.3SGF
"the door (has) closed"

(23a) *Il bicchiere è rotto*
the glass is break-PP.3SGM
"the glass is broken"

(23b) *Il bicchiere si è rotto*
the glass PRM is break-PP.3SGM
"the glass has broken/broke"

(24a) **Il treno è fermato*
the train is stop-PP.3SGM

(24b) *Il treno si è fermato*
the train PRM is stop-PP.3SGM
"the train has come to a (complete) stop"

Notice that again the b sentences show a [+eventive] reading. The a sentences indicate situations and therefore have a [+coincidence]+[+resultative] reading. (24a) is not grammatical since *fermare* is a verb which does not lexicalise the situation produced by the event *fermare*. Therefore the [-resultative] character of *fermare* explains the agrammaticality of (24a). An adjective like *fermo* will do the job.

7.2 *The [+durative] verbs and the 'aspectual si-construction'*

Let us now consider the verbs *bruciare* and *ingiallire*. The Aktionsart of these verbs is shown in Table 6 below:

| **bruciare** | [+durative] | [+trasformative]/[+dynamic] | [+resultative] |
| **ingiallire** | [+durative] | [+transformative]/ [+dynamic] | [+resultative] |

Table 6: '*The [+durative] Verbs*'

These verbs belong to a class that allows both constructions with and without the aspectual *si*-marker (see also *fondere, ghiacciare* etc.) . Let us consider some examples in the present and the past:

(25a) *la casa brucia*
the house burn-PRES.3SG
"the house is burning"

(26a) *la carne brucia*
the meat burn-PRES.3SG
"the meat is burning/burns"

(27a) *la carta ingiallisce*
the paper turn-PRES.3SG yellow
"the paper turns yellow"

(28a) *la casa bruciò*
the house burn-SPP.3SG
"the house burnt"

(29a) *la casa bruciava*
the house burn-IMP.3SG
"the house was burning"

(30a) *la casa è bruciata*
the house is burn-PP.3SGF
"the house (has) burnt /is burnt"

(31a) *la carne è bruciata*
the meat is burn-PP.3SGF
"the meat (has) burnt/is burnt"

(25b) *la casa si brucia*
the house PRM burn-PRES.3SG
"the house burns"

(26b) *la carne si brucia*
the meat PRM burn-PRES.3SG
"the meat burns"

(27b) *la carta si ingiallisce*
the paper PRM turn-PRES.3SG yellow
"the paper turns yellow"

(28b) *la casa si bruciò*
the house PRM burn-SPP.3SG
"the house burnt"

(29b) *la casa si bruciava*
the house PRM burn-IMP.3SG
"the house was burning"

(30b) *la casa si è bruciata*
the house is burn-PP.3SGF
"the house (has/got) burnt"

(31b) *la carne si è bruciata*
the meat PRM is burn-PP.3SGF
"the meat (has/got) burnt"

The combination of the features [+durative]+[+dynamic] allows both a [+eventive] and a [-eventive] reading. If the tense morpheme carries the [-perfective] reading, then the interpretation can be either [+habitual] as in (27a) or [+progressive] as in (26a) and (29a). In the case of the Present tense, since it can acquire a future sense, we may also have the [+eventive] reading, as in (26a) and (27a). If the tense requires only a [+perfective] reading, then the sentential result will be [+eventive] as in (28a). In the latter case, the *si*-marker seems to be redundant and would confirm the [+eventive] reading assigned by the [+perfective] tense. In the former case, the *si* would disambiguate and assign a [+eventive] reading, instead of a [+habitual] or a [+progressive] one. The evidence of this will become clear by comparing the following sentences:

(32a) *la casa si è bruciata*	[+eventive]	(32b) *la porta si è chiusa*	[+eventive]
(33a) *la casa è bruciata*	[+eventive /situational]	(33b) *la porta è chiusa*	[+situational]
(34a) *la casa brucia*	[+eventive /progress]	(34b) *la porta chiude*	[+situational]
(35a) *la casa bruciava*	[progress]	(35b) *la porta chiudeva*	[+situational]
(36b) *la casa si bruciava*	[+eventive]	(36b) *la porta si chiudeva*	[+eventive]
(37b) *la casa bruciò*	[+eventive]	(37b) *la porta chiuse*	------------
(38b) *la casa si bruciò*	[+eventive]	(38b) *la porta si chiuse*	[+eventive]

Consider further the following examples:

(39a) *il bosco è bruciato*
the wood is burn-PP.3SGM
"the wood is/(has)burnt"
[+eventive]//[+situational]

(39b) *il bosco si è bruciato*
the wood PRM is burn-PP.3SGM
"the wood (has/got) burnt"
[+eventive]

(40a) *il bosco è tutto bruciato*
the wood is all burn-PP.3SGM
"the wood is all burnt//(has) burnt all"
[+situational]//[+resultative][14]

(40b) *il bosco si è tutto bruciato*
the wood PRM is all burnt-PP.3SGM
"the wood (has/got) all burnt up"
[+eventive]

(41a) *il bosco ha/è bruciato per due ore*[15]
the wood has/is burn-PP.3SGM for two
hours
"the wood has burnt for two hours"
[+progressive]
ACTIVITY

(41b) *il bosco si è bruciato per due ore*
the wood PRM is burn.PP.3sm for two
hours

but:(42) *il bosco si è bruciato in due ore*
the wood PRM is burnt-PP.3SGM in
two hours
"the wood (got) burnt up in two
hours"
[+eventive]
ACHIEVEMENT

The interpretation of (29a), (40b), (41a) and (41b) would be the following (where **QE** means quantifiable **E**):

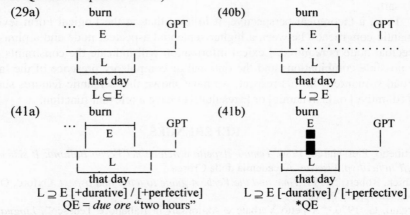

---

[14] A sentence such as *quel giorno il bosco è bruciato* "that day the wood burned" would of course only get the [+eventive] reading as in sentence (39a), since the localizer disambiguates the sequence. But in that case (40b) would maybe be preferred.

[15] Notice that it is not clear whether *bruciare* allows the auxiliary *avere*. Italian dictionaries only mention the auxiliary *essere*. Nevertheless, many native speakers also accept *avere*.

It is clear that the *si*-construction prefers to assign a [+eventive] reading, while the absence of the *si*-marker assigns a [-eventive] reading, which can be both [+situational] or [+progressive].

8. *Problems*

The construction marked by aspectual *si* can also carry the [-eventive]+ [+habitual] reading. This only happens in combination with the Present morpheme as (42) and (42b) show:

(42a) *La porta si chiude* [+eventive]   (42b) *Questa porta si chiude facilmente* [-eventive]
    the door PRM close-PRES.3SG   this door PRM close-PRES.3SG easily
    "the door closes"   "this door closes easily"

This must probably be explained by the special [-eventive] character of the present morpheme.

9. *Conclusions*

We have shown that:

a)   the pronominal marker *si*, in its intransitive use, assigns an aspectual function of the type [+eventive];

b)   this function is assigned at the sentence level, as a result of the interaction of three main parameters, namely Time, grammatical Aspect and Aktionsart.

From a theoretical perspective, it follows that, at the Logical Form level, semantic congruency between a higher sentential aspectual node and a phrasal aspectual node is required. Lexical information will indicate the constraints of the possible combinations and the optional or compulsory presence of the 'aspectual *si*-marker'. In this respect, we have shown that semantic features such as [±durative] or [±dynamic] or [±resultative] have a relevant function.

REFERENCES

Bertinetto, Pier Marco. 1986. *Tempo, Aspetto e Azione nel Verbo Italiano: Il sistema dell'indicativo*. Firenze: Accademia della Crusca.

Binnick, Robert I. 1991. *Time and the Verb: A guide to tense and aspect*. Oxford: Oxford University Press.

Borgato, G. 1976. "Aspetto Verbale e Aktionsart in Italiano e Tedesco". *Lingua e Contesto* 2.65-197.

Burzio, Luigi. 1986. *Italian Syntax: A government binding approach*. Dordrecht: Reidel.

Cennamo, Michela. 1993. *The Reanalysis of Reflexives: A diachronic perspective*. Napoli: Liguori.

Chierchia, Gennaro. 1992. "Subject and Aspect". *Golem* 2.11-14.
Comrie, Bernard. 1976. *Aspect*. Cambridge: Cambridge University Press.
Dik, Simon C. 1989. *The Theory of Functional Grammar*. Dordrecht: Foris.
Dowty, David. 1979. *Word Meaning and Montague Grammar*. Dordrecht: Reidel.
Elia, Annibale, Emilio D'Agostino & Maurizio Martinelli. 1981. *Lessico e Strutture Sintattiche: Introduzione alla sintassi del verbo italiano*. Napoli: Liguori.
Everaert, Martin. 1986. *The Syntax of Reflexivization*. Dordrecht: Foris.
Geniusiene, Emma. 1987. *The Typology of Reflexives*. Berlin: Mouton de Gruyter.
Halliday, Michael Alexander K. 1985. *An Introduction to Functional Syntax*. London: Edward Arnold.
Jezek, Elisabetta. 1997. "A Contrastive Lexical Analysis of Italian Pronominal Verbs: Proposal for a bilingual lexicographic representation". Unpublished Manuscript, University of Amsterdam, Italian Department.
Levin, Beth. 1993. *English Verb Classes and Alternation: A preliminary investigation*. Chicago: University of Chicago Press.
―――― & Malka Rappaport Hovav. 1992. "The Lexical Semantics of Verbs of Motion: The perspective from unaccusativity". *Thematic structure* ed. by Iggy Roca, 247-269. Dordrecht: Foris.
――――. 1995. *Unaccusativity*. Cambridge Mass.: The MIT Press.
Lo Cascio, Vincenzo. 1976. "On 'Linguistic Variables' and Primary Object-Topicalization in Italian". *Italian Linguistics* 1.33-75.
――――. 1995. "On the Relation between Tense and Aspect in Romance and other Languages". *Temporal Reference, Aspect and Actionality* ed. by Pier Marco Bertinetto, 273-291. Torino: Rosenberg & Sellier.
Mourelatos, Alexander P. 1978. "Events, Processes and States". *Linguistics and Philosophy* 2. 415-434.
Napoli, Donna Jo. 1976. *The two "si's" of Italian*. Bloomingtom: Indiana University Linguistic Club.
Palazzi, Fernando & Gianfranco Folena. 1995. *Dizionario della Lingua Italiana*. Torino: Loescher.
Perlmutter, David. 1978. "Impersonal Passives and the Unaccusative Hypothesis". *Proceedings of the fourth Annual Meeting of the Berkeley Linguistic Society*, 157-189. Berkeley: University of California.
――――. 1989. "Multiattachment and the Unaccusative Hypothesis: The perfect auxiliary in Italian". *Probus* 1:1.63-119.
Sabatini, Francesco & Vittorio Coletti. 1997. *Dizionario Italiano Sabatini Coletti*. Firenze: Giunti.
Salvi, Giampaolo. 1988. "La Frase Semplice". *Grande Grammatica di Consultazione*, ed. by Lorenzo Renzi, vol. I, 29-114. Bologna: Il Mulino.
Siewierska, A. 1984. *The Passive: A comparative linguistic analysis*. London: Croom Helm.
Van Valin, Robert D. 1987. "The Unaccusative Hypothesis vs. Lexical Semantics: Syntactic vs. semantic approaches to verb classification". *Proceedings of the North-*

eastern Linguistic Society 17, vol. II, 641-661. Cambridge Mass.: MIT Press.
Van Valin, Robert D. 1990. "Semantic Parameters of Split Intransitivity". *Language* 66.221-260.
Vendler, Zeno. 1967. "Verbs and Times". *Linguistics in Philosophy*, 97-121. Ithaca: Cornell University Press.
Verkuyl, Henk. 1972. *On the Compositional Nature of the Aspects*. Dordrecht: Reidel.
Wehr, Barbara. 1995. *SE-Diathese im Italienischen*. Tübingen: Narr Verlag.

SYNTACTIC OPTIONALITY AND LEXICAL SEMANTICS
THE CASE OF ENGLISH MANNER OF MOTION VERBS

STELLA MARKANTONATOU
Institute for Language and Speech Processing, Athens
and University of Cyprus

0. *Introduction*

Predicates (verbs and nouns) often admit syntactically optional predicative complements such as Adjectival and Prepositional Phrases. This kind of optionality has been treated as a random lexical syntactic property of verb predicates (cf. Levin & Rappaport 1986, Goldberg 1995), the assumption being that verbs idiosyncratically mark one (or more) of their semantic arguments as syntactically optional. Wechsler (1996), on the other hand, adopts the view that optionality of syntactic complements is reduced to optionality of semantic arguments of verbs. In this paper I will argue that certain optionality patterns which are observed with predicative complements of verbs are not random but systematic and due, first, to the semantic structure of predicates and, second, to 'Dependency' which is a general condition on the mapping from lexical semantics to subcategorisation properties (cf. Markantonatou & Sadler 1996). Furthermore, I will argue (contra Wechsler) that there exist semantic arguments of predicates which are optionally realized in the syntax. The class of verbs I take as a case study do not participate in affix mediated alternations affecting their subcategorisation patterns. However, the framework developed here can be easily extended to accommodate affix mediated alternations (such as passivization and nominalization patterns).

English manner of motion verbs will be used as a case study here. This class includes verbs such as *dance, walk, jump, march* which describe how motion is performed and must be contrasted with the class of motion verbs which denote directionality of motion such as *come* and *leave*. There is a certain controversy in the literature as to whether locative phrases are semantic and/or syntactic arguments of motion verbs or adjuncts. Syntactic optionality has been used as a diagnostic of adjuncthood, the assumption being that only adjuncts are optional. This syntactic diagnostic, however, is not a safe one. To see why, consider sentences such as *the peasant loaded the hay (on the wagon)* in which the optional locative complement is an unlikely adjunct. Because I need to draw a line between arguments of verbs and adjuncts I will use two semantic diagnostics of argumenthood and assume that semantic arguments map onto optional or obligatory syntactic arguments. According to the first diagnostic, entities which are always in our conception of the event denoted by a predicate are semantic arguments of it. For instance, it is not possible in our world to think of the event of 'eating' without thinking of an eater and an eatee. According to this diagnostic, the verb *eat* has two semantic arguments, although it is often the case that only one of them is syntactically overt. In the same way, we cannot think of a motion event without thinking of the relation between the space/location where the event took place, on the one hand, and the moving entity, on the other. According to the second diagnostic, only syntactic constituents which realize semantic arguments affect the interpretation of the head predicate. Of course, locative Prepositional Phrases (PPs) can co-occur with a wide range of semantic types of verb but, normally, they have no effect on the semantics of verb predicates. This is actually one of the well-established diagnostics of adjuncthood (cf. Bresnan 1982). Locative PPs, on the other hand, do affect the semantics of English manner of motion verbs as illustrated in sentences (1)-(7).

(1) He danced (across the room) (for an hour/ *in a minute).
(2) He danced mazurkas (across the room) (for an hour)/ *in a minute)
(3) He danced across the room (in a minute/ *for hours).
(4) He danced mazurkas across the room (in a minute/ *for hours).
(5) He danced his feet sore (in a minute/ *for hours).
(6) He danced free of his captors (in an hour/ *for hours).
(7) He danced her to oblivion (in an hour/ *for hours).

The verbs in sentences (1) and (2) admit optional predicative complements denoting the location of the motion event. Temporal adjuncts show that both sentences admit only an atelic interpretation. Both these sentences denote an activity that developed over some stretch of time in the past without entailing that the activity reached an end point. On the other hand, sentences (3) and (4) are telic. They admit obligatory locative complements and entail that the activity had an end point. In the first two sentences, the locative complement is not interpreted as the destination of the movement; it simply denotes the area where movement occurred. In the following two sentences, the locative complement denotes the destination of the movement because it identifies a particular point in the space which the moving entity reaches by participating in the activity denoted by the verb. This is reminiscent of the aspectual shift due to NP objects.

With certain verbs, when the NP denotes some delimited entity, the sentence takes on a telic interpretation (*he drank a glass of wine in three seconds/ *for an hour*) whereas when the object NP denotes some non-delimited entity the sentence takes an atelic interpretation (*he drank wine for an hour/ *in three seconds*). Because they have such an impact on the semantics of verbs (I assume that aspectual properties of sentences are recorded in the semantics of their verbal heads), locative PPs are treated here as semantic arguments of English manner of motion verbs.

In the rest of the example sentences ((5), (6) and (7)), the verbal heads admit obligatory predicative complements which denote states and they all receive a telic interpretation. Sentences (4), (5) and (7) are instances of a transitive use of the manner of motion verb. These sentences all entail that the activity was completed and that it resulted in changing the state of some entity which is not necessarily identical to the moving one. So, in (4) the moving entity is entailed to have crossed the room (by dancing mazurkas) but in (5) the entity undergoing a change of state (*his feet*) only accidentally moves. This is better illustrated with sentences such as *Commuters have run the platform thin*.

If we compare (1) and (2), on the one hand, with (3)-(7) on the other, we observe that English manner of motion verbs receive a telic interpretation only in the presence of predicative complements which introduce an end point for the motion event. The end point can be either a point fixed in space or, metaphorically, a state. A telic interpretation is never obtained from constructions with optional predicative complements. In conclusion, the telic interpretation is always obtained when a change of state is entailed and, in the case of English manner of motion verb, this coincides with the obligatory presence of predicative complements of the verb.

There are two reasons why I believe that the change of state entailment is supplied by the predicative complement rather than the motion verb. First, the entailment is missing from the sentences with an atelic interpretation. Recall that in these sentences predicative complements do not denote end points or states. Second and more important, when the entailment occurs, it is attributed to constituents which sometimes stand in no semantic relation with the verb (cf. Simpson 1983). In (5), for instance, the change of state entailment is attributed to the direct object which cannot freely co-occur with the verb predicate (8). The predicative complement, however, can be easily construed with the direct object (9). In short, the predicative complement is able to semantically support an argument which is entailed to undergo a change of state.

(8) *He danced his feet.

(9) His feet are sore.

The central idea of this paper can now be clearly stated. English manner of motion verbs do not entail that some entity undergoes a change of state; however, they may have semantic arguments which do and are realized as predicative complements. This view involves holding two assumptions about the relation between lexical semantics and syntax. First, that a semantic argument which is entailed to undergo a change of state has to be syntactically overt (unless there is some other process operating which blocks its realization). Second, that Dependency holds. Dependency is a constraint on the mapping relation between lexical semantics and subcategorisation properties which makes sure that all complements have a syntactically overt immediate semantic host, that is, they stand in an immediate semantic relation with a predicate which is syntactically overt. As a result, overt NP complements whose referents do not stand in a direct semantic relation with the verb must do so with a semantic complement of the verb which is syntactically overt. When semantic conditions of this kind do not hold, predicative complements are optional. Thus, syntactic optionality phenomena are explained in terms of the structure of the lexical semantics of predicates and of constraints on the relation between lexical semantics and subcategorisation properties.

My approach is different from the syntactic approach advocated in Simpson (1983) and Levin & Rappaport (1995), which essentially relies on the notion of an underlying syntactic object. Levin & Rappaport (1995) maintain that with manner of motion verbs an obligatory predicative complement that induces a telic interpretation co-exists with a deep structure object which is entailed to move directionally. In other words, English manner of motion verbs admitting a telic interpretation are unaccusative verbs, that is, monadic verbs whose single argument is an object at deep structure and a subject at surface structure. However, Wechsler (1996) has brought sentences such as (4) to our attention. Such sentences admit a telic interpretation, entail movement of the subject and contain an obligatory predicative complement. But they also have a surface object which entails the existence of a deep object other than the one corresponding to the moving entity. It would be difficult to argue that there are two co-existing deep objects in (4). In short, unaccusativity fails to account for the relevant data. Unaccusativity is a compelling reason to postulate that verb predicates are endowed with a syntactic level mediating between lexical semantics and surface syntax. This level is often called 'argument structure'. Levin & Rappaport also use this level to encode optionality of predicative complements. In the present account, which does not advocate an analysis in terms of unaccusativity, mapping from semantics to surface syntax is not mediated by some syntactic level of analysis and optionality of predicative complements results from the interaction of verbal semantics with the condition here dubbed Dependency.

1. *The formal apparatus*

The theory of lexical semantics which supports my treatment of syntactic optionality draws on work by Dowty (1991), Levin & Rappaport (1995) and Goldberg (1995). Lexical semantics is a level of analysis which is independent from the syntactic one. The two levels are related by a mapping relation. The syntactic level of analysis is assumed to be that of the f-structures of Lexical Functional Grammar (LFG)[1] (cf. Bresnan 1982). Traditionally LFG recognizes two syntactic levels of analysis, the c-structure and the f-structure, which are related by a mapping function. Each of these levels employs its own formal means. f-structures are represented with untyped feature structures. The so-called 'Grammatical Functions' (such as Subject (SUBJ), Object (OBJ), Adjunct (ADJ)) occur as features in LFG f-structures. My analysis introduces lexical semantics as a *third* level of analysis which employs typed feature structures and

---

[1] Abbreviations in the text and in glosses are the following:

ADJ	=	adjunct	MOT	=	motion
ARG	=	argument	OBJ	=	object
CG	=	Construction Grammar	SUBJ	=	subject
LFG	=	Lexical Functional Grammar	PRED	=	predicate

Linking relations:

caus_int_property:	*causative internal property*
ch_pp:	*change of state patient protorole*
incr_pp:	*incremental theme patient protorole*
int_contrl:	*internal controller*
int_prop:	*internal property*

link_rel:	*linking relation*
ncauser:	*non causer*
vol:	*volitional*
vol_caus:	*volitional causer*
vol_ncaus:	*volitional non causer*

Relations:

c-structure	*constituent structure*
dmtn_sc:	*directed motion with semantic constraint*
extc:	*externally controlled*
extc_dmtn_sc:	*externally controlled directed motion with semantic constraint*
extc_mtn_res:	*externally controlled motion resultative*
extc_res:	*externally controlled resultative*
f-structure:	*functional structure*
mtn_res:	*motion resultative*
mtn_sc:	*motion with semantic constraint*
nc_dmtn_sc:	*non controlled directed motion with semantic constraint*
nc_dmtn_sc0:	*non controlled directed motion with semantic constraint simple*
ndmtn_sc_tr:	*non directed motion with semantic constraint transitive*
p_exct:	*possibly externally controlled*
res:	*resultative*
sem.cons:	*semantic constraints*

multiple inheritance. The different levels are mutually constrained with the mapping relations holding among them.

Feature structures can be treated as functions from features to values. For instance, the feature structure in (10) is a function from the features **PRED, ARG1, ARG2** to the values *dance, dancer* and the embedded feature structure respectively. Feature structures may contain an unlimited number of nested feature structures. A sequence of features across nested feature structures is called a 'path': in (10) **ARG2/PRED** is a path.

The paths **ARG1** and **ARG2/ARG1** share their values. This is indicated by the box notation in (10). In this case, we say that we have a 'reentrancy'.

(10)

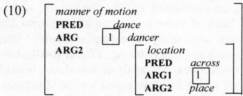

Feature structures can be typed, like the feature structures I will use to represent lexical semantic relations, or untyped, like the LFG f-structures. Typed feature structures, but not untyped ones, are each defined for a specified set of feature-value pairs. No feature or value other than the specified ones can appear in a typed feature structure. In the notation I use here, the type of a feature structure appears in italics at the top of the matrix. For instance, the type of the feature structure in (10) is 'manner of motion'.

Types may be arranged in an inheritance hierarchy. In the inheritance hierarchy shown in (11) *bird* is the supertype of both *penguin* and *canary*; *penguin* is a subtype of *bird* and so is *canary*. We say that a supertype is subsumed by its subtypes.

(11)   *bird*

            penguin   *canary*

Feature structures can stand in an inheritance relation. We say that a feature structure A inherits from a feature structure B iff all paths in B are also in A, re-entrancies are preserved, the values of the paths of A subsume the values of the corresponding paths of B and the type of A is a subtype of the type of B.

2. *Relation types*

I assume that the semantics of predicates can be understood as structured relation types which can be represented with typed feature structures. Relation types are structured to encode (a) the 'arity' of a relation, that is, the number of participants involved, (b) the role of the participants in the event denoted by a relation, (c) whether a relation is flat or nested. I will take up points (b) and (c) later in this Section. (12) is the representation of a relation type of arity one. Its type is 'first level relation'. The single participant is encoded with the first level argument **ARG1**. The relation also contains a nested relation of type 'nested relation'. **ARG1** & **ARG2** of the nested relation are second level arguments of first level relation.

(12)

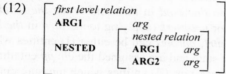

Arguments of relations which map onto referential expressions in the syntax are of type *arg* (13) which is defined for two features, **LINK** and **OTHER.LINK** is appropriate for values of type *link(ing)_rel(ation)* (14), encodes the mode of participation of an entity in the event denoted by the relation and determines the mapping from lexical semantics to syntax. **OTHER** is appropriate for a list of entailments which, however, do not affect syntax. (Which entailments affect syntax is a matter of empirical evidence.)

(13) ⎡ *arg* ⎤
⎢ **LINK** *link_rel* ⎥
⎣ **OTHER** [*list of entailments*] ⎦

I use the term 'entailment' in the same way as Dowty (1991) who elaborates on the observation that there is a range of properties attributed to the arguments of a relation which are 'entailed to hold'. To accommodate this kind of entailment in multiple inheritance networks of relation types, I define types of entailments arranged in a hierarchy relation (14).

(14)

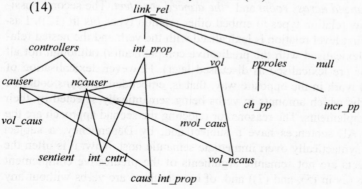

Participants in a relation are entailed to possess some of the properties appearing in (14). The names of the properties are hopefully transparent as regards their content. In what follows, I give both the full and the abbreviated name of each property together with an example context entailing it. For a more detailed discussion of the particular theory of relation types see Markantonatou & Sadler (1996). I define three most general types of properties: *controllers, pproles* and *null*. This is because the types *vol* and *int_prop* have no own subtypes. *Controllers* can be *causers* (applying to *the wind* in *the wind broke the window*, more specifically, a *non_vol_caus* or *ncausers* (applying to *the bird* in *the bird sings*; more specifically, an *int_contrl*; *pproles* can be either (I) entities which are entailed to undergo a change of state and are assigned the *ch_pp* entailment (applying to *the river* in *the river froze*) or, (II) entities which measure out the development of an activity in time and are assigned the *incr_pp* entailment (applying to *the beer* in *John drank the beer in seconds)*. Participants which cannot be attributed any of these entailments are assigned the entailment *null* (applying to *the telly* in *John watched the telly)*.

When predicative complements exist, we are clearly dealing with more than one predicative domain. One such domain syntactically realizes the semantic relation corresponding to the verb predicate and the other domain(s) the relation(s) corresponding to the predicative complement(s). In the representation framework I have adopted, there are, in principle, two architectural possibilities. The first possibility is that two predicative domains merge into a flat one. This phenomenon is called complex predicate formation. There are good reasons, however, to believe that no complex predication formation takes place with English manner of motion verbs. If the verb formed a complex predicate with the predicative complement the latter would in principle occur next to the verb in passive adjectives; however, the following constructions are not grammatical *the danced across room* and *the danced sore feet*. The second possibility is to allow relation types to embed other relation types (as in (12)). I assume that the first level relation is lexicalised with the verb and the nested relation(s) is(are) lexicalised with the predicative complement(s) (although not all nested relations are lexicalised as discussed later). However, lexicalisation of relations could work in the opposite way, that is, embedded relations could be realized as verbs which amounts to verbs being semantically selected by their predicative complements. The reasons for rejecting the second approach are the following: (I) All sentences have a subject and, by Dependency, a subject should have a syntactically overt immediate semantic host. Now, it is often the case that subjects are not semantic arguments of the predicative complement but of the verb (as in (5), and (7)) and, of course, there are verbs without any predicative complements. So, I assume that the first level relation, which is always there, is lexicalised with the verb. (II) Predicative complements themselves are subject to Dependency. Just like any other relation argument which is syntactically overt, predicative complements need an immediate semantic host predicate. Only the verb is not dependent on any other predicate and should correspond to the first level relation which is never the argument of some other relation.

3. *Motivation for multiple inheritance networks*

I now turn to the inheritance relations among relation types. The motivation for this particular formalism is twofold. First, homophonous verbs, such as the heads of sentences (1)-(7), often share a core semantics and, second, individual languages make available independent semantic patterns which merge with core verbal semantics; the combinations are lexicalised with verbs.

Let us first consider the claim that there is only one core semantics per verb. The exact interpretation of the verb *dance* varies across the sentences (1)-(7). For instance, in Section 0, I discussed the aspectual variation observed. Despite this variation, however, all the sentences entail that there was some *dancing*. We can plausibly claim that there is a certain core verbal semantics present in all the sentences discussed. I encode this idea by assuming that there is a core relation (super)type which has all the interpretations of the verb as its subtypes. Alternatively one could postulate lexical rules which would generate the different senses from a 'basic' one (for instance, one could obtain the senses of *dance* in sentences (2)-(7) from the sense of *dance* in (1)). In this way, however, unnecessary directionality would be introduced as, in general, there is no clear reason why some sense is more basic than another. For instance, it is not clear whether sense (1) is more basic than sense (3) or vice versa.

A second important assumption of the theory proposed is that language allows for semantic patterns which cut across the classes of verb meanings. Consider the semantic variation observed with sentences (1)-(7) again. There are verbs other than the manner of motion ones which also occur in constructions identical to (1) - (7).

(1') He walked around the town for hours.
(3') He ran to the station in a minute.
(4') The Magi followed the Star out of Bethlehem in a night.
(5') Felix barked the neighbors awake.
(6') The train rumbled clear of the station.
(7') The audience sneezed the napkin off the table.

Goldberg (1995), working within the framework of Construction Grammar (CG), argues that sentences (5)/(5')-(7)/(7') are instances of certain identifiable constructions of English. According to CG, 'constructions' are sentence generating templates consisting of semantic and syntactic information. Constructions combine with individual verbs and together they specify the syntax and the semantics of sentences. Constructions are designed to account for the intuition that the meaning of each of the following pairs of sentences (5)/(5'), (6)/(6') and (7)/(7') varies only as regards the meaning of the verb. For instance, the constant meaning across the pair (5)/(5') is that a certain entity has been forced by the subject of the sentence to undergo a change of state and that the subject has acted in the manner specified by the verb. This component of meaning, Goldberg argues, must be attributed to a construction, as it remains invariable across different classes of verbs.

Another important argument in support of the existence of constructions is that the semantics of sentences such as (5)/(5') and (7)/(7') is not compositional, that is, the overall meaning of the sentence is not a function of the meaning of its constituents. Consider, for instance, the sentences (5)/(5') and (7)/(7') where the subject is entailed to CAUSE the event described. The CAUSE entailment is contributed neither by the head verb nor by any other word in the sentence (it is not contributed by the head verb because it is absent from sentences (1), (2), (3), (4) and (6)). Similarly, (6)/(6') has a motion entailment related with the subject, whether the verb is a manner of motion one (6) or other (6'). These extra entailments, Goldberg says, are contributed by the construction semantics which is independent from but compatible with the semantics of the verb.

I adopt Goldberg's proposal that the semantics of sentences is sometimes the combination of independent semantic patterns with meanings of individual verbs. For instance, I assume that English has a special semantic pattern for resultatives such as (5)/(5') which contributes the CAUSE entailment. I do *not* adopt, however, the syntactic dimension of constructions. Before explaining the reasons for this decision, I will list its consequences. In my proposal, the semantics of sentences is determined solely by the semantics of their verbal heads. The semantics of verbs results from the combination of independent semantic patterns with core verbal semantics. Thus, sentences (1)-(7) are semantically and, by linking, syntactically determined by the semantics of their verbal heads.

The reasons for rejecting the syntactic dimension of the construction-based approach are two. First, there exist pervasive regularities in the mapping from lexical semantics to subcategorisation properties of verbs (I will use the term 'linking' to refer to this mapping). Constructions, as defined in Goldberg (1995), neglect these regularities which could otherwise enhance the explanatory power of the grammar. Second, and more important for my discussion, CG, as developed in Goldberg (1995), does not capture certain aspects of predicative complement optionality. There are, for instance, predicates which receive a telic interpretation both when followed by a resultative phrase (16) and in other contexts (15). Such a predicate is *hammer*.

(15) The ironsmith hammered the metal in a couple of hours.

(16) The ironsmith hammered the metal flat in a couple of hours.

(15) has three interpretations. The first is a 'holistic' one concerning not the intensity of the effect of the hammering activity on the metal but the fact that all the surface of the metal was hammered (*the metal* is an 'incremental theme' in the terminology of Dowty 1991). The second is the resultative interpretation which is relevant to our discussion here. According to this interpretation hammering has caused the metal to undergo a change of state. This interpretation is similar to that of (16) their only difference being that (16) also specifies the new state. The ambiguity of (15) shows that the resultative complement may be syntactically optional with certain predicates. This is not possible within the Goldberg version of CG whereby the resultative complement is supplied by the construction and cannot be optional by definition. If it were optional, it would allow for ungrammatical structures such as (17). Thus, the resultative complement must syntactically realize a semantic component of the verb.

(17) *Fido barked the neighbours.

One could object that, in CG, syntactic optionality can be induced by the verb predicate. However, the verb *hammer* may allow for a third, atelic interpretation of (15) which is the one in (18):

(18) The ironsmith hammered the metal for days.

To account for (18) CG would need a second entry for *hammer* without a semantic component specifying the effect of hammering on the entity undergoing it. Multiple lexical entries, however, undermine the role of constructions and, indeed, CG strongly argues against them.

To recapitulate, the theory of lexical semantics I have briefly introduced here reflects the assumption that language makes available independent semantic patterns which combine with verb meanings in order to be realized as verbs in the syntax. These semantic patterns are not independently realised in the syntax either as words or as sentences. I will use the formal means of typed multiple inheritance to encode the claim that verbal semantics results from the combination of different sources of information.

4.   *The network of relation types*

In (19) I present the network of relation types that supports my treatment of syntactic optionality phenomena as regards English manner of motion verbs and is based on the ideas and the facts discussed thus far.

The numbers attached to the leaf nodes refer to the examples in the text. First, I distinguish four types of semantic relations: *controlled* (Smith 1970), *extended, locatives* and *state. controlled* relations correspond to events, the development of which is controlled by some entity; for instance, a 'killing' event is controlled by the 'killer' but the state of sleeping is not controlled by the 'sleeper'. We will come to *extended* relations later. *state* (20) relations correspond to states. *locatives* denote locations and are lexicalised with prepositions. *controlled* has two subtypes: *extc* (21) and *p_extc* (22); *extc* are the relations which involve causation such as *murder, write*; *p_extc* are *controlled* relations with an internal controller, for instance *sneeze, sing*.

(19)

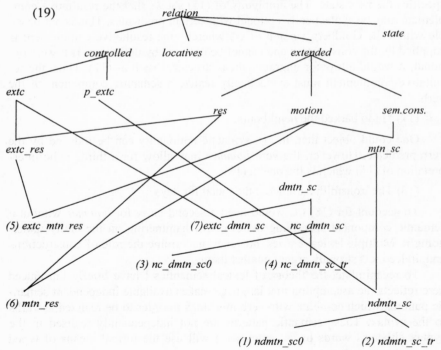

(20) $\begin{bmatrix} state \\ \textbf{ARG1/LINK} \quad pproles \end{bmatrix}$

(21) $\begin{bmatrix} extc \\ \textbf{ARG1/LINK} \quad causer \end{bmatrix}$

(22) $\begin{bmatrix} p\_extc \\ \textbf{ARG1/LINK} \quad controller \end{bmatrix}$

extended has three subtypes *res* (23), *sem.cons* (24) and *motion* (25). *extended* is different from *controlled* and *state* in that it contributes nested relations only. I have already mentioned that predicative complements syntactically realize embedded semantic structures. This clearly holds for *res* and *sem.cons.* (*sem.cons.* is lexicalised with predicative domains headed by prepositions). The semantic relation type *motion,* however, deserves further discussion. *motion* is the semantic supertype of verbs denoting motion events. It contributes an embedded relation of type *mtn_rel.*

(23) $\begin{bmatrix} res \\ \textbf{RES} \quad state \end{bmatrix}$

(24) $\begin{bmatrix} sem.cons. \\ \textbf{SEM.CONS.} \quad locatives \end{bmatrix}$

(25)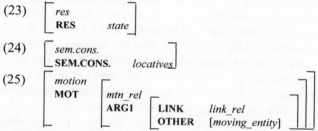

The arguments of the embedded relation are not characterized for linking purposes because **ARG1/LINK** is assigned the most general entailment type *link_rel* (14). In short, the entailment that some entity moves is not considered important to linking. This runs counter to the traditional definition of 'theme' (one of the popular semantic roles) as the entity moving along some path. Dowty (1991), however, doubts whether the motion entailment actually affects linking. Example sentences (1)-(7) support the view that linking is not sensitive to motion entailment. This is because a moving entity can turn up in both the subject (1)-(6) and the object (7) syntactic position and each time it is possible to claim that there is some other entailment type which determines linking. (1) and (2) denote activities which are normally understood as internally controlled (most probably by some *vol_ncaus*). The intuition is that the dancing activities described in (1) and (2) are volitionally controlled by the dancer. According to the linking mechanism I presented in Section 6, *controllers* always link to subject. Sentences (3), (4), (6) and (7) entail that the moving entity has undergone a change of state because it has moved to a specified position (by dancing). In such sentences, the moving entity is assigned the entailment type *ch_pp*. According to the linking theory adopted here, *pproles (pproles* is the supertype of *ch_pp* (14)) link to subject or, when a subject has already been supplied, to object. Finally, in sentence (5), the dancing entity is the *causer* of the event described and links to subject. It seems, then, that motion on its own does not determine linking. Motion denoting verbs need to have semantic supertypes other than *motion* in order to have enough semantic information for linking purposes. Consequently, the entailment *moving_entity* can be included in the list value of the feature **OTHER**.

I now turn to the relation embedded in *motion*. Assume that *motion* was defined for a first level argument linking to referential expressions, say **ARG1**, with the appropriate **OTHER** value but no specific value assigned to **LINK**. If such an argument was present we would have to observe the contrast between (5) and (7). In (5) the *causer* is entailed to move but not in (7), for instance; the subject of (7) could have been the musician playing the music accompanying the dancing (consider parallel examples such as *The general, who was yelling orders from the balcony, marched the soldiers to the barn*). In short, in order to account for (7) we have to provide for the fact that the *causer* is different from the moving entity (of course, the causer may be inferred to move but this is irrelevant). This situation must be contrasted with the situation in (5) where the *causer* of the event and the moving entity are the same entity. If there was a first level argument with the *moving_entity* entailment in the list value of **OTHER**, we would need to make sure that, when in the type *extc_dmtn_sc* (which is the relation type corresponding to (7)), the argument does not inherit from the **ARG1** of its supertype *extc* (the value of **ARG1/LINK** in *extc* is *causer*). To make sure that the **ARG1** of the supertype *extc* and the first level argument of the *motion* relation type do not necessarily point to the same entity we would need to have two different features defined; for instance, we could have defined **ARG1** as the first level argument of *motion*. This would serve the purposes of (7) (where the two features point to different participants). But, (5) would stand for a relation type defined for two semantic arguments which would point to the same entity although they would not be related with an entailment such as 'the controler acts upon himself' (as in *John shaved*). To avoid such semantic oddities, I assume that *motion* contributes an embedded relation type.

5. *The relation types for English manner of motion verbs*
I will now give the semantic relation types for the head verbs of sentences (1)-(7). Numbering will have the form 'Nr' where 'N' is the number of the corresponding example sentence and 'r' is a diacritic signifying relation type.

(1r) shows the proposed semantics for the head verb of (1). (1) denotes an internally controlled event. In the theory proposed in (19), internally controlled relations inherit from *p_extc*. The relation is defined for one first level argument and two embedded relations. As a subtype of *motion, ndmtn_sc* inherits a feature **MOT** with value *mtn_rel*. The value of **MOT/ARG1/LINK** is structure shared with the value of **ARG1/LINK** to encode the fact that the moving entity internally controls the moving event. As a subtype of *sem.cons., ndmtn_sc* inherits a feature **SEM.CONS.** with value 'location'. This is to encode the fact that the motion event does not have an end point (a destination, cf. Section 0). The value of **SEM.CONS./ARG1/LINK** is structure shared with the value of **ARG1/LINK** to encode the fact that the controller moves around (without reaching some destination point).

(1r)
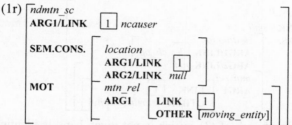

(2r) represents the semantics of head verb of (2) and is different from (1r) in that it contains an additional first level feature **ARG2** with **ARG2/LINK** value of type *null*. This feature is there to account for the transitivity of the verb in (2).

(2r)
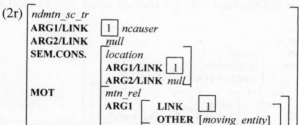

(4r) and (7r) are the representations of the semantics of the head verb of (4) and (7) respectively. Both these relation types inherit from the type *dmtn_sc* (26) which, in turn, inherits from *motion* and from *sem.cons. dmtn_sc* is the supertype of relation types denoting motion events with a destination (cf. sentences (3), (4) and (7)). It contains two embedded relation types, *destination* and *mtn_rel*. The paths **SEM.CONS/ARG1/LINK** and **MOT/ARG1/LINK** share their values to encode the fact that the moving entity undergoes a change of state (by reaching a destination).

(26)

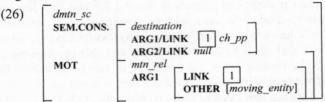

(4r) denotes an event which is not externally controlled and results in the change of state of the moving entity (4). There is no *controller* argument. The verb occurs with an object represented with the first level argument **ARG1**.

, (4r)

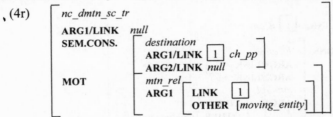

The semantics of the head verb of (3), which is not given here, is identical to (4r) without the first level argument **ARG1**.

(7r) represents the semantics of (7). The relation inherits from *dmtn_sc* (26) and from *extc* which contributes the first level argument **ARG1** with **LINK** value *causer*. *causer* is not identical with the moving entity (see Section 4 for discussion).

(7r)

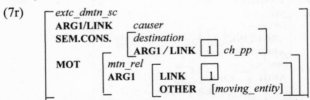

(6r) and (5r) are the representations of the semantics of the head verbs of (6) and (5) respectively. Both relations inherit form *res* (23) and denote events whereby an entity undergoes a change of state by reaching a result state (rather than a destination). The values of the appropriate paths are structure-shared to encode the fact that (6) describes an event whereby the moving entity undergoes a change of state. On the other hand, in (5) the moving entity causes another entity to undergo a change of state. So, no structure sharing is defined for the values of the paths **RES/ARG1/LINK** & **MOT/ARG1/LINK**.

(6r)

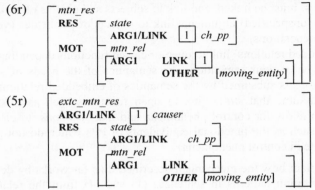

(5r)

6. *Linking*

I first describe the linking mechanism and then explain the mapping from the relation types described in Section 5 to subcategorisation properties.

The linking mechanism accounts for the regularities controlling the mapping from lexical semantics to subcategorisation properties of verbs and consists of two components. The first consists of a set of conditions on the syntax-semantics interface as listed in (27). While this linking theory is in principle compatible with any syntactic theory, the wording used assumes the formal framework of LFG and f-structures as a syntactic output hence the use of terms such as Grammatical Functions. No precise formalization of the linking mechanism will be given here. The interested reader is referred to Markantonatou & Sadler (1996) for a first formalization in LFG.

(27) Conditions on the syntax-semantics interface.

1. 'Subject Condition'. Verb predicates subcategorize for a subject.
2. 'Dependency'. Only the first level arguments of syntactically overt predicates can be syntactically overt.
3. 'Optionality'. Linking of embedded relations is optional.
4. 'Embedded Relation Completeness'. All first level arguments of all relations must be linkable.
5. 'Uniqueness'. Grammatical Functions are unique.
6. 'Correspondence'. Each syntactic argument must be linked to one semantic argument.

The linking principles show how entailments (14) affect linking.

(28) The Linking Principles
   1. 'Controllers' must be linked, and link to subjects of verbs.
   2. 'Pproles' must be linked, and link to subjects and objects of verbs.
   3. 'Null' (unspecified) arguments link to objects of predicates (verbs
      and prepositions).
   4. 'Embedded relations' link to open or closed functions depending on
      the type of their semantics. The semantics of the heads of such
      functions is subsumed by the semantics of embedded relations. (I
      will assume that *states* link to open functions such as XCOMP
      which allow for control phenomena and that *sem.cons.* to closed
      ones such as the functional equivalents of PPs which do not par-
      ticipate in control phenomena).

I will now explain how the mechanism described thus far works by deriving the subcategorisation patterns in sentences (1) and (4) from the relation
types (1r) and (4r) respectively and the linking conditions (27) and principles
(28). The first level argument of (1r) which is assigned the value *ncauser* will
necessarily map onto Subject by Linking Principle (1). Linking Condition (1) is
satisfied. To satisfy Dependency (Linking Condition (2)) we have to make sure
that the first level relation is linked to a verb form. With the first level relation
and the first level argument linked, there is no constraint forcing us to map any
other argument to syntactically overt expressions because by Condition (3) the
linking of embedded relations is optional. Furthermore, only the first level argument **SEM.CONS.** can be mapped (Principle (4)) as nothing is specified about
the mapping of **MOT**. The mapping of **SEM.CONS.** is obligatory, however, when
we want to have an overt expression denoting the location where the motion
event took place. The semantic correspondent of the location of the event is the
first level argument **ARG2** of the embedded relation *location*. By dependency,
overt first level arguments have overt immediate semantic host predicates. Consequently, the syntactic realization of the *location* relation type with a locative
PP is obligatory. The preposition functioning as the head of the locative PP is
the immediate semantic host predicate of **SEM.CONS./ARG2**. This is how my
proposal accounts for the optionality of the predicative complement in (1).

Sentence (4) contains an obligatory predicative complement. Consider its
corresponding relation type (4r). The argument **SEM.CONS./ARG1** links to subject by Principle (2). This satisfies Condition (1). However, **SEM.CONS./ ARG1**
is not a first level argument of the first level relation but of the embedded relation **SEM.CONS.** To satisfy Dependency **SEM.CONS.** links to a closed grammatical function by Principle (4). **SEM.CONS.**, in turn, is a first level argument of the
first level relation which, again by Dependency, maps to the verb predicate.

SEM.CONS./ARG2 is by Principle 3 linked to a referential expression naming the destination of the moving event. Similarly, ARG1 is linked to the object of the verb. MOT does not link, as explained above. This is how my proposal accounts for obligatory predicative complements.

7. *Conclusions*

I have presented an account of syntactic optionality patterns exemplified with the predicative complements of English manner of motion verbs which is rooted in lexical semantics.

According to this account, syntactic optionality of predicative complements is not an idiosyncratic lexical property. It is, instead, systematically determined by the semantic structure of verbs and by Dependency which is a general condition on the mapping from lexical semantics to subcategorisation properties. Dependency bears a certain similarity to the LFG constraints accounting for control phenomena in English resultatives (cf. Simpson 1983) which simultaneously introduce a subject an its syntactic host predicate. However, the LFG constraints are syntactic in nature and run into the problem of unaccusativity, whereas my account is semantic and avoids questions concerning the existence of a deep structure or an argument structure.

This framework can be extended to account for affix mediated alternations such as passivisation and nominalisation patterns. One can rely on the widely held assumption that affixes have their own semantic content which combines with the semantic content of verbal roots. Linking rules may differ slightly between the various parts of speech; for instance, we may need to define a new set of linking rules applying to deverbal nouns. In this way, the systematic correspondence between lexical semantics and syntax will be treated in a unified way across part-of-speech distinctions and alternations whether they are mediated by affixes or not.

REFERENCES

Bresnan, Joan, ed. 1982. *The Mental Representation of Grammatical Relations*: Cambridge, Mass.: MIT Press.

Dowty, David. 1991. "Thematic Proto-Roles and Argument Selection". *Language* 67.547-619.

Goldberg, Adele. 1995. *Constructions: A construction grammar approach to argument structure*. Chicago: Chicago University Press.

Levin, Beth & Malka Rappaport. 1986. "The Formation of Passive Adjectives". *Linguistic Inquiry* 17.623-661.

——— . 1995. *Unaccusativity*. Cambridge, Mass.: MIT Press.

Markantonatou, Stella & Louisa Sadler. 1996. "English Resultatives Revisited". Unpublished Manuscript, Essex University.

Simpson, Jane. 1983. "Resultatives". *Papers in Lexical Functional Grammar* ed. by Annie Zaenen, Lori Levin & Malka Rappaport, 143-57. Bloomington: Indiana University Linguistics Club.

Smith, Carlotta S. 1970. "Jespersen's 'Move and Change' Class and Causative Verbs in English". *Linguistics and Literary Studies in Honor of Archibald A. Hill, vol. II: Descriptive linguistics* ed. by M. A. Jazayery, E. C. Polome, & W. Winter, 101-9. The Hague: Mouton.

Verspoor, Cornelia. 1996. "Manner of Motion Verbs and Resultative Constructions". Unpublished Manuscript, University of Edinburgh.

Wechsler, Stephen. 1996. "Explaining Resultatives Without Unaccusativity". Unpublished Manuscript, University of Texas at Austin.

LABILE ORDERS AND GRAMMATICAL FUNCTIONS
THE FUNCTIONAL REPRESENTATION OF ONE-ARGUMENT STRUCTURES

ROSANNA SORNICOLA
Università di Napoli Federico II

0. *Introduction*

The general aim of this work is to reconsider the relationship between order and the representations of grammatical functions (henceforth GFs). It will be claimed that the traditional view which considers order merely as a dependent variable with respect to functional representations cannot be maintained. Order has traditionally been aprioristically and unproblematically conceived in linguistic theory as a means of coding GFs and/or pragmatic functions. It will be argued here that order can also be studied as an independent variable and that this can help to develop new models for the representation of functional structure. Considering order as an independent variable does not mean, of course, disregarding the role order plays in the grammar, but starting with a preliminary investigation of the properties of order per se and then trying to correlate them with functional representations.

This aim will be pursued through examination of the problems raised by what have been elsewhere defined 'one-argument' structures, that is structures with a verbal operator whose domain is a single argument at some level of representation.[1] Thus the structures that will be taken into account contain either verbs of movement, like It. *andare* "to go", *venire* "to come", or verbs of process, like

---

[1] Cf. Bernini (1995); Sornicola (1995). The problem of determining the level of representation is interesting. It concerns the difference between the set of properties of a given verbal item as they are represented in its lexico-functional grid and the actual selection of these properties in the syntactic environment in which the verbal lexeme occurs. In this model the properties of the virtual grid and those of the actual construction may be at variance. As is well known, however, this is not the only possible model for the description of verbal items. For example, one could conceive of as many distinct lexico-functional grids as there are properties of the actual constructions of a given verbal lexeme. This problem concerns us here insofar as the so-called 'pseudo-intransitive' verbs are involved. It should however be kept separate from the problem of the argument representation

suonare "to play (a musical instrument)", *echeggiare* "to echo", *fiorire* "to flower" as well as verbs of saying in the construction (or in the lexico-functional grid) with a single argument. These lexical classes share the property of being intransitive, but they can be divided into different subclasses, according to the syntactic properties expressed in the phrasal codification of the single argument (as in the distinction between ergative and unaccusative verbs in generative grammar) or according to the semantic properties of Animacy and Agentivity, as in current typological research. Other structures that can be considered 'mono-argumental' are those with reflexive-intransitive and passive verbs.

An interesting property shared by these verb classes is 'labile order',[2] meaning that the relative order of the verb and its single argument is highly unstable, oscillating according to a combination of factors (cf. Section 3.). This property is typologically conditioned with respect to basic word-order (cf. Section 3.). It will be argued that in languages with labile order of one-argument structures such a property poses a serious challenge to the determination of the underlying functional representation. It can be interpreted as an indication of either neutralization of the GFs Subject (S) and Object (O) or of an underlying distinct GF, which is neither S nor O.

1. *The problem of the representation of order*

Since the XIXth century order has been conceived of as a notion partly related to syntax and partly related to what would now be defined 'pragmatics'. Yet there has been no consensus as to how the relation between the two levels should be framed with respect to order. To the extent that formalist models have defined pragmatic factors in terms of syntactic structure, they have always emphasized the importance of the syntactic (structural) level. Functionalist models, on the other hand, have always underlined the need for an integrated representation or interplay of the syntactic, semantic and pragmatic levels.

This notion of 'interplay' has been expressed variously. One of the ideas that has received wide consensus is that languages vary according to the different degrees of influence that syntactic and pragmatic factors exert; this has led to a distinction between languages with syntactic vs. pragmatic Word Order (WO).

The model proposing an interplay of syntax and pragmatics in patterns of order should not be taken for granted as an uncontroversial *a priori*, one reason being that the precise shape it must assume is a problem per se.

What most interests us here is the fact that in both formalist and functionalist

---

of verbs in structures like reflexives and passives.

[2] I use here Daneš' terminology (cf. Daneš 1967).

descriptions order is seen as the realization of a more abstract property. However, formalist models express such a property in terms of syntax, while functionalist models express it in terms of semantics. In both cases order is thought of as a dependent variable. But if we consider order as an independent variable at the outset, it soon emerges that the correlation of order and the more abstract functional representations (whatever they may be) is more difficult.

'Order' is not a unitary concept, but has multiple 'strata' which it would be appropriate to distinguish:

(a)   Order as a non-linear relation between arguments of the verb: in this meaning one refers to 'first' or 'second' argument of the verb.

(b)   Order as a combinatory relationship between at least two constituents. This is not necessarily a linear relationship as the notion of 'combination' implies only a constructional link. Obviously, this model is concerned with a level at which argument structure has been mapped onto constituent structure.

(c)   Order as a set of positions, each characterized by a relational property defined in terms of the overall syntactic configuration. This notion implies linearity and concerns the realization of GFs.

(d)   Order as an actual sequence of constituents. This notion also implies linearity, though it concerns the level of the utterance, whereas the notion in (c) concerns the structure of the sentence.

At the level of the sentence any given pattern of order involves the three notions (a)-(c), while at the level of the utterance it involves the four notions (a)-(d).

2.   *Some methodological and theoretical assumptions*

Let us now make some of the assumptions of the present work more explicit. The first assumption is that in order to obtain plausible 'descriptions' the range of structures that are associated with a given order must be constrained. For example, here the concern is with 'order' in structures with a one-argument predicate.

A second assumption is that order has to be conceived of as a complex of notions which can be analysed along the lines of (a)-(d). Furthermore, there are regularities in order that may not emerge if the notion of order is considered merely a dependent variable, i. e. as a means of codifying GFs.

A third assumption is that the study of principles of order cannot only be tackled at level of abstraction related to the analysis of a given structure, but that it requires close scrutiny of data from corpora of real texts. For example, in recent generative models it has been claimed that structures with unergative or unaccusative verbs behave differently in terms of order, i.e. that the lexical properties of one-argument verbs determine the patterns of order in which such verbs may

appear. Yet the actual patterns of order which are found for one-argument structures diverge in an interesting way from what is expected at the level of the theoretical description of properties of order that realize the basic GFs. These diver-
gences are consistent and merit proper description and account, they cannot be
explained simply by pragmatic factors. The properties of order we will deal with
are not the mere reflex of performance facts, but indicate more general relational
properties.

3. *Constructions with one-argument verb and 'Labile Orders'*

In Romance and Slavonic languages, intransitives, reflexive-intransitives and
reflexive verb constructions tend towards the labile VS order. Close investigation
of Italian has drawn a clear division between two-argument (S, O) structures and
one-argument structures (cf. Bernini 1995; Sornicola 1994; Sornicola 1995). The
former have strong WO stability for different text types and moderate variability
with respect to pragmatic function effect, while the latter as a whole show labile
patterns with an almost equal probability of SV/VS which applies to spoken rather
than written texts (cf. Sornicola 1995, for an examination of Italian and Spanish).
Oscillations of the ideal balance of SV = 50%, VS = 50% depend on the type of
one-argument construction, the type of text and pragmatic factors such as themati-
cisation vs focalisation, backgrounding and foregrounding. However, individual
data show that certain semantic factors cause a considerable shift of the equi-
probable distribution of SV and VS. These are the lexical class of the verb, its
'Aktionsart' features and the value of the Animacy feature of S. Certain verbs
which denote a change of state (for example, *apparire* "to appear", *crescere* "to
grow", *aumentare* "to increase") are associated with the VS pattern at a much
higher rate than 50%. Verbs with the feature [+Durative] tend to occur with the SV
pattern, while verbs with the feature [+Punctual] are more frequently associated
with a VS pattern (cf. Sornicola 1994:36-37). The Animacy value of S is very
important: in both Italian and Spanish one-argument verbs constructed with an NP
(S) [-Animate] occur with VS pattern in a high percentage of cases (cf. Sornicola
1995).

The factor of Inanimacy is strictly correlated with the 'eventive' value often
associated with structures with VS order: the entire construction describes an event
or process without an agent, with the constituent with the GF S having the semantic
and syntactic properties typical of an O: this is semantically involved in the process as a Patient and the position to the right of V may be considered a sort of
syntactic incorporation of N to V (cf. *brucia la casa* lit. "burns the house", i. e.
"the house is burning", *maturano le mele* lit. "ripen the apples", "the apples are
ripening", etc.

The asymmetry between two-argument and one-argument structures and 'labile orders' are typologically conditioned. SVO languages in fact show greater asymmetry than VSO and SOV languages suggesting that there are structural reasons which contribute significantly to determining the division (cf. Sornicola 1999).

4. Stability, instability and argument structure

Stability does not depend on transitivity or intransitivity of the verb, but on a property of argument structure, i. e. the occurrence of two arguments. A piece of evidence for this is the fact that both structures with a two-argument intransitive verb and structures with agentive passive are stable with respect to order (i. e. they show almost no oscillation in patterns of order), as are structures with two-argument transitive verbs.

It is possible that the presence of labile patterns SV, VS is related to a probabilistic rule: in a statistical examination of Czech texts Uhlířová (1969) has demonstrated that there is a correlation not only between the number of constituents in a sentence and the number of possible patterns of order it may have, but also between the number of constituents in a sentence and the degree of oscillation between one pattern and another. That is, increasing the number of constituents increases the rigidity of WO, while decreasing the number of constituents decreases the rigidity of WO.

This suggests that the 'lighter' a given structure is the more unstable it is and the heavier it is the more stable.

5. The relationship between order and GFs

But how is instability of order in one-argument structures to be accounted for? Several hypotheses can be made concerning the various notions of order listed under (a)-(d) above.

Oscillation of the single argument (let us call it 'x') between the two positions, one on the left and one on the right of V, suggests that there is a 'virtual space' in the sentence whose shape is determined by the typological properties of two-argument structures. The frame of the 'virtual space' must have at least two distinct virtual positions for 'x1' and 'x2', i. e. each position corresponds to a possible site for one of the arguments. One may suppose that what is constant within the variation of the sentence type is not the GFs but the structure of the virtual space of the sentence; in other words, topological or spatial properties remain unaltered, while relational or functional properties are variable, as we shall see shortly (cf. Section 7.).

However, instability poses the problem of the relationship between GFs and order as a means of codification. As two-argument sentences are characterized by stable order and one-argument sentences by unstable order, can we argue that order functions in a different way in different sentence structures? Two possibilities may be considered:

a) The properties of order diverge in two-argument and one-argument structures, but this does not effect determination of the functional representations of the latter, i. e. GFs remain unaltered with respect to variation in argument structure and order. In this scenario we have three formal properties of order and two GFs. The three formal properties could be expressed by formulas (1)-(3) below:

(1) $x1$ V

(2)   V $x2$

(3) $\underset{\underset{x}{\llcorner \quad \lrcorner}}{\overset{\uparrow \; \mathrm{V} \; \uparrow}{}}$

(1) and (2) are related to the complex property of stability, which can be defined in the following way: 'the canonical position of the argument x1 is before the verb; the canonical position of the argument x2 is after the verb'. (3) is related to the property of instability; it states that x may occur either before or after the verb, with no canonical position, at least in the sense of (1) and (2).

We then have to map the properties expressed in (1)-(3) onto the set of GFs. As is clear, (1) correlates with S, (2) with O. Consequently, the problem arises of how to determine the GF that corresponds to (3). It could be claimed that this is either S or O – the solution that has been proposed in generative treatments, in which S and O coexist at different levels of representation.

But on the basis of what criterion do we identify the single argument of the verb as S or O? In generative models some structural tests have been established to assign the single argument x the GF S or O (cf., for example, Burzio 1986). Neither of them, however, is conclusive and – above all – neither seems to be cross-linguistically valid (cf. Sornicola 1999).

It may be possible to resort to 'external' criteria, that is to other means of codification, like Agreement or – in languages provided with it – morphological Case. Yet the relationship of either Agreement or Case (or both) to functional representations is not unproblematic, in that the very nature of these 'phenomena' is far from clear (for a concise presentation of the problems involved in analysis of the two phenomena, cf. Anderson 1994; Corbett 1994). Another difficulty is the fact that the relationship itself should be expressed as a necessary rather than a sufficient condition. For example, – as far as Indo-European languages are concerned – in order to assign the GF S to a given constituent, it must necessarily trigger the Agreement feature of the verb, or, in languages like German and Russian, it must necessarily be case-marked Nominative. However, the claim that it is sufficient for such a constituent to have either or both of these properties in order to be identified as S seems to be too strong, in that in the languages in question Agreement and/or Case are morphological features that must always be assigned.

Whatever the solution to this problem, it seems clear that in this scenario order is 'deprived of its authority' as a means of determining the functional representations of one-argument structures.

b) The properties of order diverge in two-arguments and one-argument structures and the GFs diverge too. In this scenario three different formal properties correspond to three different functions, i. e. there is a one-to-one mapping of form into function. These functions, which for the time being are named S, O and X respectively can be correlated with properties of order in the following way:

(1') x1   V   S

(2')   V x2   O

(3')   V   X
            x

This seems intuitively plausible – at least as far as the level of an abstract (i.e. oppositional or formal) representation of GFs is concerned. As a matter of fact, the function S as defined in transitive sentences, or – more generally – in two-argument sentences, is in syntagmatic opposition[3] to another function (i. e., O or, more generally, the second argument of the verb), while the function of the single argument of the verb in one-argument structures is not opposed to anything else in the sentence (cf. Section 7.).

The idea that GFs remain constant across sentence types has long been established in the Western grammatical tradition.[4] For example, the notion of 'Subject' has been used for both one of the two arguments of a transitive verb and the single argument of an intransitive verb. This view has been revised in the last decades with the increase in empirical/descriptive studies of so-called 'ergative-absolutive languages' and the development of a theoretical debate about 'grammatical function'. Neither of these threads of research, however, has been conclsive. For example, no consensus has been reached in typological studies on whether the function S corresponds to the constituent which is marked by Ergative (Erg) Case or to the constituent which is marked by Absolutive (Abs) Case. It has also been suggested

---

[3] For the notion of 'syntagmatic opposition' cf. De Groot (1939) and Kuryłowicz (1964:18ff.).

[4] A few notable deviations from the mainstream may be noted, as in theXIXth century doctrine of 'thetic' and 'categorical' sentences. This, however, was a philosophical rather than a linguistic doctrine and although it has occasionally been adopted in linguistic circles, its reformulation in linguistic terms seems problematic.

that (S, O) and (Erg, Abs) are different subsets of GFs. The crux of these analyses seems to lie in the central role which has been assigned to case-marking.

Generative studies have approached the difficulty by adopting a universal inventory of GFs – like S and O – and the interaction of multiple layers of syntactic representations. Each of these determine different relational representations. Given that different positions determine different GFs, a given constituent may be positionally S at some level of representation and positionally O at another level of representation. However, the choice here is restricted to a constituent being either S or O or both. There seems to be a sort of circularity in the correlation of linear and functional properties. Other theories that have tried to investigate this correlation have postulated a set of universal GFs which are to a certain extent independent of sentence structure.

The problem discussed so far may prove to be a thorny one. Witness Hjelmslev's authoritative view that (Hjelmslev 1935-1937:48):

> les définitions présupposées par la théorie syntaxique peuvent être de deux espèces seulement. Ou bien les 'termes de la phrase' sont d'ordre extra-linguistique, étant définis sans égard à l'expression par la langue. Ou bien la théorie constitue un circle vicieux, en définissant d'abord implicitement les termes de phrase par le cas qui les expriment, et ensuite explicitement les cas par les termes de phrase.

6.   *Oppositional conceptions in syntax*

GFs are purely relational concepts. They must be defined independently from both Semantic Roles and the level of realization where phenomena like Agreement and morphological Case appear. The independent level at which GFs must be defined is properly relational in that it is differential and oppositional in the structuralist sense. This view differs from approaches which define GFs primarily according to their coding and behavioural properties (cf. Keenan 1976, some of the contributions in Plank 1984 or, in a different way, generative treatments) as well as from approaches which define them as primitives of linguistic theory (cf. Perlmutter 1983; Perlmutter & Rosen 1984). Closer to the structuralist tradition is the definition of theoretical units in terms of differential or oppositional relations. As is well known, this idea was used in both phonology and syntax in seminal works by De Groot (1939), Jakobson (1936), Kuryłowicz (1964). These scholars, however, preferred to explore the paradigmatic/syntagmatic dimension of Case rather than Grammatical Functions. This is a crucial choice, which may have been prompted by the desire to investigate language-specific properties and to avoid pseudo-universal linguistic notions.[5]

The view maintained here is that – regardless of whether in current empirical

---

[5] This preoccupation was expressed, for example, by Hjelmslev (1935-1937:48-50).

studies of individual languages one starts with the analysis of forms or functions and regardless of the direction of the correlation itself between form and function – there must be a level at which GFs are defined in terms of differential and oppositive notions. It is presumably at this level that a definition of GFs should be sought that is neither circular nor external to language-specific properties.

As at other levels of analysis, Bühler's distinction between '*Systembedingt*' and '*Feldbedingt*' oppositions is useful here, although it must be admitted that the nature of syntactic relations casts it into a particular mould. In fact, *Feldbedingt* have a logical priority over *Systembedingt* oppositions, i. e. the latter are derived from the former.

6.1 *Substantive vs. formal aspects in the definition of GFs*

GFs may be defined as a subset of the syntagmatic relations which are established between V and its arguments. A distinction between substantive and formal aspects of such relations should be made here. As to their substance, GFs may be defined in terms of determination. For example, the functions S and O can both be defined in terms of their relationship with V, with the constituents carrying the functions S and O the determining elements and V the determined element. O may be defined as the first determining argument and S the second determining argument This model is an attempt to represent the fact that the relationship between V and O is closer than that between V and S. As is well known, this relational asymmetry is reflected in a number of properties of realization in the languages of the world. On the other hand, the relationship between V and its arguments can be expressed in terms of 'linking'. No syntagmatic relationship can be established between x = S and x = O unless through V. Both S and O are thus relationships that V imposes on its two arguments at the level of syntagmatic representations. Note that while GFs imply morpho-syntactic coding, arguments do not.

The notion of determination pertains to both semantics and syntax. Though not in itself linear, it is inherently syntagmatic, i. e. it concerns the combinatory/associative dimension.[6] It also pertains to semantics in that it deals with the general meaning of syntagmatic relations. This is to be understood as the most general property fixing the conditions for syntactic/contextual modifications of the meanings of lexical items carrying a given function, as well as those of lexical items carrying the linking function.[7]

---

[6] Linearity and syntagmatics can in fact be conceived of as different notions.

[7] Note that in traditional theories of syntagmatic relations determination has often been associated with 'abstract Case' (cf., for example, Hjelmslev 1935-1937). This depends on the choice of starting point for a model of syntagmatic relations.

As far as the formal dimension is concerned, GFs may be defined in terms of the set of differential (oppositional) relationships they establish with respect to other GFs. These are defined at a distinct level from that of the relationship between V and the arguments of V. In fact, while the latter are of first rank (let us call them 'primary syntagmatic relationships'), the relationships between GFs defined at the first rank are of second rank (let us call them 'secondary syntagmatic relationships'). Functional representations thus need to be defined at two levels: primary relationships are contextual, while secondary relationships are systemic. This seems to be an important property of functional representations and one that differentiates them from constituent representations. In fact, syntagmatic relationships between constituents are defined over sets of elements, while syntagmatic relationships between functions are defined over sets whose elements are themselves relationships.[8] At the formal (systemic) level each GF is differentially defined with respect to the others.

The above discussion implies that at the secondary (i. e. systemic) level GFs always need a syntagmatic environment to be differentially defined. This can be either 'intra-sentential' or 'cross-sentential'. An example of intra-sentential opposition is that between S and O, two functions which can be in opposition within one and the same sentence structure. Examples of cross-sentential oppositions are those between GFs that can never occur in the same environment, i. e. in the same sentence structure, such as O of a transitive sentence and S of a passive sentence. As is obvious, however, the environments of cross-sentential oppositions can be defined in terms of transformationally interrelated structures.[9]

Traditional generative models have used cross-sentential oppositions for representations of the same structure at different levels. This treatment is consistent with traditional models of American structuralism which describe phonemes as alternating sound patterns which correlate with morpho-phonological representations at different levels. In both phonemic and syntactic representations two crucial principles hold: (a) the principle of multi-layered representations of theoretical entities, be they units or relationships; (b) the principle of subjacent representations containing different structures or relationships that are transformationally interrelated to subsequent representations.

7. *What is the function of the single argument of one-argument structures?*
We should now try to define the function of the single argument of one-

---

[8] The primary relationships of GFs may be considered similar to the syntagmatic relationships between constituents. As a matter of fact, both cases concern relations between elements.

[9] This was also Kuryłowicz's proposal (cf. Kuryłowicz 1964, ch. I).

argument structures. Let us denote such a function 'X'. At least three alternative solutions may be envisaged in addition to that discussed in previous sections (i. e. X is a variant which is related to both S and O at different levels of representation):

(a) S and X are variants of the same function;

(b) O and X are variants of the same function;

(c) X is a function distinct from both S and O.

The problem of choosing between these alternative solutions is similar to the traditional phonological problem of assigning allophonic variants to a given phoneme (cf. the excellent historical overview of this problem in Anderson 1985). As is well known, the solution which was adopted by European structuralism is that two phones form a phonological opposition if and only if they have a differential functioning, i. e. if and only if the result of the commutation test in minimal pairs they set up is positive. But what kind of test can we conceive of to decide whether X is a variant of either S or O, or a separate function? Is a commutation test possible for GFs?

A few difficulties arise here. Although theoretically interesting, the parallels between phonology and syntax may not be that close. First of all, in phonology the opposed units are primarily constituents each forming a segment of one of the members of the commuting pair and only secondarily forming differential relationships at the systemic level, whereas in syntax the opposed units are themselves relationships, which then at the systemic level form second rank relationships. A second difficulty is the fact that in phonology the commutation test always works with units belonging to the same class or category.

Neither difficulty is unsolvable. As regards the first, we can accept the commutation test for functions with the proviso that:

(a) the commuting units are not 'constituents' but relationships which are defined in a given structural context;

(b) the structural context is either intra-sentential or cross-sentential.

As to the second difficulty, the condition of 'sameness' of class or category could be satisfied in terms of the class of syntagmatic relationships which are defined in specified syntactic structures.

However, what seems relevant to the parallel between phonological and syntactic oppositions is that in both cases a principle of 'maximal functional differentiation' of two units may be adopted. This principle is grounded in the relative value of the physical differences between units: there being no absolute criterion for the discrimination of units into classes, the maximal difference between two actual units (i. e. the difference that is amenable to their assignment to different classes) is the one that has the functional power of discriminating the meanings of the broader contexts, namely words in phonology and sentences in syntax. This is what guarantees the perceptual discrimination of differences by listeners. Maximal differences are thus rooted in the functioning of units in context, as well as in the action of meaning and perceptual factors.

Though the application of the commutation test to the study of syntactic oppositions poses a few problems, the general principle of maximal differentiation is the same in phonology and syntax. All languages of the world seem to have realizational means (be they coding and/or behavioural means) of discriminating the first determinant of V from the second.[10]

The principle of maximal differentiation allows the distinction of a pair of sentences such as

(4)   John loves Mary
         S   V   O

(5)   Mary loves John
         S   V   O

To the extent that GFs are always relationally defined with respect to the context, the opposition of GFs requires that syntactic minimal pairs be always couples of sentences. In order to commute GFs, one must consider not only two positions, but two lexically-realized sentence structures.

The isomorphism of phonological and syntactic oppositions suggests that neutralization can be considered as a model for functional representation of the single argument. In fact, properties like Order, Case and Agreement can be conceived of as realization features of GFs, which parallel distinctive features of phonological theories. For example, the patterns of order __V/V__ [11] can be considered the two variants of the feature 'Order', in the same way as the feature 'Voicing' can be specified as either [+Voiced] or [-Voiced] in phonology. In SVO languages, the two variants of the feature 'Order' are the distinctive markers of the functions S and O respectively. Labile orders can thus be conceived of as markers signalling that the opposition of S and O is neutralized in the context of one-argument structures. The following empirical facts, already mentioned in Section 3, are of particular interest:

(a)   In one-argument structures either of the two patterns __V/V__ may occur.
(b)   The occurrence of either pattern depends on textual features of the environ-

---

[10] I will not pursue this point here. For a discussion of typological properties of order related to S and O in the languages of Europe, cf. Sornicola (1999).

[11] This notation must be read as 'the position preceding V' vs. 'the position following V'.

ment (for example, thematization vs. rhematization, lexical properties of the verb, lexical properties of the argument of the verb; cf. Sornicola 1995). This constitutes a close parallel with phonology, where allophonic variants are often determined by the phonological environment.

(c) The statistical equi-distribution of the two variants in spontaneous spoken language is further evidence that the choice of either pattern is random in those conditions in which textual features are balanced (i. e. there is no bias towards a particular textual or contextual feature).

An alternative but equivalent treatment would be to employ the model of 'under-representation' of features in a given environment, which is typical of American phonological theories. In the context of one-argument structures, the single argument presents an under-representation with respect to Order features, i. e. its functional representation is the sum of Order features of both S and O.

Whatever the model may be – neutralization or under-representation – context plays a fundamental role, to the extent that the opposition of GFs collapses in a given environment.[12]

This picture seems to fit one of the four cases of neutralization described by Trubetzkoy, i. e. the case in which both members of the opposition represent the archiphoneme.[13] In such a situation, in fact, one of the variants occurs in a given environment while the other occurs in a different environment.

The difficulty with the neutralization model is that the opposition of S and O would be neutralized only with respect to the feature Order, while features like Agreement and Case may – in some languages – keep their role of realization markers of the opposition. Thus S and O would not be fully neutralized. It may be decided that X is a variant of either S or O, a conclusion which seems unsatisfactory as far as the level of functional representation is concerned.

On the other hand, if one starts with the analysis of functional representations, the following network of differential features emerges:

S = the function which is syntactically opposed to O in transitive structures;

O = the function which is syntactically opposed to S in transitive structures;

X = the function which is not opposed to any other function in intransitive (or intransitive-like) structures.

As is clear, this approach is from function to form. The criterion according to which S and O are differentially defined in the same structural environment sup-

---

[12] The European model employs the principle of maximal functional differentiation, while the American model makes use of the properties of the formal representation.

[13] Cf. Trubetzkoy ([1939:79-83] and especially 82).

ports the conclusion that X is a distinct function in cross-sentential opposition to both S and O. At the realization level, evidence of this is that X does not have the typical coding properties of asymmetry that S and O have. In this model labile orders are seen not as the bearers of a neutralization of the opposition between S and O, but as a structural consequence of the fact that the principle of maximal functional differentiation simply cannot apply in one argument structures.

REFERENCES

Anderson, John M. 1994. "Case". *The Encyclopedia of Language and Linguistics* ed. by R. E. Asher, vol. II, 447-453. Oxford & New York: Pergamon Press.
Anderson, Stephen R. 1985. *Phonology in the Twentieth Century: Theories of rules and theories of representations*. Chicago: Chicago University Press.
Bernini, Giuliano. 1995. "Verb-Subject Order in Italian: An investigation of short announcements and telecast news".*Sprachtypologie und Universalienforschung* 48:1/2.44-71.
Burzio, Luigi. 1986. *Italian Syntax*. Dordrecht: Reidel.
Corbett, Glenville G. 1994. "Agreement".*The Encyclopedia of Language and Linguistics* ed. by R. E. Asher, vol. I, 54-60. Oxford & New York: Pergamon Press.
Daneš, František. 1967. "Order of Elements and Sentence Intonation". *Intonation* ed. by Dwight Bolinger, 216-232. Harmondsworth: Penguin.
De Groot, W. 1939. "Les Oppositions dans les Systèmes de la Syntaxe et des Cas". *Mélanges de Linguistique Offerts à Charles Bally*, 107-127. Genève: Georg et Cie, Librairie de l'Université.
Hjelmslev, Louis. 1935-1937. "LaCatégorie des Cas: Étude de grammaire générale".*Acta Jutlandica* 7:1.I-xii + 1-184; 9:2.i-vii + 1-78.
Jakobson, Roman. 1936 [1971]. "Beitrag zur Allgemeinen Kasuslehre: Gesamtbedeutungen der russischen Kasus". *Selected Writings II: Words and Language*, 23-71. The Hague: Mouton.
Keenan, Edward L. 1976. "Towards a Universal Definition of Subject" *Subject and Topic* ed. by Charles N. Li, 305-333. New York: Academic Press.
Kuryłowicz, Jerzy. 1964. *Inflectional Categories of Indo-European*.Heidelberg: Winter.
Perlmutter, David M., ed. 1983. *Studies in Relational Grammar*, vol. I. Chicago & London: Chicago University Press.
——— & Carol Rosen, eds. 1984.*Studies in Relational Grammar*, vol. II. Chicago: Chicago University Press.
Plank, Frans, ed. 1984. *Objects: Towards a theory of grammatical relations*. London: Academic Press.
Sornicola, Rosanna. 1994. "On Word-Order Variability: A study from a corpus of Italian". *Lingua e Stile* 29:1.25-57.
———. 1995. "Theticity, VS Order and the Interplay of Syntax, Semantics and Pragmatics". *Sprachtypologie und Universalienforschung* 48:1/2.72-83.
———. 1999. "Basic Word-Order from a Pragmatic Perspective" *Pragmatic Organization*

of Discourse in the Languages of Europe ed. by Giuliano Bernini. Berlin: Mouton De Gruyter.

Trubetzkoy, Nikolaj S. 1939 [1969]. *Principles of Phonology*. Berkeley & Los Angeles: California University Press.

Uhlířová, Ludmila. 1969. "Vztah Syntaktické Funkce Větného členu a Jeho Místa ve Větě" [Le Rapport de la Fonction Syntaxique du Membre de la Phrase et sa Place dans la Proposition]. *Slovo a Slovesnost* 30.358-370.

GENERAL INDEX

Note: This index does not claim to be exhaustive. For instance, very familiar subjects with no special relevance to the discussion have been left out. When the terms selected are frequent enough, the page number is followed by *ff.*, indicating that this term is referred to often throughout the relevant paper. The abbreviation *n.* indicates that the item is referred to in a footnote.

GENERAL INDEX 309

Full Interpretation principle (FI) 196*n.*,
208, 208*n.*, 210
Fiorentino 196, 205, 210
Focus
Focus 3, 4, 101, 102, 105, 109*n.*, 110,
110*n.*, 175*ff.*, 182, 186*ff.*, 195*ff.*, 224,
231
broad Focus 110, 196
in situ Focus 109, 110, 226, 227
narrow Focus 110, 111, 178, 182,
184, 195, 196
prosody of Focus 199
Focus Criterion 197, 224
Focus marker (FM) 110*n.*, 207*ff.*, 232*ff.*
Focus phrase (FP) 183, 197*ff.*, 222
Focus prominent language(s) 233, 237
Focus projection 182, 183*n.*, 189, 190,
223
Focus structure 5, 196, 200, 232, 234,
236*ff.*, 242*n.*
formative 12, 15*ff.*, 27, 28
French 20, 25, 35*n.*, 93*n.*, 159*ff.*
f-structure 74, 75, 76, 77, 84, 89, 92, 275,
276, 287
function
discourse-semantic function 4
semantically restricted function 243,
245*n.*, 249
semantically unrestricted function 243,
245*n.*, 249
functional projection 2, 12, 18, 46, 98, 113,
114, 115*n.*, 183, 184, 196*n.*, 197*n.*,
201*n.*, 204, 209, 210, 244*n.*

G.
Generative Syntax 106
German 25, 81 121, 122, 123, 296
Given Primary Time (GPT) 260, 267
grammatical relation
primary syntagmatic relationship 300
secondary syntagmatic relationship 300
grammaticalization
grammaticalization chain *see* Chain
grammaticalization theory 2, 5, 121,
135, 151
Greek (Modern) 226
ground 175*ff.*

H.
head
head movement 2*n.*, 99, 100*n.*
head parameter 111, 111*n.*
Head-driven Phrase Structure Grammar
(HPSG) 176, 184*ff.*, 191, 192
head-marking languages 1
Hebrew (Modern, MH) 43, 44, 45
honorification 180, 184, 191
Hungarian 13, 183, 223*ff.*

I.
identification
exhaustive identification 219, 220,
222*ff.*
imperfect
imperfect indicative 15, 16, 18, 18*n.*
imperfect subjunctive 15, 16, 18
incorporation
noun incorporation 47*ff.*, 116
incorporated root 2
incremental theme 281
inflection
verb(al) inflection 11, 151, 180, 207
inflectional class 77, 78, 78*n.*, 83, 90, 94
information
information structure 185*n.*, 186
information state 176, 178, 182, 188*n.*,
192
Information Status (IS) 183, 184, 187,
189*ff.*
insertion 35, 36, 42, 43
interrogative
interrogative complement 159*ff.*, 168
interrogative construction 167
interrogative predicate 159*ff.*
interrogative pronoun 159*ff.*, 168, 169,
173
interrogative reinforced form/
reinforcement 160, 165, 173
interrogative simple form 162
interrogative subject 159, 160, 161
intonation 175, 176, 182, 183
Iroquoian 49, 98
island 222*n.*, 240*n.*, 247, 248
Italian 4, 16, 17, 21, 23*n.*, 25, 26, 32*ff.*, 77,
78, 81, 82, 84, 86, 90, 91, 110, 111, 159,

phonetics
  phonetic shift 145
  phonetic erosion 153
phonology
  diachronic phonology 22
  phonological evolution 18
phrase
  compound-like phrase 39, 41, 42, 44, 45
  'also' phrase 219, 227
  'even' phrase 219, 227
Polish 137*ff.*
polysynthesis
  polysynthetic language(s) 2, 3, 97, 98, 103, 106, 108, 109, 112*ff.*
  Polysynthesis Parameter 2, 97, 98, 110, 111
pragmatics
  pragmatic function 3, 231, 232, 245, 291
  pragmatically-based system/type 3, 232
precedence
  linear precedence (LP) 186, 191
predicate formation 278
predicative complement 271, 272, 273, 274, 278, 279, 281, 283, 288, 289
prefix 121*ff.*
preposition 121, 125
present (tense)
  present indicative 15, 17, 19, 21*n.*, 22, 25, 26
  present subjunctive 15, 18, 19, 26, 27, 28
preterite
  preterite indicative 137*n.*, 138, 138*n.*, 141, 145, 146, 147, 148
Principle and Parameter (Theory) 2, 217
pro-drop 210, 248, 248*n.*
productivity 53, 54, 55, 58, 69
prominence
  main prominence 195, 198, 201, 202, 202*n.*, 211
pronominal argument languages 1, 2*n.*, 3
Pronominalization
  pronominal affix 2
  pronominal marker 253, 258, 268
  pronominal prefix 56*ff.*
  pronominal verb 253

prosodic constituent/structure 199, 200*n.*, 202

Q.
quantifier
  universal quantifier 218, 219, 227, 229

R.
reentrancy 276
Relation (semantic)
  first level relation 277, 278, 279, 288
  nested relation 277, 278, 283
  relation type 276, 277, 278, 279, 282, 284, 285
relative clauses 206*n.*, 232, 235, 236, 239, 240, 240*n.*, 241, 245
repair strategy 196, 210
restricted paradigm 207, 234, 235
resultative
  resultative complement 281
  resultative phrase 281
resumptive pronoun 233, 237, 244*n.*, 245, 247, 247*n.*, 249
reversive (prefix) 93*n.*

S.
Selayarese 196, 204, 204*n.*, 205, 206, 208, 209, 209*n.*
Semitic 99, 238*n.*
sentence
  intra-sentential 300, 301
  cross-sentential 300, 301, 304
separability 122, 123*n.*, 124*n.*, 125*ff.*
separation 31
sign (HPSG) 185, 187, 189*ff.*
Somali 97*ff.*, 196, 207, 207*n.*, 211, 211*n.*, 213, 231*ff.*
Sonogno 23*ff.*
Spanish 16, 81, 93*n.*, 159, 261*n.*, 294
Spell-Out 181, 182, 183, 184, 198, 198*n.*, 200, 201, 203
stress
  nuclear stress 176, 183
s-structure 99, 197, 224
structure sharing 185, 193
subcategorisation
  subcategorisation patterns 271, 288

The *Current Issues in Linguistics Theory* series (edited by E. F. Konrad Koerner, University of Ottawa) is a theory-oriented series which welcomes contributions from scholars who have significant proposals to make towards the advancement of our understanding of language, its structure, functioning and development.

Current Issues in Linguistics Theory (CILT) has been established in order to provide a forum for the presentation and discussion of linguistic opinions of scholars who do not necessarily accept the prevailing mode of thought in linguistic science. It offers an alternative outlet for meaningful contributions to the current linguistic debate, and furnishes the diversity of opinion which a healthy discipline must have. In this series the following volumes have been published thus far or are scheduled for publication:

1. KOERNER, Konrad (ed.): *The Transformational-Generative Paradigm and Modern Linguistic Theory.* 1975.
2. WEIDERT, Alfons: *Componential Analysis of Lushai Phonology.* 1975.
3. MAHER, J. Peter: *Papers on Language Theory and History I: Creation and Tradition in Language. Foreword by Raimo Anttila.* 1979.
4. HOPPER, Paul J. (ed.): *Studies in Descriptive and Historical Linguistics. Festschrift for Winfred P. Lehmann.* 1977.
5. ITKONEN, Esa: *Grammatical Theory and Metascience: A critical investigation into the methodological and philosophical foundations of 'autonomous' linguistics.* 1978.
6. ANTTILA, Raimo: *Historical and Comparative Linguistics.* 1989.
7. MEISEL, Jürgen M. & Martin D. PAM (eds): *Linear Order and Generative Theory.* 1979.
8. WILBUR, Terence H.: *Prolegomena to a Grammar of Basque.* 1979.
9. HOLLIEN, Harry & Patricia (eds): *Current Issues in the Phonetic Sciences. Proceedings of the IPS-77 Congress, Miami Beach, Florida, 17-19 December 1977.* 1979.
10. PRIDEAUX, Gary D. (ed.): *Perspectives in Experimental Linguistics. Papers from the University of Alberta Conference on Experimental Linguistics, Edmonton, 13-14 Oct. 1978.* 1979.
11. BROGYANYI, Bela (ed.): *Studies in Diachronic, Synchronic, and Typological Linguistics: Festschrift for Oswald Szemérenyi on the Occasion of his 65th Birthday.* 1979.
12. FISIAK, Jacek (ed.): *Theoretical Issues in Contrastive Linguistics.* 1981. Out of print
13. MAHER, J. Peter, Allan R. BOMHARD & Konrad KOERNER (eds): *Papers from the Third International Conference on Historical Linguistics, Hamburg, August 22-26 1977.* 1982.
14. TRAUGOTT, Elizabeth C., Rebecca LaBRUM & Susan SHEPHERD (eds): *Papers from the Fourth International Conference on Historical Linguistics, Stanford, March 26-30 1979.* 1980.
15. ANDERSON, John (ed.): *Language Form and Linguistic Variation. Papers dedicated to Angus McIntosh.* 1982.
16. ARBEITMAN, Yoël L. & Allan R. BOMHARD (eds): *Bono Homini Donum: Essays in Historical Linguistics, in Memory of J.Alexander Kerns.* 1981.
17. LIEB, Hans-Heinrich: *Integrational Linguistics. 6 volumes. Vol. II-VI n.y.p.* 1984/93.
18. IZZO, Herbert J. (ed.): *Italic and Romance. Linguistic Studies in Honor of Ernst Pulgram.* 1980.
19. RAMAT, Paolo et al. (eds): *Linguistic Reconstruction and Indo-European Syntax. Proceedings of the Colloquium of the 'Indogermanischhe Gesellschaft'. University of Pavia, 6-7 September 1979.* 1980.
20. NORRICK, Neal R.: *Semiotic Principles in Semantic Theory.* 1981.
21. AHLQVIST, Anders (ed.): *Papers from the Fifth International Conference on Historical Linguistics, Galway, April 6-10 1981.* 1982.
22. UNTERMANN, Jürgen & Bela BROGYANYI (eds): *Das Germanische und die Rekonstruktion der Indogermanischen Grundsprache. Akten des Freiburger Kolloquiums der Indogermanischen Gesellschaft, Freiburg, 26-27 Februar 1981.* 1984.

23. DANIELSEN, Niels: *Papers in Theoretical Linguistics. Edited by Per Baerentzen.* 1992.
24. LEHMANN, Winfred P. & Yakov MALKIEL (eds): *Perspectives on Historical Linguistics. Papers from a conference held at the meeting of the Language Theory Division, Modern Language Assn., San Francisco, 27-30 December 1979.* 1982.
25. ANDERSEN, Paul Kent: *Word Order Typology and Comparative Constructions.* 1983.
26. BALDI, Philip (ed.): *Papers from the XIIth Linguistic Symposium on Romance Languages, Univ. Park, April 1-3, 1982.* 1984.
27. BOMHARD, Alan R.: *Toward Proto-Nostratic. A New Approach to the Comparison of Proto-Indo-European and Proto-Afroasiatic. Foreword by Paul J. Hopper.* 1984.
28. BYNON, James (ed.): *Current Progress in Afro-Asiatic Linguistics: Papers of the Third International Hamito-Semitic Congress, London, 1978.* 1984.
29. PAPROTTÉ, Wolf & René DIRVEN (eds): *The Ubiquity of Metaphor: Metaphor in language and thought.* 1985 (publ. 1986).
30. HALL, Robert A. Jr.: *Proto-Romance Morphology. = Comparative Romance Grammar, vol. III.* 1984.
31. GUILLAUME, Gustave: *Foundations for a Science of Language.*
32. COPELAND, James E. (ed.): *New Directions in Linguistics and Semiotics.* Co-edition with Rice University Press who hold exclusive rights for US and Canada. 1984.
33. VERŠTEEGH, Kees: *Pidginization and Creolization. The Case of Arabic.* 1984.
34. FISIAK, Jacek (ed.): *Papers from the VIth International Conference on Historical Linguistics, Poznan, 22-26 August. 1983.* 1985.
35. COLLINGE, N.E.: *The Laws of Indo-European.* 1985.
36. KING, Larry D. & Catherine A. MALEY (eds): *Selected papers from the XIIIth Linguistic Symposium on Romance Languages, Chapel Hill, N.C., 24-26 March 1983.* 1985.
37. GRIFFEN, T.D.: *Aspects of Dynamic Phonology.* 1985.
38. BROGYANYI, Bela & Thomas KRÖMMELBEIN (eds): *Germanic Dialects:Linguistic and Philological Investigations.* 1986.
39. BENSON, James D., Michael J. CUMMINGS, & William S. GREAVES (eds): *Linguistics in a Systemic Perspective.* 1988.
40. FRIES, Peter Howard (ed.) in collaboration with Nancy M. Fries: *Toward an Understanding of Language: Charles C. Fries in Perspective.* 1985.
41. EATON, Roger, et al. (eds): *Papers from the 4th International Conference on English Historical Linguistics, April 10-13, 1985.* 1985.
42. MAKKAI, Adam & Alan K. MELBY (eds): *Linguistics and Philosophy. Festschrift for Rulon S. Wells.* 1985 (publ. 1986).
43. AKAMATSU, Tsutomu: *The Theory of Neutralization and the Archiphoneme in Functional Phonology.* 1988.
44. JUNGRAITHMAYR, Herrmann & Walter W. MUELLER (eds): *Proceedings of the Fourth International Hamito-Semitic Congress.* 1987.
45. KOOPMAN, W.F., F.C. Van der LEEK , O. FISCHER & R. EATON (eds): *Explanation and Linguistic Change.* 1986
46. PRIDEAUX, Gary D. & William J. BAKER: *Strategies and Structures: The processing of relative clauses.* 1987.
47. LEHMANN, Winfred P. (ed.): *Language Typology 1985. Papers from the Linguistic Typology Symposium, Moscow, 9-13 Dec. 1985.* 1986.
48. RAMAT, Anna G., Onofrio CARRUBA and Giuliano BERNINI (eds): *Papers from the 7th International Conference on Historical Linguistics.* 1987.
49. WAUGH, Linda R. and Stephen RUDY (eds): *New Vistas in Grammar: Invariance and Variation. Proceedings of the Second International Roman Jakobson Conference, New York University, Nov.5-8, 1985.* 1991.
50. RUDZKA-OSTYN, Brygida (ed.): *Topics in Cognitive Linguistics.* 1988.

51. CHATTERJEE, Ranjit: *Aspect and Meaning in Slavic and Indic. With a foreword by Paul Friedrich.* 1989.
52. FASOLD, Ralph W. & Deborah SCHIFFRIN (eds): *Language Change and Variation.* 1989.
53. SANKOFF, David: *Diversity and Diachrony.* 1986.
54. WEIDERT, Alfons: *Tibeto-Burman Tonology. A comparative analysis.* 1987
55. HALL, Robert A. Jr.: *Linguistics and Pseudo-Linguistics.* 1987.
56. HOCKETT, Charles F.: *Refurbishing our Foundations. Elementary linguistics from an advanced point of view.* 1987.
57. BUBENIK, Vít: *Hellenistic and Roman Greece as a Sociolinguistic Area.* 1989.
58. ARBEITMAN, Yoël. L. (ed.): *Fucus: A Semitic/Afrasian Gathering in Remembrance of Albert Ehrman.* 1988.
59. VAN VOORST, Jan: *Event Structure.* 1988.
60. KIRSCHNER, Carl & Janet DECESARIS (eds): *Studies in Romance Linguistics. Selected Proceedings from the XVII Linguistic Symposium on Romance Languages.* 1989.
61. CORRIGAN, Roberta L., Fred ECKMAN & Michael NOONAN (eds): *Linguistic Categorization. Proceedings of an International Symposium in Milwaukee, Wisconsin, April 10-11, 1987.* 1989.
62. FRAJZYNGIER, Zygmunt (ed.): *Current Progress in Chadic Linguistics. Proceedings of the International Symposium on Chadic Linguistics, Boulder, Colorado, 1-2 May 1987.* 1989.
63. EID, Mushira (ed.): *Perspectives on Arabic Linguistics I. Papers from the First Annual Symposium on Arabic Linguistics.* 1990.
64. BROGYANYI, Bela (ed.): *Prehistory, History and Historiography of Language, Speech, and Linguistic Theory. Papers in honor of Oswald Szemérenyi I.* 1992.
65. ADAMSON, Sylvia, Vivien A. LAW, Nigel VINCENT and Susan WRIGHT (eds): *Papers from the 5th International Conference on English Historical Linguistics.* 1990.
66. ANDERSEN, Henning and Konrad KOERNER (eds): *Historical Linguistics 1987.Papers from the 8th International Conference on Historical Linguistics,Lille, August 30-Sept., 1987.* 1990.
67. LEHMANN, Winfred P. (ed.): *Language Typology 1987. Systematic Balance in Language. Papers from the Linguistic Typology Symposium, Berkeley, 1-3 Dec 1987.* 1990.
68. BALL, Martin, James FIFE, Erich POPPE &Jenny ROWLAND (eds): *Celtic Linguistics/Ieithyddiaeth Geltaidd. Readings in the Brythonic Languages. Festschrift for T. Arwyn Watkins.* 1990.
69. WANNER, Dieter and Douglas A. KIBBEE (eds): *New Analyses in Romance Linguistics. Selected papers from the Linguistic Symposium on Romance Languages XVIIII, Urbana-Champaign, April 7-9, 1988.* 1991.
70. JENSEN, John T.: *Morphology. Word structure in generative grammar.* 1990.
71. O'GRADY, William: *Categories and Case. The sentence structure of Korean.* 1991.
72. EID, Mushira and John MCCARTHY (eds): *Perspectives on Arabic Linguistics II. Papers from the Second Annual Symposium on Arabic Linguistics.* 1990.
73. STAMENOV, Maxim (ed.): *Current Advances in Semantic Theory.* 1991.
74. LAEUFER, Christiane and Terrell A. MORGAN (eds): *Theoretical Analyses in Romance Linguistics.* 1991.
75. DROSTE, Flip G. and John E. JOSEPH (eds): *Linguistic Theory and Grammatical Description. Nine Current Approaches.* 1991.
76. WICKENS, Mark A.: *Grammatical Number in English Nouns. An empirical and theoretical account.* 1992.
77. BOLTZ, William G. and Michael C. SHAPIRO (eds): *Studies in the Historical Phonology of Asian Languages.* 1991.
78. KAC, Michael: *Grammars and Grammaticality.* 1992.

79. ANTONSEN, Elmer H. and Hans Henrich HOCK (eds): *STAEF-CRAEFT: Studies in Germanic Linguistics. Select papers from the First and Second Symposium on Germanic Linguistics, University of Chicago, 24 April 1985, and Univ. of Illinois at Urbana-Champaign, 3-4 Oct. 1986.* 1991.
80. COMRIE, Bernard and Mushira EID (eds): *Perspectives on Arabic Linguistics III. Papers from the Third Annual Symposium on Arabic Linguistics.* 1991.
81. LEHMANN, Winfred P. and H.J. HEWITT (eds): *Language Typology 1988. Typological Models in the Service of Reconstruction.* 1991.
82. VAN VALIN, Robert D. (ed.): *Advances in Role and Reference Grammar.* 1992.
83. FIFE, James and Erich POPPE (eds): *Studies in Brythonic Word Order.* 1991.
84. DAVIS, Garry W. and Gregory K. IVERSON (eds): *Explanation in Historical Linguistics.* 1992.
85. BROSELOW, Ellen, Mushira EID and John McCARTHY (eds): *Perspectives on Arabic Linguistics IV. Papers from the Annual Symposium on Arabic Linguistics.* 1992.
86. KESS, Joseph F.: *Psycholinguistics. Psychology, linguistics, and the study of natural language.* 1992.
87. BROGYANYI, Bela and Reiner LIPP (eds): *Historical Philology: Greek, Latin, and Romance. Papers in honor of Oswald Szemerényi II.* 1992.
88. SHIELDS, Kenneth: *A History of Indo-European Verb Morphology.* 1992.
89. BURRIDGE, Kate: *Syntactic Change in Germanic. A study of some aspects of language change in Germanic with particular reference to Middle Dutch.* 1992.
90. KING, Larry D.: *The Semantic Structure of Spanish. Meaning and grammatical form.* 1992.
91. HIRSCHBÜHLER, Paul and Konrad KOERNER (eds): *Romance Languages and Modern Linguistic Theory. Selected papers from the XX Linguistic Symposium on Romance Languages,University of Ottawa, April 10-14, 1990.* 1992.
92. POYATOS, Fernando: *Paralanguage: A linguistic and interdisciplinary approach to interactive speech and sounds.* 1992.
93. LIPPI-GREEN, Rosina (ed.): *Recent Developments in Germanic Linguistics.* 1992.
94. HAGÈGE, Claude: *The Language Builder. An essay on the human signature in linguistic morphogenesis.* 1992.
95. MILLER, D. Gary: *Complex Verb Formation.* 1992.
96. LIEB, Hans-Heinrich (ed.): *Prospects for a New Structuralism.* 1992.
97. BROGYANYI, Bela & Reiner LIPP (eds): *Comparative-Historical Linguistics: Indo-European and Finno-Ugric. Papers in honor of Oswald Szemerényi III.* 1992.
98. EID, Mushira & Gregory K. IVERSON: *Principles and Prediction: The analysis of natural language.* 1993.
99. JENSEN, John T.: *English Phonology.* 1993.
100. MUFWENE, Salikoko S. and Lioba MOSHI (eds): *Topics in African Linguistics. Papers from the XXI Annual Conference on African Linguistics, University of Georgia, April 1990.* 1993.
101. EID, Mushira & Clive HOLES (eds): *Perspectives on Arabic Linguistics V. Papers from the Fifth Annual Symposium on Arabic Linguistics.* 1993.
102. DAVIS, Philip W. (ed.): *Alternative Linguistics. Descriptive and theoretical Modes.* 1995.
103. ASHBY, William J., Marianne MITHUN, Giorgio PERISSINOTTO and Eduardo RAPOSO: *Linguistic Perspectives on Romance Languages. Selected papers from the XXI Linguistic Symposium on Romance Languages, Santa Barbara, February 21-24, 1991.* 1993.
104. KURZOVÁ, Helena: *From Indo-European to Latin. The evolution of a morphosyntactic type.* 1993.
105. HUALDE, José Ignacio and Jon ORTIZ DE URBANA (eds): *Generative Studies in Basque Linguistics.* 1993.
106. AERTSEN, Henk and Robert J. JEFFERS (eds): *Historical Linguistics 1989. Papers from the 9th International Conference on Historical Linguistics, New Brunswick, 14-18 August 1989.* 1993.

107. MARLE, Jaap van (ed.): *Historical Linguistics 1991. Papers from the 10th International Conference on Historical Linguistics, Amsterdam, August 12-16, 1991.* 1993.
108. LIEB, Hans-Heinrich: *Linguistic Variables. Towards a unified theory of linguistic variation.* 1993.
109. PAGLIUCA, William (ed.): *Perspectives on Grammaticalization.* 1994.
110. SIMONE, Raffaele (ed.): *Iconicity in Language.* 1995.
111. TOBIN, Yishai: *Invariance, Markedness and Distinctive Feature Analysis. A contrastive study of sign systems in English and Hebrew.* 1994.
112. CULIOLI, Antoine: *Cognition and Representation in Linguistic Theory. Translated, edited and introduced by Michel Liddle.* 1995.
113. FERNÁNDEZ, Francisco, Miguel FUSTER and Juan Jose CALVO (eds): *English Historical Linguistics 1992. Papers from the 7th International Conference on English Historical Linguistics, Valencia, 22-26 September 1992.* 1994.
114. EGLI, U., P. PAUSE, Chr. SCHWARZE, A. von STECHOW, G. WIENOLD (eds): *Lexical Knowledge in the Organisation of Language.* 1995.
115. EID, Mushira, Vincente CANTARINO and Keith WALTERS (eds): *Perspectives on Arabic Linguistics. Vol. VI. Papers from the Sixth Annual Symposium on Arabic Linguistics.* 1994.
116. MILLER, D. Gary: *Ancient Scripts and Phonological Knowledge.* 1994.
117. PHILIPPAKI-WARBURTON, I., K. NICOLAIDIS and M. SIFIANOU (eds): *Themes in Greek Linguistics. Papers from the first International Conference on Greek Linguistics, Reading, September 1993.* 1994.
118. HASAN, Ruqaiya and Peter H. FRIES (eds): *On Subject and Theme. A discourse functional perspective.* 1995.
119. LIPPI-GREEN, Rosina: *Language Ideology and Language Change in Early Modern German. A sociolinguistic study of the consonantal system of Nuremberg.* 1994.
120. STONHAM, John T. : *Combinatorial Morphology.* 1994.
121. HASAN, Ruqaiya, Carmel CLORAN and David BUTT (eds): *Functional Descriptions. Theorie in practice.* 1996.
122. SMITH, John Charles and Martin MAIDEN (eds): *Linguistic Theory and the Romance Languages.* 1995.
123. AMASTAE, Jon, Grant GOODALL, Mario MONTALBETTI and Marianne PHINNEY: *Contemporary Research in Romance Linguistics. Papers from the XXII Linguistic Symposium on Romance Languages, El Paso//Juárez, February 22-24, 1994.* 1995.
124. ANDERSEN, Henning: *Historical Linguistics 1993. Selected papers from the 11th International Conference on Historical Linguistics, Los Angeles, 16-20 August 1993.* 1995.
125. SINGH, Rajendra (ed.): *Towards a Critical Sociolinguistics.* 1996.
126. MATRAS, Yaron (ed.): *Romani in Contact. The history, structure and sociology of a language.* 1995.
127. GUY, Gregory R., Crawford FEAGIN, Deborah SCHIFFRIN and John BAUGH (eds): *Towards a Social Science of Language. Papers in honor of William Labov. Volume 1: Variation and change in language and society.* 1996.
128. GUY, Gregory R., Crawford FEAGIN, Deborah SCHIFFRIN and John BAUGH (eds): *Towards a Social Science of Language. Papers in honor of William Labov. Volume 2: Social interaction and discourse structures.* 1997.
129. LEVIN, Saul: *Semitic and Indo-European: The Principal Etymologies. With observations on Afro-Asiatic.* 1995.
130. EID, Mushira (ed.) *Perspectives on Arabic Linguistics. Vol. VII. Papers from the Seventh Annual Symposium on Arabic Linguistics.* 1995.
131. HUALDE, Jose Ignacio, Joseba A. LAKARRA and R.L. Trask (eds): *Towards a History of the Basque Language.* 1995.
132. HERSCHENSOHN, Julia: *Case Suspension and Binary Complement Structure in French.* 1996.

133. ZAGONA, Karen (ed.): *Grammatical Theory and Romance Languages. Selected papers from the 25th Linguistic Symposium on Romance Languages (LSRL XXV) Seattle, 2-4 March 1995.* 1996.
134. EID, Mushira (ed.): *Perspectives on Arabic Linguistics Vol. VIII. Papers from the Eighth Annual Symposium on Arabic Linguistics.* 1996.
135. BRITTON Derek (ed.): *Papers from the 8th International Conference on English Historical Linguistics.* 1996.
136. MITKOV, Ruslan and Nicolas NICOLOV (eds): *Recent Advances in Natural Language Processing.* 1997.
137. LIPPI-GREEN, Rosina and Joseph C. SALMONS (eds): *Germanic Linguistics. Syntactic and diachronic.* 1996.
138. SACKMANN, Robin (ed.): *Theoretical Linguistics and Grammatical Description.* 1996.
139. BLACK, James R. and Virginia MOTAPANYANE (eds): *Microparametric Syntax and Dialect Variation.* 1996.
140. BLACK, James R. and Virginia MOTAPANYANE (eds): *Clitics, Pronouns and Movement.* 1997.
141. EID, Mushira and Dilworth PARKINSON (eds): *Perspectives on Arabic Linguistics Vol. IX. Papers from the Ninth Annual Symposium on Arabic Linguistics, Georgetown University, Washington D.C., 1995.* 1996.
142. JOSEPH, Brian D. and Joseph C. SALMONS (eds): *Nostratic. Sifting the evidence.* 1998.
143. ATHANASIADOU, Angeliki and René DIRVEN (eds): *On Conditionals Again.* 1997.
144. SINGH, Rajendra (ed): *Trubetzkoy's Orphan. Proceedings of the Montréal Roundtable "Morphophonology: contemporary responses (Montréal, October 1994).* 1996.
145. HEWSON, John and Vit BUBENIK: *Tense and Aspect in Indo-European Languages. Theory, typology, diachrony.* 1997.
146. HINSKENS, Frans, Roeland VAN HOUT and W. Leo WETZELS (eds): *Variation, Change, and Phonological Theory.* 1997.
147. HEWSON, John: *The Cognitive System of the French Verb.* 1997.
148. WOLF, George and Nigel LOVE (eds): *Linguistics Inside Out. Roy Harris and his critics.* 1997.
149. HALL, T. Alan: *The Phonology of Coronals.* 1997.
150. VERSPOOR, Marjolijn, Kee Dong LEE and Eve SWEETSER (eds): *Lexical and Syntactical Constructions and the Construction of Meaning. Proceedings of the Bi-annual ICLA meeting in Albuquerque, July 1995.* 1997.
151. LIEBERT, Wolf-Andreas, Gisela REDEKER and Linda WAUGH (eds): *Discourse and Perspectives in Cognitive Linguistics.* 1997.
152. HIRAGA, Masako, Chris SINHA and Sherman WILCOX (eds): *Cultural, Psychological and Typological Issues in Cognitive Linguistics.* n.y.p.
153. EID, Mushira and Robert R. RATCLIFFE (eds): *Perspectives on Arabic Linguistics Vol. X. Papers from the Tenth Annual Symposium on Arabic Linguistics, Salt Lake City, 1996.* 1997.
154. SIMON-VANDENBERGEN, Anne-Marie, Kristin DAVIDSE and Dirk NOËL (eds): *Reconnecting Language. Morphology and Syntax in Functional Perspectives.* 1997.
155. FORGET, Danielle, Paul HIRSCHBÜHLER, France MARTINEAU and María-Luisa RIVERO (eds): *Negation and Polarity. Syntax and semantics. Selected papers from the Colloquium Negation: Syntax and Semantics. Ottawa, 11-13 May 1995.* 1997.
156. MATRAS, Yaron, Peter BAKKER and Hristo KYUCHUKOV (eds): *The Typology and Dialectology of Romani.* 1997.
157. LEMA, José and Esthela TREVIÑO (eds): *Theoretical Analyses on Romance Languages. Selected papers from the 26th Linguistic Symposium on Romance Languages (LSRL XXVI), Mexico City, 28-30 March, 1996.* 1998.

158. SÁNCHEZ MACARRO, Antonia and Ronald CARTER (eds): *Linguistic Choice across Genres. Variation in spoken and written English.* 1998.
159. JOSEPH, Brian D., Geoffrey C. HORROCKS and Irene PHILIPPAKI-WARBURTON (eds): *Themes in Greek Linguistics II.* 1998.
160. SCHWEGLER, Armin, Bernard TRANEL and Myriam URIBE-ETXEBARRIA (eds): *Romance Linguistics: Theoretical Perspectives. Selected papers from the 27th Linguistic Symposium on Romance Languages (LSRL XXVII), Irvine, 20-22 February, 1997.* 1998.
161. SMITH, John Charles and Delia BENTLEY (eds): *Historical Linguistics 1995. Volume 1: Romance and general linguistics.* n.y.p.
162. HOGG, Richard M. and Linda van BERGEN (eds): *Historical Linguistics 1995. Volume 2: Germanic linguistics.Selected papers from the 12th International Conference on Historical Linguistics, Manchester, August 1995.* 1998.
163. LOCKWOOD, David G., Peter H. FRIES and James E. COPELAND (eds): *Functional Approaches to Language, Culture and Cognition.* n.y.p.
164. SCHMID, Monika, Jennifer R. AUSTIN and Dieter STEIN (eds): *Historical Linguistics 1997. Selected papers from the 13th International Conference on Historical Linguistics, Düsseldorf, 10-17 August 1997.* 1998.
165. BUBENÍK, Vit: *A Historical Syntax of Late Middle Indo-Aryan (Apabhraṃśa).* 1998.
166. LEMMENS, Maarten: *Lexical Perspectives on Transitivity and Ergativity. Causative constructions in English.* 1998.
167. BENMAMOUN, Elabbas, Mushira EID and Niloofar HAERI (eds): *Perspectives on Arabic Linguistics Vol. XI. Papers from the Eleventh Annual Symposium on Arabic Linguistics, Atlanta, 1997.* 1998.
168. RATCLIFFE, Robert R.: *The "Broken" Plural Problem in Arabic and Comparative Semitic. Allomorphy and analogy in non-concatenative morphology.* 1998.
169. GHADESSY, Mohsen (ed.): *Text and Context in Functional Linguistics.* 1999.
170. LAMB, Sydney M.: *Pathways of the Brain. The neurocognitive basis of language.* 1999.
171. WEIGAND, Edda (ed.): *Contrastive Lexical Semantics.* 1998.
172. DIMITROVA-VULCHANOVA, Mila and Lars HELLAN (eds): *Topics in South Slavic Syntax and Semantics.* 1999.
173. TREVIÑO, Esthela and José LEMA (eds): *Semantic Issues in Romance Syntax.* 1999.
174. HALL, T. Alan and Ursula KLEINHENZ (eds.): *Studies on the Phonological Word. Selected papers from the Conference on the Phonological Word, Berlin, October 1997.* 1999.
175. GIBBS, Ray W. and Gerard J. STEEN (eds.): *Metaphor in Cognitive Linguistics. Selected papers from the 5th International Cognitive Linguistics Conference, Amsterdam, 1997.* 1999.
176. VAN HOEK, Karen, Andrej KIBRIK and Leo NOORDMAN (eds.): *Discourse in Cognitive Linguistics. Selected papers from the International Cognitive Linguistics Conference, Amsterdam, July 1997.* 1999.
177. CUYCKENS, Hubert and Britta ZAWADA (eds.): *Polysemy in Cognitive Linguistics. Selected papers from the International Cognitive Linguistics Conference, Amsterdam, 1997.* n.y.p.
178. FOOLEN, Ad and Frederike van der LEEK (eds.): *Constructions in Cognitive Linguistics. Selected papers from the International Cognitive Linguistic Conference, Amsterdam, 1997.* n.y.p.
179. RINI, Joel: *Exploring the Role of Morphology in the Evolution of Spanish.* n.y.p.
180. MEREU, Lunella (ed.): *Boundaries of Morphology and Syntax.* 1999.
181. MOHAMMAD, Mohammad A.: *Word Order, Agreement and Pronominalization in Standard and Palestinian Arabic.* n.y.p.

182. KENESEI, Istvan (ed.): *Theoretical Issues in Eastern European Languages. Selected papers from the Conference on Linguistic Theory in Eastern European Languages (CLITE), Szeged, April 1998.* n.y.p.
183. CONTINI-MORAVA, Ellen and Yishai TOBIN (eds.): *Between Grammar and Lexicon.* n.y.p.
184. SAGART, Laurent: *The Roots of Old Chinese.* n.y.p.
185. AUTHIER, J.-Marc, Barbara E. BULLOCK, Lisa A. REED (eds.): *Formal Perspectives on Romance Linguistics. Selected papers from the 28th Linguistic Symposium on Romance Languages (LSRL XVIII), Pennsylvania State University, April 1998.* n.y.p.
186. MIŠESKA TOMIĆ, Olga and Milorad RADOVANOVIĆ (eds.): *History and Perspectives of Language Study.* n.y.p.
187. FRANCO, Jon, Alazne LANDA and Juan MARTÍN (eds.): *Grammatical Analyses in Basque and Romance Linguistics.* n.y.p.